British Columbia

BY THE ROAD

British Columbia by the Road

Car Culture and the Making of a Modern Landscape

BEN BRADLEY

UBCPress · Vancouver · Toronto

26 25 24 23 22 21 20 19   5 4 3 2

Printed in Canada on FSC-certified ancient-forest-free paper (100% post-consumer recycled) that is processed chlorine- and acid-free.

Library and Archives Canada Cataloguing in Publication

Bradley, Ben, author
British Columbia by the road : car culture and the making of a modern landscape / Ben Bradley.

Includes bibliographical references and index.
Issued in print and electronic formats.
ISBN 978-0-7748-3418-6 (hardcover). – ISBN 978-0-7748-3419-3 (pbk.). – ISBN 978-0-7748-3420-9 (PDF). – ISBN 978-0-7748-3421-6 (EPUB). – ISBN 978-0-7748-3422-3 (Kindle)

1. Roads – British Columbia – History – 20th century. 2. Transportation – British Columbia – History – 20th century. 3. Automobiles – British Columbia – History – 20th century. 4. Automobile travel – British Columbia – History – 20th century. 5. Landscapes – British Columbia – History – 20th century. 6. British Columbia – History – 20th century. I. Title.

FC3820.R63B73 2017   388.10971109'04   C2017-901328-9
C2017-901329-7

Canada

UBC Press gratefully acknowledges the financial support for our publishing program of the Government of Canada (through the Canada Book Fund), the Canada Council for the Arts, and the British Columbia Arts Council.

This book has been published with the help of a grant from the Canadian Federation for the Humanities and Social Sciences, through the Awards to Scholarly Publications Program, using funds provided by the Social Sciences and Humanities Research Council of Canada.

Printed and bound in Canada by Friesens
Set in Garamond by Artegraphica Design Co. Ltd.
Copy editor: Deborah Kerr
Cover designer: George Kirkpatrick

UBC Press
The University of British Columbia
2029 West Mall
Vancouver, BC V6T 1Z2
www.ubcpress.ca

Contents

List of Illustrations

Acknowledgments

The research for this book was conducted with the support of a Canada Graduate Scholarship from the Social Sciences and Humanities Research Council of Canada. A SSHRC postdoctoral fellowship at the University of Toronto provided the opportunity to complete the manuscript. *BC Studies* has kindly given permission to use a map from a summer 2011 article that was based on this research.

Ian McKay and Colin Duncan were especially generous with their time and advice as this project ranged hither and thither, occasionally speeding forward, sometimes venturing down unexpected paths, and other times getting stuck on the side of the metaphorical road. Steve Penfold's insightful comments and persistent refrain of "book, book, book" kept diversionary postdoctoral side trips to a strict minimum. Laura Cameron and Rick Rajala provided helpful feedback during the early stages.

It was my good fortune to be researching parks and landscapes at a moment when environmental history was very much on the rise in Canada. Funding from the Network in Canadian History and Environment allowed me to attend far-flung conferences and present to non-Canadianist audiences. The Quelques Arpents de Neige migratory workshop and Toronto Environmental History Network reading group offered friendly venues to test-drive some of this research. I particularly benefitted from the feedback of Jennifer Bonnell, Jim Clifford, and Jay Young, and Ruth Sandwell has been unflagging in her interest and support. For the opportunity to bounce ideas around, whether in a scholarly setting or simply over coffee, I'd also like to thank Dimitry Anastakis, John Belshaw, Claire Campbell, Jenny

Clayton, Colin Coates, Lyle Dick, Sinead Earley, Alan Gordon, Emily Hill, Beth Jewett, Frank Leonard, Jack Little, John Lutz, Richard Mackie, Ian MacLaren, Dan Rück, Joan Schwartz, Andrew Watson, and Graeme Wynn. Andrea Laforet very kindly allowed me to read her unpublished paper on the market for the coiled basketry of BC Indigenous peoples. Eric Leinberger produced the maps, and Chris Gergely advised on image work. Three anonymous reviewers generously took the time to help out along the way, like Good Samaritans stopping to assist someone changing a tire. Darcy Cullen, Lesley Erickson, and their colleagues at UBC Press helped steer the project home.

This book owes an enormous debt to the behind-the-scenes efforts of archive, museum, and library staff and volunteers, working during a period when senior levels of government have sorely neglected such institutions. I am deeply thankful for the assistance provided by the British Columbia Archives; the British Columbia J.T. Fyles Natural Resources Library and former Ministry of Forests Library; the special collections and archives at the University of British Columbia, University of Victoria, and Vancouver Public Libraries; and community museums and archives in Chilliwack, Golden, Invermere, Kamloops, Lytton, Prince George, Princeton, Quesnel, and Revelstoke.

Finally, I thank my mum, dad, and brother for their support, and my partner, Jan Hadlaw, for riding shotgun on this long and winding journey.

A Note on Mileage

Imperial units of measurement are preserved throughout this book. This is noticeable primarily with measurements of distance (miles instead of kilometres), but it also applies to area (acres instead of square metres or kilometres). Though the metric system is standard today, too often the result of converting historical figures from imperial to metric proves either imprecise or unwieldy.

Introduction

Automobility and the Making of New Kinds of Experience

The first automobile in the BC Interior began pacing the streets of Spences Bridge in 1904. Within two years, isolated examples of the species could also be found in communities such as Lillooet, Grand Forks, Vernon, and Armstrong. Single digits soon became dozens, then dozens rapidly became hundreds. By 1914, there may have been a thousand automobiles in the Interior.[1] Although they were unreliable and underpowered, they exerted a considerable sway over the imagination and grabbed many a headline, with newspapers full of stories about the first adventurous motorist to navigate his or her way from one community to another in the next valley over. Nevertheless, during the automobile's first decade in the BC Interior, it generally remained a curiosity, a plaything of the rich, the eccentric, and the mechanically inclined. Motoring did little to change the landscapes of the Interior prior to the Great War. Roads were why. The region had few roads, and the few that did exist were terrible. They were inadequate for moving bulk goods and inefficient for business travel. Railroads and steamboats easily retained their role as the predominant means of conveying people and freight over long distances.[2]

This state of affairs might be considered a pattern of transportation infrastructure that was pragmatically related to the scattered nature of the province's settlements and to the exaggerated verticality of its topography. But even in the late 1910s, many British Columbians considered it a reproach to the province's modernity. Despite the expense and difficulty of moving amidst the mountains, they were as enthusiastic as other North

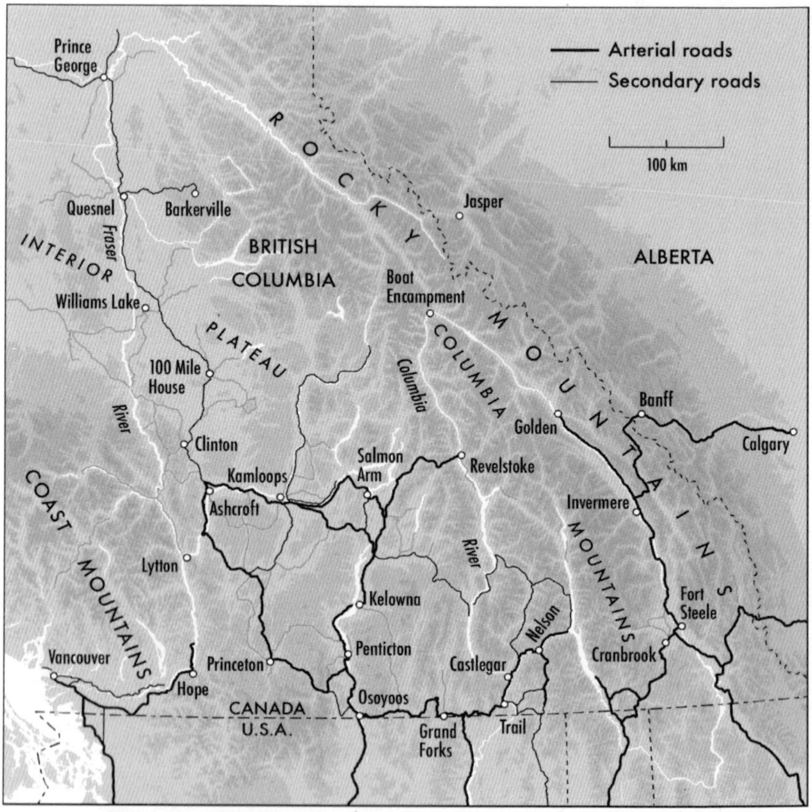

Map of BC Interior road network, c. 1925

Americans about automobiles, good roads, and motoring. They were eager to better connect the province's metropolitan centres and rural hinterlands, and sometimes as nationalistic as other Canadians about linking their province with the rest of Canada. Hence, there were cultural as well as economic and political reasons for the widespread popularity of road building during the 1920s and 1930s, followed by the even more massive program of highway development from the late 1940s through the 1960s. There were multiple compelling reasons for British Columbians to support new and improved roads, and this helps to explain why the sounds of blasting, jackhammers, and paving equipment reverberated throughout so much of the mid-twentieth century.

Between 1922 and 1972 – from the end of the sharp recession that followed the Great War to the onset of the OPEC oil crisis – automobile ownership and automobile travel were seen almost without question as social "goods" in North America. The passenger car had shed its early reputation as the rich man's plaything by the end of the First World War, and during the interwar years being part of the motoring public became an important marker of middle-class status. During that same period, the extent and condition of a province or state's network of roads came to be widely interpreted as a barometer of its modernity. There were fifty-five thousand licensed drivers in British Columbia in 1925, which was fewer than one in ten of the population. Unfortunately for them, its roads remained embarrassingly primitive. Most roads outside of major centres were impassable for much of the year, and the provincial network was so fragmented that driving between many regions was impossible, most notably between the Coast and the Interior. Forty-five years later, as North America's extended postwar boom drew to a gradual close, British Columbia had gained an extensive network of paved all-season arterial highways that facilitated year-round travel within and between every major region, as well as a larger capillary network of resource roads that reached deep into its forests and mountains. In 1970, more than a million British Columbians had a driver's licence, and half a million automobiles were registered in the province, for a ratio of one vehicle per every four residents. Ownership was still associated with middle-class status but had gone from being a relatively exclusive option to being, effectively, a universally accessible one. Most working-class families had access to motor vehicles, and all but the poorest could afford a car or truck for work and an occasional pleasure trip.

During the intervening years, huge sums had been poured into British Columbia's highway network. New roads and "democratized" automobile travel transformed the province's tourism and service industries, and driving became one of the most important ways that British Columbians encountered the province beyond their home communities. Motoring was a radically new way of viewing the province. The combination of private vehicles and public roads could make the experience of travel seem free, unconstrained, even empowering. Here was an antidote to the routines of everyday life – a therapeutic way of getting in touch with oneself and with the country. Driving could make travellers feel like active explorers of the landscapes that surrounded them, rather than passive consumers, as had been the case with the predetermined routes and timetables of railway and steamboat companies. However, "seem" and "feel like" are key words here. As *British Columbia by the Road* reveals, the individualistic "freedom of the road" and the landscape experiences that were associated with it were more tightly constrained than they seemed.

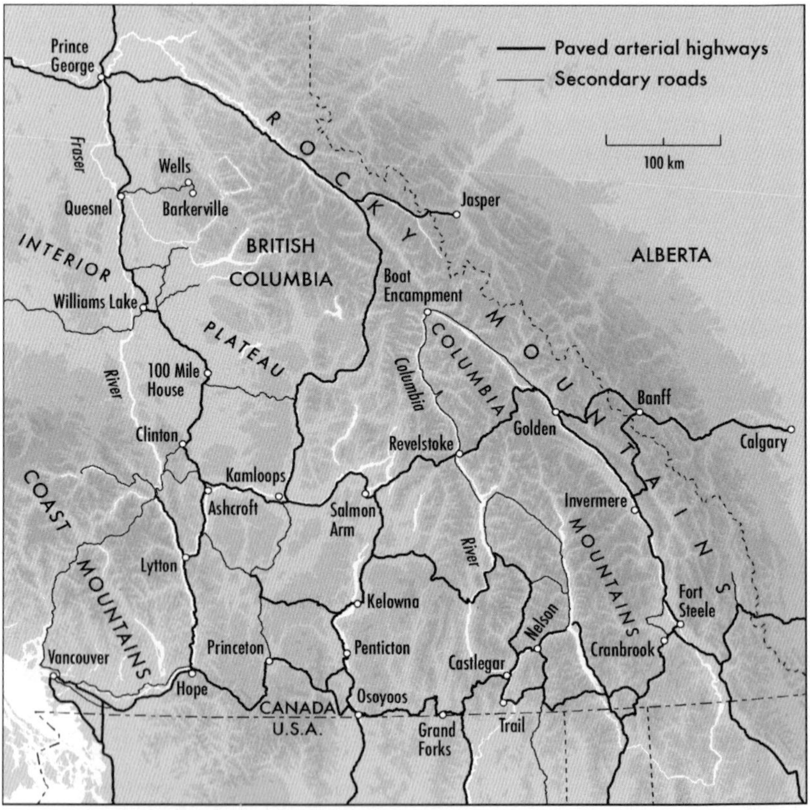

Map of BC Interior road network, c. 1970

This book shows that the millions of motorists who travelled through the BC Interior during the period 1925-70 encountered both nature and history by the road, which is meant in two ways. First, "by the road" is meant in the straightforward sense of the location of the diverse features that motorists could see as they drove along the province's arterial highways. These included landforms, flora, fauna, signs, homes, other built structures, and even entire villages and towns. More importantly, "by the road" also refers to private automobiles and public roads combining to act as a medium of landscape experience, a medium that had significant structuring effects and was one of the dominant modes of visuality in the mid-century culture of time and space associated with Fordism. Fordism was the political-economic "moment" that saw the state take an active role in regulating, stabilizing, and sometimes stimulating the economy to balance mass production and mass consumption. By doing so, it sought to avoid crises of overproduction while also legitimating its own role and liberal capitalism more generally.[3]

The BC Interior is defined here as the southern half of the province, lying between the Coast Mountains and the Rockies. About the size of contemporary Germany, most of it is mountainous, forested, and lacking in arable land. It is also sparsely populated. Throughout the period covered here, approximately two-thirds of British Columbians lived in metropolitan Vancouver or Victoria – that is, they were concentrated on "the Coast." Historian Jean Barman usefully characterizes mainland British Columbia in the early twentieth century as a fragmented archipelago of regions that were largely cut off from each other by mountain ranges and glacier fields.[4] Transportation played a crucial role in shaping its complex regionalism, as geographer Cole Harris emphasizes in his observation that its "lines of industrial transportation became those of social interaction."[5] However, the flexibility of travelling by private automobile on public roads connected the Interior's disparate regions to each other in new ways. It increasingly allowed motorists a way of understanding the Interior as a whole, yet at the same time it sharpened regional and local identities through the competitive imperative that many tourism promoters and roadside business operators shared – the need to stand out in the eyes of the motoring public through signature landmarks. Automobiles, roads, and roadside landscapes thus made the Interior simultaneously more integrated *and* differentiated during the mid-twentieth century.

The development of a network of arterial roads in the Interior followed a trajectory that was distinctive in the broader history of North American motoring, though far from unique in the mountainous west.[6] It occurred significantly later and more slowly than in most other parts of Canada and the United States. The network that emerged was comparatively thin, tenuous, and slow to change in most places due to the terrain, the distance between communities, and the high cost of building and maintaining overland transport infrastructure under such circumstances. It never came to resemble the dense, complex networks in regions such as southern Ontario or America's eastern seaboard, or even the simple but extensive ones in the grain-growing districts of the Canadian Prairies. Yet it was precisely because British Columbia's network was so thin and rudimentary that it and the road mindedness that developed in conjunction with it were so socially, politically, and culturally significant. The quality of the province's few roads was an especially important reflection of its governments. Those same roads also channelled motoring residents and visitors along a limited number of corridors, constraining their options of how to go from Point A to Point B while effectively limiting what they saw along the way. As a result, the state of modern British Columbia seemed in many cases to be plainly visible to those who experienced it by the road.

This book is first and foremost a landscape history and thus is concerned with the reciprocal relationship whereby people have continually shaped and in turn been shaped by their built and natural environments.[7] It examines how people's experiences of their surroundings were affected by individual and institutional actors, broader social forces, and also nature itself. To do this, it focuses on material conditions "on the ground," the very stuff of popular perceptions and common experiences, and refrains from speculating about the myriad possible meanings that automobile travellers might have taken away with them. As much as possible, the focus here is on landscape as a common artifact.

As motorists proceeded down public roads, they saw only some aspects of the places they passed through. The roadside was not just the border of a new kind of road but itself a new kind of place: ribbon-shaped, often complexly planned, and crowded with various and particular things, some occurring naturally, some predating the automobile, and some deliberately constructed to take advantage of their location. Far from being just the frame for the landscape, the roadside was a vital part of it – indeed, a place in its own right. Roads and roadsides came to play a crucial role in shaping automobile travellers' perceptions of communities, environments, and entire regions. People who lived and worked along the road also helped determine the character of the roadside, imbuing it with evidence of both the local economy and its level of prosperity. Like fishermen along a river, many hoped to lure custom, sometimes reaping large rewards and other times none at all. And of course, the state played a key role too. Often overlooked among Fordism's more famous topics – such as the state's construction of massive infrastructure projects – are initiatives to stimulate mass consumption through the development of public recreational and cultural amenities such as parks and historic sites. Parks and plaques served as ornaments for state-built highways and also as devices for modelling the views of an increasingly motorized citizenry.

For all the individualism and sense of personal autonomy associated with car travel, motoring was one of the century's most common and standardized activities, particularly after the Second World War, when automobile ownership became accessible to the working class. Whatever reason they drove for, motorists formed a kind of massive community in movement, which this book refers to as the "motoring public." Their travels along the beaten path of arterial road networks generated very specific shared landscape experiences, which in turn shaped (and reshaped) the image of places in the popular imagination. Communities, regions, and entire provinces and states came to be known by (and for) the roads that passed through them. Some acquired reputations as places to be sought out or avoided. Sharing in these experiences was an important part of being a modern North American, an active, observant citizen who was licensed to explore places beyond the home community, or at least gain a passing knowledge of them. *British Columbia by the Road* focuses on the intertwined histories of car culture and landscape in a particular region, but this intertwining was itself a widespread phenomenon, with places all over North America (and farther afield) becoming known by the road. Indeed, it was one of the most overarching and pervasive means by which places were made similar and at the same time differentiated during the twentieth century.

Motorists made many millions of trips along British Columbia's highways and byways during those years, seeing the same things and trying to make sense of them on an active or passive level. They doubtless found a wide variety of meanings in what they saw, depending on their life experiences and subject position. No doubt, the assumed audience that the province's white, middle-class road builders and roadside landscapers had in mind when they sought to shape the views of the motoring public was also middle class and white (during the period examined here, nine of ten BC residents identified as being of British or Continental European background).[8] However, motorists did not necessarily ascribe the same meanings to what they saw and experienced. This interpretive diversity merits greater attention from historians, but here the focus is on driving as a way by which a large and steadily growing number of people saw and knew the country, an underlying structure that tied people together as the motoring public while also linking diverse places, things, and themes together materially and experientially, "flattening" them in the sense of putting them on a common cultural plane.

This book pays particular attention to two of the most prominent and popular types of roadside feature – "nature" and "the past" – as they took form in parks and historic sites. The concept of automobility is particularly helpful for exploring how automobiles and roads could shape such broad categories of landscape, both materially and in terms of perception, for it insists that automobiles and roads are merely the central points in a constellation of related objects, spaces, images, discourses, habits, and practices. Automobility is a complex, diffuse, and non-linear system that embodies many contradictions and has wide-ranging and often unintended consequences.[9] Its central importance to experiences of modernity in twentieth-century North America can hardly be overstated. The passenger car was at once the century's quintessential *object* – the consumer durable par excellence – and its *subject,* carrier of symbolic and even political freight. It mattered enormously what sort of automobile one drove, and if one drove at all. Cars became avatars of social distinction, paradoxically as they were also symbols of egalitarianism and "democracy." It also mattered what sorts of roads were available to drive on, with the condition of arterial routes testifying to the prowess and competence of governments or, in instances where they incurred heavier-than-expected costs or ran into practical difficulties, their unfitness for office. Automobility came to dominate urban and rural space by its presence and, eventually, also by its absence. It both obscured and established boundaries between locales and between the private and public spheres. It allowed people to commune with nature and the countryside, while contributing to massive environmental degradation. Perhaps above all, the system of automobility was a key engine of twentieth-century capitalism, not only in terms of automobile production and road construction, but also in terms of how those vehicles and paths were subsequently used over the span of many years.

The flexibility of travelling in a private automobile could provide motorists with a sense of freedom and discovery, yet it paradoxically had coercive effects through innumerable laws and commonsense habits, and also because it required the use of a fixed infrastructure built and maintained by the state, often working in the interests of capital. In British Columbia, as elsewhere in North America, the automobile was a profoundly political vehicle, closely bound up with liberalism. Automobile travel simultaneously affirmed a host of liberal values, including individualism, social hierarchy, physical and social mobility, privacy, private property, consumerism, the normativity of the nuclear family, and, during the post–Second World War years, Western Cold War notions of freedom.[10] By extension, everything visible from arterial highways constituted political theatre, or a public facade, through which a growing number of residents and visitors learned about and evaluated a province's communities, environments, and overall level of development. Roadside landscapes were recognized as a means to communicate with a citizenry as well as a market. It was widely understood that the motoring public picked up "lessons" as they viewed their surroundings while driving along highways – lessons that were sometimes explicit but more often vague or implicit because they were delivered unintentionally or else intentionally through aesthetic display.

These landscape lessons – how drivers looked at things, and how things looked to them – emerged as a matter of pressing concern for many different parties, including businesses, boosters, conservationists, outdoor recreationalists, historical societies, politicians, and agencies of the state. These parties generally agreed that automobile travellers should feel that they were free to experience landscapes for themselves, without heavy-handed restrictions on where they could go or what they could look at. Middlebrow critiques of roadside commercial aesthetics notwithstanding, it was also generally agreed that property owners whose land bordered on a public right-of-way had a right to sell things to passersby and to advertise their goods and services. However, as the following chapters show, the state sometimes stepped in to manage the appearance of landscapes that were visible along the roads it had constructed. Sometimes it restricted certain industrial and commercial activities. More often it employed experts to manipulate landscapes "behind the scenery" in an effort to draw motorists' attention toward certain features and divert it away from others. And in still other instances, the Fordist state took a direct role in developing roadside amenities and attractions.

Frequently, the goal of these landscaping projects was to make a profit, as when motel and gas station owners lobbied the state to preserve appealing features (such as large trees or old buildings) that stood within view of a road that led to their community. These would attract motorists, who would then patronize their establishments. Sometimes the goal was to project a certain image around an entire community, as when boards of trade, conservationists, and historical societies co-operated to establish a park or museum. Many such efforts to differentiate a place in the eyes of the motoring public were indirectly related to the profit motive, in that cultivating distinctive attractions – even ones that did not charge an entry fee – could help lure travellers into town, where they were likely to purchase food, gas, lodging, and more. In still other cases, the goal of manipulating a roadside landscape was to deliver a pedagogical lesson, as when the Historic Sites and Monuments Board of Canada erected a monument to commemorate a person, place, or event that it deemed significant, or to divert attention away from potentially troubling features, as when the BC Parks Branch tried to hide evidence of logging or mining inside a park. These lessons about nature by the road and history by the road were often imprecise or ambiguous, for they were intended more to generate an affect than to convey specific information – for example, to encourage appreciation of natural beauty or enthusiasm for a frontier past. Nevertheless, whether their goal was to sell, promote, or instruct, these landscape cultivators ultimately sought to make British Columbia look good to a massive, amorphous, capricious, and internally diverse audience: North America's fast-growing motoring public.

Although this book focuses on British Columbia, it contributes to our understanding of the broader history of North American automobility. More than a century after Model Ts started rolling off of Henry Ford's Highland Park assembly line, historians have written far more about automobile production and road construction than about how people used those cars to drive on those roads. We know relatively little about distinctive regional histories of automobility, about the automobile as a vehicle for encountering the world, or about the culture of time and space inextricably linked with it.[11] Just as railways played a central role in what cultural historian Wolfgang Schivelbusch calls the "industrialization of time and space" in the West during the nineteenth century, automobility, as a leading instance of Fordism, did generate a new way for travellers to relate to their surroundings. The railway, as a closed system, was (and is) necessarily characterized by standardized time and hierarchical space, by rigidity and closed, top-down management. The route and means of travel were firmly conjoined, and as a result passengers' views of the places they traversed were tightly structured.[12] On the other hand, automobility, as a system, was characterized by flexible time, "public" space, dispersal, diffuseness, and a general lack of top-down management, except for a loosely enforced traffic code. The ability to travel on a timetable, pace, and route of one's own choosing was a huge part of motoring's appeal, for work and for play. The exhilaration of high speeds receives a great deal of attention from scholars of mobility (and of modernity), but the fact that motorists had the option to drive slowly, stop frequently, change route, and double back on their tracks was just as important, for it allowed them to recuperate the sense of foreground and connection to their built and natural surroundings that had seemingly been annihilated by railway travel.[13] Free to go slow or fast, to select whether to pause or go past, motorists felt themselves active participants in the landscapes they passed through, rather than passive consumers of standardized travel experiences. They could rediscover places that had been off the beaten path or mere in-between space within the rigid hierarchies of continental rail networks.

Automobile travel also offered a fuller, more sensuous experience of landscape. Railway travellers were more removed, even insulated from their surroundings, than motorists. For both, the travel experience was primarily visual, but motorists could smell a field or a forest, hear birds or a waterfall, and feel smooth and rough sections of the road. This was especially true prior to the 1930s, when open- and soft-topped passenger cars were most common. Access by automobile was a new way of getting closer to natural environments by camping, visiting parks, Sunday drives in the country, and so forth.[14] The automobile was also something of a time machine. It allowed motorists to recuperate some of the time that was seemingly annihilated in railway travel, making it possible to discern and contemplate historical features such as old buildings, trails, mines, mills, graveyards, and ghost towns. Furthermore, exposure to the elements and the unpredictability of travelling along bumpy, muddy, haphazardly maintained roads caused motorists to believe that they had a better sense of what travel had "really" been like in the past, before the advent of locomotives and steamboats. Here it is important not to exaggerate the actual degree of control in the hands of the motoring public: even so-called off-road vehicles such as jeeps and today's sport-utilities are really only bad-road vehicles, incapable of going very far without a path that has been prepared and maintained for them at someone's considerable expense. Thus, though automobile travel has been perceived by most motorists as liberating and relatively free because it was so much more flexible than travel by railway (or steamboat or stagecoach), the closer look undertaken here reveals that the practice of driving and the experience of landscapes by the road were more firmly constrained than commonly recognized. Everyone saw more or less the same thing, regardless of what kind of vehicle they were in. They were all seeing the same landscapes, even if their readings of such shared experiences might be various.

Historians and other scholars show that motorists in America and other Western countries formed communities of highly mobile subjects tied together by the flexibility of private automobiles and, ironically, the sense of individual agency and freedom engendered by driving them over public roads.[15] Their shared experiences of landscapes iconic and mundane forged deep connections between automobility and group identity. Some governments even made concerted efforts to shape drivers' ideologies through their experiences of the places they passed through.[16] Commercial activity was also an inescapable part of the motoring landscape experience, and historians have traced how the roadside economy became both big business and part of popular culture.[17] By 1920, roadside landscape features were intentionally used in many ways to communicate to the motoring public – as consumers and as citizens – including through eye-catching signs and distinctive oversize mascots.[18] In just two decades, then, automobile travel had become central to both perceptions of place and processes of place making in America.[19]

In broad terms, this pattern prevailed north of the 49th parallel. In many regions of Canada, however, automobility developed at a slower, more halting pace and on a more modest scale due to economical governments and a preponderance of undercapitalized roadside entrepreneurs.[20] As this book shows, this was particularly true for rural and hinterland areas. Precisely how automobility, landscape, and modernity became intertwined remains unexamined for most parts of Canada, even though many of the routes and landmarks popularized during the mid-twentieth century remain familiar today. In British Columbia, as in most provinces, the history of automobiles and highways has been penned mainly by retired professional drivers and engineers.[21] However, several recent scholarly studies have drawn attention to how roadsides and banal fixtures such as licence plates were made into communicative sites of memory and identity in British Columbia.[22] Historians have also traced how the province's tourism industry used roadside landscapes in its promotional campaigns.[23]

All of these writings inform *British Columbia by the Road*'s proposition that what happened in the Interior, structured as it was by the Fordist state and its infrastructure-building programs, the motoring public's unpredictable tastes and preferences, and the region's specific social and physical geography, was a more open-ended, contingent, and uncertain process than accounted for by studies of the top-down construction of automobiles, highways, and place images. By looking closely at the familiar yet unexplored terrain of the open road, by showing how an array of interested parties responded thoughtfully to what they recognized as the flexible-yet-structured pattern of automobile travel, and by situating a distinctive regional history within a larger continental or even global trajectory, this book allows us to grasp in a new way the long revolution in political economy *and* sensibility constituted by automobility, and to appreciate how it contributed to the making of modern landscapes.

British Columbia by the Road is organized as two parts or paths, both of which promise to drive readers beyond Hope. You may begin with whichever part most interests you, for they are intended to be read in any order. Route A focuses on perceptions of nature. If you would like to know how roadside landscapes inside parks were managed so as to shape the motoring public's experiences of the environment, begin with it and set out across the Cascade Mountains bound for Princeton. Route B considers perceptions of the past. If you prefer to learn how the roadsides of the Interior were used to communicate history lessons to motorists, follow the Fraser Canyon northward toward Yale.

However, before you begin for Princeton or Yale, a little context regarding transportation in the southwesternmost Interior will help set the stage while also illustrating the important effects of state-built infrastructure that channelled the motoring public along certain routes. Route A and Route B both start at the same time and place, the sleepy village of Hope in the early 1920s. Hope has long been the gateway between Coast and Interior and a junction where eastbound travellers select a route through the mountains. It sits at the foot of the Fraser Canyon, through which the river of the same name drains a basin of eighty-five thousand square miles. Hope has long been well served by modern transportation routes. The Canadian Pacific Railway (CPR) was built beside that stretch of the Fraser in the 1880s, as was the Canadian Northern Railway in the 1910s.[24] After the end of the Great War, politicians in Victoria faced intense pressure to expand and improve the provincial road network, including from boosters, boards of trade, merchants, farmers, tourism promoters, and the automobile owners who comprised the fast-growing motoring public.[25] A road that would go beyond Hope to link the Coast and the Interior was deemed essential, for the province had lacked such a connection since the 1880s, when railroad construction had destroyed much of the colonial-era Cariboo Wagon Road. Victoria acknowledged this as a priority in 1919, when it announced its intention to build a network of roads that would allow motorists to travel "from the Coast through the whole central part of British Columbia."[26]

There were only two feasible routes for such a road: one that climbed through the rugged Cascade Mountains between Hope and Princeton, and one that skirted the Cascades via the tortuous Fraser and Thompson Canyons between Hope and Ashcroft. Powerful regional interests lined up to support each option, for the former was sure to benefit the southern Interior, whereas the latter would benefit the northern and especially the central Interior. The provincial government did not make a firm commitment until 1923, by which time key components of a transprovincial highway that would span the central Interior had fallen into place. The Department of Public Works had stitched together two hundred miles of passable road between Ashcroft (on the Thompson River) and Revelstoke (on the Columbia), running parallel to the route of the CPR and thus through a number of well-established communities, including the city of Kamloops. Also in 1923, the federal government agreed to build most of a touring road between Golden, British Columbia, and Banff, Alberta. Once this was completed, only two gaps would remain in a road linking Vancouver and Calgary: one between the mountain towns of Revelstoke and Golden, and the other between Ashcroft and Hope. These developments made the Fraser Canyon route seem more of an asset than the southerly Hope-Princeton alternative. The fact that Minister of Public Works Dr. W.H. Sutherland represented Revelstoke in the provincial Legislature also boded well for central Interior motorists.[27] In early 1924, he instructed that the province's first Coast-to-Interior automobile road be built through the Fraser and Thompson Canyons.

The road opened to drivers in the fall of 1926 and quickly became an important shared landscape experience for the motoring public, renowned for its dramatic scenery and traces of the old Cariboo Wagon Road. Until 1949, it was the only automobile road that linked Coast and Interior, and as such, it played a crucial role in shaping Coast motorists' perceptions of the province beyond Hope. Driving the canyons tied people together as travellers, consumers, and citizens.[28] Simply put, that route was *the* "beaten path" of British Columbia. By comparison, places distant from or poorly connected to it seemed marginal or off the beaten path. The southwestern Interior was one such region. Its motoring-minded residents' sense of isolation was aggravated by the provincial government's stinging 1924 decision to bypass them in favour of the central Interior. By the late 1920s, however, few expected this would remain the case for long, as it seemed likely that Victoria was about to build a second Coast-to-Interior road – one that would allow the motoring public a choice in which route to follow when venturing beyond Hope.

ROUTE A

A Drive through Nature

Parks are a mixture of nature and culture, preservation and exploitation, places where sections of paradise have often been paved over in order to put up the parking lots deemed necessary for citizens and tourists to appreciate their edifying qualities. Route A maps out how the relationship between automobility and the environment was managed in two of the largest, most accessible provincial parks in the BC Interior – Manning and Hamber. Asking how the state initiative of park making intersected with the state project of road building, it looks at the construction and experience of what American park historian David Louter has called windshield wilderness, whereby the vast majority of park visitors have their encounters with nature shaped by the vehicles and infrastructure that rank among the most intrusive and extensive developments within parks.[1] Whereas several historians have traced high-level philosophical and institutional debates about the proper place of roads and automobiles in parks, the approach taken here is to look closely at conditions on the ground and at the processes and practices of managing (or not managing) park landscapes.[2]

In British Columbia, as in most of North America during the twentieth century, the popular experience of nature was shaped by parks, and the popular experience of parks was in turn shaped by the manner in which visitors reached and moved through them. Environmental historians and historians of tourism have detailed the very close relationship between railways and most of the major parks in western North America during the late nineteenth and early twentieth centuries, but the link between parks, public roads, and private automobiles has received much less attention, and this is particularly the case for Canada.[3] Between 1945 and 1970, many Canadian parks were established and managed as nation- and province-building devices. Governments saw making parks accessible to the motoring public as a good way of obtaining value from areas that had been set aside from industrial resource extraction. Developing parks alongside arterial highways was also a good way to encourage their use by tourists and citizens alike, and thus expanded investment in roads was often accompanied by increased investment in parks. In many instances, the Fordist state treated them as complementary assets. Thus, the provincial parks of British Columbia were to a large extent conceived and operated as extensions of western Canada's highway network, with the motoring public's views foremost in the mind of park promoters, planners, and day-to-day managers. Nature came to be understood as something that most British Columbians and visitors to the province experienced by the road.

For more than half a century, Manning has been one of the most popular, heavily visited, and "successful" provincial parks in the BC Interior. Its location explains much of its fame. It is relatively near Vancouver and is traversed from east to west by the Hope-Princeton Highway. This road, which forms a key section of the southern transprovincial highway, was started in 1929 but then delayed for many years, opening to drivers only in 1949. Hamber Provincial Park is an enormous tract in the Selkirk and Rocky Mountains. Hamber was traversed by the Big Bend Highway, which was started in 1929 and completed in 1940, just before war finances took up the state's attention. There were noteworthy similarities between Manning and Hamber in addition to the fact that they were both crossed by important arterial roads, but whereas Manning was lavished with attention and made into a significant asset, Hamber was sorely neglected. It saw no development and remained unknown to the public.

Before setting out along Route A, a few distinctive features about the history of parks in British Columbia need to be flagged. For most of the twentieth century, only the Canadian and American national park systems were larger than that of the province in terms of total area. For a few years, the BC system was even larger than its American national counterpart. However, most of its large wilderness parks were isolated and difficult to access before the late 1940s because of the cavalier manner in which they were created. This inaccessibility was also a reflection of the province's primitive transportation network. Whereas most of the American and Canadian national parks in the mountainous west had been opened up to drivers by the early 1930s, British Columbia's large provincial parks typically remained isolated until after the Second World War. They were, in effect, symbols that brought little material return to the province. For most British Columbians in the mid-1940s, they were little more than names on a map. Massive postwar investment in highway infrastructure changed all this.

During the late 1940s and early 1950s, the designs for BC provincial parks were very plastic. There were no firm policies in place about recreation or conservation, about allowing cabins, concessions, and other developments in the parks, or about how to manage existing parks and establish new ones. The practical men of the Parks Division, most of whom had come up within the administrative structure of the BC Forest Service, concentrated on preserving timber from forest fires, except now their emphasis was on protecting its scenic value rather than its value as an extractable resource. In 1957, responsibility for the provincial parks was transferred from the Forest Service to the newly formed Department of

Recreation and Conservation. This allowed the Forest Service to concentrate on the "productive" aspects of BC woodlands, and the parks were clearly reclassified as tourism and province-building assets. The Parks Division became the Parks Branch and started to focus more on outdoor recreation and nature interpretation.

During the 1950s and 1960s, new highways were being built and old ones were being improved throughout the BC Interior. Many of the resulting changes in provincial and national parks occurred suddenly and on a large scale, putting unanticipated strains on natural environments, facilities, and staff. For example, when the new paved, all-season route of the Trans-Canada Highway opened through the Selkirk Mountains in 1962, the growth in traffic to and through Mount Revelstoke National Park was so great and so rapid that Parks Canada closed it for two full years to upgrade its winding parkway and construct new buildings and campsites. Similar gusts of change occurred in the provincial parks, so that until the late 1960s planners and other staff usually found themselves reacting to, rather than planning for, new roads, increased traffic, and their myriad side effects. Only in the early 1970s were master plans drawn up to develop the facilities and policies needed to cope with the existing levels of traffic and the projected steady growth in the number of visitors – the vast majority of whom would pass through in a car. To a great extent, then, the postwar growth of British Columbia's provincial park system, its systematization, and the establishment of its bureaucracy were the result of new and improved highways and steadily rising rates of automobile ownership and automobile travel.

Several historians have noted what is seemingly a major contradiction in the BC postwar parks policy: although the number of provincial parks increased by almost two hundred between 1949 and 1965, the total area actually *decreased* by nearly 2.5 million acres.[4] As hundreds of small roadside picnic sites, campgrounds, boat launches, and other recreation-oriented spots were being added to the system, huge portions of older, larger parks were being deleted with the stroke of a pen, usually to facilitate enormous clearcut logging operations prior to the construction of a dam that would flood out vast areas of the country. In this light, the many small "parklets" created in the 1950s and 1960s should be understood to suggest that the provincial park system served to a large degree as an extension of the highway network. New, small parks adorned the roadsides like beads on a string, whereas large parks that were out of sight could be repurposed according the Fordist state's changing political-economic priorities.

1

Toward a Park in the Cascade Mountains

In the summer of 1929, less than three years after the crucial highway through the Fraser Canyon had provided the first direct road link between Coast and Interior, the Conservative government of Premier Simon Fraser Tolmie announced that it would begin work on a new road to connect Hope and Princeton via Allison Pass. This second Coast-Interior route would be completed by 1932, a bold claim, for building ninety miles of new road through the Cascade Mountains would not be easy or inexpensive. The area was a knot of mountains and rugged highlands, pierced by only a few narrow river valleys. There were no rail lines, communities, farms, or mines in the mountains between Hope and Princeton, only a few rough trails and a handful of prospectors' cabins. To most British Columbians, the southern Cascades were an unfamiliar wilderness, even though they were only 150 miles due east of Vancouver.[1]

The Hope-Princeton project had widespread support from residents of the southern Interior. Its motorists (and would-be motorists) looked forward to driving directly to cities on the Coast without having to follow a roundabout route via the Fraser Canyon or Washington State.[2] Orchardists looked forward to delivering their produce directly to coastal markets.[3] Hoteliers, garage owners, and many other business owners looked forward to the road bringing pleasure travellers to the region. Auto touring had become the most popular leisure activity for middle-class North Americans since the end of the war, and the southern Interior's warm, dry climate, placid lakes, and verdant valleys had long been recognized as having the potential to lure sightseers and recreationalists.[4] The provincial government did not describe the Hope-Princeton link as a touring road when it was announced, but many interested parties wanted to ensure that it would be scenic as well as efficient.

The announcement of the project could not have come at a worse time for its many supporters. The collapse of North American commodity markets in late 1929 dragged British Columbia's economy and government revenues down with it. Initially, the crisis was perceived as yet another slump among the many that had plagued the province's resource-based economy, though a particularly bad one. The Tolmie government applied the traditional remedy: reducing expenditures. Public works spending was slashed, which resulted in the Hope-Princeton project being suspended just a few months after work had begun. The unprecedented severity of the economic downturn was clear by early 1931, when the province's official unemployment rate hovered around 28 percent. Worried that unemployed, politically radicalized men from the resource hinterlands would congregate and cause disorder in coastal cities, the government in Victoria began providing relief employment through public works projects.[5]

Road-building camps were set up in isolated spots during the summer of 1931, including along the surveyed route of the Hope-Princeton road. Over the following years, camps would be established at the Sumallo River flats, Snass Creek, Copper Creek, and Cambie Creek ("Cambie Creek" refers to the uppermost section of the Similkameen River). These camps would achieve only piecemeal progress, for the construction techniques that professional building crews would normally have used were rejected to maximize the total amount of work available.[6] Prior to 1933, federal support was not forthcoming for relief work projects that were deemed to be of mere regional or provincial significance, including the Hope-Princeton. Victoria's finances quickly became overextended, and by the fall of 1932 the government was nearly bankrupt, kept afloat only by emergency funding from Ottawa. Disregarding the advice of his minister of public works, Premier Tolmie ordered the suspension of all BC relief road-building projects, except for the Big Bend Highway, a joint federal-provincial venture.[7]

It was during the early Depression years that the badly stalled Hope-Princeton project became intertwined with proposals to establish a park in the Cascade Mountains. Boosters, business owners, and tourism promoters in the southern Interior believed that a park might help spur completion of the promised road, in that motorists and recreationalists would pressure Victoria to make it accessible. In the long term, they expected that a park would differentiate the Hope-Princeton route from the park-less Fraser Canyon route, thereby helping to lure pleasure travellers and bringing increased commercial activity. By the late 1920s, there was an established pattern in western North America whereby the creation of new parks stimulated motoring- and tourism-related development in nearby communities.[8] However, the first to propose a park in the highlands between Hope and Princeton – Martin Allerdale Grainger – was not a would-be roadside commercial operator. Instead, he was a nature-loving industrialist and former senior civil servant.

Grainger was a Cambridge-educated mathematician who served as secretary to British Columbia's 1910 Royal Commission on Provincial Forest Policy and then as a ranger in the BC Forest Service. He was appointed chief forester in 1916 and held that position until 1920, when he entered the private timber business.[9] In the mid-1920s, Grainger began a recreational routine that he called "my escape from business." On Fridays in summer and fall, he would leave his office in downtown Vancouver and catch a train to Hope, where he transferred to another train on the Canadian Pacific Railway's Kettle Valley branch line. This took him to Princeton, where he kept a cabin and several saddle horses on the ranch of a local family. From this base, he spent his weekends riding in the high country between Princeton and Hope, returning to Vancouver on the last Sunday train, feeling physically drained but mentally revitalized. Grainger sometimes went into the mountains for weeks at a time, taking minimal equipment and only basic foods.[10]

Grainger tried to organize a Skyline Club that would popularize trail riding in the southern Cascades and bring riding enthusiasts together as a group that could lobby for preservation and developments that were in their interests. He also wrote a series of newspaper articles that extolled the virtues of "roughing it" in the outdoors generally and the quietude and scenery to be found in the Nicomen and Hozameen highlands specifically.[11] The 1929 announcement of the Hope-Princeton project made Grainger keener than ever to promote that area, but it also made him wary. Twenty years in the timber business convinced him that the promised road could result in commercial and industrial developments that would threaten his mountain Arcadia. He therefore set out to convince politicians and government officials to establish a park that would protect the scenic and natural attractions of the southern Cascades.

Grainger preferred the quiet and solitude of the high country, but he recognized that many middle-class British Columbians used private automobiles and public roads to escape the drudgery of the farm and the pollution and enervating pace of modern city life. Thus, he placed the

Trail riding in the Three Brothers area during the 1920s. Gowen Sutton Company postcard. Author's collection.

motoring public and its future experiences of nature at the centre of his arguments in favour of a provincial park. He made his case most comprehensively in a June 1930 letter to F.P. Burden, minister of lands in the Tolmie administration. Grainger argued that the recently opened Fraser Canyon Highway had little tourist appeal due to its gloomy scenery and "intimidating" terrain, whereas a road through the wooded and relatively open country of the Nicomen and Hozameen mountains could become the setting for "a multitude of summer cottages and tourist hotels":

> No better country for hikers or horseback riders could be found than these two ranges – they hold their own easily with Banff or Jasper Park. And the great point is that they will be right at the edge of the automobile road, so that the hikers and riders who will motor out for the weekend or the many people who will have summer camps up there will have immediate access to some of the best upland and mountain scenery on this continent.

Grainger asserted that the area's native flora and fauna were scenic assets that had to be preserved to make a good impression on future auto tourists. This was especially important along the valley floors where motorists would travel and in the subalpine areas that hikers and riders would seek to visit. "The essential thing," he implored, "is to safeguard the wild life – the flowers, the feed [grass], and the deer." Warning that "inadvertence could quite readily destroy one of the big attractions of the Hope-Princeton highway," he cited the destruction of Green Timbers on the Pacific Highway between New Westminster and the Blaine border crossing as a recent instance in which impressive natural roadside scenery had been lost.[12]

Grainger assured Burden that the proposed park would not conflict with logging or mining activity. He did anticipate a possible conflict with ranchers, but he maintained that the southwestern Interior had enough open range to accommodate them – it was not necessary to "despoil the feed and flowers of the land immediately adjacent to the new highway." He also appealed directly to Burden's political instincts by suggesting that conserving scenic and natural landscape features along the promised road would be popular with the growing number of middle-class voters who owned cars and used them for leisure travel. It would show that a tourism- and recreation-conscious government understood their desire to commune with nature through motoring. He argued that the government had to provide such amenities because the national parks in the Rockies were too far from coastal population centres: "They could not be gone to by car in a weekend as a park in the Cascade Mountains could be." Grainger concluded by suggesting that a provincial park would be "in itself, in dollars and cents, a big justification for the expense of the Hope-Princeton highway."[13]

Boosters, merchants, and agricultural producers in the southern Interior threw their support behind Grainger's proposal after the government halted work on the Hope-Princeton road project. His earliest allies in Princeton were Bert Thomas, the district road foreman, and Edgar Burr, who owned the Similkameen Garage and local Ford dealership.[14] Thomas and Burr rallied the district board of trade to the cause by pointing out that a park would bring new opportunities for profit: Princeton was an outlier in the Interior road network in 1930, with no businesses dedicated to the tourist trade. Another important supporter of the park idea was timber baron H.R. MacMillan, who had preceded Grainger as chief forester and whose brokerage firm the MacMillan Export Company was one of the province's most powerful forestry interests in 1930.[15] MacMillan had taken to trail riding in the Cascade Mountains, sometimes with his old friend Grainger and other times with his own family and friends.[16] Writing to the minister of lands in the summer of 1930, he declared the mountains between Hope and Princeton "the best piece of high country available anywhere near Vancouver" and predicted that lodges, gas stations, guiding outfits, and other commercial operations would flourish in the vicinity of a future park, allowing "quite a few people in the region to earn a steady living from the expenditures of travellers." However, he warned, "if a park is not created and the wild life not protected, the area will probably be devastated very quickly." Degradation of the scenery visible from the road would reduce the area's appeal to motorists and thus stifle development of the roadside service sector in the southwestern Interior.[17]

Sheep versus Scenery

Grainger's prediction that ranching interests would fight the proposed park proved correct. The main opponents were Willis and Sutherland, sheep ranchers out of Keremeos, forty-five miles east of Princeton, who were backed by their local board of trade and the BC Sheep Breeders Association. Willis and Sutherland had grazed their flocks in the Nicomen highlands north of Three Brothers Mountain for several summers prior to 1930. That year, eager to expand, they applied for additional grazing rights in the immediate vicinity of the Three Brothers.[18] The ranchers forecast dire economic consequences if a park were established in that area, claiming it would drive them out business and "establish a precedent which will keep stockmen from investing in this province." The BC Sheep Breeders Association pointed out that the province's mutton deficit would continue to be filled by imports if rangelands were not expanded.[19]

Park supporters were alarmed at the prospect of domestic sheep grazing near the Three Brothers, which they considered especially scenic. Sheep threatened to damage wildflower meadows and crowd mule deer out of the valley floors. The Princeton Board of Trade called on the provincial government to reserve the Three Brothers area from grazing and was supported by its counterparts in Kelowna, Penticton, Vancouver, and New Westminster. Princeton residents also petitioned Victoria to "save the Cascade region" by establishing a park. The provincial government did place a mile-wide reserve along the surveyed highway right-of-way in 1931 but more to thwart interference with construction than to preserve scenery. This reserve did nothing to prevent sheep being herded along valley floors or grazed in the surrounding highlands.[20]

When asked to decide between the interests of a few established rural producers and a coalition of middle-class outdoor recreationalists and small-town business owners, Victoria initially sided with the Keremeos ranchers. BC governments had a long history of favouring agriculture and ranching, and this was especially true under Simon Fraser Tolmie, a veterinarian, cattle breeder, and former federal minister of agriculture who styled himself as a friend to the farmer. Bigger flocks of sheep seemed a more monetarily tangible and immediate benefit to the stricken BC economy than the preservation of scenery for the viewing pleasure of people who might one day drive between Hope and Princeton. A series of reversals followed the initial issuance of a permit that allowed Willis and Sutherland to graze their sheep near the Three Brothers (which came too late for them to lead their animals into the area in 1930).[21] The following spring, the commissioner of grazing withdrew the permit in the face of sustained protest by the Princeton Board of Trade and allegations that deer were being indiscriminately slaughtered along cleared sections of the Hope-Princeton right of-way.[22] The government next put an area around Three Brothers Mountain under tentative reserve "in order to maintain it in its natural state" pending a final decision on land use. Willis and Sutherland continued to press their case and in 1934 were given special permission for "experimental" grazing in that area, which led to howls of complaint in the southern Interior. More pro-park petitions were delivered to Victoria, and Okanagan newspapers attacked the provincial government's policies on roads and tourism promotion. In the face of these protests, the new Liberal government of T.D. "Duff" Pattullo backed down. It suspended the issuance of grazing permits in the vicinity of Three Brothers Mountain and asked the BC Game Commission to provide a scientific report on the environmental consequences of sheep grazing.[23]

A damning report delivered to Attorney General Gordon Sloan in January 1936 described the destructive effects of sheep grazing on western flora, fauna, and landforms, from the crowding out of native game species to the erosion caused by stripping away ground cover. This report was accompanied by allegations that the experimental grazing permitted at the Three Brothers in 1934 had "completely destroyed" prime tracts of mule deer habitat.[24] Sloan consulted with various officials, including Chief Forester Ernest C. Manning (who recommended that grazing be permitted in the disputed zone), and concluded that the government should favour the preservationists and park promoters.[25] The Three Brothers Game Reserve was established in 1936, within which no grazing or industrial activity would be permitted. The Pattullo government was more inclined than its predecessor to treat parks as potential assets – assets that could provide much-needed short-term employment while being turned into long-term tourism and recreational attractions. This policy was no doubt influenced

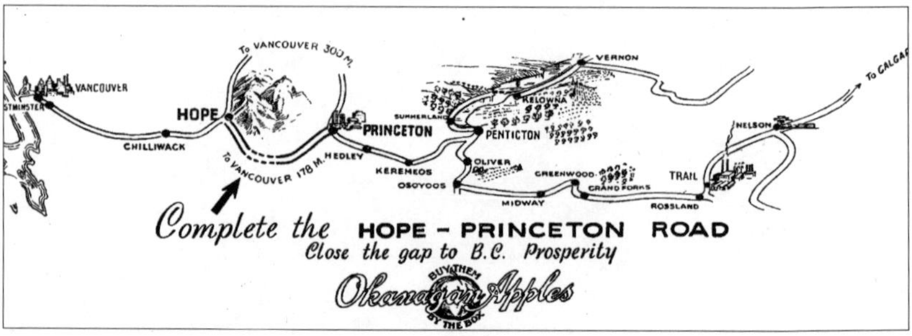

Penticton Board of Trade letterhead, late 1930s.

by the widely publicized work that the Civilian Conservation Corps had been doing in American parks since 1933.[26] British Columbia's incipient Fordist state had sided with those who proposed to develop a major attraction along an important future highway.

The government's support for scenic preservation in the Cascade Mountains was not unequivocal, however. Its decision to create a game reserve instead of a provincial park is explained by the lack of progress on the Hope-Princeton project. The work camps associated with it had opened, closed, and been transferred between various agencies and levels of government from 1930 until 1936, when Victoria shut them down permanently.[27] Ninety miles of new road had been surveyed, but only twenty-eight had been completed to a standard that was passable for passenger cars. Fifty were in varying stages of construction, and nothing at all had been done on the remaining twelve.[28] Motorists and business interests from the southern Interior continued to press Victoria to finish the road during the late 1930s, but lobbying for a park died down after the sheep menace was warded off.[29] In Princeton, where support for the park had been strongest, the preservationist impulse was eclipsed by a violent labour conflict and the closure of almost every mine in the district.[30]

Ironically, it was the outbreak of war that made completion of the Hope-Princeton seem possible. In public meetings, petitions, newspaper editorials, and letters to the premier, boosters and boards of trade in the southern Interior asserted that finishing the road was an urgent priority in the fight against Nazi Germany. They argued that Canada needed an alternative to the route through the Fraser and Thompson Canyons, where two transcontinental railroads, telephone and telegraph lines, and the province's only Coast-to-Interior automobile road all crowded through a series of treacherous defiles that had a well-deserved reputation for instability.[31]

The BC Forest Service was assigned responsibility for provincial parks in 1939, and several of its senior officials believed that the Hope-Princeton Highway would be completed in the near future. One of these was George Melrose, who had been responsible for the Princeton district during the 1930s sheep-grazing dispute and who was promoted to assistant chief forester in early 1941 following Ernest C. Manning's death in an airplane crash. In April 1941, Melrose advised the minister of lands that the Three Brothers Game Reserve was an area of "outstanding scenic beauty" that deserved to be turned into a provincial park. As Michael Dawson shows, the BC government vigorously promoted the province to American tourists in the years 1939–41 because tourism brought in hard currency that was desperately needed for the war effort. Melrose may have believed that the government would see completing the Hope-Princeton and establishing a new park alongside it as a way of drawing auto tourists from throughout the Pacific Northwest.[32]

The minister approved Melrose's recommendation, and Ernest C. Manning Provincial Park was established in June 1941. It was named after the former chief forester who had helped further the causes of conservation and provincial parks in British Columbia.[33] The fact that Manning had supported sheep grazing at Three Brothers in 1936 was conveniently overlooked. Manning Park was 170,000 acres in size and contained twenty-seven miles of the surveyed Hope-Princeton right-of-way. It had a Class A designation, which provided the province's highest level of protection against intrusion by resource development. The press release that announced the new park promoted it as a "holiday land without peer" and implied that British Columbians and visitors from afar could drive right in. "A mere jaunt by auto or train from Vancouver," it promised, "and one is at the gateway of this mountain paradise."[34] Completion of the highway and thus access to the new park were hoped to be just around the corner.

The first step that the Forest Service took in Manning Park was to erect a stone cairn with a bronze plaque in memory of its namesake. It dispatched the entire two-man staff of its fledgling Parks Division to build the monument beside the scenic Similkameen Falls near the eastern boundary of the park, at a point where it could be seen from the surveyed right-of-way. Commemorative cairns had become familiar features of Interior roadsides since the late 1920s, as shown in Chapter 5. With its very first action "on the ground" in Manning Park, the agency responsible for BC parks was seeking to shape the motoring public's future views of both nature and history by the road.[35] However, though no one could have known it in 1941, nearly a decade of construction delays would elapse before drivers saw the monument to Manning, which would also need to be relocated due to a realignment of the road. The interregnum provided boosters, botanists, business owners, tourism promoters, veterans' organizations, and government agencies including the Parks Division time to contemplate the relationship between park, highway, and motoring public, and to put forward competing proposals for how it should be managed. A key question that ran through their many plans and schemes was whether the state should develop the park with an eye toward a limited number of outdoor recreationalists – educated and well-heeled professionals like Martin Allerdale Grainger and H.R. MacMillan – or the much larger number of people who would one day drive along the highway through the park. There were class overtones to this question, as well as many practical considerations for how Manning Park should be planned and then developed.

Reconnaissance and Planning

Contrary to what senior Forest Service officials had expected in 1941, the provincial government kept the Hope-Princeton road project on the backburner for the duration of the war. The only work done was by Japanese Canadian men from the Tashme internment camp, which the BC Security Commission built on the Sumallo River flats fourteen miles east of Hope, just outside the hundred-mile Coastal Exclusion Zone. Poorly housed and paid, short of dynamite and earth-moving machinery, and resentful over their treatment at the hands of the Canadian government, the internees not surprisingly proved just as ineffective at road building as the inhabitants of the relief work camps had between 1931 and 1936.[36] The slow pace of work provided abundant opportunity for the Parks Division and other interested parties to inspect Manning and formulate proposals for its development. Some envisioned an area of refuge for educated professionals who wanted to engage in strenuous, contemplative outdoor recreational activities. However, by 1945 the Parks Division had decided to prioritize a broader and exponentially larger group that had very different viewing and travel habits: namely, the motoring public. This was an instance of what environmental historian Alan MacEachern calls "recreational democracy," in which agencies of the Fordist state thought it imperative to provide recreational opportunities for as many people as possible, starting with the middle class.[37]

In the summer of 1943, two assistant foresters from the Parks Division were dispatched to examine Manning Park and make recommendations for future development there. Ches Lyons and Mickey Trew's reconnaissance of the park was the first in a series they would undertake during the mid-1940s (their 1945 inspection of Hamber Park is discussed in Chapter 3, and Lyons's role in planning historically themed parks and plaques during the late 1950s is examined in Chapter 7). Lyons and Trew explored Manning for ten days, much of it spent riding near the treeline along mountain ridges and through subalpine meadows. Alan MacEachern argues that mountain scenery was a key yardstick for measuring Canadian park values, and Lyons and Trew clearly expected that Manning's high country would be its main attraction, enticing well-heeled visitors who could afford to buy or hire trail horses.[38] They recommended that new trails be cut and existing ones improved so that riders and hikers could reach wildflower meadows and scenic vistas. They paid far more attention to the backcountry trails than to the surveyed route of the Hope-Princeton, although they did note that it appeared "exceptionally well designed for pleasure driving."[39]

Lyons and Trew suggested that lodges with stables be developed on the uppermost Similkameen flats, near where the Lightning Lakes drained into the Similkameen River. Shallow and placid, the Lightning Lakes were linked by reedy marshes, and Lyons and Trew expected they would be popular with anglers.[40] This proposed park centre would be located a mile from the future highway and reached by an access road, effectively separating visitors from passers-through and keeping the main facilities out of sight and earshot of high-speed traffic. The lakeside lodges and high country trails that Lyons and Trew anticipated were geared toward a refined middle-class clientele who wanted independent, contemplative, and rustic types of outdoor recreation that required time, skill, and a degree of physical effort. These included fly fishing, hiking, and horseback riding. This vision of the park had echoes of the Arcadia for revitalizing "roughing it" that Martin Allerdale Grainger had advocated in the late 1920s – not exceptionally expensive or overtly exclusive but also not in line with most British Columbians' idea of a good time in the Great Outdoors.

Forest Service headquarters ordered a second inspection in 1945, apparently having revised its expectations of Manning and other provincial parks in light of the government's draft submission to the August 1945 Dominion

Provincial Conference on Reconstruction, which proposed to make significant public investment in recreational facilities such as parks. The inspection was conducted by E.G. Oldham and D.L. McMurchie, experienced Forest Service planners who had recently been demobilized from the military. Their itinerary suggests that the main problem with the 1943 reconnaissance report had been *where* Lyons and Trew had focused their attention. Oldham and McMurchie were instructed to concentrate on the valley floors, where the Hope-Princeton Highway was surveyed to run, instead of on the high country.[41]

Oldham and McMurchie's reconnaissance report emphasized that Manning was singular among British Columbia's large provincial parks for its proximity to coastal population centres and for the fact that people would one day be able to traverse it by automobile. They identified the corridor surrounding the surveyed right-of-way as requiring the most attention in any development plans because practically everyone who entered Manning Park would see it. They recognized that all motorists would share certain landscape experiences in the park, regardless of whether they were sightseeing tourists or busy commercial travellers whose "visit" consisted of driving through without stopping. As an example, they noted that anyone who drove eastward through Manning would perceive the transition from coastal to Interior climate zones, with the enormous cedars and dense underbrush on the climb toward Allison Pass giving way to a drier, sparser cover of lodgepole pine and sagebrush in the rain shadow of the Cascades.[42]

Oldham and McMurchie's main recommendation was that a large dining establishment be developed adjacent to the Hope-Princeton Highway on the Similkameen flats, at the point where an access road should branch off toward the Lightning Lakes. This restaurant would offer light meals and refreshments but not overnight accommodations and would operate in conjunction with a gas station and garage. The high country that comprised the greater part of Manning was of secondary importance in Oldham and McMurchie's plans, for they expected only a small minority of visitors to explore that area. Their vision of the park was more popular or democratic than that of Lyons and Trew, at least to the extent that it focused on motorists and what they could see and do in a short time and with minimal expense. The very fact that the second inspection was ordered indicates that during the late war years senior Forest Service officials were beginning to think of provincial parks as state-provided amenities that all British Columbians (who had access to an automobile) had a right to enjoy. It also reveals that Forest Service headquarters expected Manning to be a showcase park traversed by a showcase highway.

A lesson that the BC Parks Division drew from a half century of park development in North America was that popular and accessible examples had the best chance of being permanent. Thus, it was deemed important for British Columbians to know about and be able to visit their provincial parks, or at least know enough to *want* to visit them. In the summer of 1944, the Parks Division and the BC Government Travel Bureau organized an exclusive horseback excursion into Manning for tourism promoters, including representatives of the British Columbia Automobile Association. They wanted to show that the provincial parks – and Manning in particular – were assets that would be useful to the tourism industry once the war was over. The Parks Division's role in promoting and planning for postwar auto tourism confirms Michael Dawson's argument that during the late war years BC tourism promoters began setting the stage for increased postwar travel to (and within) the province. The excursion proved such a publicity coup that the Parks Division planned to make similar tours an annual event.[43]

The division also encouraged botanists, rock collectors, birdwatchers, and other naturalists to explore and promote Manning Park. Several naturalist organizations submitted reports to the division that expressed concern about changes they foresaw once the park was accessible by highway and offered suggestions for how it should be developed. The Vancouver Natural History Society worried that Manning's quietude and aura of wilderness would be disrupted if too many scenic areas were opened up to "portly middle-aged motorists" who were desirous of merely "parking the car ... where they can look at the country." The society predicted that "motorists who are too lazy or who are incapable of leaving their cars are going to be disappointed with the scenery of the Hope-Princeton road":

> No wide vistas can be obtained from the road on the 60-mile drive from Hope, although there are many pleasant glimpses. For 30 miles into Princeton high open ground is traversed, but it is rather bare country ... Consequently, if the motorist is to be interested, secondary roads will have to be built to carry him to scenic spots. It will be wise to forget the motor tourist for the time being and give him no encouragement.[44]

Proper park users, the Vancouver Natural History Society implied, were those who strove to know the environment up-close and in the flesh rather than passively consuming it through a windshield. The society recommended against road access to the Lightning Lakes, lest an influx of angler-motorists decimate trout stocks. Its vision for Manning Park was of a relatively exclusive retreat for the educated, refined, and physically fit – precisely the kind of development plan that the Parks Division was shifting away from by 1945.

Clifford Carl, the director of the Provincial Museum in Victoria, may have been more aware than the natural history society of the division's evolving plans. He offered the agency his findings in the belief that they might help deal with the traffic that would pass through the park once the Hope-Princeton was completed, and several of his recommendations involved the preservation of roadside natural attractions. He argued that construction should not be allowed to disturb the beaver colony on the eastern Similkameen flats, which might "prove a great source of interest to Park visitors." He suggested that the picking of rare alpine wildflowers and Pacific rhododendrons be prohibited and that this rule be "rigidly enforced." He also predicted that the (non-native) trout in the Lightning Lakes would come under severe pressure once Manning was accessible to motorists and proposed ways of manipulating the lakes to increase their "general productivity" for sport fishing.[45] Seeing the road as "a potential destroyer of wildlife," Carl predicted that deer and grouse would be "decimated ... in the first few years until they will only be seen in areas some distance from the highway." To mitigate the anticipated carnage, he suggested that signs be erected where the highway entered the park, asking motorists to avoid "the destruction of wild creatures on the road."[46] Provincial Museum staff made repeated visits to Manning over the following years; some of their findings regarding the highway's impact on animal populations are discussed in the next chapter.[47]

Naturalists were not alone in making wartime recommendations to the Parks Division about how Manning should be developed. In July 1945, the Princeton district subcommittee of the Provincial Rehabilitation and Reconstruction Committee expressed strong support for the prohibition of logging, mining, and grazing activity. "Nature has endowed British Columbia with ample and particularly attractive natural resources in the almost incomparable beauty of its scenery," the subcommittee observed, and allowing that perpetual but non-renewable resource to be marred by industrial activity would be short-sighted. The subcommittee also praised the mile-wide reserve that had been placed over Crown land along the surveyed Hope-Princeton right-of-way, thinking it useful for preventing eyesore developments:

> It needs no stretch of the imagination to see that our Government is quite right in barring the sale or lease of parcels of land within the park to private individuals who might be likely, uncontrolled, to put up unsightly gas and repair stations and tourist camps, jerry built for economy, and capable of bringing in quick returns without regard for appearances, without regard to harmony with their setting. We too have often seen such places dotted along our highways, with their sole adornment consisting of advertising signs.[48]

Princeton's forward thinkers were not opposed to roadside commerce in principle. In fact, they believed that it offered valuable opportunities for profit and self-sufficiency, and therefore urged Victoria to help returning veterans establish themselves in that kind of business – even within the boundaries of Manning Park. But they wanted to ensure that any commercial operation offering food, gas, or lodging along the Hope-Princeton would not detract from the road or the park as assets to the southwestern Interior's economy and image. The future highway corridor's reputation was foremost in mind.

Traffic Delays and Aesthetic Concessions

The end of the Second World War brought renewed interest in establishing businesses along the Hope-Princeton. A Forest Service official who visited Princeton in December 1945 found local merchants "seething with plans for taking care of the flood of travel which they anticipate will follow the opening of the road."[49] Between 1945 and 1950, the Forest Service received more than a hundred requests for permission to build cabins, camps, autocourts, gas stations, and other commercial ventures along the highway right-of-way in Manning Park. However, its long-promised, long-anticipated benefits would be deferred until the very end of the 1940s. The Hope-Princeton was resurveyed to modern Canadian standards in 1944, which required much of the existing road to be rebuilt. The completed highway would also be paved to permit all-season traffic and the passage of heavy commercial vehicles. In the blueprints of BC transportation planners, the Hope-Princeton Highway was shaping up to be one of the province's most advanced and important thoroughfares.

Manning Park and the route that spanned it remained officially closed to would-be entrepreneurs while road construction was under way and the Parks Division was drawing up development plans.[50] But not everyone was bound by the reserve on roadside Crown land, and their efforts to build cabin camps, gas stations, and other stopping places posed challenges to the Parks Division, which wanted to ensure that roadside landscapes in and around Manning would have a naturalistic aesthetic that met public expectations of a western Canadian mountain park. The Tower family owned one of the few alienated parcels of land along the Hope-Princeton right-of-way, having purchased in 1944 a 160-acre parcel from Charlie Bonnevier, an elderly and reclusive prospector who had lived near the park since 1905. This property straddled the highway and the Similkameen River near the park's eastern boundary. Planners were especially concerned about the look of any commercial development at this strategic location, so they met with the Towers to discuss their business plans and steer them toward erecting "a presentable establishment rather than a blot on the landscape." To their relief, the family proved amenable to their suggestions.[51] Other people used more creative methods of land acquisition in their efforts to establish roadside commercial operations. The most problematic case was a prospector named Hansen who in 1946 started building tourist cabins inside the park, on a mineral claim located beside the highway near Cambie Creek.[52] Chief Forester C.D. Orchard complained directly to his counterpart in the Department of Mines that Hansen was abusing his right to erect buildings on a mineral claim. He pointed out that Hansen's guest cabins, gas pump, and "advertising of tourist accommodation" were clearly unrelated to mining and argued that they presented an aesthetic problem, as the cabins had been built in a slapdash manner. Orchard insisted that the department investigate the legitimacy of Hansen's claim.[53]

The Parks Division expected that Hansen would be compelled to tear down or remove his buildings. Instead, it learned that an oversight had enabled Hansen to upgrade his mineral claim to a Crown grant, meaning the Department of Mines could no longer control what he did on it. Lacking an administrative tool with which to dislodge Hansen and his objectionable cabins, the division was forced to negotiate. The government finally paid Hansen $3,500 to let his claim lapse, after which the ranger in charge of Manning Park burned the buildings and cleaned up the site so that no trace would be discerned by passing motorists.[54] Several other rural residents who aimed to become roadside entrepreneurs attempted to revive old mineral claims and grazing permits as a means of gaining toeholds inside the park, leading Ches Lyons to warn that "a firm stand must be taken against such intrusions" if the Parks Division were to maintain a high degree of control over what was visible along the road.[55] Help came in 1949, when cabinet issued an Order-in-Council that forbade prospectors from erecting buildings or cutting trails or roads in any BC provincial park without first acquiring permission from the division in the form of a parks use permit.[56] This permit system would prove an invaluable tool in the division's efforts to impose and maintain a clean, naturalistic aesthetic along the highway through Manning, and in many other provincial parks too.

At the same time that the Parks Division was striving to find an administrative tool with which to regulate against shabby, slap-dash private developments, it also had to decide what kind of private development it did support. Roadside commercial concessions were a new feature in the provincial parks. In February 1946, F.S. McKinnon, the head of the Parks Division, sent the chief forester a lengthy report about development and commercial concessions in Manning. It concluded that the Hope-Princeton would be "the artery from which all traffic in the park will originate" and therefore recommended that a single concession be permitted inside the park: a large lodge with an estimated cost of $150,000, which would be located adjacent to the highway on the Similkameen flats, more than a mile from the Lightning Lakes. A gas station and autocourt would also be associated with the lodge. The proposed concession was clearly oriented more toward the general public than toward hikers, anglers, and backcountry trail riders.[57]

McKinnon set out the requirements expected of any future concession holder. The accommodation and dining facilities must not be expensive to the point of exclusivity, but nor were they to be overly commercial in form. The buildings were to blend in with their natural surroundings. McKinnon recommended low structures with a simple, semi-rustic exterior finish and colour scheme to be determined in consultation with park planners. The lodge would have a dining room for forty, snack bar for fifty, and public restrooms, and the upper floor would provide accommodations for thirty guests. The concessionaire would have to install a diesel-electric lighting plant, water system, and septic field, and also provide "appropriate" landscaping of the grounds. A gas station was required because running out of fuel would be a very real risk for motorists and because the planned concession site was equidistant between Hope and Princeton. Within two years of opening, the concessionaire was also expected to build an autocourt consisting of between fifteen and twenty self-contained, drive-up "cabin bungalows." All these structures were to be concentrated close together to avoid the appearance of a commercial strip.

The concession was to be the first road-accessible commercial enterprise offered in any of British Columbia's provincial parks, and Manning itself was poised to become a showcase where the cultural, recreational, and economic value of the provincial parks could be demonstrated to political and business elites as well as to the motoring public.[58] The Forest Service therefore wanted to ensure that the winning applicant had sufficient financing and construction experience to build a respectable operation that was aesthetically appropriate. Chief Forester C.D. Orchard interviewed the short-listed applicants in late 1946, consulted both the minister of lands and Premier John Hart, and ultimately awarded the concession to the Armstrong Construction Company of Vancouver. However, sharply conflicting views about what constituted appropriate uses for the lodge would prevent the company from building the concession complex.

In February 1948, Ches Lyons examined Armstrong's plans and was perturbed to learn that the company intended to operate a beer parlour in the lodge.[59] Public consumption of alcohol remained a contentious topic in postwar British Columbia. Highly regulated beer parlours had been the only public places where it was legal to drink since 1925, and they were inextricably associated with the working-class clientele that tended to frequent them.[60] The regulations that the BC Liquor Control Board imposed on beer parlours also jeopardized the Parks Division's development plans for Manning, in that cabin camps were forbidden near drinking establishments. Furthermore, a beer parlour threatened to introduce elements of "rough" working-class culture to a place where middle-class individuals and families were expected to get a sense of uplifting communion with nature. In a letter to Orchard, Parks Division head F.S. McKinnon confided, "We older people are set in our drinking habits and if we must have our liquor can afford to bring our bottle with us but it would seem to be poor policy to have beer by the glass readily available to young people out for a weekend of recreation."[61]

The premier was said to be personally interested in the development of Manning Park, which made the stakes especially high for the Parks Division and Forest Service. Any chance that a drinking establishment might get built beside a showcase highway in the middle of a showcase park was unacceptable. In February 1949, the head of the Parks Division notified the Armstrong Construction Company that it would not be issued a park use permit to erect the concession buildings.[62] C.D. Orchard had convinced cabinet that the best way to proceed with commercial development in Manning was for the government to go into the accommodation, food, and gasoline business itself by building the concession complex with public funds and then leasing its operation to a private party under strict conditions. The Fordist state would generate this key piece of tourist and

Hope-Princeton opening ceremony, November 1949. BC Archives, F-07648.

recreational infrastructure itself and thereby maintain tight control over the aesthetics of (roadside) development inside the park.

The lodge at the concession complex – which came to be known as Pinewoods – was not finished in time for the grand opening of the Hope-Princeton Highway in the fall of 1949. The ceremony was held on 2 November at the summit of Allison Pass, just a short distance from the new Department of Public Works maintenance yard, where graders, caterpillar tractors, snowplows, and other large machines were lined up for everyone to admire.[63] An arch covered in evergreen boughs and a gate sporting a provincial crest were placed across the highway for the proceedings. The road had yet to be paved, but that did not deter five thousand boosters, business owners, and driving enthusiasts from parking along its verges on each side of the gate.[64] After speeches about public works, progress, and postwar prosperity, Premier Byron Johnson used a golden key to unlock the gate, throwing the long-awaited highway open to the public. Accompanied by his packhorse, Charlie Bonnevier, the elderly prospector who had sold his property near the eastern edge of Manning Park to the Tower family, was invited to be the first to step through the gate. “I’ve been waiting for this road for 54 years,” he told the premier, while shaking his hand. Bonnevier’s appearance had been arranged by Public Works officials to show that the new highway had opened up a long-isolated part of the province to the motoring public, who were now free to seek pleasant prospects along it, albeit in a manner that differed markedly from what Bonnevier had been doing for so many years.[65] The Hope-Princeton Highway and the unfamiliar country that it traversed remained a blank slate to the public, and their image in the popular imagination was still highly malleable. As the following chapter shows, the Parks Division recognized this and went to great lengths to impose and maintain an appealing aesthetic along the highway corridor in Manning Park. Simply establishing a park and completing the road were not enough to make the high country between Hope and Princeton into a natural asset. An active and sustained program of development and maintenance was required.

2

Behind the Scenery in Manning Park

The Hope-Princeton was far and away the most advanced mountain highway in British Columbia when it opened in late 1949. Newspapers and magazines hailed it as a "superhighway" and a vital artery of trade and tourism. *Country Life in British Columbia* predicted it would "give Coast residents access to areas hitherto little known."[1] The motoring public expressed little spontaneous enthusiasm for it as a scenic route, however. Victoria grocer Leonard Coton, who was an avid auto tourist and keen observer of roadside landscapes, had only this to say in 1950:

> This highway, in all deference to those who built it and those who have used up gallons of ink writing about it since its opening, is far too highly rated. As a scenic highway it has little or nothing as compared with some of the other roads I have traveled on this trip, except perhaps for the occasional view across a canyon more or less obscured by roadside trees ... Perhaps in years to come, those trees will be cut or blown down, and then this may be a scenic attraction [but] for now it is only a road which has shortened the distance from Vancouver to Princeton by over a hundred miles.[2]

The Parks Division also regarded the Hope-Princeton corridor as neither intrinsically scenic nor particularly interesting. During the early 1950s therefore, it set out to develop a series of scenic, natural, and historical attractions that would improve both Manning Park and the highway, increasing their appeal to the public and their value to the state. Planners

Highway and roadside pullout at Skagit Bluffs. Gowen Sutton Company postcard. Author's collection.

based in Victoria and staff stationed in Manning Park worked "behind the scenery" to impose a naturalistic aesthetic along the highway corridor. They also sought to maintain this aesthetic so that park landscapes would meet motorists' expectations of nature by the road. Transforming Manning into a major asset that made British Columbia look good was not a one-time project. Instead, it was an ongoing process that required both long-term funding and expert attention.

The field inspections that the Parks Division conducted during the mid-1940s had identified several features outside the boundaries of the park that could potentially serve as attractions.[3] Most were in the uppermost Sumallo and Skagit River valleys, including the striking views where the road would traverse the towering Skagit Bluffs, twenty-eight miles east of Hope. During the final stages of road construction, the Parks Division persuaded the Department of Public Works to have its contractors build a paved pullout along the western edge of the bluffs so that motorists could safely leave the flow of traffic, exit their vehicles, and peer down into the gorge of the Skagit. Because of the crash barriers that lined the edge of the precipice, this impressive view was invisible to those who did not stop at the pullout.

The Parks Division also identified a remnant of the gold-rush-era Dewdney Trail as a potential historical attraction. British Columbia's

A remnant of the Dewdney Trail flanks the Hope-Princeton Highway. Note the small pullout at right of centre. University of Victoria Archives, Chester P. Lyons fonds.

colonial government had surveyed a wagon road between Fort Hope and the Rock Creek gold diggings in 1860 and hired Edgar Dewdney to blaze a preliminary trail through the Cascade Mountains. Plans to upgrade the trail into a wagon road were cancelled when the Rock Creek rush fizzled out, but prospectors and ranchers continued using Dewdney's trail, and several sections remained intact in the 1940s. One gracefully curving and ascending stretch was located adjacent to the Hope-Princeton Highway, seventeen miles beyond Hope.[4] No other portion was so prominently visible from the new road. A longer section farther east was especially well preserved, but it was high above the valley floor in an area where the road followed a series of sharp curves pinched between the Sumallo River and steep, rocky hillsides. Parks Division staff determined that "a dangerous traffic situation" might occur if signs were put up to indicate this gold-rush-era relic to passing motorists, so they focused their efforts on the plainly visible and easily accessible segment to the west, where a small pullout was built on the highway verge.[5] Several years later, when the BC Telephone Company strung a phone line from Hope to the Pinewoods concession complex, it was instructed to run the wire high on the hillside, away from the view of travellers who stopped to look at the trail. BC park planners were not especially interested in historically themed landscape features during the early 1950s, but this relic of nineteenth-century transportation was too conveniently located to pass up and could enhance eastbound motorists' sense that they were rediscovering a little-known part of the country.

The Parks Division also identified three potential natural attractions outside Manning's original western border that merited preservation for (and from) the public. One was the grove of wild California rhododendrons that grew on the flats twenty-three miles east of Hope. This grove marked the northernmost range of the plant and had inspired Provincial Museum director Clifford Carl to call for strict rules forbidding the removal of certain species of flora in the Cascades.[6] Division staff decided that Rhododendron Flats was one of the most unusual and interesting botanical sites along the Hope-Princeton Highway, meriting attention from passing motorists and protection from overenthusiastic admirers. As it was not inside the park, they proposed to designate it a recreational reserve.[7]

The second attraction, a very different kind of grove, lay just west of Rhododendron Flats. Between the highway and the meandering Sumallo River at mile twenty-two east of Hope was a stand of enormous, ancient western red cedars and Douglas firs, kept damp by the heavy precipitation on the windward side of the Cascades. Sumallo Grove was the tallest stand of such timber beside the new highway, and it seemed particularly spectacular in comparison with the immature growth to the west and the smaller, sparser pine forests to the east, as the highway climbed toward Allison Pass and the Interior rain shadow.[8]

The third potential attraction was on the bluffs across the river from Sumallo Grove. Prime mountain goat habitat extended southward from these bluffs, and a healthy population of around thirty goats had been observed on the bluffs in the 1940s. In the fall of 1949, however, Provincial Museum staff spotted the remains of a kid at the base of a cliff, "killed accidentally or possibly shot and unrecovered." Prospector Bill Robinson, who had a cabin downriver, reported hearing gunshots on numerous occasions, which indicated that sniping from the roadside was a frequent occurrence.[9] Hunting was forbidden inside Manning Park, as signs along the highway pointed out, but no such protection extended to the mountain goats on the Sumallo bluffs. As Clifford Carl warned,

> the area is now so easily accessible that it will be most surprising if increased hunting pressure does not drive or eliminate goats from the immediate environs of the highway. Sportsmen who desire to add this animal to their trophies should not expect to take it from a public thoroughfare. However,

Sign erected at the western edge of the Big Burn in spring 1950. University of Victoria Archives, Chester P. Lyons fonds, AR409, 4.12.5.

> when such a trophy presents itself, rare is the hunter who will pass up the opportunity. For this reason some well-publicized restrictions should be imposed in order to maintain goats on "Robinson's Ridge," where they may be enjoyed by everyone passing along the road.[10]

Park planners recognized that the clutch of potential attractions to the west of Manning could help compensate for a major eyesore at the point where the highway entered the park. The forest on the western approach to Allison Pass is arid and susceptible to fire, and large conflagrations had struck there in 1869, the late 1910s, and during the tinder-dry summer of 1946, when several thousand acres burned on the steep mountainsides bordering the highway right-of-way.[11] Observing the 1946 fire from an airplane, the Kamloops district forester had correctly predicted that the burnt-over area would be a "most conspicuous feature, in full view of any person driving through the park."[12]

Park staff concluded that the "big burn" presented "such a frightful, desolate sight" that it required explanation. They also believed that its shocking appearance could be used to promote safety in the woods. In the spring of 1950, Ches Lyons and Mickey Trew set up a large sign on the western edge of the burnt-over area that read "One camper made this 5700

Manning Park Gallows, with recently paved highway surface. University of Victoria Archives, Chester P. Lyons fonds, AR409, 4.12.3.3.

acres look like hell! Don't *you* be careless." The Department of Public Works objected strongly, not only because the sign had been erected without its permission, but also, according to Lyons, because "hell was a pretty strong word to display to public gaze in those days." As a result, the sign was redesigned to become the Manning Park Gallows. Beneath a ten-foot-long cigarette swinging by a noose, a sign read "The guy who dropped it should also be hanged. Prevent forest fires."[13]

Ironically, given that the gallows was meant to explain and reduce the impact of an enormous eyesore, it quickly became an attraction in and of itself, a colossus that borrowed from the whimsical styling of the commercial strip and carnival fairway to deliver its message. "This was a car stopper for sure!" Lyons recalled. "It was photographed and displayed in magazines near and far. I don't think there has ever been a forest fire sign with more impact than that one." The Forest Service's public relations officer received so many favourable comments about the sign that he recommended it be re-erected in 1951, with or without permission from Public Works.[14]

Having the entrance to a showcase provincial park marred by evidence of a huge forest fire raised troubling questions about the roles of the Parks Division and Forest Service as stewards of the woods. By shifting Manning's western boundary toward Hope, the division could solve two problems at once: the four potential attractions would be brought under its jurisdiction, and the Big Burn would no longer mar the western entrance. Late in 1949, ranger Mickey Trew suggested that a mile-wide parkway be established along the Hope-Princeton corridor for ten miles beyond Manning's original western edge. This, he argued, would give motorists "at least an impression of 'park' before coming to the desolation of the burned area."[15] Trew's proposal quickly gained support among division staff, for parkways had been a familiar and popular feature in North American parks since the 1920s.[16] By 1950, it was also clear that such an arrangement was the only affordable way to minimize the visual impact of the Big Burn: the division could not afford to clear thousands of charred snags and replant the slopes with seedlings.[17] Establishing a linear parkway in the upper Skagit and Sumallo River valleys and developing a series of attractions within it would form a kind of aesthetic buffer zone, bringing eastbound travellers past interesting, accessible, and clearly identified sites before they reached the burnt-over area at Allison Pass.[18]

The ten-mile-long, 4,500-acre parkway was grafted onto Manning Park in June 1950, increasing its total area to 175,000 acres. At the stroke of a pen, the Parks Division gained control over several potential roadside attractions. It placed "No Hunting" signs along the highway near the goat crags. When amateur botanists were caught picking wild flowers at Rhododendron Flats, it charged them under the provincial Dogwood and Rhododendron Protection Act, publicizing these prosecutions to notify everyone that plundering the park's newest attractions would not be tolerated.[19] The creation of the western parkway was one of the division's most ambitious and successful attempts to shape the motoring public's experiences of nature by the road. Staff were soon busy identifying sites inside the parkway where evidence of industrial activity and recent habitation required a "clean-up" to be consistent with the desired naturalistic aesthetic.[20]

Animal Attractions

Many travellers expected to see large, furry mammals when visiting mountainous parks in western North America, and the Parks Division tried to ensure the presence of several such species in Manning.[21] The beaver ponds at the eastern end of the Similkameen flats are a case in point. Their value had first been flagged in 1946 by the director of the Provincial Museum,

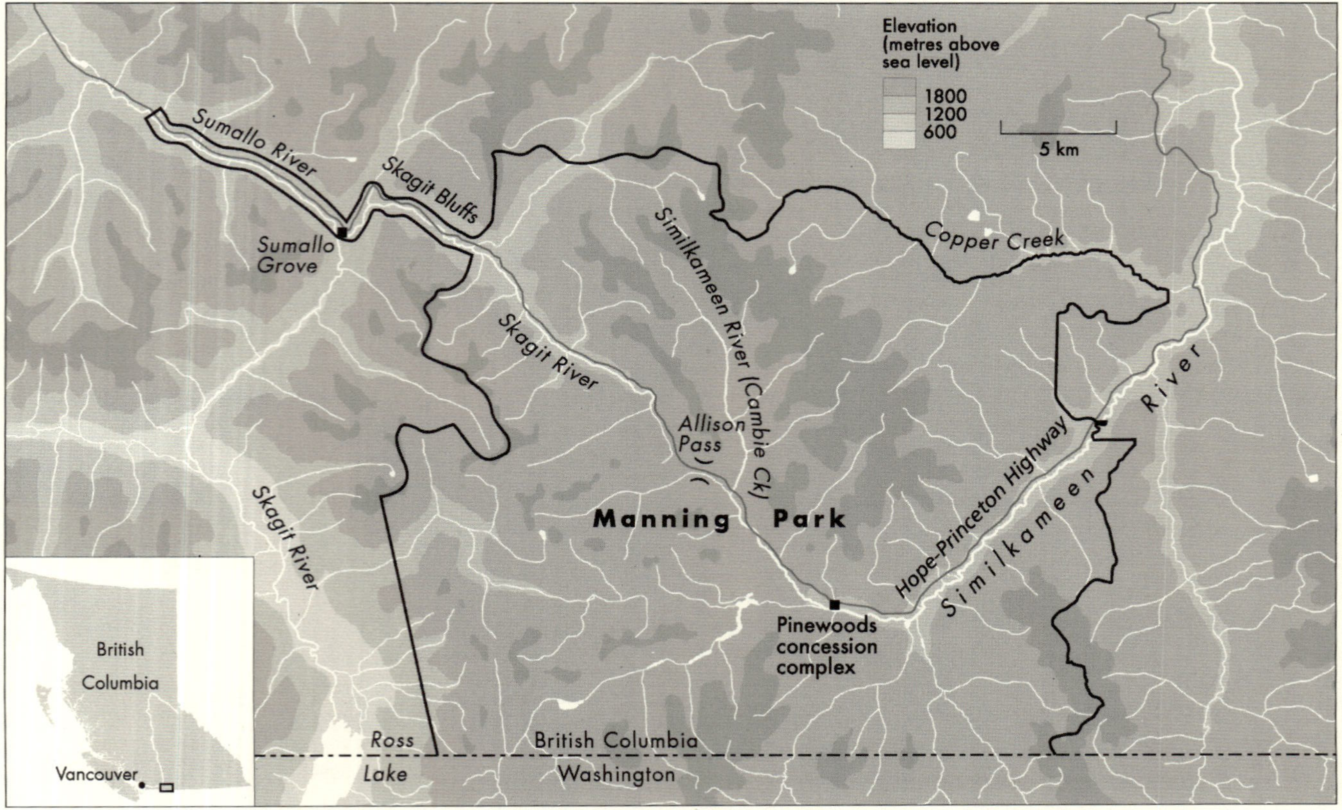

Manning Park in 1952, showing parkway extension at the park's western edge.

who recommended that highway construction not be allowed to disrupt the resident beaver colony, because it might prove popular with future visitors. The Forest Service's 1951 annual report promised "an effort to make beaver and deer more abundant and easily seen" in Manning. In the summer of 1954, park planner Ray Lowrey was sent to investigate the potential of the ponds.[22]

After studying the site and the beavers' behaviour, Lowrey concluded that the ponds could be turned into "a unique roadside attraction" to enhance Manning's tourist appeal. However, careful development was required. The highway ran along a terrace about fifteen feet above the ponds, and though the beavers appeared untroubled by traffic, they quickly submerged and retired to the safety of their lodges whenever they observed an automobile stop at the edge of the road. Lowrey determined that a small parking lot could be cleared while retaining a screen of brush and timber between it and the beavers. Unseen by the wary animals, people could leave their vehicles in the lot and walk through the trees to a viewpoint overlooking the ponds.

Lowrey also believed that the proposed viewpoint area should be tidied. "Numerous dead trees killed by [road construction] should be removed from the fringe of timber between the parking lot and viewpoint and the ponds," he reported. "Visibility, appearance, and safety will all be improved by the destruction of these snags." Interpretive signs with "interesting facts about beavers" would also be required. Finally, Lowrey considered how the ponds should be maintained as a permanent attraction. The beaver dams were quite old, and the ponds were so still and nutrient-laden that they would eventually be choked by plant growth, driving the beavers away. In effect, they were slowly becoming reedy meadows. This was a natural process, but Lowrey argued that the "beaver pond next to the highway warrants special efforts to ensure a continued production of beaver." Possible solutions included topping the dams with sandbags to raise the pond level by several feet or dynamiting a channel that would allow water from the Similkameen River to enter the ponds. To dissuade the beavers from relocating, Lowrey recommended replacing the existing vegetation with alder, willow, aspen, and cottonwood, their preferred food.[23] The Parks Division built a viewpoint based on Lowrey's recommendations in 1957, which quickly became one of Manning's most popular roadside features.[24]

The sedentary habits of beavers enabled their transformation into a sightseeing venue, but most large mammals in the southern Cascades ranged far and wide, making them unreliable as natural attractions. In the early 1950s, the Parks Division studied the use of salt licks as a way of drawing mule deer to the western Similkameen flats, which was the centre of development in the park, where many drivers pulled off the highway to picnic, buy gas, or dine at the new Pinewoods concession complex.[25] Seeing deer in this part of the valley was common but by no means assured. Following the success of Walt Disney's *Bambi* in 1947, making deer more visible seemed a good way of increasing the park's appeal to families with young children while demonstrating that the presence of humans had not disrupted wildlife populations in the Cascades.[26] Tests conducted on a pine flat near park headquarters found that sodium bicarbonate and sodium acid phosphate were the most effective deer attractants. The chief of the Parks Division instructed park staff to place salt licks "where there is public access," which meant near campgrounds, picnic sites, and Pinewoods – all of which were close to the highway and all of which the deer were otherwise likely to avoid due to automobile traffic and other human activity.[27]

The division conducted a second taste test in Manning that summer in the hope of making a different kind of large mammal less visible. Black bears loitering along the roadside and visiting parts of the park that were frequented by humans had been a problem since the completion of the highway. To learn whether cat and dog repellents would drive these bears away, staff half-filled six tin pails with Rogers Golden Syrup and hung them from trees near the park garbage dump, which was in an old gravel pit. Within an hour, bears had torn down the pails and licked them clean. Another six pails of syrup were then treated with a variety of commercial cat and dog repellents and hung up. These too were quickly torn down and licked clean. The experiment was repeated twice more with the same results, convincing staff that domestic pet repellents were not an effective way to deter bears from visiting areas of the park where humans tended to congregate.[28]

The dump was a grey area in the Parks Division's efforts to manage the relationship between bears and humans. Staff were comfortable allowing visitors to drive to the dump to watch bears scavenging through the copious amounts of garbage deposited there, provided they remained in their cars and kept their windows rolled up. A letter from Superintendent Bob Boyd to the chief forester shows that the dump was treated as an informal attraction during the early 1950s. "On the writer's recent trip to one of our large National Parks, they were reluctant to allow me to visit their garbage disposal area," Boyd complained. "We, in Manning Park, invite our tourists to look at the animals frequenting the [dump] area."[29] This practice no doubt acclimatized bears to both cars and humans, and when they began visiting picnic sites, campgrounds, and other developed areas, the division took steps to combat what was termed "the bear problem." The frequency of garbage pickup was increased in places where visitors regularly left scraps of food. Staff also stopped treating the dump as an attraction. The large sign that marked its entrance was replaced with a small, discreetly positioned sign, with another partway along the access road warning sightseers habituated to visiting the dump to stay inside their cars when bears were around.[30]

None of this dissuaded bears that had learned to associate picnic sites and campgrounds with food. Summers during the early 1950s saw numerous instances of overturned garbage cans, slashed tents, and broken car windows, and several visitors suffered minor bear-related injuries. The casualty rate for bears was significantly higher. In 1956 alone, one yearling had to be shot, another that was entering the garbage room at the administration building was frightened away only by wiring the door handle to deliver a strong electrical shock, and two attempts were made to lasso and relocate a young bear that was begging for food beside the highway.[31] Unfortunately, the Parks Division did not study animal migration patterns in the park or track mortality rates along the highway during the early 1950s, so it is impossible to calculate the impact of traffic on deer, bears, and other wildlife populations.

Ultimately, the division's efforts to make beavers and deer visible to visitors while steering bears away from them were meant to demonstrate that the highway, automobiles, and motorists passing through Manning Park had not disrupted these animals' habitat or corrupted their behaviour. The managed presence of certain large mammals in close proximity to the highway showed the public that Manning was not a *Bambi*-type scenario, with "Man" bringing death and destruction to the woods.

Coping with Eyesores

Suppressing visual blight was an important complement to protecting scenery and developing attractions in the Parks Division effort to impose and maintain a clean, naturalistic aesthetic along the highway corridor. Most of the sites/sights that it perceived as eyesores involved industrial structures and activities that were visible to drivers. Unlike the Big Burn, the dilapidated construction sites and active mining and logging operations inside a provincial park could not be pithily explained away by a clever, eye-catching sign.

Erasing traces of the highway's construction was a key aim for the Parks Division. It resented the quarries and gravel pits that lay along the right-of-way, and after years of lobbying convinced the Department of Public Works to screen them from view by strategic plantings of native trees and shrubs.[32] Old construction camps were similarly problematic, for they showed that the highway was a recent creation, not a natural path that magically transported visitors through a pristine environment. After paving was finished in the summer of 1951, the division asked Public Works to remove or demolish the buildings at its former construction camps, including the one at Copper Creek, which was outside Manning's eastern boundary. Park staff argued that these abandoned structures posed a fire hazard, might draw transients, and "detract[ed] from the otherwise very scenic highway."[33] Eventually, they were permitted to burn the buildings and clean up the work camps inside the park. Because these sites had good access to the highway and steady water supplies, several were converted into campgrounds – thus, campground development did double duty for the division, providing outdoor visitor accommodations while covering up traces of recent construction.[34]

Eyesores associated with resource extraction industries were trickier to manage. Although Manning was a Class A park, pre-existing resource rights had not been extinguished when it was established. As a result, numerous trap lines, mineral claims, and timber licences were grandfathered inside the park. Similarly, the 1950 parkway extension was superimposed over active mineral claims that had been outside the original boundaries of Manning, including the Hillside claims that served as the base camp for the Canam Mining Corporation's copper prospecting operations in the nearby hills. By 1949, the company had built a bunkhouse, workshop, and several other structures there, as well as a jeep road that connected it with promising claims in the Skagit range to the south.[35] None of these buildings or actions drew the Parks Division's attention, even though the jeep road had been built across a backcountry section of Manning without permission. However, when Canam bulldozed a new access road between its Hillside camp and the Hope-Princeton in July 1950, it trespassed (albeit perhaps unwittingly) upon Manning's recently added parkway extension.

This development was particularly problematic because the new access road was plainly visible from the highway. Moreover, westbound motorists could discern the Hillside base camp through the intervening timber. The Parks Division suggested that the situation could be resolved and a parks use permit granted for the access road if the mining company relocated a few hundred feet of the road and moved its camp "a short distance to the west, where it would be hidden from view."[36] The mine manager replied that he wanted to clear up any objections to Canam's operations in and near Manning Park, and though it would be costly, he agreed to relocate the access road.[37] Moving the entire base camp was out of the question, but the manager did offer to camouflage it. Buildings would be painted to blend with the forest; areas not used by vehicles would be sown with grass seed; and trees or a hedge would be planted between the camp and the highway. The proposed cover-up convinced the Parks Division to issue the company a parks use permit for its access road.[38]

Eyesores associated with logging were another major concern. As in most BC provincial parks, the government had granted timber licences for berths inside Manning. Most had been issued decades before the park was created, and the timber they covered had never been of much commercial value due to the area's inaccessibility. Over time, these renewable licences were bought, sold, and swapped by logging companies and brokers, but no trees were actually cut. Then, with the rise of truck logging and the impending completion of the road between Hope and Princeton in the 1940s, long-isolated berths in the Cascade Mountains – including those in Manning Park – became more accessible, more valuable, and more feasible to log.[39]

Anyone who held a valid timber licence inside Manning had the right to log in the designated berth. However, building an access road to remove the fallen timber would first require a parks use permit issued by the Parks Division. Because Manning was so far from the nearest sawmills (in Hope and Princeton), logging companies and timber brokers with holdings in the park regularly approached the division or other offices of the Forest Service to determine whether they could exchange their licences for the right to cut elsewhere on Crown land. In the summer of 1952, sawmill owner Hugh Leir suggested just such an exchange to the Forest Service. He had acquired licences that allowed him to log several berths along Cambie Creek, near the centre of Manning Park, including one that bordered the Hope-Princeton right-of-way.[40] Leir offered to trade his Manning berths for others that were nearer to his Princeton and Penticton sawmills.

The Forest Service's Kamloops district office was willing to make an exchange, but only for the licence that allowed Leir to log near the highway. Preventing logging in areas of the park that would be screened from view by standing timber and the contours of the terrain was not seen as worthwhile.[41]

Leir was not satisfied with this offer. He felt that his licences on Cambie Creek were worth more than the value of the timber alone because they were prominently located inside a newly accessible park. He may have hoped to use them as a bargaining chip toward acquiring a tree farm licence near Penticton.[42] Leir protested the Forest Service decision to his MLA – Kelowna hardware salesman W.A.C. Bennett, who had recently been elected premier – but to no avail. In late 1953, his crews logged the berth that bordered the highway, despite the fact that Forest Service staff were cruising for a suitable tract to offer in exchange. Then, having found it unprofitable to haul the logs to Princeton, Leir sold his remaining Cambie Creek licences to a broker. Several years later, when this broker approached the Parks Division about swapping the remaining "Leir licenses" for timber elsewhere in the region, he was curtly informed that "the aesthetic values we tried to protect have been lost and there is no further point to an exchange." To hide evidence of the logging at Cambie Creek, the division developed a campground on the cut-over area.[43]

The dispute over licences, logging, and roadside aesthetics at Cambie Creek was the first in what would prove a fusillade of similar situations in the coming years. The Parks Division learned an important lesson from the incident: it could not rely on other branches of the Forest Service to help preserve a clean, naturalistic aesthetic along the main travel corridor through Manning Park. It subsequently strove to keep all negotiations involving timber exchanges in Manning (and other provincial parks) "in house," which allowed it to pursue its priorities without interference from other, more production-oriented offices of the Forest Service. A top priority was to prevent people from seeing logging operations or clearcuts as they drove through the park. The division's campaign to fend off eyesores and cultivate natural attractions along the highway corridor during the early and mid-1950s illustrates the active role that state agencies played in managing the relationship between the environment and the motoring public. But imposing the desired aesthetic was not a one-time endeavour. Each success fed into an ongoing process of landscape maintenance to satisfy public expectations, not only of what a western Canadian wilderness park should look like generally, but also of what now-familiar Manning Park should look like specifically.

Maintaining Appearances

During the late 1950s and the 1960s, the BC Parks Branch struggled to maintain the naturalistic aesthetic it had imposed along the Hope-Princeton Highway in Manning Park. Like other North American park agencies, it faced problems associated with skyrocketing traffic and visitor numbers, and the growing popularity of outdoor recreation. Controversies flared up over structures and activities that were seen as incommensurate with the highway's established aesthetic. There was also pressure from logging and mining companies to allow new industrial operations inside Manning Park. With the passage of time, and the passage of millions of drivers along the highway, the motoring public's shared experience of Manning acquired more and more cultural and political significance, compelling the agency responsible for the park to continue meeting, to the best of its abilities, the expectations of nature by the road that it had done so much to create since 1949.

Parks Division surveys conducted during the mid-1950s confirmed that most visitors to Manning were British Columbians, who picked up lessons about nature as they passed through it.[44] Eighty percent of day visitors and campers were BC residents, as were 60 percent of overnight guests at Pinewoods. The park was especially popular with young working- and middle-class families.[45] Of the few complaints received, most related to overcrowding. By 1956, the five campgrounds were practically bursting at the seams between Canada Day and Labour Day. Skagit, the first campground reached by eastbound drivers, was often filled to more than double capacity on long weekends. Campers piled into one campsite, or set themselves up in parking lots, picnic sites, and even at the side of the highway. Others carved out their own unauthorized sites, cutting down branches, clearing brush, and using their cars to push aside logs and rocks.[46] Crowded, noisy, worn-out campgrounds were antithetical to the experience of nature that the Parks Division wanted people to have and that many campers had come to expect in Manning Park.

Parks officials were pleased that these surveys demonstrated Manning's value as a state-provided amenity, both as a site for recreational democracy and as a device for encouraging travel on the BC highway network. Even the complaints about crowding were evidence of its popularity. However, as the surveys indicated, it was being used more as a transient stopping place than as a destination in and of itself, a fact that troubled officials. Eighty percent of campers and 84 percent of guests at Pinewoods stayed for only one night. Eighty-six percent of visitors (defined as anyone who stopped inside the park) did so for less than an hour, confining themselves to the attractions, picnic sites, campgrounds, and concession complex that were accessible from the road.[47] Interpreting this lack of holding power as a failing, planners responded with more developments. These included new and expanded campgrounds, a road that led up Blackwall Mountain to a scenic viewpoint, a road to the Lightning Lakes, and a dam that transformed those lakes into a more recreationally appealing body of water. All of these were closely linked to the highway corridor.

So too were the pair of massive, wooden sign-sculptures that the Parks Branch erected at the park portals in 1958. The eastern entrance was adorned by a gigantic black bear and the western by a gigantic yellow-bellied marmot. Within a few years, the bear was being blamed for creating dangerous traffic conditions. Perched atop a massive stone-and-timber plinth, it lured many motorists to stop and take snapshots, just as the Manning Park Gallows had done. However, the lack of a safe place to pull off the increasingly congested highway, where traffic moved at sixty miles per hour, resulted in several accidents.[48] In the 1960s, the Parks Branch and the Department of Highways built a small parking lot at the east portal, made similar improvements for the massive marmot, and redesigned access to the beaver ponds on the Similkameen flats, where the terrain that helped hide visitors from the beavers had also obscured oncoming traffic's view of vehicles that were exiting the parking lot.[49]

Like any road, the Hope-Princeton was a work in progress. Constant maintenance was required, as were a series of major upgrades. The Department of Highways maintenance and improvement program sometimes conflicted with the Parks Branch desire to maintain a naturalistic aesthetic along the highway. In 1956, Highways announced that it would resurface twenty miles of the Hope-Princeton inside Manning Park. This led Superintendent Bob Boyd to complain to headquarters that the gravel required for the production of asphalt was bound to be excavated from borrow pits along the right-of-way, including one beside the new Mule Deer Campground. Boyd saw the borrow pits as among the worst eyesores in Manning and predicted that paving contractors would "leave behind them gaping holes and unsightly banks."[50] The Parks Division pleaded for Highways to minimize the project's impact on "aesthetic qualities along the roadside" and asked that restoration plans be drawn up for each pit that was visible from the highway.[51] In that case, the two agencies agreed to split the cost of planting native shrubs that would screen them from view. There was never any question, however, of the division actually preventing the gravel from being quarried or otherwise hindering the maintenance project.

The growing volume of high-speed traffic on the Hope-Princeton, combined with the heavy use of Manning's amenities, generated hazardous conditions at the access points to several picnic sites and campgrounds, as well as the Pinewoods concession complex. In effect, the popularity of designated stopping places inside the park conflicted with the arterial nature of the highway that ran through it, resulting in numerous crashes and near-misses. Whenever the Parks Division's aesthetic standards diverged from the safety standards of highway engineers, it was the predictable, efficient flow of traffic that won out, leaving staff to cope as best they could. The mid-1960s saw the Department of Highways make a number of significant improvements to the Hope-Princeton on the Similkameen flats in the vicinity of Pinewoods, adding acceleration, deceleration, and left-turn lanes.[52] These additions greatly improved traffic safety, but they also changed the ambience. That stretch of highway came to resemble a suburban interchange, and because it had been doubled in width, pedestrians were less inclined to cross it. Heavier traffic volumes and the higher speeds associated with a paved highway also made it necessary for motorists to exercise greater caution when slowing down or pulling over to gaze at animals, rivers, or scenic mountain peaks. Sometimes, it was effectively impossible to do so. Over the late 1950s and the 1960s, the motoring public's experiences of nature by the road in Manning Park gradually became less carefree and more narrowly delimited to those stopping places that had been built specifically to accommodate them.

Eyesores Old and New

Increased budgets and co-operation from other government agencies allowed the Parks Branch to sanitize several lingering blemishes during the late 1950s and the 1960s. The most noteworthy involved the Big Burn at Allison Pass, where the Forest Service cleared and replanted three hundred acres of scorched, desolate mountainside that was visible from the highway. In 1963, after the seedlings had taken hold and the slopes were becoming steadily greener, the Parks Branch removed the famous Manning Park Gallows and replaced it with a less eye-catching, more didactic sign to inform passersby that a government-funded reforestation program was under way. The gallows and its swinging cigarette had been a signature landmark of the Hope-Princeton since 1950, but undifferentiated "natural" forest cover was considered preferable to a famous man-made object – even one that had done so much to educate the motoring public about the need for fire safety in the woods.[53]

British Columbia's sustained postwar resource boom meant that the Parks Branch was faced with many new real and potential eyesores. Rising copper prices caused a flurry of claim staking in the park, including at locations where the Parks Branch wanted to avoid any trace of industrial activity, such as Rhododendron Flats, the giant bear sculpture at the eastern entrance, and Cambie Creek campground.[54] The aesthetic and jurisdictional challenges posed by timber licences grandfathered inside Manning became more complicated after March 1957, when the Parks Division was renamed the Parks Branch and made part of the new provincial Department of Recreation and Conservation. After being trimmed from the Forest Service, the Parks Branch could no longer acquire control over sensitive timber berths inside provincial parks by simply exchanging them for Crown timber elsewhere. Instead, timber licences that allowed cutting in prominent park areas were typically swapped for the right to cut an equivalent amount in some out-of-the-way section of the park. Thus, a growing volume of timber was cut inside provincial parks, including Manning, but almost never where the motoring public could see.

High lumber prices and lax enforcement of logging regulations during the late 1950s and the 1960s contributed to a cavalier attitude among many loggers, which led to several blatant instances of trespass inside provincial parks. In Manning, the most egregious (and untimely) example occurred during the summer of 1958, when loggers built a highly visible skid road in the park. The Huston Shake and Shingle mill in Hope was licensed to cut a stand of cedar on timber berth X65469, which straddled Manning's western border and thus the administrative boundary between the Vancouver and Kamloops Forest Districts. Because X65469 could not be seen from the highway and could be accessed by an old logging road in the Vancouver Forest District, which predated the 1950 parkway extension, the Parks Branch did not object to the removal of the cedars. The summer of 1958 was very hot and dry, and in August the Vancouver Forest District ordered a stop on all cutting and hauling operations due to the fire risk. Manning was part of the Kamloops Forest District, where no such suspension was in place, so the owner of the Huston shingle mill decided that "in order to get our logs to our mill we had to make a cat road through a section of the Park." A caterpillar tractor was used to cut a rough road through half a mile of "log jams and flooded areas" between X65469 and the Hope-Princeton. Logs were then skidded to a roadside clearing, stacked, and loaded onto trucks bound for Hope. The cedars taken from X65469 were massive: the logging trucks typically carried only three to five pieces of timber.[55]

The crude work of hauling and loading old-growth timber was supposed to have occurred away from public view, but now motorists could see enormous, freshly cut cedars being skidded around just a short distance past the new marmot sign-sculpture that clearly indicated Manning's western boundary. To make matters worse, the summer of 1958 was the high travel season for the province's centennial year. Government publicity campaigns were urging British Columbians to hit the road and encounter their province's scenic landscapes and natural, historical, and recreational features. It was crucial that the Hope-Princeton corridor be in perfect condition, especially inside such a popular provincial park, where people expected to see nature unsullied by industrial activity. At the very moment that the Parks Branch wanted to make the best impression, the shingle company's skid road and hauling made Manning look bad. Unauthorized industrial operations were a serious violation of the Provincial Parks Act, but the archival records do not indicate what (if any) penalty the company received.[56]

The Parks Branch was so sensitive to the public's views of industrial activity in Manning that it refused loggers permission to "clean up" a major defect that resulted from natural causes. In the spring of 1964, a severe windstorm produced extensive blowdown in the park. Princeton logging companies lobbied for access to the toppled timber before it started to rot and become susceptible to fire and insect infestation, so salvage operations were permitted in several backcountry areas. The clean-up effort was more complicated at the popular Mountain View picnic site, where almost no trees had been left standing and where the blowdown had wrecked picnic tables, signs, and pit toilets. In light of Mountain View's popularity, something needed to be done, and quickly, before the summer travel season began.[57] However, the Parks Branch was opposed to letting loggers bring their cats, skidders, and trucks onto the site because it might set a precedent for industrial activity in the park's frontcountry. Manning's new superintendent, Tom Moore, came up with an inexpensive solution that echoed the placement of the Manning Park Gallows at the Big Burn during the early 1950s. Moore recommended that the Mountain View site simply be left as it was (aside from relocating and replacing the demolished toilets and picnic tables) and that a large interpretive sign be erected to describe the natural phenomenon of blowdown and explain its role in forest succession.[58] This was a quick and easy way to turn devastation into an educational experience, almost a natural attraction in and of itself. It also showed that the Parks Branch was not responsible for the site's unappealing condition.[59] The damaged section of forest was allowed to regenerate according to its own timetable.

Pinewoods as Centre of Attention

Several significant infringements of the Parks Branch's naturalistic aesthetic occurred in the vicinity of Pinewoods. There, the battle against visual blight involved a surprising level of micromanagement, with modern surfaces that disrupted the complex's rustic woodsiness proving particularly troublesome. During one visit to Pinewoods, the Parks Branch chief was perturbed by shiny metal garbage cans in the parking lots, which he insisted be painted dark brown, and by a freestanding red-and-white, metal-and-plastic standard model telephone booth that the BC Telephone Company had installed in front of Pinewoods Lodge.[60] A few years later, shiny aluminum-skinned trailers that the Parks Branch used to accommodate the growing number of staff were deemed problematic. They offered a flexible, inexpensive solution to the park's housing shortage but were hard to camouflage and made the concession complex resemble one of the province's many remote resource work camps. Even worse, the first trailers were visible from the Hope-Princeton. Headquarters ordered their removal to an area that was screened from view by timber and brush, where they would not contribute to "scenic defacement of the highway."[61]

As the midway point and only significantly built-up area between Hope and Princeton, Pinewoods was a magnet for public attention, and the Parks Branch regularly faced pressure to develop new attractions and services there. Some proposals were intended to complement the experience of nature by the road, but others had the potential to confuse or detract from it. In January 1957, Pinewoods Lodge concession operator Rene Pelletier suggested that a museum be built at Pinewoods.[62] Pelletier was a personal friend of Premier W.A.C. Bennett, who regularly drove from Kelowna to meet politicians and supporters from the Coast at the lodge. Pelletier was also the biggest promoter of new developments at Pinewoods, as it was in his interest to have an array of attractions that could entice drivers off the highway and hold them in the area. He no doubt saw the addition of a historically themed venue as a way of broadening the tourist appeal of Pinewoods and recognized that the preparations for the 1958 BC centennial celebrations might convince Victoria to expedite such a project. Parks Branch experts had also contemplated the construction of an interpretation centre in Manning. Wildlife biologist Yorke Edwards argued that it would provide visitors with a better appreciation of landforms, flora, and fauna. In the spring of 1957, his lobbying combined with Pelletier's to convince Parks headquarters to build the Manning Park Nature House.

The nature house lay beside the main parking lot at Pinewoods, and admission was free. It was not actually a house or even a permanent structure for the first few years. Instead, Edwards was given a heavy old canvas camp tent with a wooden frame and floor. The original display furniture consisted mainly of pallets and boxes scavenged from the park dump, where Edwards and his student assistant "dug with the bears." The nature house was small but jammed full of educational materials about Manning's natural features, including exhibits about rocks, trees, and wildflowers, and photographs of birds, beavers, mountain goats, and deer. Edwards recalled that few people visited it prior to grade school being let out for summer; in early June 1957, most of his guests were "distressed" motorists "needing a toilet." However, due to its strategic location, it quickly became Manning's most popular attraction, recording thirteen thousand visitors in the summer of 1957. Ironically, its popularity was largely the result of its location at the centre of development in Manning Park. Many motorists visited it while parking at Pinewoods to patronize the gas station, dining facilities, public telephone, and washrooms.[63]

The nature house conveniently deflected attention from concurrent developments that diminished the naturalistic atmosphere at Pinewoods. By the mid-1950s, the lodge and detached autocourt-style cabins that the government had built in 1949 and 1950 were filled to capacity all summer. Rene Pelletier lobbied the Parks Branch to build more accommodations so that he could increase his high-season takings and was leant support by the many travellers who wrote letters of complaint when they were unable to find a room there. In 1957, these pressures led the government to tender bids for the construction of a new twenty-four-unit motel at Pinewoods, plus a store and several large, paved parking lots.[64]

The new motel's multi-unit layout was in keeping with broader trends in the accommodation industry, but even the use of rough pine siding could not disguise the fact that it was a significant stylistic departure from the far more rustic-looking earlier buildings at Pinewoods, which were

Pinewoods concession complex, c.1958, showing new crescent-shaped motel structure at right, with tennis court behind. Natural Color Productions postcard. Author's collection.

made of split pine logs.[65] By 1958, the original water, sewage, garbage disposal, and electrical systems at Pinewoods all needed upgrading. Parks Branch records indicate no hesitation on the part of planners or field staff regarding the expansion and modernization at Pinewoods, or the development of new recreational features such as tennis courts. These were simply seen as "democratic" responses to Manning's popularity. Nevertheless, with the widened highway, the large new motel, power lines, and the growing number of cars parked in asphalt lots at the concession complex, Pinewoods increasingly resembled a commercial strip. Attempting to make the new structures blend in, the Parks Branch installed landscaping that would "duplicate the alpine meadows" in Manning's high country. It planted seventy evergreens around the complex (only in spots where they would not obstruct motorists' views) and seeded the lawns with wildflowers.[66] These seemingly run-of-the-mill efforts to manage the grounds at Pinewoods show that by 1960 at least some Parks Branch staff were anxious that the concession complex no longer satisfied public expectations of nature by the road inside a major park.

Even commonplace seasonal maintenance could be an issue for the Parks Branch. In the summer of 1966, staff discovered that the Department of

Highways or the BC Telephone Company had sprayed a chemical herbicide along their shared right-of-way between Pinewoods and Hope to control brush. The Hope-Princeton right-of-way extended fifty feet from each side of the centreline, but overspray had damaged plants at twice that distance. The worst damage was between the massive marmot sculpture and Pinewoods, with "a most ugly avenue of defoliation" in the first half mile above the western portal. Staff were outraged to find that "even almost bare rock faces and road cuts are being sprayed," resulting in the loss of "fine patches of pentstamon and other wild flowers." They reported getting "quite a lot of complaints from travellers [about] the unsightly mess. To these people, the park is anything they see – but especially the few feet either side of the road." The deputy minister of recreation and conservation ordered an investigation to find out who was responsible for the "ugly blighting and desecration of the roadside." "Elimination of this sort of thing is essential," he declared, "not only for the Park as such but for the many thousands of travellers who enjoy driving through Manning."[67] This incident demonstrates that the Parks Branch's desire to maintain its aesthetic was sometimes at cross-purposes with other agencies that were charged with moving people and things through Manning in a safe, efficient manner. The observation that most travellers invested "the few feet either side of the road" with special significance indicates that park managers continued to see the motoring public's views as a top priority during the mid-1960s.

Traffic, new services, and modern surfaces steadily degraded the rusticity of Pinewoods. In 1972, Parks Branch headquarters dispatched planner Mel Turner to examine the concession complex and make recommendations for its future management. Turner described Pinewoods as suffering from "mini urban sprawl."[68] The park buildings were still concentrated on the western Similkameen flats, just as the reconnaissance reports of the 1940s had recommended, and no other commercial developments had been allowed to sprout alongside the Hope-Princeton corridor within the park. However, development at Pinewoods had spread considerably along the highway, with the result that buildings and other structures were visible to motorists along most of the western flats. There was also a confusing array of access points to and from the highway, and roadside signs had proliferated to help visitors find their way around. In 1972, parking lots, utility lines, multi-unit motels, left-turn lanes, directional signs, and traffic congestion were familiar aspects of everyday life for most British Columbians and visitors from elsewhere, but a mountain park was precisely the kind of place where they sought temporary respite from these spaces and routines of suburbia. Since the mid-1960s, there had been a resurgence of concern among North American middlebrow critics about sprawl, visual blight, loss of open space, and commercialization.[69] Pop star Joni Mitchell's reference to "paving paradise to put up a parking lot" had entered common parlance. Furthermore, British Columbians who followed the news were cognizant of recent controversies surrounding the Social Credit government's willingness to allow the reduction of provincial parks for industrial purposes and its reluctance to act on environmentalists' requests for new "wilderness" park areas that would see minimal development, including in the Skagit River valley southwest of Manning.[70] Thus, not only was Pinewoods decidedly less naturalistic and rustic looking in the early 1970s than it had been during the early 1950s, when many motorists had gotten their first impression of it, but some BC residents were increasingly likely to criticize both it and other roadside developments in Manning Park.

With new cultural and political freight attached to the look and atmosphere of the concession complex, the decision to conduct a review of the site in 1972 can be seen as an effort to protect the reputation of Manning, the Parks Branch, and the provincial government generally. Mel Turner prescribed a dose of mini urban planning to help make Pinewoods look better. His main recommendation was to rationalize the complex by dividing it into four zones that would be defined by function. Maintenance and administration would be confined to the north side of the highway, whereas visitor services and "natural environments" would be concentrated on the south side. Such a configuration, Turner argued, would permit a sharp reduction in the number of points where automobiles entered and exited the highway, thereby simplifying traffic patterns, improving safety, and clearing up visual clutter. Most of Turner's suggestions were adopted by the Parks Branch and implemented over the following years, and went on to shape the first master plan for Manning in the early 1980s.

Exiting Manning Park

When Mel Turner reviewed Manning in 1972, it was the most heavily visited provincial park in the BC Interior. By this yardstick, it was a significant asset to the province: accessible and with a wide array of attractions, it both adorned the Hope-Princeton Highway and justified its expense. BC residents and visitors had made millions of trips through the park since the road had opened in 1949. Many had stopped to experience its scenic and natural features or spent time at its picnic sites, campgrounds, and concession complex. Others had been content simply to look out the window as they drove through it. Either alternative provided lessons about nature by the road: some didactic, others implicit. The Skagit Bluffs, Rhododendron Grove, Sumallo Grove, Big Burn and Manning Park Gallows, beaver ponds, and Pinewoods Lodge had become common landscape experiences. So too had relatively undifferentiated stretches of highway from which logging and mining had been excluded. To most motorists, Manning seemed perfectly natural. After all, few knew anything of its history or realized how closely it was intertwined with that of the Hope-Princeton. Even fewer knew how carefully and consistently agents of the state had manipulated and modified its landscapes in order to shape their views.

The construction of the Hope-Princeton had fuelled the movement to establish a park in the southern Cascades during the 1930s, when park proponents had cited the economic importance of the public's views to call for the preservation of flora, fauna, and scenery. After Manning was founded, the Parks Division and Forest Service tailored it to the tastes of the "democratic" motoring public rather than a smaller number of well-heeled outdoor recreationalists. During the 1950s, the division imposed a naturalistic aesthetic to encourage the use of the road and the enjoyment of the park. Ironically, both proved so popular that new developments and upgraded infrastructure became necessary, a fact that often posed difficulties for park managers as they struggled to gratify public expectations.

Manning Park proved a valuable asset to the Fordist state, though a strange one, in that it generated little direct revenue. In fact, the case is even stranger. In building and sustaining Manning as a roadside amenity, the state had had to deal with several complicating factors that involved both expense and political friction. Road and park supporters – many of them working within the state – had to convince skeptical politicians and bureaucrats of its value; resolve conflict with ranchers, loggers, miners, and would-be entrepreneurs; and cope with nearly a decade of delay in completing the highway. They then faced numerous unexpected pressures and costs associated with mass tourism, recreation, and automobility. The case of Manning Park and the Hope-Princeton demonstrates the munificence and commitment that British Columbia's emerging Fordist state could marshal. It poured substantial resources into one asset – the park – that helped justify much larger public investment in another – the road. Few other provincial parks were as carefully and lavishly tended as Manning was: it was a crown jewel of the park system. But in the next case – that of Hamber Provincial Park and the Big Bend Highway – we see another side of the same state, not only less generous and dedicated to creating appealing experiences of nature by the road, but in the end actively destructive of its own achievements.

3

The Politics of Roads and Parks in the Big Bend Country

Few British Columbians today have heard of either Hamber Park or the Big Bend Highway. Fragments of both still exist, but they are isolated and widely separated from each other, so that nothing remains on the ground to suggest that they were once closely linked. No Route 66–style nostalgia surrounds the "lost" Big Bend Highway, which was extremely unpopular in its time, and even those who can recall navigating the road are unlikely to have known that it traversed an enormous provincial park for the better part of a hundred miles. In fact, Hamber Park was practically unknown to the motoring public during the middle decades of the twentieth century. Neither the road nor the park shaped the public's experience of landscape in a manner that was deemed valuable by the state. Whereas private interests and government agencies successfully cultivated a major asset in the southern Cascades, a similar scenario on the opposite side of the Interior came to an entirely different conclusion.

With their intertwined histories, Hamber Park and the Big Bend Highway were both counterparts of and counterpoints to Manning Park and the Hope-Princeton. They were counterparts in that they shared significant similarities. All were located in mountainous, unpopulated, inaccessible sections of the Interior that were unfamiliar to most British Columbians. Both roads were started in the summer of 1929 and took more than a decade to complete. Both parks were established in 1941, with many of the same individuals and agencies involved in their management. However, whereas Manning and the Hope-Princeton show that the Fordist state could choose to make a park into a major asset, Hamber and the Big Bend reveal that pairing an arterial highway and a large "wild" park was no guarantee of either popularity or permanency.

Hamber is a noteworthy example of a "failed" park. Parks that failed – that did not get past the planning stage or were set up only to be reduced or dissolved – deserve to be treated as integral to the larger history of Canada's provincial and national park systems.[1] They provide important context for the better-known success stories, in that they illustrate the changing political, economic, and aesthetic criteria involved in constructing present-day parks. They also help denaturalize or demythologize existing parks by revealing the myriad actors and interests that determined which ones "succeeded" and which fell by the wayside.

The origins of parks and roads were intertwined in the Big Bend country and involved the most high-level political negotiations. The area could plausibly have been an important addition to Canada's national parks during the mid-1930s and the early 1940s but was rejected by the federal government and subsequently perceived by the Province as little more than a white elephant. As Alan MacEachern shows in his study of national parks in the Atlantic provinces, a dynamic existed between the federal and provincial governments during the interwar years whereby provinces were willing to give land for new national parks in exchange for a commitment from Ottawa to invest in the development of regional infrastructure, most often in the form of roads.[2] Thus, the history of BC parks during the middle decades of the twentieth century – including both the many success stories and the few failures – needs to be recognized as having been linked to intergovernmental politics and competing infrastructure priorities. The BC government established Hamber Park as part of a scheme to have Ottawa incorporate it and several other provincial parks into the national park system – Hamber was intended to be given away. This was part of a larger effort to get Ottawa to build and maintain roads in the Selkirk and Rocky Mountains. Hamber's size and location make it particularly important. One of the largest parks in Canada, it was contiguous with Jasper, Banff, Yoho, Glacier, and Mount Robson Parks. To understand why British Columbia created this enormous, strategically situated park with the expectation that Ottawa would take it over, we must go back to the late 1920s, when a network of auto touring roads was beginning to emerge in the mountains of western Canada.

Coming on the heels of the opening of British Columbia's first Coast-to-Interior road link through the Fraser Canyon, the completion of a touring road between Lake Louise, Alberta, and Golden, British Columbia, in the summer of 1927 meant that the only gap in the Vancouver-Calgary route lay between the towns of Golden and Revelstoke, a distance of less than seventy miles as the crow flies. The road that connected Lake Louise and Golden had been built by the engineering service of the National Parks Branch in conjunction with the BC Department of Public Works. After it was completed, many observers expected those agencies to move their construction crews west and co-operate on creating a link between Golden and Revelstoke via Glacier National Park, which had been world-famous for its mountain and glacier scenery around the turn of the century but had gone into steep decline after the First World War and was not connected to a road network.[3] However, engineers were reluctant to build a road via the infamous Rogers Pass, where avalanches had killed hundreds of Canadian Pacific Railway (CPR) employees and passengers between 1884 and 1916, when the CPR completed a tunnel beneath the summit of the pass. Instead, Ottawa and Victoria agreed to co-operate on putting in a road that would loop to the north of the Selkirks and follow the U-shaped course of the Columbia River, known as the Big Bend.[4] The Province would construct the western section of the road – from Revelstoke to Boat Encampment, an old fur trade rendezvous at the apex of the Big Bend – and the National Parks Branch would build the eastern section, from the outskirts of Golden northward to Boat Encampment. The road would not cross any national parks, but Ottawa justified the National Parks Branch's participation on the basis that it would comprise an important section of a future Trans-Canada Highway while also connecting Mount Revelstoke National Park to Yoho and Banff. Thus, the Big Bend road was initially envisioned as a means of encouraging auto tourism and leisure travel in the mountains of western Canada.

Aside from avoiding the Rogers Pass, the advantages of the roundabout Big Bend route are difficult to discern. It would traverse a veritable howling wilderness for nearly two hundred miles. There were no farms, mines, or logging camps in the Big Bend country, only a few trappers' cabins and half obscured trails.[5] The area typically saw a fraction of the snow that the Rogers Pass did, but the western slope of the Selkirks still experienced heavy snowfall, receiving between fifteen and thirty feet each winter. Dense forests with jungle-like undergrowth climbed high on the mountainsides, and many stretches of the Columbia were unnavigable between Revelstoke and Golden, which meant that during the short construction season all supplies would need to be delivered by pack trains hacking their way through the forest. The two governments had a hopelessly optimistic timetable that called for completion by summer 1932. No one could have guessed

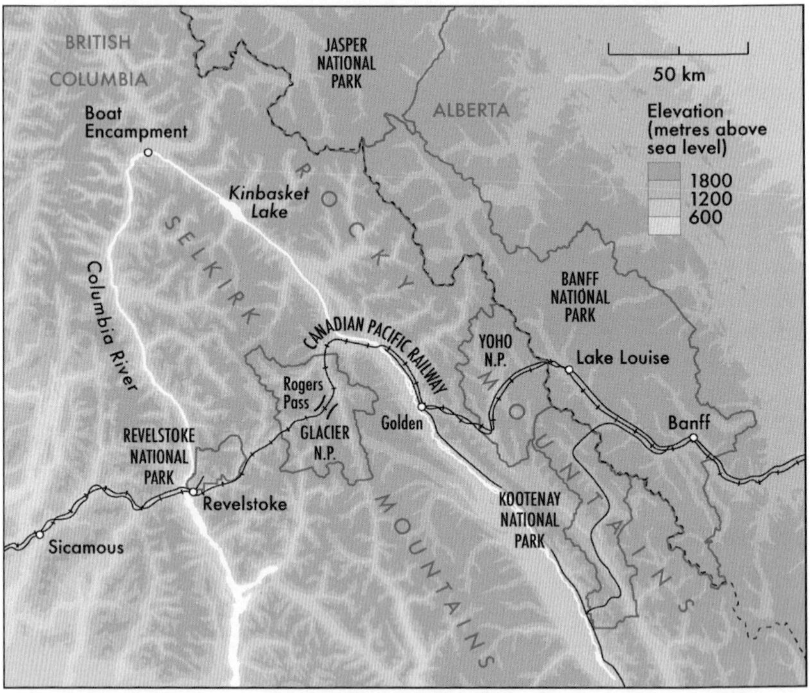

Transportation routes and national parks in the Rocky and Selkirk Mountains, 1927.

it in 1929, but they could not have chosen a worse moment to begin such an ambitious project.

Construction began in early 1930 and was immediately slowed by the difficult terrain and inaccessibility, and by the downturn in the economy. Victoria converted its construction camps into relief work camps in 1931 but managed to keep them open in 1932 due only to emergency funding from Ottawa. In 1933, the Department of National Defence took control of relief camps nationwide, which meant that the federal government was paying for the entire Big Bend project, with the National Parks Branch overseeing work on the eastern section and the Canadian Army on the western.[6] It was during the summer of 1932, when British Columbia was in its direst financial straits, that the National Parks Branch approached the provincial government with a proposal to protect scenic timber along a stretch of the Big Bend road. This was a very modest step toward recognizing roadside landscapes as assets that would appeal to the motoring public, but it ended up becoming a flashpoint for a bigger debate about the future road and the environments it traversed.

Road Finances and Park Schemes

J.M. Wardle was the National Parks Branch's chief engineer, responsible for overseeing major construction projects throughout western Canada. In August 1932, he asked the provincial government to establish a quarter-mile-wide reserve along twenty miles of surveyed right-of-way between Kinbasket Lake and Boat Encampment.[7] He believed that the tall, ancient firs and cedars in this area were worth preserving as an attraction (or distraction) for the motorists who would spend many hours driving through the unpopulated Big Bend wilderness. Wardle's request said nothing about creating a national park in the Columbia River valley, but provincial politicians may have wishfully interpreted it as an overture to just such a proposal. There was precedent for this. The Big Bend road situation seemed to echo the two governments' experience with the Banff-Windermere Highway and Kootenay National Park a decade before. In 1919, Ottawa had agreed to complete the cash-strapped province's section of the Banff-Windermere Highway project in exchange for 320,000 acres of Crown land on which it established Kootenay National Park.[8] Thus, the idea of swapping park land for road construction in the mountains of eastern British Columbia was familiar to provincial politicians.

The BC deputy minister of lands informed Wardle that his government supported the preservation of scenic timber along the Big Bend road, at least in principle. He also pointed out that Victoria had issued numerous timber licences in the Big Bend country, including in the strip of forest that Ottawa wanted to protect.[9] Due to the area's inaccessibility and the impossibility of running logs down the rapid-riddled Columbia, no cutting had been done. Nevertheless, logging companies and timber brokers held onto their licences as speculative investments, making it impossible to say when the timber rights might revert to the Crown. These parties would demand compensation if their cutting rights were curtailed in the cause of scenic preservation. The lingering question was who should provide that compensation.

There the issue was left until early 1934, when Minister of the Interior Thomas G. Murphy wrote directly to T.D. "Duff" Pattullo, the new premier of British Columbia, to draw his attention to the National Parks Branch's desire for a roadside timber reserve. Murphy explained that his department was "naturally interested in the scenic attractions of the Big Bend Highway." The ancient forest between Kinbasket Lake and Boat Encampment deserved to be protected from unsightly resource exploitation, he argued, because it was "the only stretch of virgin timber of fairly large size along

New road through old timber south of Kinbasket Lake. Library and Archives Canada, Parks Canada collection, e010836790.

the whole route of the Trans-Canada Highway from the Atlantic to the Pacific." Murphy urged Pattullo to act and predicted a "storm of protest from the general public" if logging were allowed to mar the scenery along this section of the Big Bend Highway.[10]

Pattullo agreed that the timber reserve would make driving the highway more enjoyable for auto tourists. However, though it was fine for the National Parks Branch to desire unspoiled scenery along the new highway, expecting the impoverished Province to bear the cost of acquiring it was unfair. He suggested that if Ottawa truly saw the matter as one of national importance, it should purchase the timber licences in the area.[11] Pattullo, it is important to note, had been the BC minister of lands in 1919, when the Banff-Windermere Highway agreement was negotiated and the land base for Kootenay National Park transferred to Ottawa. By dragging his feet on the scenic timber reserve, he may have hoped to coax Ottawa into proposing a new national park in the Big Bend country.

Pattullo's reluctance to take action must have struck Thomas Murphy as rather ungrateful, given that Ottawa had been paying for all the Big Bend construction since 1932. He reminded Pattullo that the Department of the Interior had agreed to participate in the project in 1929 on the basis that it was intended "primarily to increase the revenue from tourist traffic." It was therefore "of first importance that the scenic advantages of the road be duly capitalized." If the scenic advantages were not treated appropriately, further federal involvement in the project would be called into question.[12]

If Murphy had expected this veiled threat to bring Pattullo to heel, he must have been taken aback by the response it generated. "The time has come," Pattullo's minister of public works asserted in November 1934, "when the Canadian National Parks [Branch] can advantageously assume the whole of the Columbia-Revelstoke Highway, together with a strip of land 1/4 mile wide on either side of the road which will be available for park purposes." The Province argued that the completed road would form "an integral part of the National Parks System connecting [Mount] Revelstoke Park with the Rocky Mountain and Yoho parks to the east." Thus, it was logical for Ottawa to establish a linear national park (or parkway) along the entire road and assume permanent responsibility for its maintenance. Once Ottawa agreed to this, the provincial government would pass legislation along the lines of the 1919 bill that had transferred provincial Crown land to the federal government for Kootenay National Park.[13] Such an arrangement would permanently relieve British Columbia of the cost of maintaining almost all the roads between Revelstoke and the BC-Alberta boundary. The Province had little to lose by this proposal, for the forests of the rugged Big Bend country were of little value to timber companies in the days before truck logging.

British Columbia's offer was received with surprise in Ottawa. Pattullo was informed through political back channels that the federal government was not interested in a new park if it meant taking permanent responsibility for the road.[14] Then, shortly before the 1935 construction season began, Murphy delivered an ultimatum to Pattullo. The National Parks Branch had nearly finished the eastern section of the road between Golden and Boat Encampment, and once it was done, Ottawa would be under no obligation to do further work on the project. Murphy was willing to have the agency take over construction of the western section, but only if the

Province agreed to maintain the completed road and "conserve in perpetuity" the desired strip of tall trees between Kinbasket Lake and Boat Encampment.[15]

Victoria had to drop its proposal for a new national park in the Big Bend country to get Ottawa to finish the road. Pattullo agreed to maintain the highway and to preserve the strip of timber, which satisfied Murphy, who instructed the National Parks Branch to complete the road's western section.[16] After the trees were under reserve, congratulatory messages poured onto Pattullo's desk from tourism promoters, boards of trade, and motoring associations throughout western Canada, commending him for his foresight in protecting such an important natural attraction.[17] Discussions about parks and scenery along the Big Bend Highway then disappeared from Pattullo's correspondence with Ottawa for several years. However, though the parkway proposal had failed, the idea of a national park in the Big Bend country was not abandoned.

Boosters, business owners, tourism promoters, and park supporters lobbied for scenic and natural landscape features to be preserved along the entire Revelstoke-to-Golden road corridor. In 1938, the Canadian National Parks Association asserted that the public had a "moral right" to see "alluring forest scenery" along the Big Bend Highway. Arguing that public roads in the mountains of western Canada should be used to "attract the world's tourist trade" rather than to "provide cheap transportation for the lumberman," the association recommended that logging be forbidden "within sight of the highway." Ironically, it suggested that the National Parks Branch pressure Victoria to establish a linear provincial park along the entire highway.[18]

In the BC Interior, Revelstoke booster Earle Dickey was the most outspoken advocate for scenic preservation along the Big Bend Highway. Dickey worked as an electrical engineer at Revelstoke's municipal power utility. He was also a postcard photographer, chairman of the board of trade's tourism and publicity bureau, and district correspondent for the *Vancouver Sun*.[19] In June 1937, Dickey submitted a story to the *Sun* in which he stated that a "fringe" of roadside scenery should be protected along the Revelstoke-to-Golden highway to stave off the "real menace of forest mutilization [sic]" that was posed by logging companies about to get access to the Big Bend country. The following month, Dickey preached the gospel of scenic preservation to Revelstoke City Council. People who lived in heavily forested districts were complacent about "the scenic value of trees," he warned councillors. "Would the prospect of a motor journey through bleak, burnt-up Saskatchewan fill you with enthusiasm? I don't think so! Yet visualize our Big Bend Highway with the timber gone and we have just such another picture." Dickey suggested that the dense, damp forests of the Big Bend country could make the drive between Revelstoke and Golden a special experience, singular even among the nearby national parks, which were characterized by sparser forest cover. But the future highway's appeal would be greatly reduced if evidence of logging or other industrial activities were visible from the road.[20] Like Martin Allerdale Grainger in his campaign to preserve the scenery in the southern Cascades, Dickey recognized the importance of being a step ahead of resource companies, which would be difficult to dislodge if they gained footholds in newly accessible areas.

Earle Dickey's campaign was backed by the district board of trade and also the local branch of the Native Sons of British Columbia, a nativist organization that usually dedicated itself to commemorating the province's Anglo-Saxon heritage.[21] He also claimed to represent general opinion in Revelstoke, telling council that many residents had approached him to indicate their support for protecting forest scenery and promoting auto tourism in the region. Like their counterparts in Princeton and many other Interior communities during the interwar years, Revelstoke boosters and merchants looked to auto tourism as an economic lifeline after the collapse of local resource industries.[22] They came to view scenery and parks as practical business concerns, in that they could lure pleasure travellers who would purchase food, gas, lodging, and other goods and services. The better the quality of the highway, both in terms of engineering and the attractions that were visible along it, the better business would be for local commercial interests. They supported preserving the landscapes along the Big Bend road, even if it meant restricting how timber resources could be used. Neither Dickey nor the Canadian National Parks Association called directly for a new park along the Big Bend Highway, but it is noteworthy that their arguments closely echoed the Pattullo government's 1934 parkway proposal.

First Impressions of the Big Bend Country

The Big Bend Highway opened to the motoring public in June 1940, a full decade after construction had begun. The opening ceremony at Boat Encampment was presided over by Premier Pattullo and attended by hundreds of tourism promoters and highway boosters, including a "See BC First Caravan" co-sponsored by the Vancouver Chamber of Commerce

Big Bend Highway opening ceremony at Boat Encampment, June 1940, showing steel bridge over Columbia River and Wooden Head looking on from left of centre. Earle Dickey photograph. Revelstoke Museum and Archives, Earle and Estelle Dickey collection, 2903.

and the BC Government Travel Bureau. The souvenir program claimed that completion of the highway was of no less national significance than the driving of the last spike of the CPR near Revelstoke in 1885.[23] Now the only "gap" left in a Canadian transcontinental highway was along the rocky north shore of Lake Superior.

The proceedings also saw the unofficial unveiling of what would become the Big Bend Highway's best-known curiosity. While working at a relief camp, Revelstoke resident Peter Fuoco fashioned an enormous human head out of a stump and scrap lumber. Impressed, the construction foreman had the ten-foot-tall head guillotined from its base and trucked to Boat Encampment, where it was positioned atop a bank that overlooked the approach to the steel bridge over the Columbia. The head was accompanied by a sign that warned, "Don't be Wooden Headed! Drive Carefully. You'll live to enjoy the scenery more and longer." This whimsical and conspicuous colossus reminded motorists about traffic safety and marked the apex

BC Government Travel Bureau advertisements for Big Bend Highway, 1940.

of the Big Bend. As the approximate midway point between Golden and Revelstoke, Wooden Head indicated to drivers that they were turning back toward the south, and civilization. As a memorable hand-crafted curiosity, "he" also served to humanize the lonely wilderness of the Big Bend country.[24]

The provincial government made the Big Bend Highway the centrepiece of its 1940 publicity campaign to entice American tourists northward. Brochures and magazine ads described it as "a splendid new highway extending for 200 miles through a scenic wonderland," providing motorists with "a thrilling travelogue of mountain peaks, glaciers, and entrancing views of the mighty Columbia River."[25] A few promotional materials mentioned the area's ties to the nineteenth-century fur trade, which had been a favourite theme among western Canadian tourism promoters since the late 1920s due to its connotations of discovery and adventure (as discussed in Chapter 5). Most, however, emphasized the primeval nature of the Big

Bend country, noting that the new road enabled drivers to experience a wilderness previously inaccessible to all but the hardiest adventurer, a "virgin territory" that offered "a unique travel experience with all the thrill which attaches to the new and unexpected." "The scenery here is magnificent," boasted one pamphlet. "Every tangent of the highway reveals fresh vistas of glittering peaks, rank behind rank into the dimness of infinity, a vast new playground thrown open for the first time."[26]

For all the fervent publicity, doubts soon emerged about how splendid and thrilling the new highway really was. Driving the Big Bend was an endurance test, taking between five and seven hours. The unpaved road was narrow, rough, and twisting in many places, and had no verges. In hot, dry weather it was incredibly dusty, which made driving unpleasant and sometimes hazardous. The dust raised by passing vehicles coated the roadside foliage, turning the immediate scenery drab and lifeless.[27] Promotional materials in the early 1940s neglected to mention that no food, gas, or lodging was available in the "200 miles of virgin territory" between Revelstoke and Golden.[28] Indeed, the only buildings that motorists passed were abandoned construction camps and a solitary forest ranger's cabin at Boat Encampment. The *Revelstoke Review* acknowledged the lack of commerce but presented it as a distinctive and appealing quality:

> Today your modern traveller is anxious to penetrate into the unknown [where] nothing spoils the wilderness ... For those who think that neon lights and gaily illustrated billboards are the acme of modern accomplishment and living, the Big Bend is not their highway. For on this carefully planned route there is not even a humble "hot dog" advertisement. You are not harassed by being directed to Mac's or Joe's fine foods or to dine-and-dance nite spots ... These modern outcroppings of the great national desire for travel, food, and entertainment simply do not exist, are not allowed to mar the perfection of a virgin wilderness.[29]

Rocks and debris fell onto the road in numerous places. Heavy runoff damaged culverts and bridges, requiring detours at creek and river crossings. To cap it off, the highway was open for only half the year. From late October to mid-May, it was closed due to heavy snow.

Even in 1940 and 1941, there were signs that the highway might not become popular with auto tourists. Washboard and potholes were common. "I have just been over that stretch of road," one BC motorist wrote to Premier Pattullo, "and have been told that you have had the consummate nerve to spend money advertising the Big Bend road in American

Typical section of the Big Bend Highway, August 1939. Library and Archives Canada, Parks Canada, e010836789.

newspapers and magazines. You should be ashamed of yourself!"[30] Austin Cross, travel writer for the *Ottawa Citizen,* savaged the route in an article on the nascent Trans-Canada Highway. "It is positively the loneliest road in North America," he complained, "not a town, not a village, not a hamlet, not two houses together, not a suggestion of civilization." The road itself was "villainous ... built by people whose minds must be back in the 1920s." Even the tall timber along the highway failed to impress Cross, for the dense, seemingly endless forest crowded claustrophobically close. In terms of scenery, Cross declared, "the much-touted Big Bend Highway could play second fiddle to many another British Columbia turnpike." He recommended that auto tourists who wished to travel between Golden and Revelstoke should ship their vehicles by railcar.[31]

There were even rumblings of dissatisfaction in Revelstoke, where boosters would bend over backward to present the road in a positive light. One month after the official opening ceremony, the Revelstoke Board of Trade reported to Premier Pattullo that "not a day goes by that we do not have two or three accidents." This was not the fault of the highway itself, the board asserted, but rather the drivers, "most of whom are from the Prairies and not accustomed to driving mountain roads."[32] The following summer, a Revelstoke resident who drove to Golden and back encountered "too many chuck holes and too much washboard to make the journey a happy one." He believed that the road could be made "a humdinger of a tourist attraction" but that in its present state it did a disservice to the province's reputation. He cited an encounter with an American motorist who had told him "one trip over that road was enough for a lifetime."[33]

By the summer of 1941, the *Revelstoke Review* was full of worrisome stories and anxious editorials about the new highway. Some concerns seemed trifling. An editorial titled "Road Signs Needed" claimed that travellers were "ready to launch a vigorous complaint over the absence of adequate signs" to identify points of scenic, natural, and historical interest, as well as hazards such as sharp curves.[34] A more serious topic was addressed two weeks later, after two Winnipeg women drowned when their car struck a boulder that had fallen onto the road, went over an embankment, and landed upside down in the Columbia. This followed a similar accident, in which a family of three on their way from Vancouver to Calgary had died after their car went over an embankment north of Revelstoke. The editor of the *Review* called for greater safety measures that would protect the road's reputation. The Big Bend section of the Trans-Canada Highway was very much in the public eye, he wrote, and though it was safe, provided it were driven as a mountain road ought to be, "it will have to be guarded as much as possible against unfavorable publicity." Anything that could be done to enhance the impression of safety would help. "Prairie motorists are not accustomed to driving on mountain roads and the smallest incline contributes to their mental hazard," he claimed. "One way to eliminate much of this inherent fear would be to place guard rails along sections where the highway skirts the Columbia."[35] For those who wanted to increase Revelstoke's tourist and roadside service trade, the only thing worse than having the highway labelled boring or unappealing would be for it to acquire a "killer" reputation, as several sections of road in the BC Interior already had.[36]

A Gambit toward a New National Park

Despite the bad publicity for the Big Bend Highway – or perhaps because of it – Duff Pattullo decided to make another effort at convincing Ottawa to assume responsibility for its maintenance and improvement.[37] Having a new national park established in the Big Bend country remained the easiest way to get the federal government involved in the highway's upkeep, but securing Ottawa's co-operation was tricky. Its rejection of the 1934 proposal for a half-mile-wide ribbon of national park along the road could be taken to indicate that it saw the strip as too small for a proper

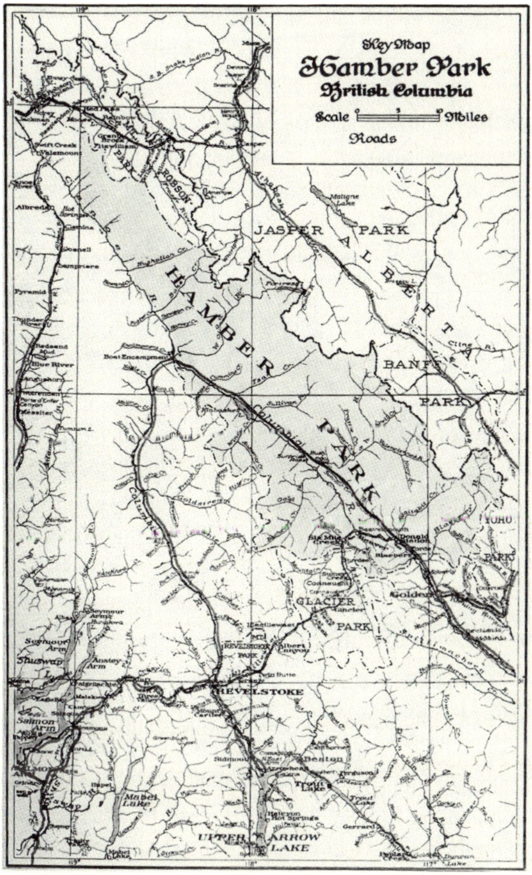

Map of Hamber Provincial Park, from the pamphlet *Hamber Park, British Columbia, Canada* (1942). Courtesy of the British Columbia Ministry of Forests and Range.

national park. Thus, the obvious solution was to establish a much larger provincial park that would then be made available for transfer to the national park system. The creation of BC provincial parks remained a cavalier process during the early 1940s, and Pattullo had the executive authority to establish a new park that might prove tempting to Ottawa. As his biographer Robin Fisher notes, the premier believed that brevity was a virtue in day-to-day government affairs and made many policy decisions "instantly, rather than pondering them at length."[38] Abruptly and with little consultation, he issued an Order-in-Council on 16 September 1941 that created an enormous new park in the Big Bend country.[39]

Named after a former lieutenant-governor, Hamber Provincial Park was nearly 2.4 million acres in size. Consisting of archetypal BC wilderness, it was mountainous, glaciated, heavily forested, cleft by icy watercourses, and almost completely uninhabited. Large areas had never been surveyed or accurately mapped. Hamber encompassed the eastern slope of the Selkirks and the western slope of the Rockies, stretching from the CPR mainline in the south to the Canadian National Railways mainline in the north. It took in the eastern section of the Big Bend Highway and had been carefully designed to act as a kind of land bridge: it bordered against Mount Robson Provincial Park in the north, Jasper and Banff National Parks on the east, and Glacier and Yoho National Parks to the south. Pattullo must have been sure that this magnanimous and rather spontaneous gesture would finally persuade Ottawa to take over British Columbia's other provincial parks in the Rockies, for an unbroken chain of national parks covering both slopes of the Rockies from Mount Robson in the north to Radium Hot Springs in the south was bound to be a great tourist draw, even during wartime. Underlying it all was the expectation that if the federal government did assume responsibility for Hamber Park, it would be obliged to maintain and improve at least half of the Big Bend Highway and to undertake other possible infrastructure developments.[40] Unlike Manning Park, which the Pattullo government had established three months earlier, Hamber was not intended to be a state asset for British Columbia. Its primary purpose was to lure Ottawa into shouldering responsibility for a long road that traversed a very rugged and sparsely populated section of the country.

This bold scheme quickly fell apart. In 1941, the Mackenzie King administration was focused on the war effort, and it had previously informed British Columbia of its desire to have national parks spread all around the country rather than concentrated in the Rockies.[41] Probably the most important factor in Hamber's failure as a gambit toward a new national park was a lack of opportunity to discuss the subject. Duff Pattullo was abruptly pushed out of the premiership by members of his own party on 3 December 1941, just weeks after he had won his third term as premier and less than three months after Hamber had been established. It is unclear whether a tentative proposal to incorporate Hamber into the national park system had been made by then, but losing the architect of the scheme would have scuttled any plans that had been discussed. Then, four days after Pattullo was forced out, Japan attacked the American Pacific fleet at Pearl Harbor. In September 1941, before America entered the war, it might have seemed reasonable to gamble that the federal government would favour the establishment of an enormous new national park along the route of the emergent Trans-Canada Highway. However, once the United States had been drawn into the conflict, the pleasure travel of American motorists was bound to be curtailed.[42] Thus, the immediate rationale for establishing Hamber Park was lost, and British Columbia found itself stuck with a giant park of questionable utility.

Early Responses to Hamber Park

Following Pattullo's departure, the provincial government displayed little enthusiasm for Hamber Park. Senior Forest Service and Parks Division officials felt slighted at not having been consulted about its creation, and field staff were put in the embarrassing position of learning about it from irate loggers and timber brokers who had read the news in the provincial gazette.[43] Shortly after Hamber was established, a memo circulated around Forest Service headquarters, proposing that its protective status be downgraded from Class A to Class B so that new industrial activity could be permitted within it.[44] This memo was written by the assistant to F.S. McKinnon, head of the Parks Division, which strongly suggests that the official in charge of BC parks was set against Hamber from the start. However, this proposal was blocked by Assistant Chief Forester George Melrose, who had recently played a key role in establishing Manning Park.[45] Disagreement about what to do with Hamber was indicative of a larger split within the Forest Service during the early 1940s. Some officials saw provincial parks as real assets that could encourage tourism, outdoor recreation, and enthusiasm for natural landscapes. Others saw parks as mere publicity devices and were opposed to letting them permanently lock up valuable resources. This latter group viewed Hamber as an egregious example of parks being established without due consideration for their long term effects on the province's forest industry.[46]

The industry was undergoing rapid changes during the war, with high prices and new harvesting and transportation techniques making it feasible to profitably cut trees that only a few years earlier would have been considered useless and best left as a scenic backdrop. Wise use of BC forest resources came to be associated with small operators who employed innovative truck logging techniques for selective cutting. Flexible, gas-powered, labour-saving technologies such as chainsaws, caterpillar tractors, multi-axle trucks, and portable sawmills combined with the expanding road network to allow loggers to reach timber that had previously been inaccessible, including on steep slopes and swampy terrain, and then haul it long distances overland. Truck logging made large tracts of Interior forest suddenly appear useful for more than just their scenic value, including forest lands recently made accessible by the Big Bend Highway.[47]

Loggers and sawmill operators in Revelstoke and especially Golden complained that Hamber Park would stifle the revival of the forest industry in their districts, where it had been moribund since the late 1920s.[48] They were supported by Golden MLA Thomas King, who pointed out in a letter to the minister of lands and forests that the Big Bend country was full of "over mature" trees that had passed their peak commercial value and were becoming susceptible to rot, disease, insect infestation, fire, and blowdown. King argued that truck loggers could remove large amounts of this "decadent" timber without detracting from Hamber's scenic value because they tended to "cream" the berths, selectively extracting valuable cedars and pines while leaving the rest intact.[49] At his urging, the question of Hamber's protective status was reopened in the spring of 1945, shortly after park advocate George Melrose had been transferred from the Forest Service to the Department of Lands. Premier Hart was informed that Hamber's Class A designation interfered with commercial development along the Big Bend Highway, and he therefore issued an Order-in-Council that downgraded it to Class B status.[50] This allowed the Parks Division to issue permits for new industrial activity such as mining and logging within its borders. Hamber was now a more flexible or malleable asset in the hands of senior officials and their political masters.

By the summer of 1945, the Parks Division was planning for increased pleasure travel as part of the transition back to peacetime conditions in North America. Driving ranked high among the anticipated activities of Canadians and Americans, and the national parks in the Rockies were expected to remain popular with auto tourists. In August 1945, with heavy peacetime traffic predicted on the Big Bend Highway, Ches Lyons and Mickey Trew were sent to conduct a reconnaissance, formulating plans for Hamber's development. They had explored most of the large parks in the Interior since 1943, including Manning, Wells Gray, Tweedsmuir, and Garibaldi, but none of these had been accessible by automobile, and thus Hamber represented a departure from their reconnaissance routine, in that it had been superimposed over an existing road. Their instructions specified that they inspect both Hamber and the Big Bend Highway corridor, providing further evidence that during the last months of the war senior Forest Service officials were beginning to see highways and the views of the motoring public as centrally important to the future of BC provincial parks. It is noteworthy that Lyons and Trew were sent to examine Hamber at almost the same moment that their colleagues E.G. Oldham and D.L. McMurchie were conducting the second reconnaissance of Manning Park, in which they paid so much more attention to the Hope-Princeton corridor than Lyons and Trew had.

Trew and Lyons spent a day and a half in the Big Bend country and made no attempt to explore beyond the immediate vicinity of the highway right-of-way.[51] Their report was profoundly unenthusiastic, and dissatisfaction with the highway shaped their conclusions. They described it as "well built from a constructional point of view, but poorly located from the aesthetic point of view."[52] The road was decent. The country had scenic features. But the relationship between the road and the landscape made the drive between Revelstoke and Golden unappealing. The road ran through dense forest in a steep-walled valley, which meant that for long stretches motorists could see neither the Columbia River below nor the glaciers and mountain peaks above. The highway had originally been conceived of as a parkway or touring road, but auto tourists and their viewing habits had been forgotten over the course of its decade-long construction. Funds had not been available during the Depression for such frills as pullouts, scenic vantage points, or the pruning of timber to improve sightlines. Lyons and Trew echoed the verdict of many motorists when they complained about the highway's "tendency to being monotonous." The two-hundred-mile drive between Revelstoke and Golden was time consuming, physically and mentally taxing, and ultimately unrewarding for most pleasure travellers due to the undifferentiated scenery and lack of attractions and services. As a scenic route, the highway was a failure compared to what was available in nearby Banff, Kootenay, and Yoho Parks.[53]

Lyons and Trew enumerated instances in which scenic, natural, and historical features could have been cultivated but had not. Silvertip Falls was striking enough that the Revelstoke Board of Trade had co-operated with the district branch of the Native Sons of British Columbia to build a roadside viewing platform there, but a forest fire had subsequently burnt the surrounding timber, "leaving but snag and rock," and nothing had been done to restore it.[54] The 12-Mile, Priest, Rockslide, and Death Rapids on the Columbia River above Downie Creek were impressive cataracts linked to the fur trade and gold rush days by tragic and gruesome stories of drowning, starvation, murder, and cannibalism.[55] However, these interesting features were not visible from the road and were not marked, so motorists passed them without realizing they were there. The same was true for Surprise Rapids upstream from Kinbasket Lake. Even the captions that Lyons and Trew applied to the photographs pasted into their reconnaissance report emphasized the paucity of good views and the fleeting nature of the few that were available. A photo of Frenchman's Cap and the Columbia River near Downie Creek was labelled "one of the few open vistas along the road." Others identified a "potential scenic vista," a mountain peak "glimpsed through the trees," and a "scenic vista barely visible from the road."[56]

The Columbia Valley was particularly steep, narrow, and damp on the western slope of the Selkirks, so that for long stretches between Revelstoke and Boat Encampment the road undulated through a seemingly impenetrable and unbroken forest. From Golden to Boat Encampment, the Columbia River flows through the Rocky Mountain Trench, which is somewhat broader and also drier due to the rain shadow effect, with forest cover that is correspondingly less dense. These factors provided motorists with slightly better views, and Lyons and Trew deemed the eastern section of the highway inside Hamber more scenic (or at least less monotonous) than the western. Between Boat Encampment and Kinbasket Lake, the road passed through the ancient timber that the National Parks Branch had been so keen to preserve during the 1930s. Lyons and Trew pronounced this part of the drive "rather attractive." The highway also skirted along Kinbasket Lake, offering impressive views of Mount Trident and other glaciated peaks of the Adamant range. However, the lake itself had little recreational potential and a notorious reputation. It was icy cold and heavily silted, which prevented swimming and sport fishing, and strong winds made boating hazardous.[57] The Bush Lakes midway between Kinbasket Lake and Golden were Lyons and Trew's favourite part of Hamber; they described them as "the type of lakes which are painted with a rising morning mist and a moose feeding offshore or flights of ducks and geese coming in to feed." Unfortunately for drivers, these picturesque lakes were "so effectively screened off by a narrow belt of trees that the average traveler does not know they are there."[58] In noting these potential attractions that were not visible from the road, Lyons and Trew were implicitly criticizing the engineers and project administrators of the 1930s for failing to make the best use of the country's scenic resources.

Lyons and Trew also took note of the roadside commercial operations that had opened along the Big Bend Highway. In the early 1940s, the two hundred miles between Revelstoke and Golden had featured no buildings except abandoned road construction camps and a lone Forest Service cabin at Boat Encampment. Drivers who were unfortunate enough to break down or get into an accident had found themselves in a very difficult situation. By August 1945, however, three family-owned businesses had opened beside the highway. On the western section, the Nichols family had a gas station, tearoom, and basic cabins at Downie Creek, forty miles above Revelstoke. On the eastern section, seventy miles north of Golden where the Middle River emptied into Kinbasket Lake, the Chapman family ran a gas station and auto camp. At Boat Encampment – the apex of the bend – the McKinnon family of Revelstoke had a gas station and lodge by the large steel bridge that spanned the Columbia River.[59] Lyons and Trew described these commercial ventures as adequate for the time being but unlikely to encourage visitors to stay in the Big Bend country for long. The auto camp at Downie Creek had "no particular view," Boat Encampment had "no outstanding attractions," and the Middle River Auto Camp stood on a "barren delta" of gravel deposits and scrub brush.[60]

Although Ches Lyons and Mickey Trew were not inspired by the scenery along the Big Bend Highway, they nevertheless recommended that it be "aesthetically developed and protected."[61] Forming a crucial part of the nascent Trans-Canada, the road was a kind of gateway to the BC Interior, and they therefore believed that it deserved to be managed as an asset. The first priority was to develop a series of roadside picnic and campsites at Silvertip Falls, Boat Encampment, and Kinbasket Lake. These facilities would reduce the fire hazard posed by travellers who pulled off the road to cook and camp wherever they found it convenient. Lyons and Trew's second priority was to improve the scenic aspects of the road, both inside and outside the boundaries of Hamber Park. They suggested asking the Department of Public Works to clear pullouts where motorists could pause and gaze toward mountain peaks, glaciers, tall trees, and the Columbia River. They also suggested that the district Forest Service office assemble a "mobile crew" to work on the "improvement of scenic vistas" by cutting down trees and clearing brush along the highway, thereby providing better sightlines. The crew would also erect signs to identify landscape features and build trails so that motorists could walk to attractions that lay a short distance from the right-of-way, such as the dramatic rapids on the Columbia.[62] Cumulatively, the measures proposed by Lyons and Trew were meant to improve the public's experience of a road that was not considered intrinsically attractive. They would provide a kind of redemption through stagecraft, helping to punctuate an otherwise undifferentiated wilderness.

Lyons and Trew were positively brusque in discussing the portions of Hamber Park that lay beyond the Big Bend Highway corridor, explaining that "the nature of this park together with its history and local information did not warrant such a reconnaissance at this time." They criticized the 1941 decision to create Hamber for saddling the Parks Division with "3,800 square miles of park which are, except for spot areas, utterly useless for park purposes." Access beyond the highway was extremely limited, and little of the scenery was visible. There were no alpine meadows or other areas of open country. Big game was scarce and fishing poor. The only recreationalists who might appreciate Hamber's vast backcountry were mountaineers, who might be drawn to its many unscaled peaks. Wilderness, then, was not park-worthy in and of itself.[63]

Lyons and Trew believed that Hamber should be cancelled, but they recognized that getting rid of a relatively new park whose area made up nearly a quarter of the total provincial park system might pose "an awkward problem to the Government." They therefore proposed two ways of ameliorating its deletion. The first option called for a series of small roadside parks or recreational reserves to be established between Golden and Revelstoke, which would contain campgrounds, picnic sites, viewpoints, and scenic attractions. This dovetailed with their general recommendations for development along the Big Bend Highway. In the second option, Hamber would be replaced with a half-mile-wide parkway running along the highway from Revelstoke to Golden. This echoed the Province's 1934 proposal for a linear national park, although nothing in Lyons and Trew's report suggests that they were familiar with this failed scheme.[64]

The Parks Division's first inspection of the Big Bend country gave the region a failing grade on two counts. The highway was long and tedious, and though Hamber was amply supplied with prominent peaks, glaciers, lakes, tall timber, and large furry mammals – all classic elements of North American mountain parks – few were either visible or accessible to motorists. As experienced from the road, Hamber had virtually nothing to offer – almost no attractions or recreational venues. Since the 1920s, a visual-vehicular relationship between road corridors and the surrounding environment had come to be considered normal in the mountain parks of western North America, whereby auto tourists and pleasure travellers expected to encounter roads with wide verges, or at least a large number of scenic viewpoints and open vistas, supplemented by clearly demarcated natural and historical attractions and interspersed with convenient, respectable commercial operations. By this yardstick, Hamber Park and the Big Bend Highway failed to measure up, and it was questionable whether either could be sufficiently upgraded to become a major asset to British Columbia.[65]

Ches Lyons and Mickey Trew were the Parks Division's experts on reconnaissance and development plans, and their unenthusiastic assessment of the Big Bend country provided valuable ammunition for those within the Forest Service who saw Hamber as a barrier to restructuring the Interior forest industry. Even though the park had already been downgraded from Class A to Class B, Lyons and Trew argued that the limited amount of appealing scenery along the highway could be protected (and even improved) without retaining such an enormous provincial park. They found no convincing reason to keep Hamber. However, as the subsequent lack of development inside the park would show, senior officials in the Parks Division and Forest Service were not bound to follow the recommendations put forward in 1945.

4

The Failure of Hamber Park and the Big Bend Highway

The decline and eventual fall of both Hamber Park and the Big Bend Highway was protracted, and after the park was eviscerated in 1961, massive environmental changes occurred that were removed from the motoring public's view. The few historians and park advocates who touch on Hamber focus on its truncation in 1961 and give the impression that this was purely the result of rapacious resource companies pressuring an acquiescent state into freeing up forest land for logging and hydroelectric development.[1] Although there is some truth to this, it does not explain why such a large, accessible, and strategically located park was so vulnerable to these industrial incursions at a time when auto tourism and the popularity of provincial parks was growing by leaps and bounds. A fuller understanding of Hamber's failure must take into account the antipathy that the Parks Division and most motorists felt for the road that traversed it.

The Fordist state's treatment of Hamber contrasted starkly with its cultivation of Manning Park as a significant asset. Park managers saw the Big Bend Highway and the landscapes visible along it as having little to offer the public. They therefore made no concerted attempt to popularize Hamber or cultivate it as a major attraction during the 1950s. Only limited efforts were made to protect the landscapes that were prominently visible from the highway. Hamber was kept in a state of limbo, being neither developed within nor excised from the provincial park system. The widespread disdain for the Big Bend Highway was key to the Parks Division's hands-off management of Hamber during the 1940s and 1950s, and also to British Columbians' lack of awareness of the park. As in other areas, the public's experiences of the environment in Hamber were shaped by faraway planners and politicians, and by loggers, commercial operators, and other actors working "on the ground." Yet indifference and inaction also played key roles, leading to the failure of both Hamber Park and the Big Bend Highway.

The same arterial road that brought drivers into the Big Bend country also allowed loggers and sawmill operators to contemplate the profitable cutting of its timber and engineers to imagine the construction of dams on that section of the Columbia River. Prior to 1940, large-scale resource extraction and building projects had effectively been impossible in the region due to the difficulty of moving people and materials in and out. Completion of the road between Golden and Revelstoke opened up a whole new realm of possibilities, making the sparsely populated area a contested terrain.

During British Columbia's postwar resource boom, Hamber was subjected to many of the same pressures from logging and mining companies as Manning Park, the other large provincial park in the Interior that was traversed by an important highway. However, Hamber proved far more susceptible to their advances than Manning did. This was due in large part to the poor reputation of the Big Bend Highway and the Parks Division's associated decision not to develop amenities or attractions in Hamber or even indicate its existence. It was the motoring public's negative experiences of nature by the road along the lonely, monotonous highway that ultimately left Hamber open to incursions by industrial resource extraction and megaproject schemes. Hamber was kept in an undeveloped state for many years until the early 1960s, when it and the Big Bend country were designated a kind of "sacrifice area," where government agencies countenanced irreparable damage to extensive swathes of land in the name of progress and the greater good.

Hamber in Limbo

By the summer of 1945, the war in Europe had ended, and increased pleasure travel was anticipated as part of the transition back to peacetime.[2] The national parks in the Rockies were expected to remain popular with auto tourists. Traffic over the Big Bend section of the Trans-Canada Highway was also expected to include many western Canadians who were maintaining family links: by 1950, 250,000 of British Columbia's 1.1 million residents were migrants from the Prairie provinces, and many British Columbians had also moved from the Interior hinterlands to the cities of the Coast.[3] Forest Service officials did not rush to eliminate Hamber Park in 1945. Nor did they implement the modest developments recommended by Lyons and Trew. Instead, Hamber was left in obscurity. No mobile crew went out to cultivate scenery and attractions along the highway. No campgrounds, picnic sites, or pullouts were built. No promotional materials were produced, and no signs were erected – not even at the points where the highway entered and exited the park. The Parks Division avoided drawing attention to Hamber and dissuaded would-be entrepreneurs from applying to start businesses such as hunting lodges inside it.[4] As a result, most people who drove between Golden and Boat Encampment had no idea that they were crossing one of the largest parks in North America.

Motorists responded to the lack of designated stopping places by carving out their own. In 1947, the forest ranger stationed at Golden reported to Parks Division headquarters that

> during the tourist season a very considerable number of people travel with trailers or camping units along the Big Bend Highway through Hamber Park ... They search in vain for good camping places and end up making camp wherever there is room [beside the road] to park their car or trailer. Practically every small level spot, gravel pit, etc. has its overnight occupant every night for a period of about two months.[5]

The ranger recommended that small public campsites be established at regular intervals along the highway, but to no avail. The lack of such amenities would not have been unusual in the late 1940s, but it persisted through the 1950s, by which time the public was coming to expect the presence of government-maintained picnic sites and campgrounds along the province's arterial highways. The absence of basic facilities in the two-hundred-mile drive marked the Big Bend Highway as a kind of secondary road and thus reinforced the impression that the surrounding country was trackless wilderness.[6]

Most motorists experienced the Big Bend country as a featureless, meaningless, timeless landscape – a seemingly endless journey through dense forests punctuated by only a handful of buildings and a few brief glimpses of distant snow-capped peaks. There were no elevated vistas over wide expanses of land, endowing a magisterial sense of ownership; no spectacular views of looming mountain peaks; just mile after mile of dark, dense, undifferentiated forest.[7] Bears, moose, and mountain caribou

Typical section of the Big Bend Highway, late 1950s. Author's collection.

lived in the Big Bend country but were relatively scarce and rarely seen, doubtless to the disappointment of tourists who were accustomed to spotting furry quadrupeds when driving through the Rockies. The mosquitoes, on the other hand, were "horrific" and discouraged many people from leaving their vehicles.[8]

With few traces of human activity other than the road itself, driving the Big Bend Highway was a journey into the wilderness sublime, with as much reason for worry and fear as for admiration and awe. Vehicles that went off the road could plunge over a cliff and disappear into the river or dense brush, potentially never to be found. As if to emphasize the danger, the mangled remains of vehicles that had come to grief along the road were typically pushed to the shoulder and abandoned there due to the impracticality of towing them away. An intermittent stream of accidents occurred on the highway, including some of a spectacular nature, which simply reinforced its reputation as simultaneously monotonous *and* dangerous.[9]

The dullness of the scenery, the relatively primitive state of the road, and the loneliness of passing only a handful of occupied buildings during many hours of driving instilled a sense of isolation and vulnerability. Between the outskirts of Revelstoke and Golden, the highway was a thin, tenuous, unpaved line of modernity, snaking through a wilderness that struck many as desolate, even repellent.[10] Despite its arterial road, the Big Bend country was not a modern landscape, tamed for the pleasure of the motoring public. Nor was it an anti-modern landscape, full of scenic wonder and recreational opportunities. It was simply long, wild, and boring. Given that parks were especially valorized environments, the public's experiences of the Big Bend country might have been different had they known that they were traversing one of Canada's largest parks as they drove between Golden and Boat Encampment.

Plotting the Big Bend Highway's Future

Canadians' perceptions of what constituted a proper highway were changing rapidly by the late 1940s. "Highways" that had narrow, dusty, gravel surfaces and that were closed in winter no longer seemed adequate or up to date.[11] Whenever a new paved highway was opened or significant improvements were made to an older road, the shortcomings of the Big Bend Highway were thrown more sharply into relief. The Department of Public Works found it difficult to maintain. One Golden resident who travelled it regularly during the 1950s recalled "gaping holes straight down into the canyons below, scary stuff to drive over."[12]

Thousands of western Canadians drove the Big Bend road, and like other arterial highway corridors, it became a shared landscape experience, something they had in common. In most cases, that experience was a negative one. The highway's reputation as a route to avoid spread by word of mouth among tourists and casual travellers. Commercial trucks and most buses that went between the Prairies and the Coast chose the Crowsnest Pass and emergent southern transprovincial highway.[13] Boosters and businesses in other parts of the Interior were not shy about using the Big Bend Highway's unpopularity and perceived shortcomings as ammunition in their campaign to have different routes designated as the BC section of the Trans-Canada Highway.[14] Canada's primitive transcontinental road was of little practical value to any but the most adventurous auto tourist during the 1940s. Plans to modernize it were supported by automobile associations, tourism boosters, the nascent trucking industry, and industrial groups that shared an interest in encouraging Canadians to purchase and use an automobile.[15] Under the terms of the Trans-Canada Highway Act, which was passed in December 1949, the federal government agreed to help the provinces build a paved, high-quality, all-season highway that followed "the shortest practicable east-west route." Ottawa would pay half the cost of new construction and the entire cost in national parks and Indian reserves. The act set out minimum standards of grade, curvature, and permanence that must be met if construction were to be eligible for federal funding.[16] These would be very expensive to implement in the mountainous Interior of British Columbia, and it was also difficult to reconcile the Big Bend Highway's circuitous course with the goal of following the "shortest practicable east-west route." Furthermore, the road was closed during the winter. In 1952, the Social Credit government of W.A.C. Bennett announced that it wanted to modernize the highway in partnership with Ottawa. However, the same year saw the BC Department of Public Works begin investigating other possible routes for the Trans-Canada between Revelstoke and the BC-Alberta boundary. The key question was whether to upgrade the existing road or replace it with new one that followed a different route.[17]

The Parks Division and Forest Service were not consulted about what to do with the section of the Trans-Canada that ran through Hamber Provincial Park. During the late 1940s and early 1950s, their main concern in Hamber was to manage truck logging operations so that they would not negatively affect motorists' experiences of nature by the road. Their goal was the same as in Manning and other provincial parks that were crossed by arterial roads, but the situation in Hamber was complicated by its Class B status. Not only did it contain many grandfathered timber licences, but loggers were free to apply for the right to cut other Crown timber, and most such applications applied to trees that were easily accessible – and in most cases also visible - from the highway.

Pressure to allow logging inside Hamber and elsewhere along the Big Bend corridor came from both large and small players in the forest industry. There was an enormous proliferation of small truck logging operations in the Interior between 1940 and 1950. The beginnings of large-scale corporate influence could be also discerned by 1950, when Columbia Cellulose – the Canadian subsidiary of US-based Celanese Corporation – announced plans to develop the first pulp mill in the Interior at Castlegar, at the confluence of the Columbia and Kootenay Rivers 150 miles south of Revelstoke.[18] This mill would need a huge supply of wood fibre, so the company – called Celgar by local residents – purchased sawmills at Castlegar, Nakusp, and Revelstoke during the early 1950s to gain control of their timber holdings.[19] In 1952, Celgar also began negotiating with the provincial government for cutting rights on nearly 3.5 million acres in the Columbia watershed between Castlegar and Boat Encampment. The river and the region's fast-developing road network would serve as a kind of conveyor belt, feeding wood fibre to the pulp mill's chemical digesters.[20]

During the late 1940s and early 1950s, the Forest Service and Parks Division were barely able to keep up with the applications to cut timber in Hamber Park. By the mid-1950s, several logging operations were active inside it. Most were small truck logging ventures like that of Walter and Adolph Roosdahl, who hauled a home-built, diesel-powered "gypo" sawmill to their timber licences near Surprise Rapids.[21] Small operators like the Roosdahls tended to "cream" their berths, selectively removing the most valuable trees, roughly processing them, and having them hauled to faraway planer mills in Golden or Revelstoke. However, large-scale clear-cutting was becoming common in the Golden district by the mid-1950s. This was the case with Selkirk Spruce Mills, whose timber licences spanned a long stretch of the Big Bend Highway fifteen miles north of Golden and which eventually had two portable sawmills and a planer mill working inside Hamber Park.

The Parks Division usually acquiesced to new logging activity in Hamber, provided it did not create eyesores that would be visible to motorists. It did conduct a few strategic timber swaps to preserve scenic roadside landscapes, and in a few instances it turned down logging applications for aesthetic reasons. A 1949 application to cut cedar poles on the lower slopes of Mount Trident, on the opposite side of Kinbasket Lake from the Middle River Auto Camp, was rejected because it would be "impossible to conceal [from drivers] and could conceivably spoil the aesthetic values of a very beautiful piece of parkland." Not only would skid roads and landings leave ugly scars, but the operation would produce considerable waste wood. The timber applied for consisted largely of "decadent Upper Columbia cedar," which from the outside appeared perfect for utility poles but that often turned out to be riddled with crown, heart, and butt rot. Felling these cedars generated large amounts of unsightly waste from culls (rotten trees that were simply discarded) and long butting (trees cut high above the ground to avoid rot in the base). Park planners also worried about the safety of hauling forty- to ninety-foot-long cedar poles along the highway during the summer tourist season.[22]

Within the Parks Division, opinion was divided about how to balance the forest industry's interests with the public's experience of Hamber.

Kinbasket Lake, with Mount Trident in the distance. Byron Harmon postcard. Author's collection.

Planner Robert Ahrens, who had ruled against the application to log on Mount Trident, contended that roadside aesthetics should be closely controlled because the highway was an important artery and would remain so for the foreseeable future. On the other hand, Mickey Trew favoured allowing logging and other resource extraction operations inside the park. In a 1949 report to the head of the Parks Division, he argued that Hamber had been "set aside for a reason only remotely related to its recreational values" and thus "should not be a park to start with." Trew predicted that the Big Bend road would not be modernized or retained as part of the Trans-Canada Highway, because it was "a long, dreary, and disappointing drive." He therefore proposed that Hamber be treated more as a forest reserve than a provincial park and suggested that its managers limit their efforts to protecting the tall timber and shoreline views between Boat Encampment and Kinbasket Lake. In effect, he argued that worrying about logging-generated blight along the highway made little sense because traffic would soon be rerouted away from the Big Bend country.[23]

Despite the continuing critiques of Hamber from within the Parks Division (and elsewhere in the provincial government), it was easier to do nothing with the park during the late 1940s and early 1950s than to develop it or to delete it. The uncertain future of the highway did nothing to inspire decisive action on the matter. The Parks Division continued to discourage outside parties from publicizing the park, which suggests that senior officials hoped to avoid having people know or care about it.[24] The efforts to keep Hamber out of the public eye can be explained by the agency's lingering sense of resentment regarding the park and also by the more general dissatisfaction with driving the Big Bend Highway. In the mid-1950s, however, a number of more concrete reasons to prevent the public from knowing or caring about Hamber began to arise.

Development Plans in the Mid-1950s

Hamber and the Big Bend country started to emerge from limbo during the mid-1950s due to the growing likelihood that a series of dams would be built along the BC section of the Columbia River. The Canadian Pacific Railway (CPR) had studied the feasibility of hydroelectric development in the area during the early 1920s.[25] In 1944, the International Joint Commission began researching how the Canadian Columbia could be regulated to reduce downstream flooding while also maximizing its power generation and determined that most of the river's storage capacity was located in the Big Bend country. In 1951, the commission identified a narrow point in the valley at Mica Creek, seventy-five miles north of Revelstoke, as the best site for a storage dam on the Columbia. The envisioned seven-hundred-foot-high dam would hold approximately 15 million acre feet of water, with one acre foot being the volume of water necessary to fill an acre-sized area to the depth of twelve inches. It would also destroy Kinbasket Lake and the eastern half of the Big Bend Highway.[26] British Columbia's Social Credit government was so keen on hydroelectric development that it briefly entertained the idea of letting a consortium of Washington State power utilities build a dam at Mica Creek. This scheme did not advance far, but the idea of a large dam at Mica was subsequently incorporated into the discussions that led to the Columbia River Treaty.[27]

The mid- and late 1950s were full of intense, sometimes acrimonious, constitutional and diplomatic wrangling between the federal and provincial governments about the sites and sequence of dams that might be built on the Columbia.[28] However, all proposals called for a very large dam at Mica Creek, and this was less controversial than the dams proposed for upstream and downstream areas, where dozens of communities and thousands of people would be affected.[29] If there was any section of the Columbia Valley that many British Columbians could be convinced was an empty, unproductive wilderness and therefore a suitable sacrifice for a megaproject, it was the Big Bend country. It contained no communities, no designated recreational areas, and virtually no scenic, natural, or historical attractions. So far as most people knew, it contained no parks either: there were no picnic sites, campgrounds, boat launches, viewpoints, or signs to indicate Hamber's existence. Many western Canadian motorists would happily seen the long, boring Big Bend Highway drowned, provided it was replaced by a shorter, more modern, and ideally more scenic road.

There was no guarantee that dams would be built on the BC section of the Columbia.[30] In June 1954, park planner Robert Ahrens observed that "interest waxes hot and cold over such projects, sometimes for many years," and recommended that the Parks Division continue to exercise a degree of control over resource extraction in Hamber until it was clear whether a dam (or dams) would be built.[31] The fact that the Trans-Canada ran parallel to the Columbia River for nearly two hundred miles was a major stumbling block to the crucial Mica Dam project, one that historians who have studied the Columbia River development in Canada have tended to overlook. Hamber Park was also a stumbling block, albeit a less significant one, given the Social Credit government's demonstrated willingness to axe provincial parks that stood in the way of lucrative industrial developments.[32]

The larger of these two stumbling blocks was abruptly removed in late 1955, when the BC Department of Highways submitted the results of its surveys for a future route of the Trans-Canada between Revelstoke and Alberta. Its engineers had determined that a new all-season highway could be built through the Selkirks for approximately the same cost of improving the Big Bend Highway to modern standards of gradient, curvature, permanence, and safety.[33] A highway between Golden and Revelstoke via the avalanche-scarred Rogers Pass would be half as long as the Big Bend route. Better yet – at least from the provincial government's perspective – most of it would run through Glacier and Mount Revelstoke National Parks. Under the terms of the Trans-Canada Highway Act, Ottawa would have to pay for almost all the new construction, as well as for future maintenance and the elaborate avalanche defences that would be necessary to keep the highway open in winter.[34]

In March 1956, Victoria officially notified Ottawa that it wanted to re route the Trans-Canada through the Rogers Pass. Barely fifteen years after the opening of the Big Bend Highway, the provincial government had manoeuvred Ottawa into paying for a second road between Revelstoke and Golden. The unpopular, roundabout Big Bend Highway had become expendable, and thus the Big Bend country was available for dam development.[35] Hamber Park was now the only impediment to the construction of dams that would transform the Big Bend of the Columbia into an enormous reservoir.

After a decade of stagnation, things started to change rapidly in Hamber. During the summer of 1956, it was thrown open to logging, including areas that were visible from the highway. Construction of a dam at Mica Creek was now "only a question of time," planner Robert Ahrens explained in a memo to the head of the Parks Division, adding that the dam "promised to raise water over Kinbasket Lake by approximately 200 feet." Huge tracts of timber that had previously merited preservation were suddenly destined for inundation, so there was no good reason to block applications for logging in Hamber Park, even in especially scenic areas such as the lakeside slopes of Mount Trident. Ahrens dryly noted that it was "better to take the timber now than to leave it for flooding later."[36] The Forest Service began automatically approving all applications to log below the elevation 2,450 feet above sea level, which was the anticipated maximum height of the future reservoir.[37]

Clearing the valley floor became an urgent priority. This meant abandoning the pretense of managing Hamber as a park: there was no point worrying about protecting scenery and natural landscape features along a route that would probably be underwater within a decade. Loggers were now allowed to cut right up to the edge of the road. Old commitments to preserve scenery were also jettisoned. The tall, ancient trees that lined the highway between Kinbasket Lake and Boat Encampment, and which Duff Pattullo had agreed to preserve "in perpetuity" in 1935, were made available to loggers in early 1959.[38] The Parks Act and Forest Act were violated in numerous instances, including unauthorized road construction, unapproved operation of portable sawmills, excessive slash left behind, unsatisfactory disposal of sawdust and slabs, and sawmills burning wood waste without adequate safety measures to prevent forest fires. This gradual breakdown of control was the result of inadequate supervision, the marginal profitability of logging in the Big Bend country, and a sense of urgency due to anticipated dam construction. By 1958, senior Parks Branch officials were contemplating the "elimination of a large portion of the park."[39]

Looking Forward to the End of the Road

News that the Big Bend Highway would be replaced by a shorter, paved route that would be kept open year-round was warmly embraced by western

Canadian motorists, tourism promoters, business groups, and journalists. Many magazine and newspaper articles that looked forward to the new highway took the opportunity to disparage the existing road between Revelstoke and Golden. The *Vancouver Sun* dismissed the "gravel, narrow, twisting, and lonely" Big Bend route as the "weak link" in an otherwise safe and pleasant drive between Vancouver and Calgary. "Some of these faults might be forgiven if it were scenic, but it is not. Most of it is just a road through the trees and plainly boring." *Sun* columnist Jack Scott boasted that the "fantastic speedway" being built through the Rogers Pass would eliminate "the loop of 193 nasty miles of washboard, dust, and gravel known far and wide as the Big Bend." *Vancouver Province* columnist Eric Ramsden expected that the new route would offer "breathtaking scenery and a wide modern road," in contrast to "the slightly-less-than-exciting Big Bend gravel road."[40] The *Brandon Sun* denigrated the existing road as "a cow path" and a "failure."[41] In 1960, *Weekend Magazine* warned would-be auto tourists that "for the moment, the notorious Big Bend Highway (and that last word is used advisedly) is the only all-Canadian way over the Rockies for a car." Tapping into the wealth of "tall tales" that surrounded the unpopular road, the article reported that

> stories have circulated for years about gibbering patients being held in Calgary hospitals until they have regained sanity after a car ride over the Big Bend. I drove it and can half believe the stories. But [with completion of the Rogers Pass route] we will be able to forget about such things, for Canadians will have their nation-wide highway, dreamed of for so long.[42]

In an article for *Imperial Oil Review,* Bob Metcalfe positively rejoiced at the impending demise of the old road. The roundabout route had always been a "highway horror," he explained, and "nobody is shedding a tear" that it would soon be redundant. "Only loggers, miners, sportsmen, and the adventurous and foolhardy will use it," he predicted, "and then the Columbia River power project will deliver the *coup de grace.*"[43] The Big Bend Highway's reputation for monotony and danger had spread far and wide among western Canadians since 1940. Its replacement by a modern highway through the Rogers Pass seemed a tangible marker of postwar progress. The new way promised a faster, safer, easier drive along a paved road with substantial verges – *and* it would traverse a national park with wide-open mountain scenery of the classic western Canadian variety. Superior in every respect, it would vastly improve the motoring public's experience of nature by the road.

The Parks Branch began preparing for a wholesale retreat from the region. In September 1960, its director circulated a confidential consultation document on the topic of deleting Hamber Park.[44] A few months later, Minister of Forests Ray Williston urged his cabinet colleague Minister of Recreation and Conservation Earle Westwood to remove barriers to industrial activity in what he called the "underutilized" Big Bend country. Wanting to use the reservoir-clearing process to jumpstart the forest industry in Golden, Williston proposed the establishment of the Kinbasket Sustained Yield Unit, 2.2 million acres that would correspond more or less with Hamber Park.[45] Approximately half a million of its acres would consist of "accessible productive forest," which would provide a long-term resource base; an additional 55,000 acres of valley bottom timber would need swift extraction from the projected flood area behind Mica Dam. Williston impressed on his junior cabinet colleague the "urgent" need for a decision, since companies would need to set up new timber processing facilities in Golden by the time full-scale reservoir clearance got under way.[46]

The Forest Service's plans for large-scale logging in advance of dam construction and the impending completion of the Rogers Pass route combined to remove the last reason for continuing the charade that Hamber had become. In the spring of 1961, the provincial government pressed forward with its elimination. The briefing document that recommended this step could not explain why Hamber had been created in the first place and pointed out that its deletion had been recommended several times since 1945.[47] Hamber was described as lacking accessible, high-quality scenery and as having limited recreational appeal. Parks Branch headquarters predicted little public opposition to its departure – after all, it was essentially unknown to British Columbians. More worrisome was the fact that deleting its 2.4 million acres would reduce the total area of the provincial park system by nearly a third, which was bound to draw attention following on the heels of controversial hydroelectric developments in Tweedsmuir and Strathcona Parks. There was a risk that the government, the Department of Recreation and Conservation, and the Parks Branch would be exposed to embarrassing criticism about how BC parks were being managed – partly on the basis of an emerging environmental politics and also because of the widespread popularity of the parks during the postwar years. Driving through Hamber on the Big Bend Highway had never made British Columbia look particularly good, but its termination could still make the government look bad.[48]

Parks Branch officials devised a plan to minimize the potential political fallout, while at the same time leveraging Hamber's cancellation for maximum institutional gain. The branch had been trying to get a large provincial park established in the Cariboo region since the early 1950s.[49] This would encompass the scenic Bowron Lake chain, which was expected to become a popular destination for boaters and backcountry campers. It would also be located a short distance from Barkerville Historic Provincial Park, a gold-rush-era ghost town that the branch was developing as a major attraction. However, senior Forest Service officials had repeatedly blocked the Bowron scheme because they wanted to encourage pulp mill development in the northern Interior and saw the area as a valuable source of wood fibre.[50] Minister of Forests Ray Williston – who represented a Cariboo riding – had expressed his desire to transform the eastern section of the Big Bend country into a sustained yield forest management unit, so the Parks Branch indicated that it would be willing to expedite Hamber's cancellation if the Forest Service dropped its opposition to the Bowron proposal. Bowron would be one-tenth the size of Hamber, but according to branch headquarters would nevertheless offer "a far superior park area." On the verge of being sacrificed to facilitate dam development, Hamber could finally do something positive for the branch by serving as a bargaining chip in its bid to create a major new recreational asset in the faraway Cariboo. In turn, establishing the park at Bowron could be used to divert public attention away from a significant decrease in the province's total park area.[51]

On 6 June 1961, an executive Order-in-Council liquidated almost all of Hamber Park.[52] Only a 56,000-acre rump was retained around Fortress Lake, isolated high in the Rockies, bordered by Jasper National Park on three sides, and accessible only by floatplane. The Parks Branch concern that this step might provoke an outcry proved unfounded. It drew nary a whimper from the public, for few realized that the park had ever been there, and most of the few who did either saw it as an impediment to logging or associated it with the detested Big Bend Highway. After Hamber was reduced, the total area of the provincial park system was smaller than it had been in 1940, despite the fact that the number of parks had increased from 46 to more than 150 during the intervening years. Still, senior Parks Branch officials claimed that getting rid of Hamber demonstrated their willingness to make "drastic adjustments ... in the light of proper recreational assessment."[53] The system had been purified, in a sense, and would no longer be burdened by a huge tract that was unappealing to the motoring public and largely inaccessible. Ironically, Hamber had been precisely the kind of park that a growing number of North American environmentalists and outdoor recreationalists were beginning to extol as "wilderness areas" during the 1960s, free from the cars, crowds, and concessions found in such popular parks as Manning.[54]

Floods, Fires, and Forgetting

The summer of 1962 saw duelling opening ceremonies for the new Rogers Pass section of the modernized Trans-Canada Highway. At a July ribbon cutting in Revelstoke, Premier W.A.C. Bennett declared the highway finished. Two months later, Prime Minister John Diefenbaker declared it open at a ceremony in Glacier National Park. In the populist blacktop politics of the early 1960s, both men were keen to claim credit for a crucial piece of infrastructure that would appeal to sightseers, business travellers, and commercial truckers alike. Neither ceremony acknowledged that the new stretch of highway that made Glacier National Park accessible to motorists had also eased the way for the destruction of a little-known but much larger provincial park.[55]

The Rogers Pass section of the Trans-Canada proved more popular than its biggest advocates could have predicted. Its smooth asphalt surface, passing lanes, and gentle curves and grades were perfectly suited to the powerful, low-slung, glassed-in touring cars of the time. It could also be used by heavy buses and transport trucks. The relationship between the new highway and the surrounding environment provided an experience that differed radically from that of the route it replaced. The open terrain, wide verges, and high speeds permitted by the paved and superelevated surface gave the impression of cruising along at the top of the world. Indeed, the route through Glacier Park and the Rogers Pass was regularly deemed the scenic high point of a motor trip over the Trans-Canada. A few travellers, however, observed that easy access and high speeds seemed to reduce the sublimity of the mountain landscape. The Saskatchewan English professor Edward McCourt found the road "child's play for even the timidest tourist to drive" and, as a result, deemed the summit of the pass "an anti-climax ... definitely not overpowering."[56]

The new highway implicitly conveyed lessons about progress made possible by scientific expertise, heroic infrastructure, and active government. Newspaper and magazine stories boasted that engineers had studied the environment of the pass before designing the highway's winter defences. Electronic sensors read air temperature, humidity, and the consistency of the snow pack, and transmitted this information to Glacier National Park's administrative and road maintenance complex. Berms, dikes, and catch basins deflected and contained snow slides, and reinforced concrete snowsheds sheltered the highway where it ran through major avalanche paths. Gun emplacements allowed the Canadian Army to accurately fire high explosive shells onto cornices and avalanche routes, thereby dislodging snow in a controlled manner. The triumphal nature of the new highway, with its monitoring systems, earthworks, and battlements, was further emphasized when Parks Canada repurposed the ruined CPR snowsheds as historical attractions. The timber sheds had been part of the CPR mainline before the 1916 completion of a tunnel beneath the summit of the pass. These and other scenic pullouts, picnic sites, and interpretive signs along the new road through Glacier Park heightened its contrast with the Big Bend Highway, whose landscape was bereft of designated stopping places and explanatory information.[57] Postcards, magazines, and newspapers emphasized that the new route allowed drivers to travel through the Selkirks safely and easily at any time of the year. Modern engineering and technology were presented as having tamed one of Canada's most dangerous environments, seemingly without damaging its scenery or ecology.[58]

The Big Bend country was abandoned to logging trucks and construction machinery after the summer of 1962. Away from public view, work proceeded on the enormous dam at Mica Creek through the 1960s. In 1965, survey crews and fallers cut out the high-water line of Mica Dam's future reservoir, and loggers spent the next decade clearing timber below that elevation. Certain species of wildlife were also haphazardly removed from the area. In 1967 and 1968, the moose hunting season in the Big Bend country was extended through the winter to exterminate animals that would otherwise be displaced by timber clearing and flooding.[59] One of the few people who left a description of driving the Big Bend Highway after 1962 was Donovan Clemson, a farmer and photographer from the Okanagan who decided to travel the old road one last time "before it goes underwater."[60] The Clemson family found the eastern section "pretty much as it was in former times," with traffic almost non-existent except for logging trucks. However, the Boat Encampment area had changed dramatically. Heavy blasting was under way, and the Clemsons became caught up in a convoy of massive dump trucks hauling fill to the dam site. South of Mica, the old highway had been rebuilt and realigned to handle 175-ton loads, with the result that some attractions, such as Silvertip Falls, had disappeared from view. Clemson's 1970 article was singular for its faintly nostalgic approach to the highway. Virtually everyone else appears to have felt that nothing of value was lost when the Big Bend country was flooded.[61]

Clearcut zone and floating debris behind Mica Dam. Courtesy of BC Hydro.

Mica Dam became operational in March 1973. As the diversion tunnels that had redirected the Columbia around the construction site were closed off, the river slowly and inexorably rose behind the completed dam. The reservoir took three years to fill to capacity and at maximum level had a surface area of 130,000 acres – approximately three-quarters the size of Manning Park. It inundated sections of the Columbia, Canoe, Wood, and Bush River valleys that had once been part of Hamber Park, as well as the eastern half of the Big Bend Highway. It destroyed the habitat of moose, elk, deer, mountain caribou, wolves, bears, beavers, river otters, migratory birds, and Columbia River sturgeon. The BC Fish and Wildlife Branch calculated that 207 miles of valley bottom and 71 miles of tributary creeks and streams were flooded, constituting "most of the high quality wildlife habitat in the valley." The reservoir blocked the migration patterns of the region's surviving large mammals, many of which moved seasonally from one range to another. The barrier effect was exacerbated by debris floating on the reservoir surface and the steepness of its shoreline.[62]

The public relations arm of BC Hydro, the provincially owned power utility that built and operated Mica Dam, promised that the Kinbasket

Reservoir would offer "boundless recreational opportunity" in an "unspoiled wilderness."[63] However, the reservoir proved inimical to recreation. The water level fluctuated by nearly a hundred feet, and the drawdown zone was an unsightly moonscape littered with dead stumps. The surface of the reservoir remained matted with floating debris for many years; the water was icy and turbid; the valley plagued by high winds. Sedimentation and changing temperature structures killed most of the desirable sport fish, and big game populations had been decimated. The state had permitted the Columbia to be turned into a massive storage lagoon and the Big Bend country into a kind of sacrifice zone, but most British Columbians were unaware of this because both dam and reservoir were invisible from the new route of the Trans-Canada. Out of sight and out of mind, the Big Bend country was again an unfamiliar wilderness to most BC residents, just as it had been prior to 1940.

Cultivating and Disposing of Nature

If few people knew of Hamber Park's existence between 1941 and 1961, even fewer have heard of it today. On the rare occasion that scholars mention it, they inevitably focus on its truncation, overlooking its many years of obscurity and its origins in the intertwined politics of roads and national parks. Yet its dramatic dismemberment takes on a new significance in light of the fact that it was created solely to be given away. Hamber was never intended to serve as a major asset for British Columbia. Instead, it was a counter in Victoria's ongoing campaign to offload responsibility for building and maintaining roads in the Selkirk and Rocky Mountains. In retrospect, this may seem a questionable basis for establishing such an enormous park, but it made sense in the political context of the day.

Unlike Manning and many other BC parks, Hamber remained essentially unknown and invisible in the years following the Second World War. This illustrates the selective role that state agencies played in cultivating roadside landscapes. Although Hamber had been accessible to drivers for many years before Manning and the other large provincial parks, the Parks Division (and Forest Service) chose not to promote or develop it. In the 1950s, political leaders and park officials concentrated on Manning, relegating Hamber to the sidelines. Almost no one knew of its existence precisely because the state preferred it that way.

In Hamber Park from the late 1950s onward, the Fordist state can be seen directly intervening in the fate of a large swathe of country by permitting severe environmental modifications. Perceiving neither Hamber nor the Big Bend Highway as assets, it destroyed its own investment in them by building a dam that was massive in itself and also a component of an even bigger megaproject. Moreover, it permitted loggers to do largely as they pleased in the Big Bend country. In this, its new priority can be seen pushing aside the older one. It could be argued that the disposal of Hamber is a textbook illustration that the Fordist state valued abstract growth above all other considerations and was indifferent to the fate of particular places. In sacrificing Hamber, the Big Bend Highway, and much of the Big Bend country to logging and a hydroelectric megaproject, the state was, in a sense, acting like a capitalist enterprise, writing off fixed infrastructure that was deemed inadequate, outdated, or otherwise surplus to its search for bigger gains.

When compared to the success story of Manning and the Hope-Princeton, and of other provincial parks traversed by a major road, the failure of Hamber and the Big Bend Highway invites speculation about how things could have turned out differently. One cannot help but wonder what might have happened to the Big Bend country if Hamber had become a national park or been promoted and protected as a provincial park. Could its roadside landscapes have been cultivated into a cherished asset? If so, how might this have affected the plan to build Mica Dam? These kinds of questions show how examining a failed park or road can offer insights into the history of their more successful and familiar counterparts. The drive through nature taken by Route A shows how the Fordist state, explicitly favouring automobility for its citizens, was willing to build massive infrastructure, to valorize some natural environments and landscapes, and to destroy others. Although what happened in the Big Bend country is far from typical, it is particularly noteworthy because of the great size of Hamber Provincial Park, because of the forests, river, and highway that lie drowned beneath the Kinbasket Reservoir, and because all this happened just a short distance from the crown jewels of Canada's national park system. But more broadly, the story of the unknown park and unpopular highway reveals that there was nothing natural or inevitable about the Fordist state's decisions to accept or develop certain areas as assets or attractions – even areas that were readily accessible by automobile. Instead, it was a highly selective process. Some were showered with attention; others were effectively ignored.

ROUTE B

Paths to the Past

When motorists travelled through the BC Interior, they were presented not only with a managed view of nature but also of history. The province's past was presented to them by the provincial highway network and by parties who manipulated landscapes with the intention of shaping their views. Profit-seeking businesses played a much greater role in shaping history by the road than they did nature by the road. Rarely were these big, well-capitalized firms. More often they were local boosters and small businesses. During the interwar years, dozens of family-owned and -operated concerns such as autocourts, hotels, and gas stations sought to differentiate themselves in the motoring public's eyes (and thereby capture some of their trade) by placing relics of the BC fur trade or gold rush days in front of their establishments or by boasting that their buildings were linked to the frontier past. Some even founded private museums. This pattern continued into the postwar period, when the state began to play an active part in developing major roadside historical attractions.

The Fordist state filled multiple roles: as a builder of roads, manager of landscapes, developer of attractions, and promoter of both tourism and automobile travel. During the interwar years, the provincial government did not involve itself in cultivating history by the road in the Interior, except to the extent that its arterial roads made certain places accessible (and others inaccessible). Instead, the federal Historic Sites and Monuments Board of Canada was the government agency that sought to shape motorists' views of the past.[1] It erected a series of relatively standardized cairns and plaques, most notably along the Fraser Canyon and Cariboo Highway corridors. These solemn monuments were scattered amidst a much larger number of relics and ruins, as well as small businesses that tried to associate themselves with the past. Together, they contributed to making modern highways serve as avenues into yesteryear, paths to the past.

We know little about automobility as a means of getting in touch with the past. Museums and historic sites became common features of middle-class North American touring itineraries during the interwar years, when car ownership and auto touring were on a meteoric rise. Many historians of tourism and the public past have noted the congruence of these cultural and economic trends, yet the precise manner in which popular mid-century understandings of the past were shaped (actively and incidentally) by automobility remains poorly understood.[2] These scholars usually examine how the past was moulded for the benefit of tourists at fixed and neatly bounded sites – how it was given a semblance of rootedness and permanence. James Opp and John C. Walsh argue that mobility and perceptions of the past are also intrinsically connected, in that "moving through specific locations [can] produce or confirm memories," but few others have paid close attention to how historical attractions were shaped by the routes and means via which they were reached.[3]

The literature on the history of "heritage" tourism and historical sites in Canada provides a particularly useful concept for understanding important aspects of how history by the road emerged, was cultivated, and was experienced in the BC Interior. In their study of how Nova Scotia's image was recast to appeal to middle-class tourists during the early twentieth century, Ian McKay and Robin Bates coin the term "tourism/history" to describe an easily digestible yet essentializing way of representing history, a way that evokes a vague yet palatable sense of pastness.[4] They show that tourism/history was produced by a range of interconnected interests, including agencies of the state, large companies such as railways, and a bevy of historians, archivists, authors, and promoters. To differentiate Nova Scotia from other touring destinations during the 1920s, the province was represented as an unchanging land of innocence in which one could escape the routines of modern everyday life. The production of tourism/history was not just an intellectual project. It was necessarily accompanied by the development of infrastructure that included museums, heritage sites, monuments, and other historically themed attractions. McKay and Bates note that transportation networks – first, railways and later automobile roads – played a key role in bringing tourists to and through these sites/sights.

The concept of tourism/history offers a powerful device for understanding tourists' perceptions and experiences of the past in a particular region. However, this study uses "history by the road" instead of tourism/history to signal its concern for a broader and more inclusive category of traveller. Tourists were certainly part of the motoring public but not all members of the motoring public were tourists. Everyone who drove the highways of the Interior during the middle decades of the twentieth century saw the same landscape features – not just sightseers and pleasure travellers from afar. As much as any tourist from out of province, BC residents were likely to pick up certain implicit and explicit lessons about the past when driving. Thus, the identification, development, and promotion of historical and historically themed attractions was as much a way to shape the views of citizens as to steer the consumption patterns of tourists.

First, however, some background information on the public past in British Columbia will help contextualize what will be seen – and also not seen – along Route B. The study of commemoration and the public past is underdeveloped in British Columbia, with the result that the emergence of popular themes such as exploration, the fur trade, gold rushes, and old trails and wagon roads remains little understood, even though they endure today.[5] As certain topics were elevated and valorized, others were marginalized or downplayed, and it is no coincidence that "adventuresome," "pioneering" subjects began rising to prominence in western Canada after the First World War, when North Americans thought of the frontier as something that had closed and of colonization as a completed project – something that had occurred in the past.

Daniel Francis observes that "Indians" were less and less sought out by tourists to western Canada after 1918, and the following chapters support this contention.[6] First Nations were largely absent from the motoring public's experiences of British Columbia by the road during the period examined here and therefore are noticeable in the following chapters primarily by their absence. Historians John Lutz and J.R. Miller describe relations between Indigenous people and settlers during the first half of the twentieth century as characterized by a widening socio-economic gulf whereby most whites were separated from and disinterested in Indigenous peoples and issues.[7] The First Nations of British Columbia grew all through the period 1921–71 yet declined sharply as a proportion of the total population. As First Nations employment plummeted in rural industries such as logging and farming, the urbanization of the province's population and many important economic motors reduced everyday interaction between First Nations and the faster-growing number of settlers. Business openings generated by the new roadside economy bypassed First Nations because most reserves were situated away from the prime valley bottom lands where farms, towns, and arterial highways were located. Residents of reserves that did not suffer this disadvantage – such as those in the Fraser and Thompson River canyons – were cut off from roadside entrepreneurialism in part because they could not use their property as collateral for business loans, and also because many travellers did not feel comfortable stopping on Indian reserves and patronizing First Nation-run businesses.[8] Furthermore, there were legal and racist obstacles to First Nations people finding waged work in hotels and restaurants, such as restrictions on their employment in places where alcohol was sold and a belief among proprietors that white customers did not want to be served by non-whites. Marginalized geographically and occupationally, First Nations were barely visible to the motoring public. Beyond an occasional fleeting mention, it is rare to find a travelogue or guidebook that steered attention toward Indigenous cultures or communities, and few asked why this was the case. With Indigenous peoples out of sight and out of mind, most of the motoring public's experience of history in the Interior fed into the "vanishing American" discourse that had been prevalent during the late nineteenth century and that lingered through subsequent decades.[9] Even as Canadians' interest in western history picked up, Indigenous people – who might simplistically have been seen as closely connected to the past and therefore as intrinsically historical – were sidelined from the benefits that automobility and history by the road delivered to boosters, business owners, and, indirectly, the state.

The few monuments and museum displays that gave a cursory nod to the province's original inhabitants tended to treat them as the supporting cast for the overland explorers and fur traders of the early nineteenth century, sometimes portraying them as helpmates and sometimes as obstacles to travel through the region. None of the major historical attractions or tourist icons of the Interior drew in any significant way on local Native cultures and histories. There was no Interior equivalent to the totem poles of the Coast; these had been made into regional tourist icons by non-Indigenous boosters and businesses, and had become so synonymous with British Columbia that the provincial government stamped them on its licence plates during the 1950s.[10] Handicrafts such as coiled cedar baskets, the "cowboy Indians" who competed at the Williams Lake Stampede, legends such as the Ogopogo of Lake Okanagan – all of these were deployed at different times and with varying levels of enthusiasm by boosters and business owners, curators and authors, and planners and other experts working for government agencies in order to differentiate particular places so that they would appeal to the motoring public.[11] As spectacles, souvenirs, or mascots, none become particularly famous or synonymous beyond a limited section of the Interior. Nor did they further non-Indigenous understanding of First Nations, past or present. This was underscored during the late 1950s and the 1960s, when Indian-themed businesses proliferated along the highways. Owned and operated by non-Indigenous people but festooned with stereotyped totem pole, thunderbird, and tipi motifs, they soon outnumbered the handful of Indigenous-run enterprises. Ultimately, the roadside economy's use of visual and material culture as narrative devices helped to mask a politics of dispossession and appropriation, naturalizing and legitimizing the province as a resettled space with only lingering, isolated pockets of "Indian" country.

In twentieth-century British Columbia, most early efforts to commemorate historical events and personalities, and to mark and preserve sites and structures associated with them, were driven by such nativist organizations as the Pioneer Society and the Native Sons of British Columbia. Based in the cities of the Coast, they tended to focus on historical topics and themes with a coastal bent, including maritime navigators, the remnants of old fur trade posts such as Fort Victoria and Fort Langley, and overland explorers who managed to reach tidewater, including Mackenzie, Thompson, and Fraser. They were more concerned with filiopietism, patriotism, and demonstrating their enthusiasm for the British Empire than with attracting tourists. Residents of the Coast also dominated the membership of the more scholarly BC Historical Association, which was formed in 1922 to "encourage historical research and public interest in history [and] promote the preservation of historical sites and buildings."[12] Prior to the late 1920s, history enthusiasts in large cities showed relatively little interest in promoting or preserving historically significant sites in the Interior. The land-based fur trade, the gold rushes of the late 1850s and the 1860s, and turn-of-the-century railroad construction seemed too distant, too recent, too commercial, or too polyglot (too American, too Asian) to be deemed important. The Interior – a veritable sea of sterile mountains, a hinterland region of a hinterland province – seemed historically and geographically marginal to most national and imperial grand narratives.[13] Railway companies said little about the Interior's past in their guidebooks and publicity materials. Even the Historic Sites and Monuments Board of Canada (HSMBC), a quasi-autonomous board that advised federal bureaucracies on questions of historical commemoration, ignored British Columbia during its first few years.[14]

The Interior's status as a commemorative backwater made it ripe for new "discoveries" as the provincial road network was expanded and improved during the interwar years, allowing ever larger numbers of motorists to travel to ever more corners of the province. As the following chapters show, the HSMBC erected cairns beside the Fraser Canyon Highway and the Cariboo Highway at about the time when they opened to the motoring public. However, early development of historical tourist attractions and cultivation of popular historical images in the Interior was driven primarily by small-town boosters, rural and small-town business owners, small-town journalists, and amateur historians. This period of the "amateur" is examined in Chapters 5 and 6. Old buildings, other landscape features, and artifacts were pressed into service to attract visitors. Such "recoveries," it was hoped (only sometimes realistically), would generate increased economic activity. Few tried to convey a specific idea, attempting instead to create an ambiance – a sense of old-timey-ness – by invoking a handful of popular themes, including exploration, pioneering, and the importance of transportation for wresting wealth from a resource frontier.

Route B first explores the Fraser Canyon and Cariboo Highways during the interwar years, focusing on how drivers experienced these roads as corridors into the province's past. During the first decade after the Second World War, which was a period of massive economic growth in the Interior, many British Columbians were uneasy about the rapid and dramatic modernization of the area and called for the preservation of familiar historical features that provided concrete links to the past. Between 1955 and 1970, a period when the provincial government began to actively cultivate history by the road, it supported the foundation of local museums, established a network of historical markers, churned out reams of motoring-related promotional material, organized commemorative celebrations that travelled along provincial highways, and developed major historical tourist attractions, including the ghost towns at Barkerville and Fort Steele. Governments across Canada saw living history museums as a new way to cash in on tourism during the 1950s, and the BC government latched onto the trend enthusiastically, for multiple reasons.[15] Like generating a system of roadside provincial parks, creating a "system" of roadside historical attractions was a way of encouraging the public to travel along the highway network the state had built with such heady abandon since the end of the Second World War, consuming goods and services while contemplating their role as citizens. It was also a way of building up the tourist industry and diversifying certain regional and local economies. Finally, British Columbians' concerns about Fordist modernity could be soothed by the preservation and development of historical landscape features that suggested industrial resource extraction, an active state, and rugged individualism all played an essential role, not only in the past, but in the present and future as well.

5

Tracing the Route of the Cariboo Wagon Road

The five-hundred-mile stretch of highway that ran through the Fraser and Thompson River canyons and into the Cariboo was the first and most important "historical" automobile road in the BC Interior. It approximated the route of the old Cariboo Wagon Road between Hope, the gateway to the Interior, and Barkerville, the traditional capital of the northern goldfields, and thus it boasted many historical and history-themed features. Most of these were ruins, relics, and remnants: the detritus of a hinterland economy that had been stagnant for decades. But interspersed among them were a growing number of new markers, monuments, and museums that were created by rural and small-town boosters and business owners who hoped to benefit from the passage of the motoring public.

During the interwar years, the provincial government played a relatively minor role in cultivating history by the road. This inactivity is particularly noteworthy, given that Victoria built and maintained the road, and was becoming increasingly involved in tourism promotion, as Michael Dawson shows.[1] There was no concerted, top-down effort to develop any major historical attractions along the highway between Hope and Barkerville during the interwar years. Nevertheless, the route constituted the province's premier drive into the past due to the sheer number and variety of historical and history-themed artifacts and landscape features that were visible along it.

When motorists from the Coast headed north from Hope to Barkerville, they saw things in more or less the same order as they travelled through three distinct sections: the Canyon Highway, which ran through the Fraser and Thompson Canyons, and joined the communities of Hope and Ashcroft; the Cariboo Highway, between Ashcroft and Quesnel; and the Quesnel-Barkerville Road, which linked Quesnel and Barkerville.

Building Anticipation

Provincial politicians in the early 1920s had to choose between two routes for the first road to link the Coast and the Interior: a southerly option that crossed the Cascade Mountains between Hope and Princeton or a more central one that skirted the Cascades via the Fraser and Thompson Canyons. Initially, the former was favoured, but by 1923 the latter appeared more promising because it would connect with a road that spanned the central Interior from Ashcroft in the west to Revelstoke in the east and that seemed likely to connect with Calgary in the not-too-distant future. It would also do double duty in the province's emerging road network, as Ashcroft was the railhead for supplying the scattered ranches and mines of the Cariboo country. Since the 1880s, cargo, passengers, and mail had been unloaded at Ashcroft's rail yards and transferred onto northbound freight wagons, stagecoaches, and sleighs pulled by teams of up to a dozen horses. In 1910, however, the BC Express Company (BX) added a pair of powerful Winton Six automobiles to its Cariboo stage service, and by 1918 several freighters were experimenting with trucks. By the mid-1920s, gasoline-powered vehicles had supplanted the draught animals and wagons that had plied the road since the mid-1860s, putting teamsters, leatherworkers, and animal breeders out of work.[2]

There was a third reason for choosing the canyon route, one whose significance is difficult to quantify in terms of cost or potential economic value. The route had already been the most important transportation link between the Coast and the Interior for more than half a century. In 1858, the discovery of placer gold in the canyons had drawn thousands of fortune-seekers, leading to the establishment of the colony of British Columbia. The discovery of extensive goldfields on the northeastern Cariboo Plateau during the 1860s then led the colonial government to build the Cariboo Wagon Road, which linked the lower Fraser River to the diggings four hundred miles to the north. The Canadian Pacific Railway (CPR) was built through the Thompson and Fraser Canyons in the 1880s, destroying much of the wagon road in the process. It was followed by the Canadian Northern in the 1910s, which became part of Canadian National Railways

(CNR). Boasting two transcontinental railroads plus telegraph and telephone lines, the Fraser and Thompson Canyons comprised one of the most important transportation corridors in all of Canada. Squeezing an automobile road through the canyons posed serious engineering challenges, but for politicians facing pressure from the motoring public and an array of business interests to connect the Coast and Interior, it must have been appealing for its familiarity and accessibility. It was the traditional way between the province's metropolitan centres and mountainous hinterlands, and thus one of its most widely shared and important landscape experiences. As the boosters of the Kamloops-based BC Trans-Provincial Highway Association put it in 1923, building a road through the canyons would allow motorists to "travel historic ground."[3]

In May 1924, the Liberal government of John Oliver announced that the first automobile road between Coast and Interior would in fact be built through the Fraser and Thompson Canyons. Contracts were let in October, and construction commenced soon after.[4] The contractors who built the road doubtless perceived the irony of doing so in the very place where a wagon road had been constructed at considerable expense sixty years earlier. Provincial road engineers who had studied the possibility of restoring the old wagon road in 1919 had criticized the railways for unnecessary damage done to the route. They reported that forty-four of seventy-seven miles between Yale and Spences Bridge had been damaged beyond use by railway construction and flooding, including nineteen of twenty-five miles "practically entirely destroyed" along the Thompson River.[5]

Railway passengers had long glimpsed remnants of the Cariboo Wagon Road as they sped through the canyons. Most got the impression that they were the ruins of a bygone age, abandoned as the natural result of progress. As a traveller put it in 1916,

> One sees relics of it here and there from the train on the far side of the canyon, a streak along the face of an almost perpendicular cliff, a flimsy looking bridge across a gully, half-destroyed by time, a bit of cribbing to support the road along the side of a precipice; It looks scarcely possible for any one to have travelled over such a road and reached the end of the journey alive![6]

The railway companies' publicity departments did little to dispel this notion: the CPR and CNR sold scenic grandeur on their BC lines, not history. Their guidebooks ignored the gold rushes of the 1850s and 1860s, even as historians were arguing that they were the pivotal events in the province's past. This was most clearly the case in the multi-volume *British Columbia from the Earliest Times to the Present,* published in 1914 by provincial librarian E.O.S. Scholefield and New Westminster jurist Frederic Howay. In it, the 1858 Fraser River gold rush marked the transition between the province's "ancient" and "modern" history, and thus the Fraser Canyon represented the crucible of British Columbia. Howay frequently described the Cariboo Wagon Road as the colony's Appian Way, at once an instrument of communication, civilization, commodity extraction, and agricultural colonization.[7]

By the early 1920s, some of the key ideas from scholarly works such as *British Columbia from the Earliest Times* were trickling into middlebrow writings that were closely intertwined with automobility in British Columbia's middle-class consumer and literary cultures. These included pamphlets, guides, travelogues, and popular histories such as *Early History of the Province of British Columbia* (1926), written by Bruce McKelvie, a newspaperman and senior officer of the Native Sons of British Columbia.[8] Newspapers in Vancouver and Victoria printed hundreds of stories about auto touring, scenic landscapes, and the history of western North America during the mid- and late 1920s. Saturday editions of the *Vancouver Sun* devoted an entire section to automobiles and auto touring, which included a regular column called "Outlines of the History of British Columbia."[9] Many automobile owners on the Coast shared the sense of being cooped up in the southwestern corner of the province, with nowhere to go for an extended pleasure drive except south into the United States. Ottawa promoted the national parks in the Rocky Mountains, but they were effectively inaccessible to motorists from the major population centres of British Columbia, who could not even drive between the Coast and Interior without dipping into Washington State. An automobile road through the Fraser and Thompson Canyons was expected to provide a bevy of new opportunities for auto touring, thereby allowing patriotic citizens from the Coast to better know the communities, natural environments, and past of their own province.[10]

The road promised to throw new light on BC history. The valorization of western themes in middlebrow Canadian historical writing during the early 1920s had middle-class residents of the Coast primed to explore the Interior hinterlands with an eye toward the history of discovery and adventure. An article in *Pacific Coast Motorist,* the magazine of the Automobile Club of British Columbia, captured the spirit of anticipation regarding the new highway and its associations with the old wagon road. "That we are living in a different age will be appreciated as we drive over the reconstructed road," the author predicted, "thinking twenty and thirty miles an hour as slow travelling":

> The Canadian Pacific Railway stole from the road its most dangerous sections through the canyons – the portion which visitors most admired and dreaded. For forty years that section has been abandoned; its well travelled roadbed has been a weed and grass grown stretch; its stone embankments a home for the pack rat; its bridges and wooden supports food for beetles and bugs. Now in 1925, a new Cariboo Road comes into being to replace the old one and to be used not by the slow-paced mules, or by creaking, groaning freight wagons, but to be used by vehicles unknown when the old road existed, and by people who come to see the land the pioneers discovered. The tourist, as he passes Chapmans Bar, may imagine the scene of 1858, when those bars were covered with struggling men, endeavouring to wrest some of the treasures from the golden goddess. Or we may see the old road itself, crowded with a throng of men, freight wagons, and stages, hurrying into the wilds of Cariboo to continue the struggle.[11]

Anticipation was also keen among Interior boosters, businesses, and would-be roadside entrepreneurs. Eager to be connected to coastal markets and western North America's emerging interregional highway network, they were doubtless inspired by predictions like that from an American expert who told the BC Automobile Association that 90 percent of the traffic on the road would come from out of province. The *Prince George Citizen* foresaw that completion of the Canyon Highway would be "one of the most important events in the history of this province."[12]

Building the Canyon Highway was an elaborate, expensive endeavour. Tunnels were blasted through impassable granite bluffs, and many bridges and cribbings were built, yet the new road ended up no wider, and in some places significantly narrower, than the old wagon road had been. In several places, it clung to sheer cliffs on precarious-looking grasshopper trestles. It was a highway in name only, more akin to a mountain touring road than to the broad, concrete-surfaced thoroughfares that were starting to link major American cities. The new Alexandra Suspension Bridge was a key part of it, carrying motorists over the Fraser River at a narrow point in the gorge just upstream from Spuzzum, at the same spot as the 1863 bridge of the same name. Crossing the Fraser was one of many dramatic points in the drive. Gazing down into the river's churning, muddy waters, the journalist Bruce Hutchison deemed it "forever hostile"; another auto tourist

Fraser Canyon Highway, late 1920s. Verso reads "This place just opened up." Author's collection.

Postcard of the Fraser Canyon between Hope and Yale, late 1920s or 1930s. Gowen Sutton Company postcard. Author's collection.

Highway tunnel in the Fraser Canyon, late 1920s. Gowen Sutton Company postcard. City of Vancouver Archives, P544.

characterized it as "fierce and repellant."[13] The Alexandra Bridge was also memorable because a hefty toll was charged to cross it, much to the chagrin of Interior tourism promoters and drivers of modest means.[14]

The canyon route had many other features that emphasized the power of nature. For long stretches, dark, frangible cliffs loomed above the narrow road, and it was common to see evidence of rockfall. Traffic was frequently stopped for days or even weeks so that slides could be cleared away or washouts filled in. Fog, rain, and snowfall were not uncommon in the timber-clad Fraser Canyon, which could be damp and gloomy even when points to the east and west were sunny and dry. This was due to the surrounding mountains, which caused weather systems coming off the Pacific to cool and release their accumulated vapour. In stark contrast, the Thompson Canyon, which lay in the rain shadow of those same mountains, was one of the hottest and most arid parts of Canada, with sagebrush, cacti, and rattlesnakes.[15] In most places, the new road rose high above the canyon floor, displaced by the railroads, which ran along the water grade; in several spots, the river and tracks were visible more than a thousand feet below, down near-perpendicular cliffs. In other sections, as at Sailor Bar in the Fraser Canyon and Tank Hill in the Thompson, the river boiled and swirled just a few feet below the road, and these low-lying sections were regularly flooded by summer freshets.

To reassure drivers, timber railings and thick, thigh-high rock walls were placed along many of the road's highest, tightest, most precarious, and dizzying sections. Nevertheless, many found that driving the Canyon Highway evoked a not irrational sense of dread: of tumbling over the edge of a precipice, of being crushed from above without warning, of colliding with a car rounding a near-blind corner. The striking but forbidding landscape induced contemplation of oblivion and one's own mortality as well as a series of kinesthetic thrills. Edmund Wragge, a young lawyer who drove from Vancouver to the Cariboo in the fall of 1926, recorded in his diary that when passing through the canyons one of his companions sat on the floor "so as not to see the tightrope road we were driving on." Frank White, who was a child when he drove through the canyon with his father in 1928, recalled "a feeling of adventure as we ... entered the storied goldfields of the Fraser ... I felt some kinship with the old miners of the 1860s." Schoolteacher Ernest Harris, who drove from Vancouver to Horsefly in 1931, described the road as "a narrow shelf hacked out of the mountain side" and concluded that motoring through the Canyon Highway was not dissimilar from the exploits of a hero-explorer such as Simon Fraser.[16]

The Canyon Highway lent an aura of adventure to an automobile journey between Coast and Interior, which was enhanced and given a dash of romance by the knowledge that it followed the same route as the Cariboo Wagon Road. A 1926 travel guide published by the provincial government explained that the Department of Public Works had "reconstruct[ed] this part of the famous old highway," a claim echoed by the *Vancouver Province,* which called the highway the "new-old Cariboo Road" and noted "there are still places where your balloon tires turn on the very foundations of the old road."[17] Traffic was light and slow enough during the late 1920s and the 1930s that pleasure travellers could safely stop on the side of the road to admire (and photograph) scenic vistas, sleepy villages, old or ruined buildings, and traces of the gold-rush-era wagon road. Thus, driving the province's most important arterial road became closely linked to historical narratives that involved journeys of discovery, fortune hunting, and struggles against nature. Whether they thought about the romance of bygone days or saw history as a steady march of progress, many people were inspired to contemplate the BC past when driving through the canyons. As discussed below, the highway's association with nineteenth-century gold rushes was especially heightened during the 1930s, when a spike in gold prices caused a modern-day rush to the auriferous bars of the Fraser Canyon and the Cariboo beyond. With its intermingling of sublime scenery, intimidating terrain, and remnants from the past, the Canyon Highway became British Columbia's premier drive, synonymous with both its history and natural environments. As the only automobile road between the Coast and Interior from 1926 until 1949, it was one of the most important and widely shared landscape experiences of British Columbians, and it remained so into the 1990s.

On the Very Bones of the Gold Road

Once they reached Chilliwack, motorists heading inland from Vancouver and other coastal centres began to sense the narrowing of the Fraser River Delta, as the sawtoothed peaks of the Skagit Mountains loomed ever larger to the south. The village of Hope, a hundred miles east of Vancouver, effectively marked the boundary between Coast and Interior. There, the mountains closed tight around the Fraser, constricting its channel and making its muddy waters rush and churn, hinting at the cataracts upstream. Hope had been established as a Hudson's Bay Company (HBC) trading post in the late 1840s and in 1858 had briefly been the uppermost point of navigation for sternwheel steamboats carrying fortune-seekers bound for the gold diggings. By the mid-1920s, it was home to just 250 people, but the new highway spurred the development of roadside businesses, including rustically styled stopping places such as the Cariboo Auto Court, Silver Creek Cabin Camp, and Restmore Lodge, where passersby could shop for Indigenous crafts and watch Teddy the soda-drinking black bear, who was kept chained in a pen beside the road. Hope boasted one of the oldest churches in British Columbia, a timber-frame Gothic Revival structure that had been built by Anglican missionaries in 1861. In 1925, while work was under way on the new road, the Historic Sites and Monuments Board of Canada (HSMBC) erected a cairn near the village centre, on a narrow strip between the highway and the riverbank where sternwheelers had once tied up. The bronze plaque mounted on the cairn commemorated Hope as a former HBC post.

There had been relatively little business activity in the canyon communities beyond Hope since the construction of the CPR in the early 1880s, aside from a few years of bustle during construction of the Canadian Northern. Most buildings were old and rundown, and the damp climate of the canyon caused neglected structures to deteriorate and be reclaimed by the bush. Motorists could see the remnants of old rancheries along the highway, as well as cribbings, retaining walls, and other traces of the 1860s wagon road, which reinforced the impression of picturesque old-timey-ness amidst the rugged terrain and sublime scenery. Old and new rubbed elbows due to the lack of room for road building; many of the businesses that sprang up to cater to drivers stood on the site of old roadhouses that had similarly sprung up to provide food, lodging, and animal shelter during the colonial gold rush days.

Ten miles beyond Hope, the road passed the Emory Lodge and Auto Court, near the point where Emory Creek flowed into the Fraser. Emory Bar had been one of the richest placer diggings in the lower canyon during the 1858 rush, and people who drove through the canyon during the 1930s got a tangible reminder of its gold rush past. In the early Depression years, hundreds of unemployed men panned for gold at Emory Creek, and then, from 1935 to 1939, the provincial government operated a camp in which young men were taught to prospect for gold and "look after themselves in the hills."[18] A few miles upriver from Emory Lodge was the village of Yale, which, like Hope, had been established as an HBC trading post in the 1840s. It too was home to a gold-rush-era church: St. John the Divine, which had been built in 1863. Yale had supplanted Hope as the head of steamboat navigation on the lower Fraser, becoming a centre of commerce, administration, and debauchery during the gold rush days and then again when the railroad was built in the 1880s. Its role as a port and transshipment point had left a legacy of fine old buildings, including the All Hallows Girls' School, an Anglican boarding school that had operated from 1884 until 1920.[19] Shortly after the new canyon road was completed, the Crawford family purchased the former school and established the All Hallows Auto Camp on its grounds. Their advertising promoted Yale as "one of British Columbia's most interesting and historical places."[20]

Yale was one of the first sites in western Canada to be recognized by the HSMBC – it was at the top of Judge Frederic Howay's list of priorities when he joined the board in 1923.[21] The following year, an oblong boulder was erected beside the surveyed route of the new highway at a point overlooking the riverfront, with a plaque affixed to it that commemorated Yale as the "beginning of the Cariboo Wagon Road," which had extended four hundred miles northward to Barkerville. Combined with the dull roar of the fast-flowing Fraser and the grey bluffs that crowded in on every side, the monument might well have elicited a sense that essential aspects of the landscape and the journey through the canyon remained unchanged from the gold rush days. The plaque and cairn at Yale were officially unveiled in 1925, while the new road was still under construction. The ceremony was organized by Judge Howay, who invited his friend Justice Denis

Murphy of the BC Supreme Court to be the guest speaker. Murphy was the son of pioneer roadhouse operators, having been born at the 141 Mile House in the Cariboo. In his speech, he outlined the Cariboo Wagon Road's social and economic importance to the gold colony and recounted what growing up beside it had been like. Murphy declared himself pleased that the new highway would allow the motoring public to explore the central and northern Interior. "Almost from where we stand can be heard the crash of falling trees and the reverberations of mighty blasts, for men are busy rebuilding the old road," he observed. "Soon again will it stretch in a long white ribbon from Yale to Cariboo."[22]

Motorists traversed a series of Indian reserves and rancheries between Yale and the village of Spuzzum, just downstream from the Alexandra Bridge.[23] Guidebooks and travelogues of the interwar years said next to nothing about these communities or their residents, as was the case with the rest of the Canyon Highway and most other arterial roads in the Interior. A few motoring publications did mention Indigenous salmon fishing, an activity that could be glimpsed from the road in a few spots during the summer months. Indigenous techniques of catching and drying salmon were typically described as ancient but also as primitive, implicitly reducing any contemporary claims that the First Nations might make to the land and its resources.

The publications failed to mention a monument that Indigenous people placed beside the stretch of highway connecting Yale and Spuzzum. Though it referred to the canyon's history, it was not intended for the edification of passing motorists. In 1938, members of the Sto:lo communities who had familial roots in the Fraser Canyon, but who lived for much of the year on reserves downriver in the Fraser Valley, erected a stone memorial at a point known to them as Eayem, or I:yem. This lay in a constricted section of the canyon, where the highway and the CPR mainline ran close together. Used primarily as a summer fishing site since the turn of the century, it had been a village before that and had a cemetery in which bodies had been reinterred during the 1880s after their original burial plots were disturbed by construction of the CPR. The monument was a granite cross set atop two concrete blocks, one of which displayed a bronze plaque with the inscription "Erected by the Stallo Indians - In memory of many hundreds of our forefathers buried here. This is one of six ancient cemeteries within our five mile native fishing grounds which we inherited from our ancestors. R.I.P."[24] The monument had many layers of meaning: at once a grave marker, an assertion of traditional territorial and resource rights, and a memorial to a village that many Sto:lo with roots in the area had forgotten by the 1930s.[25] It is also significant that, in a very general way, it resembled the cairns that the HSMBC and other parties had recently installed at Hope, Yale, and various points along the Canyon Highway. They too were built of stone and were of about the same size. Although they did not incorporate religious symbols, they did honour the ancestors and history of those who raised them. They also sat right beside the highway, where they would catch the eye. The I:yem monument may have been partly intended as a retort to those erected by British Columbians whose history in the canyon went back only a few generations. It was clearly part of a cemetery, surrounded by a white picket fence and flanked by several headstones, which together indicated that it was not to be casually approached by curious passersby.[26]

The motoring public was far more interested in Indigenous-made coiled cedar basketry. Though not valorized by any marker, it was available for purchase at several roadside operations. Indigenous women from up and down the canyon delivered hand-woven cedar baskets for sale at the Spuzzum general store and gas station, which promoted itself in tourism pamphlets and on a signboard out front as the "home of Indian Baskets."[27] Indigenous handicrafts usually brought poor returns to their producers, but the baskets and related products of the type sold at Spuzzum were very popular with tourists, especially Americans from the Pacific Northwest.[28] At once exotic, authentic, and regionally distinctive, they were both souvenirs of a visit to the Interior and collectibles, in that their value was widely expected to appreciate as Indigenous cultures faded away – the popular discourse of the vanishing American had not disappeared by the 1920s.

As noted above, the Alexandra Suspension Bridge, located just upstream from Spuzzum, was one of the most prominent structures along the new road. Many motorists paused there for a brief respite or to photograph the bridge, whose concrete towers and gleaming suspension cables contrasted sharply with their gloomy natural surroundings. In 1927, the Engineering Institute of Canada and the Association of Professional Engineers of British Columbia applied for and were given permission to erect a ten-foot-tall cairn beside the bridge's western approach. It commemorated the Royal Engineers who had surveyed and supervised construction of the canyon section of the Cariboo Wagon Road, and like the HSMBC cairns in Hope and Yale, it sat right beside the new road.[29] Its bronze plaque conflated the old and new roads, crediting the Royal Engineers for building a key section of "the original Cariboo Highway." Also like the HSMBC cairn at Yale, it cultivated a historical theme that can be called heroic infra-

Alexandra Bridge, showing cairn to Royal Engineers. Phillip Timms photograph. City of Vancouver Archives, AM54-S4-: Br P32.

structure. Both valorized the colonial roads and road builders that had enabled affordable and predictable long-distance travel through difficult terrain, thereby facilitating the resettlement of British Columbia and the exploitation of its resources. They presented roads as part of a continuous process of opening up the country, embodiments of order, material progress, and scientific and administrative enlightenment. By implication, heroic status also extended to the railroad builders of the 1880s and 1910s, and even to the highway engineers and bridge builders of the mid-1920s, who had made it possible for motorists to enjoy the landscapes of the Interior safely and at their own pace, free from the railways' inflexible routes and impersonal timetables.

A mile north of the Alexandra Bridge was Alexandra Lodge, a stopping place built in 1926 on the approximate site of a gold-rush-era roadhouse. It had modern amenities such as electrical lighting and a clutch of autocourt-style cabins, but the main building's heavy timber beams, large porch, and balcony gave the lodge a rustic appearance that echoed the roadhouses of the past – an association that was cultivated by its proprietors.[30] Past the gloomy Black Canyon, the new road helped revitalize the gold-rush-era village of Boston Bar, which the CPR had bypassed during the 1880s.[31] On a flat just north of Boston Bar, motorists passed the ruins of the old Boothroyd roadhouse, which had been a popular stopping place during the 1860s. The highway reached its greatest heights – and some of its most dramatic and cringe-inducing points – in the vicinity of Boston

Bar, at Hell's Gate, Jackass Mountain, and China Bar Bluff. Motorists wondered that stagecoaches and freight wagons had ever dared to traverse those dizzying precipices. The new highway seemed to have been constructed "on the very bones of the gold road," journalist Bruce Hutchison reported in 1930. "In places you can see abandoned stretches of the old road itself, narrow with steep grades, clinging to the canyon side, and a few ruined houses that once glittered with light as the stagecoaches stopped to changes horses." For Hutchison, these relics elicited a pleasing sense of bygone days, of the romance of travellers who in seeking their fortunes had struggled against distance and inhospitable environments:

> In the evening, when the shadows move suddenly down the mountains, and the mountains turn into a flat wall of darker darkness at arm's length – then even a stranger, standing by the old road on the lip of the canyon, with the steady gurgle of the Fraser far below, can surely hear the sound of the stagecoaches rolling along in the dust, the beat of hooves, the marching feet.[32]

Descending from Jackass Mountain, drivers negotiated twisting stretches near Kanaka Bar before crossing several Indian reserves on the approach to the village of Lytton. Indigenous cemeteries along the road testified to the canyon's long history of occupation. In Lytton, visiting motorists who ventured off Main Street – which was part of the highway till after the Second World War – and came across the memorial to the Nlaka'pamux chief David Spintlum would have found further evidence of that history. Erected by members of the Lytton Indian Band in April 1927, forty years after Spintlum's death, it stood at the edge of town on a promontory overlooking the confluence of the Fraser and Thompson Rivers. Like the I:yem memorial of a decade later, it was a complex statement about the history of the Fraser Canyon. It was comprised of a large stone cross set atop squared stones that were inscribed with Spintlum's birth, death, and baptism dates (1812, 1887, and 1872). It was not a grave marker, however, for Spintlum was almost certainly buried at a nearby church cemetery. The memorial identified him as "Chief of the Thompson Tribe of Indians," and the inscription on a white marble slab that was attached to the base honoured him as a peacemaker in the violent conflicts associated with the 1858 Fraser River gold rush – an aspect of local history that the cairns recently erected by whites had failed to mention. The inscription also asserted contemporary Nlaka'pamux claims to the surrounding territory, noting that "when the White Men discovered British Columbia the Indians were using the land ... David Spintlum made his posts at Spuzzum, at Lillooet, at Stathshone and at Sheheouos, and these four posts are the limits of Thompson Tribal Territory." The Spintlum memorial was more than a block off the highway, so most people who drove through Lytton did not see it. Nevertheless, the fact that it was built shortly after the HSMBC erected cairns at Hope and Yale suggests that it may have been partly inspired by those monuments and meant to remind passersby of parties who had been left out of their explanatory inscriptions.

On the Lytton Indian Reserve, which bordered the town's main commercial area, drivers also saw evidence that Indigenous populations and cultural traditions persisted in the region. Cedar baskets, moccasins, buckskin, and other handicrafts were sold to passing motorists at a large store operated by a First Nations woman named Rose Skuki.[33] This entrepreneurialism contrasted with the arrangement down the road at Spuzzum (and a few other points between Vancouver and Quesnel), where similar items were sold from a white-owned business. The store run by Skuki stands out as a rare instance of direct First Nations participation in the Interior roadside economy of the interwar period. However, like the Spintlum memorial, it was not mentioned in travelogues or promotional pamphlets, so how the motoring public viewed it remains unknown.[34]

Many drivers paused at a lookout just a short distance from the Lytton town centre to view the confluence of the Thompson and Fraser Rivers, with the blue-green waters of the former inexorably absorbed into the muddy, sullen flow of the latter. The Thompson River section of the Canyon Highway had fewer commercial stopping places than its Fraser counterpart, largely due to the difficulty of obtaining potable water. Cactus and sagebrush attested to its blazing summer heat, and the sharp contrast between the two canyons played an important role in shaping the public's landscape experiences along the route. Due to the sparse forest cover and the generally lower elevation of the highway in the Thompson Canyon, motorists had better views of the river and the mountains, with all their geological instability. At many spots, the effect was more unsettling than reassuring. As one motorist put it, "the Fraser Canyon is clothed, wherever the cliffs are not perpendicular, with lush growth of trees, but the steep rocks of the Thompson Gorge stand out, bare and menacing."[35] No state-sanctioned monuments were installed along this section of highway, but the Thompson's arid climate did preserve old and neglected structures that would never have survived in the damp Fraser Canyon. Sun-bleached cribbings, corrals, and cabins could be seen all along the

Highway in the Thompson Canyon, 1930s. J. Fred Spalding postcard. Author's collection.

road between Lytton and Ashcroft. As a result, the olden-days ambiance of the Thompson seemed particularly natural and uncontrived.

Traversing the Canyon Highway was one of the most dramatic, popular, and widely shared landscape experiences for drivers in British Columbia during the interwar period. The route became imbued with special cultural significance precisely because nature and history seemed so inseparable there, and also because it was the province's *only* road link between Coast and Interior until 1949. As one early commercial trucker recalled, "Whether you ran from Vancouver to Bralorne or Kamloops or Vernon or Clinton or Prince George or Vanderhoof, or even Burns Lake, the [canyons] were there to contend with."[36] The motoring public, which still consisted largely of white, educated, middle-class automobile owners, could see themselves as part of a continuum, retracing the steps of Simon Fraser, the prospectors of 1858, and the stagecoach drivers of the wagon road days. They could imagine themselves facing the same risks of travelling through a dangerous, seemingly eternal environment. Every decaying building, hair-raising precipice, and trace of the old Cariboo Wagon Road seemed redolent with romance and adventure. Every bridge, tunnel, and elaborate work of highway engineering seemed part of a heroic, ongoing effort to open up the riches of the BC Interior.

Northward to the Goldfields

Unlike the Canyon Highway, the Cariboo corridor between Ashcroft and Quesnel crossed rolling, open terrain – the relatively undifferentiated scenery of the Cariboo Plateau. A "big sky" country, it lacked the dramatic vistas and exaggerated verticality that tourism promotion materials traditionally associated with the Interior. A ranching region, it was thinly populated, and its economy had been stagnant for decades, with the result that it had few traces of the modern utilities, building styles, and consumer culture that were becoming part of everyday life for middle-class residents of the Coast. These factors combined to make historical landscape features stand out along the Cariboo Highway. Unable to use its natural scenery as a tourist draw, boosters and roadside business owners sought to transform underdevelopment into an asset by cultivating associations with the past, thereby making a trip along the Cariboo Highway seem like a journey through yesteryear. They frequently displayed or referred to stagecoaches and freight wagons, which had been the gold-rush-era equivalents of modern-day passenger cars and commercial trucks, and to the roadhouses that had served travellers until just a few years earlier.

At the outskirts of Ashcroft, motorists reached a junction where they had to choose between heading north toward the Cariboo or east toward Kamloops and the central Interior. This crossroads lay a short distance from Ashcroft Manor, a famous ranch and stopping place on the Cariboo Wagon Road. By the late 1930s, an autocourt, service station, and teahouse had been established among the ranch buildings, and the words "Ashcroft Manor" were spelled out in huge white letters on the roof of the main house to attract the attention of motorists. The manor house burned down in 1943, but the gold-rush-era roadhouse survived. The owners of the nearby TU Auto Camp, which was in a shady, inviting stand of trees beside the highway, put up a large sign to advertise their services and surrounded it with an eye-catching arrangement of old ox yokes, freight wagon wheels, and sun-bleached cattle skulls. Postcards show that the TU Auto Camp also displayed an old stagecoach beside the highway, enclosed in a lean-to that sheltered it from the elements.

For motorists heading northward, these roadside relics were the first of many that alluded to the days of horse-drawn stagecoaches and freight wagons.[37] Whether haphazardly heaped or artfully presented, they evoked a sense of kinship with the travellers of yesteryear, with the fortune-seekers, camp followers, and pioneer agriculturalists who had trudged along the

Postcard showing TU Auto Camp advertising at Cache Creek, 1930s. Author's collection.

same road that they themselves now sped over. These displays were typically produced by individuals and families, with minimal participation by the state, academic experts, or big business. Except in a few instances where a local board of trade got involved, they seem not to have co-ordinated their efforts. They seem also to have selected their themes because suitable material was readily at hand: the use of stagecoaches and freight wagons had continued well into the 1910s, and many businesses on the Cariboo Highway were housed in buildings that dated from the gold rush days.

Ashcroft boosters latched onto these regional symbols with particular enthusiasm. As early as 1929, they erected a giant hoarding beside the highway that pronounced Ashcroft the "Gateway to the Golden Cariboo."[38] A few years later, they were proposing that a famous nineteenth-century stagecoach known as the Dufferin Coach should be repatriated from the New Westminster chapter of the Native Sons of British Columbia so that it could become a local tourist attraction.[39] The editor of the *Ashcroft Journal,* R.D. Cumming, found it galling that such an important relic of the Interior was languishing in a city on the Coast. "It isn't likely that anyone living in New Westminster today knows what the Dufferin Coach is," he complained. "To them it is merely a waggon."[40] Cumming wanted the provincial government to exhibit the coach "in a dignified shelter in a conspicuous place" along the new highway, ideally somewhere closely

Postcard of restored freight wagon at Ashcroft. Author's collection.

Postcard showing restored stagecoach at Clinton. Author's collection.

connected to the Cariboo Wagon Road, such as Yale or Ashcroft Manor. After this proposal came to nothing, Cumming took it upon himself to develop historical attractions that would lure the public into Ashcroft. Under his editorship, the *Journal* spearheaded a campaign to restore and preserve an abandoned freight wagon that had been used on the Cariboo Wagon Road until the 1890s. Local residents raised funds to help repair

The Clinton Hotel and Cariboo Highway, 1930s. Gowen Sutton Company postcard. Author's collection.

the wagon and erect a protective shelter. This wagon initially stood in the town centre, near the CPR station, but was later situated beside the road that led into Ashcroft, thereby echoing the stagecoach at the TU Auto Camp and serving as a prosaic substitute for the famous Dufferin Coach. In 1933, Cumming also opened a museum on the second floor of the *Journal* building. This consisted of his own private collection of artifacts, photographs, and old documents. It was the second historical attraction in the Interior to be referred to as a museum; the first was located less than an hour's drive north in Clinton.[41]

The northbound route climbed steadily from Ashcroft to Clinton, with the arid climate, steep sidehills, and sparse pines of the Interior dry belt gradually giving way to cooler temperatures, rolling hills, and denser stands of fir and spruce. Ranching dominated the economy of the south Cariboo, proof of which was visible everywhere: hayfields, split-rail fences, browsed timber, and grazing cattle and horses – sometimes right on the verge of the road. Clinton, twenty-five miles north of Ashcroft, was one of the most intact and intrinsically old-timey towns in the Cariboo, for the scourge of fire had spared most of the log cabins and false-front stores on its main street, which formed part of the Cariboo Highway. With a population of about four hundred, it was the commercial and administrative centre for a much larger ranching district. Cowboys commonly rode into town, and most businesses and government buildings were equipped with

The Payne family's private museum at the Pine Tree Auto Camp, 1930s. B.C. Printing and Litho Company postcard. Author's collection.

hitching posts out front. Postcards show that by 1940 the town greeted motorists with a display of old wagon wheels, freight wagons, and a restored BX stagecoach, which echoed the gold rush motifs at Ashcroft and Cache Creek.[42]

The Clinton Hotel was the town's most prominent landmark. It had been built as a roadhouse in 1861, and its owners proudly promoted it as the oldest hotel in British Columbia. During the interwar years, it looked essentially the same as it had at the turn of the century, despite the addition of diesel-electric lighting, a gas pump, and a summer ice cream parlour. Clinton also had a small privately owned museum at the Payne family's Pine Tree Auto Camp, just across the road from the hotel. It is not clear exactly when or how the Payne family established their museum, but it was open in 1930, and a photograph from the following year shows a hand-painted sign advertising it to customers of the family's gas station. Another photo shows the museum as a wood-frame garage crammed full of items related to the gold rush and wagon road, including patent medicine and liquor bottles, blacksmith's tools, rifles, ox shoes, and gold pans. A modest private collection, the museum was founded for the enjoyment and edification of passing motorists and customers of the gas station and auto camp. It received no support from any government agency or historical society and served to differentiate the Payne family's operation from those of competitors. It was the first historically themed attraction in the Interior to be described as a museum.[43]

Northbound from Clinton, the road passed 59 Mile House and 70 Mile House, the first of a series of roadhouses whose names indicated their distance from Lillooet on the original Cariboo Wagon Road. After the First World War, many roadhouses had adapted to serve automobile traffic, but cars and trucks did not need to stop every ten or fifteen miles as stagecoaches and freight wagons had, with the result that the roadhouses were in decline even as tourists from the Coast started driving the Cariboo Highway.[44] Many reverted to use as private homes. Several were lost to fire. Others were bypassed by road realignments that were intended to accommodate the new automobile technology: long tangents with the occasional steep section were deemed safer than the erratic ramblings of the wagon road, which had meandered this way and that, staying as level as possible to avoid overtaxing draught animals. As the Cariboo Highway was incrementally realigned for safety and efficiency, motorists saw a growing number of spots where the wagon road diverged from the path of the modern road, running parallel to it for a short distance before disappearing behind trees or hills, only to rejoin it farther along. The wandering old way served to remind them of the Cariboo's long history of fortune-seeking travellers.[45]

In the 1920s, several Cariboo roadhouses began to generate extra income by operating as dude ranches that gave city people a chance to try their hand at riding, roping, and range living. Others promoted the Cariboo as a destination for big game hunting and sport fishing.[46] The motifs associated with these recreational activities further enhanced the atmosphere of bygone days at many roadhouses. Animal skulls and horns were mounted on gateposts and outbuildings. Wagon wheels, old carts, surplus saddlery, and various relics that might otherwise have been discarded, but that vaguely suggested the olden days of the open range, were displayed around the yard.[47] Even the roadhouses that offered modern goods and services such as gasoline, soda, and indoor plumbing tended to be weather-beaten and look a bit down at the heel. These undercapitalized businesses were often ancillary to a larger ranch operation and were kept afloat by family labour. Few brought in enough money to adequately maintain their buildings, let alone expand or improve them. The construction of a new lodge at 100 Mile House on the Bridge Creek Ranch was a singular event during the interwar years, explained by the fact that the fifteen-thousand-acre ranch was owned by the Marquess of Exeter, a wealthy British aristocrat.[48] The new 100 Mile House Lodge was a rustic-looking log structure

Cariboo Highway and 70 Mile House, late 1920s. Author's collection.

styled loosely after its namesake, and a restored BX stagecoach was displayed at the end of its driveway, which had been adorned with old wagon wheels. Many Cariboo old-timers expressed regret when the original 100 Mile House burned down in April 1937, but there was no real loss to the ranch: the dilapidated building had sat empty for years.[49]

One of the oldest roadhouses in the central Cariboo was the 122 Mile House at Lac La Hache, midway between 100 Mile House and Williams Lake. When members of the Auto Club of Southern California stopped there for lunch in 1930, they imagined themselves transported back to the days of the gold rush:

> Could we have rolled back the years we would have found in the identical setting a stagecoach party refreshing itself much in the same manner as were we ... These hostelries in the days of their splendour were the stage stations along the Cariboo Road, wherein the weary, dust-laden stagecoach passenger was rested and refreshed. Many of them stand today, as then, providing comforts within their log walls in an atmosphere still pregnant with romance of times gone by.[50]

The inveterate Cariboo booster Louis LeBourdais stopped at the 122 Mile House in 1935 and was pleased to find the old roadhouse still operating.

However, he lamented the fact that "a gasoline pump has taken the place of the watering trough" used by oxen and horses, and that a tennis court had been built in the yard where teamsters and stagecoach drivers had tended to their animals in the days of his childhood.[51] During the interwar years, the 150 Mile House remained a popular stopping place: Edmund Wragge and his friends stayed there in the fall of 1926 and pronounced the accommodations "unchanged from the stagecoach days." A few miles to the north was the 153 Mile House, run by the Crosina family. Built in 1902, it was not especially old but was part of an active ranch. In addition to gasoline, oil, and tires, Lilly Crosina sold local Indigenous beadwork, buckskin, and birchbark baskets from her general store.[52]

In 1936, the HSMBC erected a cairn and plaque beside the Cariboo Highway at Alexandria, forty-five miles north of Williams Lake. It commemorated the nearby site of Fort Alexandria, a fur trade post that had been established by the North West Company in 1821. Judge Frederic Howay asked Louis LeBourdais to help him select "some suitable point for the memorial as nearly historically accurate as the matter of publicity will justify." More specifically, Howay intended that the monument should be "of course near the highway."[53] He also organized its dedication ceremony and invited local rancher Harry Moffatt (who had arrived in the Cariboo in 1875) to unveil it. Few traces of Fort Alexandria remained: the last original buildings had been torn down for firewood more than a decade earlier. There was little for visitors to see at desolate Alexandria, which was primarily a crossroads, where a number of ranch roads intersected the main highway.[54] Indeed, the north Cariboo was even more sparsely populated than the southern and central, with undifferentiated scenery relieved only by occasional glimpses of the muddy Fraser.

After passing the small, scattered ranching communities of Soda Creek, Australian, Kersley, and Dragon, the road finally reached Quesnel, which had a population of 450 in the late 1920s. It was the commercial and administrative centre of the north Cariboo, having supplanted Barkerville in that role in 1913.[55] It was also an important transportation hub, and in the highlands to the east were the famous but long quiescent Cariboo goldfields. Selling goods and services to tourists and other pleasure travellers was an economic afterthought in the Quesnel district until motorists started arriving from points south in late 1926.[56] By 1927, however, local boosters were expecting "an epidemic of visitors," and business owners were building new facilities to serve them.[57] The Quesnel Board of Trade established one of the Cariboo Highway's most elaborate roadside historical attractions, right in the centre of town: one visitor called it an "open-air

Quesnel outdoor museum beside the Cariboo Highway, c. 1932. Author's collection.

museum."[58] The first artifact put on display was an old HBC freight canoe, which was hauled ashore and mounted in cement cradles near the foot of the new bridge over the Fraser River. A signboard explained that Indigenous boatmen had hewn the canoe from a single cottonwood at Takla Lake, three hundred miles to the northwest, many years before, but it said nothing more about the crucial role First Nations people had played in the fur trade economy, which was treated as part of the distant past.[59] In the summer of 1930, the BC Institute of Mining and Metallurgy arranged to have an old Cornish pump waterwheel transported to Quesnel from a gold mine in the hills, where it had not been used since the turn of the century. The twenty-foot-tall waterwheel was placed between the freight canoe and the bridge, with a small plaque identifying it as "a memorial to the pioneer prospectors of the Cariboo."[60] Quesnel's roadside collection gained a third item in 1932, when the HSMBC unveiled a cairn and plaque that commemorated the town as the northernmost point reached by the Collins Overland Telegraph, which had been under construction on its way toward Alaska and Siberia when the scheme was scuttled in 1867.[61] This tribute to modern communications was the only HSMBC cairn along the Hope-to-Barkerville highway that did not relate to exploration, the fur trade, or the gold rush. Nevertheless, it did tie in with the common theme of heroic infrastructure and the "annihilation" of time and space through modern technological networks.

From Quesnel to the Goldfields

During the interwar years, many auto tourists capped off their trip to the Cariboo by savouring the romantic decrepitude of Barkerville. Many deemed the site to have special value, a kind of living link to the gold rush past. Leaving Quesnel, the route to the main goldfields followed the Fraser River two miles north before branching eastward onto the Barkerville road. It climbed steadily from the valley floor: in the fifty-five miles between the two communities, it rose from 1,500 to 4,000 feet above sea level. Barkerville sat on the outermost edge of the Cariboo Plateau, close enough to the mountains that temperatures could drop below freezing at any time of the year. The drive between Quesnel and Barkerville was not particularly pleasant: the road was quite primitive, and the forest cover was scrubby and patchy due to many years of logging, firewood cutting, and forest fires, which made industrial landscape features all the more prominent.[62]

The only gold-rush-era roadhouse left on the Quesnel-Barkerville road was Cottonwood House, on a ranch eighteen miles east of Quesnel. The Boyd family had owned the ranch and roadhouse since 1874 and proudly displayed the guest register that dated back to the mid-1860s. By the late 1930s, Cottonwood House had a gas pump out front and colourful metal signs on its walls that advertised soda and cigarettes. However, its squared log construction and weathered facade were evocative reminders of the days when stagecoaches and freight wagons had stopped there to look after their animals. Anyone who drove between Quesnel and Barkerville could not help but notice Cottonwood House, for the road passed through the centre of the ranch, squeezing between the roadhouse and the clutch of barns and outbuildings that crowded around it. American tourists who paused at Cottonwood House in 1930 described it as infused with "the Cariboo's romantic history."[63]

Fifteen miles beyond Cottonwood House, evidence of the district's placer mining history began to appear. Hydraulic monitoring had been the preferred method of mining in the Cariboo goldfields since the 1890s, and it created deep, gaping, boulder-strewn gulches, with waste rock deposited wherever was most convenient.[64] Remainders of hydraulic and other mining operations were visible all along the Quesnel-Barkerville road: washed-out gulches, huge piles of churned-up gravel, culverts, ditches, flumes, and rusting pipes. Motorists also passed the remnants of several gold rush communities. Almost nothing was left of Van Winkle, which a mining company had purchased and burned down to make space for tailings extracted from Lightning Creek. LaFontaine was also completely

Barkerville in 1930. Asahel Curtis photograph. University of Washington Libraries, Special Collections, CUR1562.

abandoned: by 1930, only a few subtle traces could be spotted mouldering in the bush. Stanley still had twenty or thirty residents, as well as a post office, the Kwong Lung Kee general store, and the old Grand and Lightning Hotels. Edmund Wragge drove through Stanley in the fall of 1926 and described it as an "old camp ... where some placers were still being worked in a small way." Four years later, members of the Auto Club of Southern California found it "practically deserted ... a relic of the past."[65]

Inactivity, roadside detritus, and the handful of dilapidated ghost towns along the rough, narrow road to Barkerville lent the goldfields an air of bleakness and decay. For anyone who made the drive during those years, it must have seemed like a trip into the past: a formerly bustling resource frontier bypassed by modernity and in seemingly irreversible decline. In Barkerville itself, which provincial librarian John Hosie described in 1929 as "still and silent as the grave," nothing dispelled the impression of decay.[66] Gold mining, which was essentially the district's only industry, had been in decline for decades, and Barkerville had only 150 year-round residents by the mid-1920s, including 35 to 50 elderly Chinese men who lived in the dilapidated Chinatown at its upper end. The town's buildings were cramped along a narrow strip of creekbed, hemmed in between famously auriferous Williams Creek and steep, wooded bluffs. Its narrow main street was lined by weathered log cabins and old timber-framed structures, some of which were still connected by elevated wooden sidewalks.[67]

One of the first motorists to drive from the Coast to Barkerville was lawyer Edmund Wragge, who made the trip in the fall of 1926. When he and his friends arrived in town, they found it redolent of frontier days. They checked in at the Kelly Hotel,

> the old original log hotel which we were told was unchanged from the sixties when it was built. Meals were served at a long table as they always had been, the piano which had been packed in during the golden days was still there, and some beautiful glass that no doubt had come around Cape Horn by sail was still to be seen.

A resident whom Wragge called "a real old timer" showed his party the partially overgrown cemetery at the lower end of town. They also drove a mile up Williams Creek to the abandoned site of Richfield to see the old district courthouse, which had not seen court in session since 1913. The badly dilapidated structure was one of the last vestiges of Richfield, and when Wragge peeked through a window he thrilled at the sight of the judge's bench coated with cobwebs.[68]

Once leisure travellers started driving into the north Cariboo during the late 1920s, district boosters and business owners began to see auto tourism as a valuable addition to an otherwise stagnant economy. Some focused on preserving and promoting Barkerville as an exemplar of gold rush days, for the town was regionally distinctive yet also tied in with North American middlebrow and popular culture's enthusiasm for frontier and Wild West themes. This scheme hinged on two key factors: the Cariboo Highway and Quesnel-Barkerville road had to be kept in good repair by the provincial government, and residents had to maintain the townsite more or less the way it was, neither improving it too much nor allowing it to deteriorate much farther. Some middle-class Cariboo boosters and tourism promoters doubted that the residents were capable of recognizing the potential value of their decrepit surroundings and the economic importance of preserving them. In April 1927, a front-page editorial in the *Cariboo Observer* (which was owned by a Quesnel hotelier) noted that a "close observing tourist" who had visited Barkerville the previous fall had remarked that "the town should be put in a museum" and went on to bemoan residents' failure to maintain an active volunteer fire brigade and to keep "the appearance of the city within the bounds of respectability."[69] That many residents were elderly, impoverished, and of

Chinese ancestry simply sharpened the sense that they themselves were relics of a bygone age.

In late 1927, the *Observer* reprinted a story from the *Vancouver Province* in which the BC Historical Association (BCHA) expressed alarm at the condition of the old Richfield courthouse. Describing the building as a "unique relic of the great gold stampede" and "one of the most important landmarks of the province," the BCHA complained that it sat unprotected and uncared for "in the wilderness [and] ruins of the old town." The front of the courthouse was overgrown with brush, and miners had heaped tailings against the back:

> In the building, entirely unprotected, are documents of almost priceless historical value – old court records and other papers that tell the romantic history of the gold days ... These, as well as many other historical objects still preserved in the neighbourhood, should be protected for posterity ... No other relic of the gold rush equals the old courthouse in historical importance.[70]

The BCHA proposed to transform the courthouse into a "historical museum," and Cariboo boosters must have found it reassuring that experts from the Coast had acknowledged Barkerville's potential value as a tourist attraction. Some began to collect papers and artifacts relating to the gold rush.[71] However, nothing came of this proposal: establishing a museum a full mile away from a small, dwindling community that was already an extreme outlier in the Interior road network was clearly impractical.

Former BCHA president Frederic Howay did manage to obtain a measure of official recognition for Barkerville through his membership in the HSMBC. In August 1929, an HSMBC cairn and plaque were unveiled beside the Quesnel-Barkerville road on the lower outskirts of town. Instead of the usual country rock, the cairn had been specially fashioned from quartz stone taken from Williams Creek, the richest of the many auriferous creeks in the Cariboo goldfields. The plaque commemorated Barkerville as the northern terminus of the Cariboo Wagon Road, which tied it to other monuments, relics, and historical landscape features that lay along the Cariboo Highway. For motorists entering the townsite, the cairn was a reminder of the many fortune-seekers who had passed there before them, reaching the goldfields after arduous journeys through canyons and forests. It also revealed that they themselves had arrived at their destination, striking tourist gold at the epicentre of what scholarly and popular historians deemed the most important event in British Columbia's past.

Approach to Barkerville in the early 1930s, showing Historic Sites and Monuments Board of Canada cairn at far right. Author's collection.

The ceremony to unveil the HSMBC cairn was treated as a special occasion in the north Cariboo. In Quesnel, fifty-five miles to the west, the village commissioners declared a local holiday. The *Cariboo Observer* predicted that the influx of motorists and dignitaries would "surpass anything of this nature that has taken place since the sixties – the days of the real gold rush." Cariboo politicians past and present attended the event, along with Judge Howay and provincial librarian John Hosie. The guest of honour was eighty-six-year-old Harry Jones, "the oldest pioneer of the district," who had come to Barkerville in 1863 and still lived down the road in Stanley. After pulling away the Union Jack that had been draped over the cairn, Jones shared a few "off colour jokes" as well as some memories of digging in the gravels of nearby Williams Creek and of life in Barkerville before the great fire of 1868 destroyed the original town.[72] The *Observer* pronounced the occasion an enormous success, reporting that Quesnel had been "overrun with motor cars and tourists." It estimated that a thousand visitors travelling in 250 cars had attended the proceedings. That so many people had come all the way to Barkerville from communities outside the Cariboo seemed to bode well for future tourist interest in the district's gold rush past.[73]

Although the HSMBC cairn gave Barkerville an official stamp of approval, it did nothing to overcome the substantial constraints on tourist traffic to the goldfields. Barkerville was more than five hundred miles and three days' drive from Vancouver, at the end of a rough road from Quesnel. Furthermore, it was a dead end. It could not be incorporated into a loop trip, meaning that visitors were compelled to backtrack through country they had already seen and that was not too scenic to begin with. The town consequently saw no tourism-related development during the 1920s and early 1930s: things carried on much as they had since the end of the First World War, when gold mining had last gone bust. Gasoline could be purchased from a hand pump on the porch of the old Kelly Hotel, but no one opened a business that was oriented toward tourists or the motoring public.

Members of the Auto Club of Southern California who stayed in Barkerville in June 1930 described it as "charged with the memories of old and better days" but concluded that it was a "ghost city," destined to crumble and disappear in the not-too-distant future.[74] Provincial librarian John Hosie, who sat on the BC Historical Association executive council, travelled to Barkerville that same summer to remove historically significant papers from the derelict gold commissioner's office and Richfield courthouse to the safety of the archives in Victoria. The journalist Bruce Hutchison also visited Barkerville in 1930 and was inspired to pen a highly romantic account of the town as an epitome of old-timey-ness. "When I first saw Barkerville it was a ghost to make you shudder deliciously," he declared. He stayed at the Kelly Hotel, where he played billiards "on a table carted on the backs of mules over the Cariboo Road," and visited the decrepit Theatre Royal, where he imagined the miners and townsfolk of yesteryear watching "melodramas and dancing girls." With its slumped economy, lack of modern utilities, and array of weather-beaten surfaces, Barkerville exuded an air of past greatness and inevitable decay that appealed to Hutchison. He described its main street thus:

> The single street of drunken cabins was crushed between the churned gravels of Williams Creek and the shoulder of the hill. No house was in place, none level, all mounted on tipsy stilts ... The rain drummed on the broken roofs and the creaking sidewalks, and it trickled in eerie sound from the eaves. Every black cabin door was filled with presences that you did not seek to discover.[75]

Whether or not they detected spectres from the frontier era, most visitors to Barkerville in the late 1920s and early 1930s would have agreed that its best days lay far behind it. That the boom times of the 1860s might ever recur seemed out of the question. However, the Depression of the 1930s, which brought so much upheaval to British Columbia, ironically spurred a new gold rush to the Cariboo, which temporarily breathed some life into the old town beside Williams Creek.

A New Cariboo Gold Rush

The cratering of the BC forestry, mining, and fishing industries during the early 1930s drove hundreds of unemployed men to try their hand at panning for gold in placer diggings. The initial wave of unemployed gold seekers came to the Cariboo in the years 1930–33 and eked out a living sifting through tailings and "sniping" in patches of ground previously passed over.[76] A second, much larger wave began in early 1934, when the official price of gold leapt more than 33 percent overnight: the reported value of gold mined in British Columbia would increase from $3 million in 1929 to $14 million in 1935.[77] Many long-dormant hydraulic operations were reactivated, and the development of the Cariboo Gold Quartz (CGQ) mine five miles west of Barkerville was one of the brightest spots in the provincial economy during the Depression. The CGQ was a large, well-financed hard-rock mining operation that founded a new town called Wells, which had a population of two thousand by the end of 1934. Journalists frequently claimed that the new gold rush was reminiscent of the 1860s, despite the fact that most people who moved to the goldfields were seeking waged employment rather than hunting for their fortune in the district's creekbeds.[78] Politicians and mining promoters regularly used the historic gold rushes and popular frontier figures such as the ruggedly independent prospector to reassure British Columbians: events in the Cariboo pointed toward economic recovery and a rosy future, as they proved that the province was still laden with resource wealth just waiting for enterprising individuals to discover it.

The boom in Wells affected communities all along the Cariboo Highway. Machinery, construction materials, fuel, food, and consumer goods all had to be trucked in, and many old roadhouses stayed open through the 1930s by serving the growing volume of traffic that passed along the road.[79] The economic importance of the CGQ also led the provincial government to improve the Quesnel-Barkerville road. Several portions were surfaced with gravel, and a dangerous section at Devil's Canyon near Stanley was re-aligned. Hard-rock mining, unlike placer mining, could be done all year

Winter in Barkerville in the mid- or late 1930s, showing electrical wires, street lights, and an automobile used as a "Bennett buggy." Author's collection.

round, so keeping the road passable in winter was a key priority. The Department of Public Works deployed caterpillar tractors fitted with plow blades to keep it clear of snow.[80] Newspapers and magazines clamoured for stories about the Cariboo goldfields, and seemingly every journalist who went to Wells also went out of their way to visit Barkerville and draw parallels between the two communities. Visitors regularly commented on the contrast between bustling, electrified Wells and sleepy, weather-beaten Barkerville: even the Department of Mines juxtaposed the new against the old in a series of side-by-side photographs printed in its 1936 annual report.[81]

Within the Cariboo, the benefits derived from the new gold rush accrued primarily to Wells and Quesnel. A little money was put into maintenance and repair in Barkerville, but several historic landmarks were lost, including the Royal Cariboo Hospital, the Masonic Hall, the old town hall, and the famous Theatre Royal.[82] In her 1938 travelogue on the Cariboo Highway, Winnifred Futcher blamed Wells for having "robbed Barkerville of much of its prosperity," yet she also reported that "nearly every cabin in town is occupied." New mines opened. Old ones were reactivated. The winter population increased from 125 in 1929–30 to almost 400 in 1934–35. Squatters built cabins and shacks at the lower end of town, below St. Saviour's Church. Tailings from the new Shamrock Mine were carried above the Quesnel-Barkerville road on an elevated conveyor belt and deposited on the other side, a short distance from the HSMBC cairn that had been raised in 1929. Barkerville's narrow main street was crowded with cars, trucks, and caterpillar tractors.[83]

During the mid- and late 1930s, most first-time visitors to Barkerville found it highly evocative of BC frontier days. However, many who had become familiar with the town during the 1920s and early 1930s believed that the new mining boom had disrupted its romantic association with the gold rush of the 1860s. Bruce Hutchison was disappointed on his return to the goldfields in the late 1930s, nearly a decade after he had deemed Barkerville a "ghost to make you shudder deliciously." Wells struck him as an agglomeration of "modern conveniences suddenly dumped into the wilderness," and Barkerville had changed too much for his liking. Several fine old buildings that had caught his fancy during his previous visit were gone, and the power lines and automobiles that lined the main street had disrupted its atmosphere of decay. "Barkerville is no longer the ghost town we used to know," Hutchison lamented:

> It has been repaired, reroofed, cleaned up, painted, so that only the old [St. Saviour's] church at the end of the street, beautifully brown and weathered, remains as an authentic touch of the gold rush – the church and the miles of gravel along the creek, where gold was washed ... We drove away from Barkerville secretly sad at its rebirth.[84]

Few who visited Barkerville during the 1920s would have guessed that a modern-day gold rush might threaten to efface the traces of the 1860s gold rush that were so central to its tourist appeal. However, anyone who knew about the history of gold mining in British Columbia would have recognized that bust was bound to follow boom. The value of gold production in the province plummeted from $24 million in 1940 to $7 million in 1945. Hydraulic operations were the first to close; then the CGQ scaled back production, and hundreds of people left Wells.[85] Auto tourism was severely curtailed by gas rationing during the war, but boosters and business owners were conscious of the need to keep up appearances for the few people who did visit the region during the war and strove to protect its assets, including the "outdoor museum" in Quesnel and the abandoned Richfield courthouse.[86] Following the war, the gold mining industry failed to rebound, and people drifted away in search of other opportunities. By 1950, the populations of Wells and Barkerville had dwindled to four hundred and seventy respectively, and Stanley was practically abandoned.[87]

After teetering on the edge for decades, Barkerville seemed poised to join the ranks of the many Cariboo ghost towns. However, a coalition of boosters, business owners, and history enthusiasts rescued it from oblivion by eventually convincing the provincial government to develop it as a major tourist attraction, more than thirty years after it had first been suggested that "the town should be put in a museum."

6

Changing Times and Crisis amidst Prosperity

British Columbia did not suffer a postwar recession during the 1940s, as it had after the First World War. Demand for most of its natural resources either increased or remained steady, with the result that much of the province experienced high employment, rising incomes, and a sense of optimism during the first postwar decade. The provincial government began pouring huge sums into the construction and improvement of roads, expansion of the electrical grid, and extension of the Pacific Great Eastern (PGE) railway northward from Quesnel, all of which helped stimulate economic growth in hinterland communities. These infrastructure projects also served as tools for province building, tying regions closer together, ameliorating some of their disparities, and in the process taking the edge off traditional regional identities. For many Interior residents, new road infrastructure was the most concrete expression of how Fordism played out in the province.[1] The arrival in the Interior of what historian Jean Barman calls "the good life" was also strikingly expressed by the proliferation of new automobiles travelling over its roads – Fords, Chevrolets, and Chryslers; sedans and station wagons; and pickups and logging trucks. In postwar British Columbia, as in most other parts of North America, "democratized" automobility seemed to epitomize the triumph of liberal capitalism.

Although the provincial government strove to modernize the highway network and also increased its support for the tourism industry, its new hands-on involvement in the economy did not extend as far as cultivating history by the road – at least not during the first decade after the war.

Through the late 1940s and most of the 1950s, this was left to private individuals and private organizations, just as it had been during the interwar years. Boosters, boards of trade, and roadside business operators were joined in their efforts by a growing number of local and regional historical societies, many of which had their origins in an undercurrent of anxiety about the pace and scale of social and economic change. British Columbia's postwar prosperity and atmosphere of material progress fused with Fordism's rhetoric of egalitarian all-in-it-togetherness to obscure the fact that not everyone benefitted from the resource and infrastructure-building boom. It had losers as well as winners. Several industries went into decline during and after the war, dragging communities down with them. The collapse of gold and silver mining had negative consequences for the Bridge River valley, parts of the Kootenays, and the Wells and Barkerville area. Coal mining did not wane as sharply, but several large mines shut down as railways switched over to diesel fuel, and as oil and natural gas replaced coal as a source of domestic heating. Furthermore, some communities and districts remained isolated within or peripheral to the provincial road network.

Hundreds of British Columbians were displaced by infrastructure projects during the first postwar decade. This typically resulted when the government expropriated private property to build new roads or improve existing ones, but giant industrial developments also played a role. A dramatic example was the Kenney Dam, which was built in the early 1950s to reverse the flow of the Nechako River so that it could be used to produce electricity for the new Alcan aluminum smelter at Kitimat. Hundreds of people in the Nechako and Ootsa Lake watersheds lost some or all of their homesteads due to this megaproject. Members of the Cheslatta Indian Band fared worst: they were given only two weeks to leave their reserves, after which their homes were razed and their cemeteries inundated. For these and other residents of the province's hinterlands, the pace and scale of postwar modernization were more than just disorienting – they were positively threatening. The feeling of being marginalized or cast aside in a seemingly inexorable march of progress generated undercurrents of anxiety and even a sense of crisis.[2]

The Forest Industry

After the wartime collapse of the BC gold mining industry, the economy of the north Cariboo would have returned to the doldrums of the 1920s if not for the expansion of the forest industry. The growth of logging and sawmilling in the Interior during the late 1940s and early 1950s was driven primarily by petty producers: small, undercapitalized operators who used flexible truck logging techniques to selectively cut the most valuable trees in a given timber block. Hundreds of truck logging operations and "gypo" sawmills sprang up around the province, providing work for thousands. Between five and twenty-five men worked on a typical Interior gypo operation, and in 1947 there were sixty-one sawmills in the Quesnel district alone, nearly twice as many as the previous year. By 1952, 180 mills lay within a thirty-mile radius of Quesnel.[3] This boom was closely associated with the widespread availability of gas-powered technologies such as chainsaws, caterpillar tractors, and surplus army trucks, and with the development of small truck-portable sawmills that could be hauled straight into the bush. It was also closely linked to the construction of a capillary network of logging roads and, less obviously, to the improvement of secondary and arterial highways so that they could accommodate trucks hauling heavy loads of timber. The expansion of the Interior forest industry went hand-in-hand with that of the Interior road network – the same network that invited a growing number of working- and middle-class motorists to explore the landscapes of their province, learning about nature and history by the road.

The postwar forestry boom was imbued with a kind of frontier mentality, even though it was heavily reliant on state-built infrastructure. Truck loggers and gypo sawmill operators saw themselves as the modern-day equivalent of the prospectors, teamsters, and pioneer ranchers of the late nineteenth century: small bands of men, often family and friends, they were determined to be their own bosses and to eschew waged employment in the cities of the Coast. They prized rugged masculinity and liberal values such as independence, self-reliance, innovation, and personal initiative. They called for level playing fields and equal opportunities, and preferred to imagine that they were not dependent on government policies or political favours, even as they clamoured for the Forest Service and Department of Public Works to build more and better roads that would "open up" the country.[4]

The Interior forest industry had traditionally concentrated along the east-west railway lines, but the rise of truck logging techniques allowed it to expand into new areas, one of which was the Cariboo. Trucks laden with logs, poles, and lumber became a common sight along its arterial roads, including the Cariboo Highway. The Cariboo saw some of the most dramatic growth in the Interior forest industry. By the early 1950s, planer mills, plywood plants, and drying kilns stood at multiple points along the route of the PGE, including at 70 Mile House near Clinton, 100 Mile House, Williams Lake, and Quesnel. The growth of the industry in the Cariboo was overshadowed only by its spectacular expansion in northern British Columbia. Prince George became the industry's undisputed northern capital after 1952, when the "Prince George Eventually" finally reached town. As the most important junction in the northern transportation network, Prince George was a prime candidate for a pulp mill, as were crossroads communities such as Quesnel in the northern Interior, Kamloops in the central Interior, and Castlegar and Cranbrook in the southern Interior.[5]

The industry began consolidating in the early 1950s, as Victoria implemented sustained yield policies that were intended to make more efficient long-term use of timber resources. These policies benefitted large operators backed by international capital, particularly those who purchased tree farm licences, which provided perpetually renewable tenure over enormous tracts. Big mills bought up small mills and their associated timber leases, then contracted truck loggers and other small operators to build their logging roads and do their cutting and hauling. By the early 1950s, truck loggers had begun to fear that government policies, which favoured the big players, would squeeze them out. Interior communities felt a sense of crisis even in the midst of an economic boom. Petty producers worried about losing access to resources and markets, and the hinterland ideals of independence and self-mastery seemed to be threatened by faceless bankers, indifferent politicians, and technocratic experts in distant cities. Gordon Hak shows that this undercurrent of anxiety helped propel the populist and avowedly pro-free-enterprise Social Credit Party to power in 1952.[6]

The Roadside Service Industry

British Columbia's postwar boom was not driven exclusively by the forest industry. Mining for base metals such as lead, zinc, and copper remained strong. Construction of power transmission lines, pipelines, smelters, mills, waterworks, new and improved roads, and schools and government buildings provided employment for thousands. Substantial growth also occurred in the service and hospitality sector, where increased business travel was overshadowed by an enormous rise in auto tourism and outdoor recreation.

The boom in leisure travel was made possible by savings accumulated during the war, steadily rising incomes, increased rates of working- and middle-class automobile ownership, and the paid vacation time that was built into most union contracts. It was facilitated by the improvement and expansion of the provincial highway network and encouraged by the development of free public amenities such as the provincial parks, with their campsites and diverse attractions. It was also stimulated by the myriad promotional efforts of roadside business operators, automobile manufacturers, and oil companies, all of whom stood to profit from increased consumption of their goods and services. Furthermore, Victoria became more actively involved with tourism promotion, treating it as an industry that merited direct support. The BC Government Travel Bureau conducted extensive publicity campaigns, marketing the province in print and on film, at tradeshows and on billboards, to visitors from afar but also to residents, who were encouraged to take to the road and learn about their own province, to "see BC first," to "know British Columbia better."[7]

Although many aspects of the leisure travel boom were novel, particularly its extension to the working class, it was part of a longer trajectory. Michael Dawson shows that BC boosters and businesses never completely abandoned tourism promotion during the Depression or the war and that their work planted seeds of curiosity and desire that came to fruition after hostilities ended.[8] It is also important to consider the changing social geography of western Canada. In 1951, a quarter million British Columbians – fully 20 percent of the province's population – had moved there from the Prairie provinces, most since 1930.[9] A large percentage of residents in coastal cities and fast-growing regional centres such as Kamloops and Prince George were migrants from smaller BC hinterland communities. With so many urbanites having rural and small-town backgrounds, it is reasonable to assume that much of the intra- and interprovincial travel that passed for tourism during the postwar years actually revolved around the maintenance of family ties and participation in traditional rural activities such as fishing, hunting, and camping. Thus, for many western Canadians, the arterial highways of the Interior provided an affordable way to keep in touch with friends and family while enjoying themselves en route.

The postwar years held great promise for roadside commercial operators. Like truck logging, ownership of an autocourt, campground, cafe, lodge, or gas station provided an opportunity to be one's own boss in an industry that appeared poised for a boom. As during the interwar years, most roadside commercial venues that opened during the first postwar decade belonged to families, occasionally with financial backing from an oil company. Family-owned operations dominated the service sector in the Interior through the 1950s and 1960s. These small businesses faced new opportunities and challenges as the provincial government poured money into modernizing the highway network and as the rapid motorization of the working class expanded the market for food, gas, lodging, and other services.

As with the Interior forest industry, there were reasons for anxiety. The boom brought many more potential customers, but it also spawned many more competitors, which put pressure on established operators. New businesses sprang up along existing roads, and new and improved routes changed established travel patterns. The Hope-Princeton Highway provides an excellent illustration of this. From 1926 to 1949, every automobile driven between the Coast and the Interior had gone by way of the Fraser and Thompson Canyons. As shown in the previous chapter, this drive was one of the province's most widely shared and culturally significant landscape experiences. By offering a more direct route between the Coast and the southern Interior, the Hope-Princeton spurred the growth of the roadside service sector in the Similkameen and Okanagan Valleys. The Okanagan underwent some of the greatest changes, with a profusion of fruit stands, ice cream vendors, motels, and campgrounds. The Hope-Princeton also diverted a significant proportion of the traffic that had traditionally passed through the canyons. Business owners along the canyon route complained about Manning Park's free campgrounds and elaborate government-owned concession complex. They accused Victoria of unfairly competing against them and of acting as a commercial monopoly along the Hope-Princeton. They even complained when the Parks Division put up signs to indicate the distance to Pinewoods Lodge, declaring they were a type of advertising forbidden elsewhere in the province. Once the Department of Public Works turned its attention to modernizing the highway through the Fraser and Thompson Canyons, these same people complained about the associated detours and delays, claiming they were driving customers away and themselves out of business.[10]

The modernization program led to the expropriation of many properties that bordered on rights-of-way, including those of businesses that depended on the passing traffic. For them, modernization was a double-edged sword, and every widening, realignment, bypass, or commercial signage restriction that affected them generated a bevy of complaints and accusations.[11] They wanted good roads, because a poor road might get a bad reputation and steer customers away, but the detours and delays of new construction might keep them away in the short term, and they themselves might lose some or all of their property to expropriation. They also worried about the appearance of highway corridors, frequently complaining that the government did not maintain or manage roadside landscapes properly. They cited litter, junkyards, wandering livestock, logging clearcuts, gravel pits, the presence of signage, the absence of signage, traffic going too slow, traffic going too fast, unregulated roadside development, over-regulated roadside development, and all manner of perceived eyesores.[12] This issue took on an increasing significance, for they understood that the aesthetics of the highway shaped the reputation of regions and communities in the eyes of the motoring public.

Changes along the Canyon Highway

In 1946, after twenty years of complaint by pleasure travellers, commercial truck drivers, and Interior tourism promoters, the toll charged to cross the Alexandra Suspension Bridge near Spuzzum was finally eliminated.[13] Its removal symbolically declared the BC Interior open for business and invited the public to enjoy the "freedom of the road" after five years of gas rationing and proscriptions against leisure travel. It eliminated a material barrier to the rapidly growing number of automobile owners on the Coast who wanted to visit family, go sightseeing, or participate in recreational activities in the Interior. Politically, removing the toll was necessitated by the impending completion of the toll-free Hope-Princeton Highway: the government did not want to be seen as favouring the new route into the southern Interior.[14] During the late 1940s, Victoria began to upgrade the road through the Fraser and Thompson Canyons, which had comprised part of the Trans-Canada Highway since 1940. By 1951, coastal motorists who ventured beyond Hope could enjoy paved surfaces all the way to Clinton in the north, Kamloops in the east, and Princeton in the south. Hope went from being an insignificant village to an important junction point, where drivers had to choose which route to follow into the Interior. By 1949, it had twenty-one campgrounds, autocourts, motels, and hotels, capable of accommodating up to four hundred people. In the 1950s, local boosters were promoting Hope as the "Gateway to Holidayland."[15]

Modernization of the Fraser Canyon Highway changed the motoring public's experience of history by the road. Stone retaining walls, timber cribbings, and other familiar traces of the Cariboo Wagon Road were destroyed or obscured by realignments, lane widening, and efforts to stabilize

Colonial-era masonry wall incorporated into Fraser Canyon Highway, late 1950s. University of Victoria Archives, Chester P. Lyons fonds.

frangible cliffs. "The old road can still be seen, but is now mixed with long stretches of new highway," perambulating Victoria grocer Leonard Coton recorded in his diary during the early 1950s. The new paved surface also allowed motorists to travel at higher speeds. This, in combination with a steady growth in both the volume of traffic and the size of vehicles on the road, made it increasingly difficult to experience the landscape at a leisurely pace.[16] Instead of pulling over wherever they pleased, as had generally been possible during the interwar years, drivers were effectively restricted to stopping at places that the Department of Public Works had set aside for that reason. For safety purposes – and often at the urging of tourism promoters, the Parks Division, or the BC Government Travel Bureau –

Unimproved section of highway at China Bar Bluff in the Fraser Canyon, 1961. University of Victoria Archives, Chester P. Lyons fonds.

Public Works constructed a series of paved pullouts at points where there were scenic views or interesting natural features such as a waterfall. This work was akin to what was being done at the Skagit Bluffs, the roadside remnant of the Dewdney Trail, and other points of interest along the new Hope-Princeton Highway. The Parks Division also established several small roadside parks in the Fraser and Thompson Canyons during the early 1950s, including Emory Creek, Skihist, and Goldpan. With their picnic sites, free campgrounds, and pit toilets, they quickly became popular.

Although the Canyon Highway was considerably improved during the late 1940s and the 1950s, it never lost its sense of the sublime, the possibility that danger – and thus adventure – might lurk around every corner. Sections remained narrow and precarious, especially when compared to new arterial roads such as the Hope-Princeton. The tunnels in the Fraser Canyon remained incapable of accommodating two full-size cars side-by-side. The Alexandra Bridge retained its steel open-grate deck, which afforded a nerve-wracking view of the river churning below. The harrowing one-lane timber grasshopper trestle that swung out over the abyss at China Bar Bluff remained in place until the early 1960s.

Motorists could still enjoy history by the road, but it was less readily discernable. One travelogue writer made a dangerous recommendation to tourists who wanted to get a sense of what travelling the canyons had been like during the gold rush:

> Leave your car at one of the viewpoints on the fine new paved highway north of the suspension bridge and scramble down the rocky bank to the old [wagon] road. You will find at almost any place you happen to choose examples of engineering skill that will astonish you ... Reconstruct in your imagination the narrow road clinging to the rocky abutments and following their steep grades. Put yourself in a six-horse stagecoach and go rocketing around those curves and down those grades at top speed. Then you will have some idea of what was done here.[17]

In the early 1950s, Leonard Coton complained that "Lytton, for all its great history, was a disappointment." The town had lost most of its gold-rush-era buildings to fire and done nothing to identify or interpret those that remained. Coton believed that the locals ought to "make some attempt to interest the tourists" by cultivating "places and things which might perpetuate those old days." Conversely, he heaped praise on Ashcroft and Cache Creek, where boosters and businesses still kept old, familiar stagecoaches and freight wagons "well displayed by the roadside," thereby evoking the romance of the Cariboo Wagon Road.[18]

The motoring public's experience of the landscape also became more tightly structured in the Fraser and Thompson Canyons during the late 1940s and the 1950s. Historical features, primarily in the form of monuments and plaques, such as the HSMBC cairns at Hope and Yale, were gradually concentrated at a limited number of state-designated stopping places. Higher speeds and traffic volumes discouraged many travellers from pulling off the highway, even at those spots. Furthermore, several sections of the Canyon Highway were realigned to divert traffic from the "main street" of communities such as Yale, Spuzzum, and Lytton. This was intended as a safety measure. At Yale, realignment had the effect of bypassing the HSMBC cairn installed beside the highway more than thirty years earlier, as well as the Sto:lo cemetery at nearby I:yem. The market for coiled cedar basketry and other First Nations handicrafts went into steep decline after the Second World War, which was when the highway was adjusted to bypass Spuzzum, where the general store had been selling these goods, as well as the handicrafts store on the Lytton Indian Reserve.[19] Ironically, "Indian" motifs grew more popular as the modernized form and route of the highway detoured the public away from even a modicum of interaction with Indigenous people.[20] In Lytton, an old boarding house was rebranded

Historic Sites and Monuments Board of Canada cairn at Yale bypassed by highway realignment, 1957. University of Victoria Archives, Chester P. Lyons fonds.

the Totem Motel and Auto Court during the early 1950s. Around the same time, the Tee-Pee Café opened near Boston Bar. Wood-framed and stucco-coated, it took the shape of a thirty-foot-tall tipi. Painted with southwestern Indian motifs such as cattle skulls and cacti, the Tee-Pee was a popular landmark until the late 1950s, when the Department of Highways expropriated and demolished it to widen the road.[21] Between the widened road, faster traffic, and changing commercial forms, the landscapes along the Canyon Highway were losing much of their power to evoke the trudging prospectors, creaking freight wagons, and racing stagecoaches of the gold rush days. The route retained its sublime scenery and many of the kinesthetic thrills of the interwar years, but its historical assets were gradually becoming streamlined or de-featured.

Changes along the Cariboo Highway

The public experience of history by the road was also affected by changes along the plateau section of the Cariboo Highway. As indicated above, the scale and pace of postwar industrial change were especially dramatic in the Cariboo, and thus the contrast between past and present was particularly sharp. These changes generated a sense of crisis in some circles, a sense that important and sometimes irreplaceable links to the past were disappearing in an era of big business and big government. Some Cariboo residents lamented the loss of pioneer values. Others worried about the effects of commercial and industrial eyesores on scenic landscapes. Still others grew anxious about the loss of old buildings and other historical features, many of which had been familiar to the motoring public since the late 1920s. The absence of a well-known landmark could be quite obvious along the Cariboo Highway due to the region's relatively undifferentiated scenery and the great distances between towns.

Gold-rush-era roadhouses were becoming fewer and farther between, continuing the decline that had briefly been arrested by the gold mining (and trucking) boom of the 1930s. Several were demolished or bypassed when sections of the highway were paved, widened, or realigned to allow heavier loads, higher speeds, and greater safety. Near Clinton, the 59 Mile House burned down shortly after it was bypassed by a realignment, causing neighbours to suspect a case of "insurance fire." Also lost during the immediate postwar years were the 74 Mile House north of Clinton and 122 Mile House at Lac La Hache. The original 83 Mile House was also bypassed, but its owners secured a bank loan that allowed them to build a motel and diner beside the new alignment. In 1955, Kersley House, a former roadhouse fifteen miles south of Quesnel, was destroyed by a fire, along with numerous relics contained inside.[22]

Other historical features were obscured by their proximity to new commercial developments. In the late 1940s, a service station selling British American Oil products was built at Alexandria, right beside the cairn erected by the HSMBC in 1936. In the early 1950s, that section of highway was widened and paved, with the result that the service station became the only practical place for people to park if they wished to inspect the cairn that commemorated fur-trade-era Fort Alexandria. A large sign for the service station stood at the foot of the broad mound that was topped by the cairn, which could be taken to imply that the monument was somehow sponsored by the business. At some point in the late 1950s, a sign advertising five-cent pony rides was placed beside the mound, further distracting from the cairn, which was effectively overshadowed by the modern look and garish commercialism of the service station.[23]

Quesnel was an important centre of the Interior forest industry by the late 1940s. It got a new plywood plant in 1950 and had many planer mills – only Prince George, seventy-five miles to the north, had more. There were serious proposals to dam the Quesnel River for hydroelectric power

Service station and Historic Sites and Monuments Board of Canada cairn at Alexandria, mid-1950s. University of Victoria Archives, Chester P. Lyons fonds.

and talk that a pulp mill might be built one day, which would create hundreds of year-round industrial jobs. Quesnel's population leapt from 650 in 1941 to 1,500 a decade later. The town was becoming more stable and prosperous, one of the emerging regional centres associated with the booming resource economy, the kind of town that local boosters believed could afford civic amenities such as a museum that would encourage auto tourists to stop for a few hours.

Quesnel still had its open-air "museum" on Front Street, but it was in embarrassingly bad condition. By the end of the war, the HBC freight canoe had been on the verge of disintegrating and was removed from the display soon after. The local board of trade struggled to maintain the Cornish pump waterwheel, which the *Cariboo Observer* called the town's "most famous landmark." Only the stone-and-bronze HSMBC monument that commemorated the Collins Overland Telegraph seemed impervious to the elements. The growing volume of cars and trucks that travelled along Front Street – which remained a section of the Cariboo Highway – also made it less safe and less appealing for people to stop and examine these fur trade and gold rush artifacts. Quesnel's boosters and tourism promoters concluded that the town required a new historical attraction.[24]

In 1946, Quesnelites were invited to submit proposals for a memorial that would honour district residents who had served in the war. A front-page editorial in the *Cariboo Observer* suggested that the most fitting memorial would be a civic building, which would house a library, public restrooms, and a "museum of Cariboo relics." Cariboo MLA Louis LeBourdais was set to throw his support (and perhaps his personal collection of gold-rush-era papers and relics) behind this scheme, but when he passed away it was shelved for several years.[25] The idea of a museum for Quesnel was resurrected in 1950, when village commissioners revived their plan to construct a public restroom for the convenience of visitors. The washroom proposal inspired several community groups to argue that a museum should be built in conjunction with it, including the district's Women's Institutes and the North Cariboo Growers Co-operative, which both offered to help raise funds. Although the scheme bogged down, it did bring Quesnel's various history enthusiasts together. They co-operated to collect artifacts and old documents, and arranged for them to be stored in the basement of the post office, one of the town's few brick structures. This teamwork eventually led to the establishment of the Cariboo Historical Society, as discussed below.[26]

The rapid postwar growth of regional centres such as Quesnel, Williams Lake, Kamloops, and Prince George was accompanied by an increasingly modern look, with new mills, new government buildings, new hard-surfaced streets, new traffic lights, new signs and advertisements, a growing volume of car and truck traffic, plus a growing number of homes with electricity, indoor plumbing, telephones, and oil-burning furnaces. Amidst these transformations, which were proudly trumpeted in local newspapers, some smaller, older Interior communities that had been bypassed by the boom – that did not get a large new sawmill or were situated away from a main highway – became increasingly appealing to history buffs and auto tourists. Their relative scarcity enhanced their perceived cultural and economic value. Barkerville was one such place. It had slipped into decline after the gold mining boom fizzled and by the late 1940s was again on its way to becoming a ghost town. In 1947, the old government assay office was condemned and demolished. So were the former HBC store and the Scott Saloon, the latter one of the few buildings to survive the great fire of 1868. The remaining residents of Barkerville and Wells were not shy about pilfering useful fixtures from abandoned buildings and sometimes tore down disused cabins for firewood. The badly dilapidated structures in the uppermost Chinatown section of the townsite were particularly susceptible to this fate. Antique collectors and souvenir-hunting tourists entered vacant buildings and removed almost anything that was portable.[27]

In Stanley, where only a handful of people lived after the war, the Grand Hotel (which was owned by Bill Hong of Wells) was consumed by flames in 1948. No one was hurt, but none of its many old fixtures and furnishings could be saved. Eight months later, in January 1949, fire broke out in the attic of Barkerville's famous Kelly Hotel, which had been built in 1870. Disaster was avoided because its tin roof slowed the spread of the flames, allowing time for the Barkerville and Wells Volunteer Fire Brigades to arrive and save the hotel, with only minimal damage. The Kelly family had made the hotel's saloon into a kind of informal repository for gold rush items collected by enthusiasts. As firefighters battled the blaze, volunteers raced to remove these treasures to the safety of the street, indicating growing local acceptance that the town's historic legacy was an asset meriting preservation. In 1951, the Boyd family sold Cottonwood House on the Quesnel-Barkerville road, severing ties with a famous landmark they had owned since the 1870s.[28]

These losses and near-losses in the north Cariboo were part of a broader trend during the first postwar decade. Familiar historical features were vanishing at an alarming rate. They had become important parts of a shared culture since the late 1920s, a culture that revolved around landscape experiences structured by public roads, private automobiles, and the practice of driving. Their disappearance was particularly obvious in the Cariboo, a sparsely populated district whose relatively flat terrain and gently rolling plateau lands gave highway planners greater leeway for new alignments than was possible in mountainous areas. The loss was also acute on the approaches to town centres, where property was both affordable and desirable for the construction of new commercial operations and light industrial plants. In the Cariboo, as in many parts of the Interior, postwar prosperity also prompted the replacement and renovation of old, weathered structures, which had been neglected during the war years (when materials were scarce) and the Depression (when cash was scarce). Building a brand new home or business was often easier than refitting an older one with insulation, electrical wiring, a new heating source, and indoor plumbing. Some old buildings were torn down, but many more were simply left to decay and eventually collapse under the weight of winter snow.

In the midst of a boom driven by resource extraction and the construction of modern infrastructure, there seemed to be little thought of protecting (let alone restoring) antiquated buildings and other fragments of the past. For some Cariboo residents, the loss of these landmarks stirred up great concern. Not only were they part of local and regional identities, but in many cases they were also part of a popular, distinguishing image or atmosphere that had been cultivated since the late 1920s – that is to say, they were historical, and they had a history of being recognized as such. Any district, community, or highway corridor that lost enough of them was at risk of becoming undifferentiated, of losing its appeal, of failing to meet the motoring public's expectations. Having invested in their cultivation and promotion, the boosters, tourism promoters, and small-business owners of the Cariboo had good reason to worry about the postwar thinning of history by the road, for they lacked spectacular scenery to fall back on.

Responses to the Crisis

Tension between new and old, progress and prudence, the impulse to modernize and the impulse to preserve was writ large in the pages of *Northwest Digest,* a bimonthly magazine established in Quesnel in 1945.[29] Focusing on northern BC and the northern Interior, *Northwest Digest* represented the interests of small-town merchants, independent construction contractors, and petty producers such as truck loggers. Its main fare consisted of stories (and advertisements) related to logging, farming, ranching, commercial hauling, hunting, and fishing. The magazine was enthusiastic about opening up the province for new resource extraction activity and about Victoria building new infrastructure. *Northwest Digest* had a "frontier" mentality and was unwavering in its support of free enterprise, but it was not altogether uncritical. It complained about government policies that favoured large corporations and ran stories that highlighted some of the unevenness and contradictions of the postwar boom. *Northwest Digest* also supported tourism, conservation, and outdoor recreation, and therefore condemned visual blight and wasteful practices. It regularly promoted the Interior and northern British Columbia as destinations for pleasure travel and sightseeing, and printed editorials about the importance of protecting the attractions of these areas, whether they be scenery, wildlife, game fish, totem poles, or historic buildings. It also printed many stories about BC history.

A 1951 editorial by Quesnel resident F.W. Lindsay captured *Northwest Digest*'s concern about the neglect of the past. Titled "We Never Think," it criticized modern British Columbians for their failure to recognize the cultural and potential economic value of ghost towns and historical landscape features:

> We admire the United States and its people for the reverence and homage they pay their heroes. We in British Columbia, however, are far more practical. We don't honor our dead, we don't cherish our shrines or our history. We cherish nothing but the Dollar (spelled with a capital, as though it were either Holy or Royal). We cherish dreams of hydro plants, paper plants, pulp plants, and other kinds of plants which grind out money and industrial diseases of many sorts. We never think of painting a fence around a graveyard, or protecting the oldest courthouse in BC, or keeping green the memory of [the] gallant company of adventurers who lie so silently in the bedraggled burying ground at Barkerville.
>
> One time there was a war-canoe at Quesnel. It was a relic of past times. It rotted and fell away. In the central and eastern provinces the memories of the past are part and parcel for the present and future history ... Throughout the east there are countless small and well kept museums and these prove to be among the greatest tourist attractions.
>
> There must be some tourist attraction in ancient history and relics. If there is not perhaps someone would explain in words of not more than one syllable why the Americans buy Indian totem poles from Masset and Sandspit and Bella Coola and other points to use in their parks and museums.
>
> If money is the chief end of man in British Columbia it seems as though we are defeating our own ends by letting the past die out. Yale is a forgotten town and Soda Creek and all the towns between. The thousands of [gold rush] argonauts are forgotten. One wonders what tourist will come as far north as Quesnel to see a hydro-electric plant? ... Cariboo is the cradle of BC. The next generation may well wonder what kind of insensate creatures preceded them. A stone cairn stating "Alexander Mackenzie passed here" will be a mute testimony to our lack of imagination ...
>
> For years a handful of people in Barkerville have tried to keep some of the points of historic interest intact. [However,] the Richfield courthouse above Barkerville is now a skeletal structure whose walls have been profaned, whose windows have been broken and whose history has been all but forgotten. Imagine a building such as that in Washington or Oregon falling into such disrepair ... There is no museum in Quesnel. One or two people have saved historical curios throughout the years but there is no building in which to house them.

> It is not enough that roads are being built and the country opened up in the interests of Industry. There should be more to life than jobs and the creation of jobs. Possibly if there were a little more accent placed upon the pioneer and a little less upon [economic] security we might have time to glance about us and get our house in order.
>
> We personally feel greatly embarrassed whenever a tourist points at the Quesnel cemetery and says, "Is THAT your cemetery?" We feel like crawling under a stone whenever a tourist talking about Barkerville says "Well why the dickens don't you people do something about it?" And we feel like screaming when some large rotund politico says "Of course these things will be attended to ... but first of all we must look to the future."[30]

The *Prince George Citizen* echoed elements of Lindsay's eloquent lament in a 1953 editorial titled "Keep Our History Alive." Like Lindsay, the *Citizen* pointed toward the potential tourism value of the province's myriad historic sites and landscape features. But unlike Lindsay, it offered a specific prescription for how value could be extracted from them. It recommended that more markers and interpretive signs be erected along arterial roads to make them legible and meaningful to tourists, the vast majority of whom travelled by automobile:

> British Columbia's colorful past will be lost to the motoring public if something is not done to preserve and mark our historic sites. The BC Automobile Association asks are we missing the boat in not providing a running commentary on signs along the highways telling tourists some of the highlights of our early days.
>
> The people in the province have been so preoccupied with building the future that already many historic sites have been destroyed. In those instances all that can be done is to "mark the spot" [after the fact]. Buildings connected with our pioneering days need to be rebuilt and preserved. The entire town of Barkerville, for example, could be made into a historic site with so much attraction that tourists would drive miles out of their way to see it ... In every community there are forgotten stories of our past. This province is a treasure trove of exploratory history. The men who first crossed our mountains and came down our valley deserve to be remembered ... The Fraser Canyon, the famous Cariboo, and Fort George regions are literally abounding in sites of historic interest, and we might ask why more of these sites are not marked. A running commentary on signs beside the highway would greatly add to tourist enjoyment of Central BC.[31]

Significantly, the *Citizen* did not specify who should organize and pay for this ambitious program.

Rather than waiting for some state agency (or the BC Automobile Association) to step in or relying on the munificence of business owners, middle-class history buffs in many parts of the Interior banded together to preserve sites that were at risk of demolition or decay. In Quesnel, the Cariboo Historical Society (CHS) was formed in 1951. It had three main goals: to amass documents and artifacts related to the district's past, to build a museum in which that collection could be displayed, and to protect old buildings and other historical landscape features. Members of the CHS were particularly concerned about the dwindling number of gold-rush-era structures along the Cariboo Highway corridor and in the vicinity of Barkerville. The CHS acquired a substantial collection of artifacts from the Boyd family after they sold Cottonwood House on the Quesnel-Barkerville road in 1951. It also marked several historical sites with wooden signs during the early 1950s.[32] Although the CHS was based primarily in Quesnel, it established chapters elsewhere in the Cariboo, including in the Alexandria district and at Williams Lake. It also encouraged the 1952 formation of the Wells-Barkerville Historical Society, with long-time property owners Hazel Kelly and Bill Hong serving as president as vice-president, respectively. The launch of a historical society in the goldfields revived long-forgotten talk of building a museum at Barkerville.[33]

Other historical associations were formed in the BC hinterlands during the early 1950s. In the southern Interior, the Boundary Historical Society was established in 1951. Like the CHS, it adopted a regional perspective: its membership was centred in Grand Forks but took an interest in a region that extended along the southern transprovincial highway from Rock Creek to Nelson. In northern British Columbia, the Prince George Rotary Club formed a "Canadian history committee" in 1951, with the goal of collecting objects for a future museum.[34] Many of these new societies wanted to establish their own museum, but few managed to do so during the early 1950s. The South Cariboo Historical Society opened a museum in Clinton in September 1953, housing it in one of the town's few brick buildings, the former schoolhouse that had been built in 1892 and donated by the provincial government. Many of the items held in the museum had been provided by the Payne family, who had owned the Pine Tree Auto Camp and its associated private museum since the early 1930s. The new museum inspired the chairman of the local chamber of commerce's publicity committee to erect a roadside cairn of his own design, fashioned from fieldstone

Cariboo Highway in downtown Clinton, 1955. R.B.A. Cragg photograph. Kamloops Museum and Archives, 4087.

gathered at various points along the Cariboo Wagon Road.[35] Clinton remained one of the most old-timey towns on the Cariboo Highway and the Clinton Hotel its most famous historical landmark. Nevertheless, the narrow strip of highway that comprised its main street saw significant changes during the early and mid-1950s. Hitching posts disappeared as increased traffic made it unsafe to ride horses into town. Utility lines were strung overhead. Several false-front stores were remodelled, their logs and whipsawn lumber covered over with stucco and tin siding. Others were torn down and replaced by modern-looking autocourts and gas stations.

Seeing new museums open in small towns must have been inspiring as well as frustrating for Barkerville boosters. Few people in Barkerville or Wells had any money, the two communities were far off the beaten track, and they were shrinking rather than growing, with only about sixty and four hundred residents, respectively. Many Barkervillians were quite elderly and too poor to relocate even if they had wanted to. The Wells-Barkerville Historical Society did count local business and property owners among its members, but they produced nowhere near the income of the 1930s boom. Old-timers such as the Tregillus and Wendle families donated important records and artifacts, but preserving (let alone restoring)

Barkerville's many historic buildings lay far beyond the reach of locals. The poor condition of the Quesnel-Barkerville road and the fact that motorists would need to double back along the same route after visiting the goldfields were also strikes against the development of any tourist attraction there.

Lack of progress in getting a public museum at Barkerville inspired long-time resident Fred Ludditt to establish the Barkerville Historic Development Company in 1953. Ludditt owned one of the last hydraulic mines still operating in the district, and he harboured dreams of making Barkerville into a tourist draw. He imagined leasing or purchasing its remaining dilapidated properties and then fixing them up in a manner that would appeal to auto tourists who were interested in ghost towns and western historical themes. He hoped to raise funds for this scheme from private investors and doubtless expected members of his family, who owned a construction company in Quesnel, to assist with the repair and maintenance work. However, Ludditt was unable to do much more than install a few signs that identified some of Barkerville's oldest remaining buildings.[36] Between Ludditt, the Wells-Barkerville Historical Society, and the Cariboo Historical Society, many people hoped to breathe some life into the two declining towns by playing up the district's gold rush past, but none had the capital or expertise required to do so beyond the smallest scale. They scoured the area for relics of the nineteenth century, trying to prevent them from falling into the hands of antique dealers and souvenir hunters who might remove them from the region or province. Large items collected by members of the Wells-Barkerville Historical Society were kept in a disused warehouse, whereas most of the smaller ones continued to be stored in the saloon of the Kelly Hotel. By the mid-1950s, the Kelly family operated the saloon as a kind of private museum, with several hundred visitors each summer, each paying two dollars to enter.

Visitors to Barkerville continued to be impressed by the many weathered buildings that lined its narrow main street and by its general atmosphere of bygone days. Some complained that residents did not appreciate its worth as a tourist asset, and some even suggested that it be placed under the control of experts, who would know how to preserve, promote, and extract value from it. An Edmonton lawyer who visited Barkerville in 1954 was appalled at the condition of the Richfield courthouse, which was badly weathered and nearly overgrown with trees and brush on every side. Believing that it should be saved, "in view of its great historical background," the lawyer promised to lobby the provincial government and BC Bar

Society for its restoration.[37] Every fire or demolition that destroyed an old Cariboo roadhouse, and every instance in which a goldfield ghost town such as Stanley or Quesnel Forks lost yet another year-round inhabitant, increased the sense of urgency to preserve Barkerville.

The Clinton Hotel, the oldest hotel in British Columbia, burned down in May 1958, with the loss of four lives. Built in 1861, it had long been one of the most famous roadhouses on the Cariboo Highway, a prominent landmark and favourite subject for photographers passing through town. A tourist who drove through Clinton shortly after the fire remarked that it was "not very prosperous looking" and could "ill afford to lose its principal attraction, the old roadhouse, heirloom from a vanished age." Clinton did retain one roadside historical attraction – the museum that the South Cariboo Historical Society had opened in 1953 – but it was not as arresting or as evocative as the old hotel, which to the motoring public had been a familiar, authentic, and tangible link to the days of the gold rush and Cariboo Wagon Road.[38]

The destruction of the Clinton Hotel did not spell its end as an attraction, however. Shortly after the fire, a franchisee of the Standard Oil Company purchased the lot and built a large, modern-looking service station with canopies, floodlights, and a glassed-in front. Hoping to exploit the familiarity of the site, he added a rustic cabin-style shelter around the back, which contained a scale diorama of the old hotel, historical photographs, a map of the Cariboo Wagon Road, and several items that had been rescued from the fire. A sign out front – "Here! See Model of BC's Oldest Hotel!" (with "model of" in smaller letters than the rest) – invited customers to visit. The BC head office for Standard Oil later lobbied the provincial government to erect a special commemorative marker at the site. For years, the Clinton Hotel lived on as a kind of a phantom venue, a place where, as the *Prince George Citizen* had put it in 1953, all that could be done was to "mark the spot." As during the interwar years, private businesses played an important role in cultivating history by the road along the Cariboo Highway.[39]

Ironically, the Clinton Hotel burned down one day after the '58 Centennial Stagecoach Run had passed through town and posed in front of it with an authentic gold-rush-era stagecoach. With rollicking Wild West pageantry, the Stagecoach Run was one of the many history-themed and highway related events that the provincial government organized to mark the hundredth anniversary of the mainland colony of British Columbia. Agencies of the state would play an increasingly active role in cultivating history by the road in the Interior during the late 1950s, treating museums, monuments, ghost towns, and other historical sites as both cultural and economic assets. The 1958 centennial celebrations played a pivotal role in that shift.

7

On the Road for the 1958 Centennial

The year 1958 marked the hundredth anniversary of the colony of British Columbia's foundation. In celebration, the Social Credit government decided to construct a major province-building initiative around the centennial, as a kind of cultural counterpart to the large-scale infrastructure projects that the state had built since the end of the war. It arranged for an elaborate series of centennial celebrations to be spread across the province. Many of these were closely tied to the highway network and drew on historical themes, symbols, and objects that would have been familiar to most motorists who had driven around the Interior since the late 1920s.

In her study of the various BC centennial celebrations between 1958 and 1971, Mia Reimers argues that the 1958 centennial's panoply of historically themed events aped the American Wild West popular culture of the 1950s. These events did occur during the second golden age of the Hollywood western and amidst a torrent of western-themed comic books, pulp novels, and television programs that were as popular in British Columbia as anywhere else in North America. However, many of the centennial's key themes and symbols had been used for decades in the Interior: stagecoaches, wagon roads, and gold rush prospectors were all part of a well-established tradition.[1] Aside from the state's considerable role in organizing and paying for most of the festivities, it was tone rather than any specific theme that distinguished them from earlier proceedings, such as the unveiling of the various cairns erected by the Historic Sites and Monuments Board of Canada (HSMBC) since the mid-1920s. As Reimers points out, Victoria strove to generate a party atmosphere around the centennial. It was supposed to be lively, fun, casual, and optimistic rather than serious-minded, didactic, and patriotic. Publicity materials regularly referred to it as "British Columbia's 100th birthday party."[2] As consumers and as citizens, British Columbians were encouraged to explore the new frontiers that modernized highways had thrown open since the end of the war, including the many amenities that the government had developed alongside them. Prior to 1958, these amenities consisted almost exclusively of "natural" provincial parks, but in the lead-up to the centennial Victoria turned its attention to history.

Preparing for the 1958 Centennial

In late 1955, the provincial government began preparing to celebrate the 1858 establishment of the colony of British Columbia, which had been precipitated by the Fraser Canyon gold rush. The Social Credit cabinet struck the British Columbia Centennial Committee to organize centennial events and appointed Deputy Provincial Secretary Lawrie Wallace, a former schoolteacher and principal from Vancouver Island, to serve as its chairman. The provincial secretary's office was primarily concerned with administrative and ceremonial matters, including the designation of official historical sites.[3] The government's early planning for 1958 was no doubt influenced by events elsewhere during the summer of 1955. Alberta and Saskatchewan had marked their golden jubilees of provincehood with historically themed events, the erection of roadside interpretive markers, and the promotion of tourist attractions such as Fort Battleford and Fort Macleod. In the western United States, the sesquicentennial of Lewis and Clark's explorations was honoured with monuments and museum exhibits, and western legislators and tourism promoters had lobbied for a stretch of interstate highway between Missouri and Washington State to be designated the Lewis and Clark Memorial Highway.[4] Enthusiastic public responses to these state-sponsored commemorative projects prompted the BC government to prepare its own show for 1958.

As an exercise in cultural province building, the 1958 centennial celebrations complemented the government's efforts at social and economic province building through investment in fixed infrastructure. They also functioned as a kind of pedagogical device for educating British Columbians about the nature of the province's regions, landscapes, and economy.

As a 1956 editorial in the *Vancouver Sun* argued, the centennial promised to "unite British Columbians as never before," and therefore its "first business should be to acquaint residents with their own all-too-strange province."[5] By valorizing frontier archetypes such as the solitary prospector, stagecoach driver, and pioneer rancher, it could address the sense of crisis that had arisen among many petty producers and small-business owners who were concerned about the pace, scale, and unevenness of postwar change. Representing these figures as timeless archetypes who were essential to the province's past (and by extension to its future) could soothe anxieties about the place of the "little guy" in a fast-changing economy. Furthermore, playing up historical themes that were related to exploration and travel, such as old trails and wagon roads, could encourage British Columbians to explore their province during the summer of 1958. In and of itself, this would be a shared experience that drew them together. Crucially, the festivities could also help raise the Social Credit government's profile. Unveilings and grand openings would occur in every corner of the province, and each would associate W.A.C. Bennett and his party with prosperity and progress.[6]

Much of the planning and execution for the centennial revolved around roads and interregional automobile travel. In fact, the highway network was the stage on which many of the most attention-grabbing events played out. The best example of this was the Centennial Stagecoach Run. This travelling spectacle (and spectacle of travel) involved an authentic gold-rush-era BC Express stagecoach being taken on a tour of the province, with stops at the gold-rush communities of Hope, Yale, Ashcroft, Clinton, and Quesnel on its way to Barkerville. Local organizing committees were invited to use the stagecoach's arrival to stage mock hold-ups, shoot-outs, and vigilante trials, which were meant to evoke the rough and ready Wild West atmosphere of the gold rush. Provincial highways played a central role in other events, including the Historic Caravan, the Magic Nugget and BC Centurama theatrical tours, the Changing of the Guard, and the Vintage Car Run. Other events that revolved around travel and transportation were the inaugural run of the Pacific Great Eastern (PGE) from Prince George to Dawson Creek; the Canadian National Railways Museum Train; the Fraser River Brigade; and Princess Margaret's whirlwind tour of the province, which entailed travelling by jet, seaplane, ship, train, automobile, and even stagecoach.[7] It was British Columbia's growing transportation network, and especially its network of modern highways, that made everything possible and tied it all together. Furthermore, it was the highway

The Centennial Stagecoach Run enters Hope. Note the palisaded "Fort Hope" set up for the occasion. British Columbia Centennial Committee, *The Report of the British Columbia Centennial Committee* (Victoria: The Committee, 1959).

network that allowed British Columbians and visitors to participate in the celebrations. The Centennial Committee, the BC Government Travel Bureau, and private tourism promoters distributed reams of publicity material urging residents to "see BC first" in 1958, while also inviting auto tourists from throughout western North America to swing by and catch the party.[8]

All these events were spectacular, but they were ultimately ephemeral: a clutch of touring shows that criss-crossed the province during 1958 before shutting down for good. Yet Victoria also took steps to develop a more lasting legacy. It distributed grants to nearly every community in the province, which were typically used to construct or repair community halls, cenotaphs, pioneer cemeteries, libraries, municipal parks, and recreation facilities. Several communities put their grant money toward the construction of a museum, including Ashcroft, Grand Forks, Kaslo, and Princeton. The provincial government also initiated several ambitious, large-scale, permanent developments, two of which were the Stop of Interest program and Barkerville Historic Provincial Park.

The Centennial Stagecoach Run pauses at the Clinton Hotel, which burned down the following day. British Columbia Centennial Committee, *The Report of the British Columbia Centennial Committee* (Victoria: The Committee, 1959).

The Stop of Interest Program

The planning for the 1958 centennial generated one of British Columbia's most focused and sustained discussions about history by the road. Archivists, planners, and historians were brought together to discuss practical aspects of conveying lessons about the past to the motoring public. They evaluated previous efforts and considered how the centennial could be used to improve the existing patchwork of marked historic sites. Their deliberations led to the Stop of Interest program, a venture that had widespread and long-term effects on how (and what) motorists in British Columbia learned (and continue to learn) about its past. The gold-on-green Stop of Interest markers that have been familiar to the motoring public for more than half a century have so far eluded historians' attention. Here they are shown to have been conceptualized and implemented as a pedagogical system organized around the provincial highway network.

One of the Centennial Committee's very first steps was to create the Historic Sites and Publications Subcommittee, which was dedicated to commemorating and popularizing the past.[9] Its chairman was provincial archivist Willard Ireland, a professionally trained historian who also edited the *British Columbia Historical Quarterly.* Deputy provincial secretary and Centennial Committee chairman Lawrie Wallace also sat in on several meetings. As a former teacher and the main liaison between the Centennial Committee and cabinet, he wanted to know what kinds of "lessons" any site-marking program would offer the public. The subcommittee had three citizen members, all of whom were white, middle-class experts from the Coast. Madge Hamilton had worked for many years as a researcher at the Provincial Archives and since retiring had advocated for the preservation of old buildings in Victoria. Bruce McKelvie was a retired newspaperman and popular historian who also lived on southern Vancouver Island. He had been a senior official of the Native Sons of British Columbia, a speechwriter for Conservative premier Simon Fraser Tolmie, and the first head of the Provincial Information Bureau, which was the precursor to the BC Government Travel Bureau. Dr. Walter N. Sage had recently retired as a professor in the Department of History at the University of British Columbia and had been the BC representative on the HSMBC since 1943, when Frederic Howay had passed away.[10]

The subcommittee also had two staff members. Wilson Duff was curator of anthropology at the Provincial Museum in Victoria and an expert on Northwest Coast Native groups. Duff had been working for several years to get legislation that would protect the province's archaeological sites.[11] Ches Lyons was in charge of special projects for the Parks Division, which to a large degree entailed driving around and looking for places to establish new parks. Having thoroughly surveyed the main highway corridors for the division, he was the province's leading expert on the cultivation of public roadside attractions. Lyons would play a key role on the subcommittee, including overseeing the implementation of its decisions on the ground.[12]

The subcommittee first met in September 1956 to decide on general policies for selecting and marking sites of special significance.[13] Ireland outlined the province-building nature of the planned centennial events. He also reported that several museums and local historical societies already intended to mark sites associated with the gold rushes of the late 1850s and the 1860s. For example, the Cariboo Historical Society expected to place more than twenty stone tablets and bronze plaques at former roadhouses and other stopping places along the route of the Cariboo Wagon Road.[14] To avoid duplication and to identify regions that were densely or sparsely marked, Ireland distributed copies of an inventory that listed existing site markers and monuments. It revealed that all three levels of government, as well as boosters, historical associations, service groups, and professional organizations, had set up monuments. It also showed that these were unevenly distributed, both geographically and in terms of the themes they covered. They were concentrated on the Coast, with relatively few in the hinterlands. Except for the Cariboo Highway corridor, most regions of the Interior were very thinly covered, and the northern half of the province had only three marked sites. Historical markers in the Interior were almost exclusively related to three themes: western exploration, the fur trade, and gold rushes. The inventory also showed that almost every monument, cairn, plaque, and other marker that had been erected in the BC Interior prior to 1956 was located beside or near an arterial road.[15]

The subcommittee discussed how the centennial could be used to improve this patchwork of marked sites. Every member asked whether funding would be set aside for the preservation and restoration of old buildings and other landscape features. McKelvie, for example, wanted to know if funds would be available to clean up neglected colonial-era cemeteries in Yale and Barkerville, and Indigenous cemeteries such as the ones visible from the highway in the Fraser Canyon. The three citizen members were eager to support these kinds of projects, expressing the anxiety among middle-class history enthusiasts about the disappearance of familiar landmarks. They agreed that old buildings and other tangible features helped evoke a sense of connection between the present and the past. "Looking at a sign is not as interesting as living history," was how Lyons summarized this argument. However, Ireland sought to dampen their enthusiasm. He explained that their mandate was limited to identifying and marking sites. Any project that involved purchase, preservation, restoration, or reconstruction was likely to be very expensive and would require consultation with professional architects and curators.[16]

With the mandate apparently settled, conversation turned to the appearance of the markers. Stone cairns and bronze plaques like the ones the HSMBC had used since the 1920s were deemed "inadequate" for the centennial: they were too serious and didactic. Wooden signboards, such as those used by Saskatchewan for its 1955 golden jubilee, were inexpensive and allowed a lot of information to be displayed but had proven vulnerable to vandalism and the elements. Lyons reported that recent US marking programs had found cast aluminum "absolutely the best" material for free-standing signs. Aluminum was durable and light, and could be made in various colours and finishes. Lyons proposed to use aluminum signs with a forest-green background, gold lettering, and a dappled, rustic-looking finish: gold and green were the official centennial colours, representing mining and forestry, the foundations of the province's past and present-day economies. The subcommittee agreed that the markers should be standardized, just like the traffic signs put up by the Department of Highways. They would also have to be conspicuous, with lettering big enough to be read by anyone sitting inside a parked car (for the benefit of the elderly and infirm, and for when the weather was inclement). Most markers would require a pair of pointer signs to give drivers advance warning that they were approaching a government-designated attraction.

The subcommittee devoted considerable attention to questions of marker location, both in terms of which regions and which kinds of places. The centennial celebrations were meant to be a province-building exercise, so ideally the unevenness of previous marking efforts would need to be corrected. "We should try to serve each of the principal areas of the province," Sage declared. "We must sell BC to the people of the province and to tourists, in that order." That meant the hinterlands were due for a large percentage of the new markers, which neatly meshed with the fact that the provincial economy was being driven by the regional boom in resource extraction and infrastructure building. Lyons recommended that the markers not be so abundant that the public would become indifferent to them. He reported that between fifty and a hundred was usually enough to "saturate a state."

It was unanimously agreed that the provincial highway network would be the skeleton around which the program would take shape, just as it had been with the provincial park system since the end of the war. As Lyons told the subcommittee, US programs had discovered that marked historic sites located alongside arterial roads received by far the most public attention:

> You want as many people as possible to see these [markers] adjacent to heavily travelled highways. For our purposes we have to stick to highways ... The new trend in the eastern states is to develop off the highway parking and bolster the desire to stop by putting in drinking fountains or picnic sites ... You must get [motorists] off the shoulder of the road. You must not antagonize the highway department.

Everyone on the subcommittee stressed the importance of tying the marking program to the road network. "We must mark things on the highways," said Sage. "You want them where they can be seen," McKelvie chimed in.

Lawrie Wallace emphasized that the sites "must be accessible." The history experts on the subcommittee had dedicated themselves to preserving archival records and writing about the past, but they all knew that the general public's understanding of BC history was inextricably tied to landscapes experienced by the road.

The subcommittee understood that harnessing the program to the highway network would result in constraints. Some significant sites were far from any major road. Others stood near a major highway but not close enough to be visible from it. Still others would be better off if they were hidden from the motoring public. Wilson Duff specifically recommended that pictographs, middens, burial caves, and other First Nations archaeological sites be left unmarked to protect them from pilfering. At first glance, this appears to be another case of what Mia Reimers identifies as the centennial's tendency not to erase the presence of First Nations totally, but instead to greatly reduce their role. However, the concealment was deemed necessary due to the small but growing number of unregulated hobbyist-collectors who were pillaging many unprotected archaeological sites during the 1950s. Duff's insistence that the markers not encourage or provide information to these amateurs proved both prudent and prescient in subsequent years, when they began printing their own guidebooks on convenient, road-accessible digging spots.[17] The subcommittee also anticipated problems with locations in which the road was congested, constricted, or otherwise dangerous to enter and exit. Ireland cited the winding section through the Fraser and Thompson Canyons as the kind of highway that would be difficult to adorn with new markers.

Restoration Reconsidered

The second meeting of the historic sites subcommittee took place two months after the first, in November 1956.[18] Willard Ireland found it impossible to draw up a budget without first clarifying the subcommittee's position on preservation and restoration projects. This topic required further discussion because many letters had been received from local and regional historical societies who requested the subcommittee's assistance to preserve or restore old buildings and other structures. Many of these requests came from the hinterlands. From the Cariboo came calls to help save the old townsite of Barkerville; history buffs in the east Kootenays wanted help with the ghost town at Fort Steele. Most such proposals involved the preservation or restoration of buildings, but several pursued the popular theme of frontier transportation. For example, isolated communities along Kootenay Lake and the Arrow Lakes asked for help to preserve the SS *Moyie* and SS *Minto,* sister Canadian Pacific Railway sternwheelers that had provided crucial transportation links but that had been made redundant by the completion of new mountain roads. The historical societies hoped to transform these steam vessels into distinctive attractions, following the lead of Penticton, where the SS *Sicamous* had been hauled ashore on a city beach in 1951 and turned into a museum.[19] The subcommittee judged many of these projects worthwhile and was disappointed that they fell outside its purview. Ireland reiterated that the subcommittee did not have funds for such ambitious projects. Expensive endeavours involving preservation or restoration would need to be treated as "special projects" and proposed directly to the Centennial Committee.

With the parameters of its work clarified, the subcommittee turned to getting its markers erected in time for the 1958 summer travel season. Ches Lyons had done more research on aluminum signs. One particularly appealing feature was the fact that they could be much larger than was possible with bronze: an impressive amount of text could be fitted onto a thirty-two- by forty-inch aluminum plaque, which would weigh only forty pounds. Walter Sage initially had reservations about using such a modern material, for as the long-time BC representative on the HSMBC he preferred the traditional stone cairn and bronze plaque, which had a certain gravitas. However, Sage was eventually brought around to the aluminum idea on the basis that the metal was an important product of British Columbia, what with the development of a new smelter at Kitimat. Lyons recommended that the subcommittee look beyond 1958 to a moment when the provincial government would establish an agency with permanent responsibility for marking, interpreting, preserving, and promoting historic sites. As he noted, the matrix that would need to be designed and cast to produce the standardized centennial markers could be used for many years – even decades – if care were taken to ensure that its form was not too specific to the year 1958.

Having agreed on the general form of the markers, the subcommittee contemplated the crucial question of their placement. McKelvie and Sage both reiterated the need for careful distribution. "Victoria and Vancouver are hogging too much," argued Sage, whereas "nobody pays attention to Vanderhoof." McKelvie concurred and suggested that residents of the hinterlands tended to "feel very neglected" by politicians and bureaucrats based on the Coast. The subcommittee agreed on the importance of prioritizing the hinterlands, which was where the resource boom was under way, where anxiety about postwar modernization was greatest, and where Social Credit's power base was located. Having studied how to erect the markers, Lyons suggested the cheapest, most efficient way – assigning the task to a mobile Parks Division crew, which would handle the installation of markers, pointer signs, picnic tables, and pit toilets. He reported that the Department of Highways was enthusiastic about the project and had promised its co-operation, but he warned that even with support from Highways, putting up certain markers might prove impossible. Ultimately, traffic conditions and the structure of the road would determine which sites were feasible. The meeting concluded with a suggestion by Ches Lyons that the signs highlight what he called "points of interest." Liking the name "point of interest," the subcommittee approved his idea. It was neither too solemn nor too specific in the sense of identifying a precise site. Thus, a marker could speak to the general history of a community, district, or entire region. The phrase also allowed the program to extend beyond historical events and personalities to encompass noteworthy scenic, natural, and even industrial features. Over the following eighteen months, "points of interest" evolved into "Stops of Interest," reflecting how closely the program was tied to the highway network and the viewing habits of the motoring public.

Parallel Marking Committees

After its first two meetings, the historic sites subcommittee lapsed into dormancy for more than a year. During the interval, Ches Lyons drove throughout the province, investigating possible locations for historical markers and other points of interest. With Willard Ireland's approval, Lyons also organized a technical committee comprised of experts from government agencies including the Parks Branch, Forest Service, Provincial Museum and Archives, and Departments of Mines and Highways. Its goal was to assemble a list of existing and potential roadside pullouts that could feasibly accommodate Stop of Interest signs.

Lyons and Ireland sidelined the historic sites subcommittee because its citizen members knew little about highway planning, traffic engineering, right-of-way regulations, or the management of landscape aesthetics. Most of the bureaucrats on the technical committee had no background in researching or promoting history, but they did have practical experience in co-ordinating roadside development. Lyons later explained the genesis of the technical committee in a report on the marking program:

> In attempting to fit theoretical plans to conditions as found in the field it was apparent that certain governing factors existed. Few historic sites such as a building, campground, trail, etc. occur adjacent to the highway system. If they do, it often is impossible to provide a suitable parking area ... In general we are forced to choose certain viewpoints already constructed and adapt the text theme to what can be seen.[20]

Dozens of signs needed to be cast, delivered, and set up in time for the 1958 summer vacation. When the historic sites subcommittee reconvened in February 1958, Lyons urged it to approve the shape, finish, and colours of the markers as soon as possible.[21] However, the citizen members objected to being rushed. They complained that they were being treated as a rubber stamp, with the technical committee having effectively usurped control over the project, making important decisions about locations and topics and even proposing the wording of some markers. Walter Sage was the most vocal in his displeasure, criticizing the "inconsistent" and "corny" tone of several proposed inscriptions. "I have not seen anything here that would get past the Historic Sites Board," he huffed. "It is amateurish."[22]

Anthropologist Wilson Duff, who sat on both the historic sites subcommittee and the technical committee, tried to assuage Sage's concerns. He reminded the subcommittee that the centennial was meant to be colourful, playful, and imbued with a sense of optimism. In the midst of an economic boom, the Stop of Interest program would teach all British Columbians about their province, its past, and its landscapes. It was not intended to fixate on obscure dates or dull details about "great men." Duff also defended the draft inscriptions that Lyons had submitted, arguing that he was "always going for the public appeal" because he recognized that their audience would be the motoring public, most of whom learned about history from reading popular literature, visiting museums, and observing landscapes, rather than from dense academic texts or memorizing details inscribed on solemn monuments. Lyons and Duff asserted that adopting a casual style akin to a travelogue or guidebook would ultimately make the Stop of Interest markers more effective. Some could take a heroic, romantic, or tragic tone. Others could be wry, whimsical, or humorous. Some could deal with success and progress; others could focus on failure or disaster. Some would cite impressive and precise figures about the value

Stop of Interest marker on the outskirts of Yale. Department of Recreation and Conservation photograph. James K. Nesbitt, *Historic Sites of British Columbia* (Vancouver: Home Oil Distributors, 1962).

of gold pulled from a creekbed; others would invoke mythical creatures, such as Ogopogo, the serpent-like denizen of Okanagan Lake whom tourism promoters and the board of trade in Kelowna had adopted as a municipal mascot. The key concern was that the inscriptions not be predictable or boring. Mixing up their tone and keeping their messages relatively simple would encourage all kinds of people to stop and look at them, and would help generate memorable experiences of history by the road.

In the end, the citizen members of the subcommittee resigned themselves to the fact that because roads and traffic would play such an important structuring role in the program, the technical committee was in the driver's seat. Their third meeting ended with a discussion of the inscriptions for the first ten signs. Members voted on their preferences and suggested minor revisions. There were a few differences of opinion about the most significant person or event to commemorate at certain stopping places. Mostly, there were questions about the geographic distribution of signs. Did the Dewdney Trail deserve to be marked in two places along the southern transprovincial highway corridor: in both Manning Park and the city of Trail? Should so many markers be clustered in the Fraser Canyon and

Stop of Interest marker at roadside pullout above Osoyoos on the southern trans-provincial highway. The smaller plaque mounted beneath the main one states that it was erected as part of the 1958 centennial celebrations. G. Morris Taylor photograph. Author's collection.

along the Hope-Princeton Highway? "You must mention Kelowna," insisted Centennial Committee chairman Lawrie Wallace, doubtless wanting to ensure that W.A.C. Bennett viewed the program favourably.

The two committees worked through the spring of 1958 to have markers in place for the summer.[23] Their number was scaled back to thirty-eight, and erecting even that many proved a complicated process because not every pullout was ideally suited to accommodate them. The pullout on the outskirts of Yale was found to be located just a few hundred yards from the cairn that the HSMBC had unveiled in 1925. Field staff wondered whether it was appropriate to have the two monuments so close together, especially as they both commemorated Yale as the southern terminus of the Cariboo Wagon Road. At Ashcroft Manor, concerns were raised that having cars enter and exit the flow of traffic to view the proposed marker would cause a serious hazard. In the Cariboo, with its lack of long sightlines, trees had to be removed at most Stop of Interest pullouts to improve the view. They were also cut down on the Westbank Indian Reserve to provide a better view of Kelowna. At another pullout overlooking Okanagan Lake, the view was found to be marred by utility poles and telephone lines. An otherwise desirable vantage point overlooking Shuswap Lake was plagued by illegal dumping.[24]

By May 1958, the two committees were scrambling to ensure that every major highway corridor received a fair share of Stop of Interest markers. The main highways through the Kootenays and on Vancouver Island were deemed to need more, as was the Okanagan, which was Premier Bennett's riding. A two-hundred-mile gap along the Cariboo Highway between Ashcroft and Quesnel was considered unacceptable (even though there was the HSMBC cairn at Alexandria), so a marker was put up near the hamlet of Soda Creek to commemorate the sternwheeler steamboats that had once plied the Fraser River upstream from that point. Thirty of the thirty-eight signs erected in 1958 were in the Interior, twenty-five of which addressed the three historical themes that had been most closely associated with the Interior since the mid-1920s: exploration, the fur trade, and gold rushes. Considerable attention was also paid to resource extraction and transportation. Ten of the markers in the Interior were directly related to mining, ranching, and pioneer farms, whereas twelve involved trails, wagon roads, steamboats, roadhouses, and other transportation and infrastructure topics. Women, workers, and First Nations people were given short shrift, but so were premiers and other politicians.

The Stops of Interest proved enormously popular with the public, leading both the Centennial Committee and the Parks Branch to pronounce the program a great success. More signs would be raised in the following years, particularly during the lead-up to the 1966, 1967, and 1971 centennials. Ninety-one had been installed by the end of 1966, when the Parks Branch published a brochure that invited motorists to "Stop, Look, and Learn" whenever they spotted one. As a system, the Stops of Interest remained closely tied to the highway network, just as their name suggested they must be.[25] Individually and collectively, they probably did nothing to draw auto tourists to British Columbia. Yet on a banal level, they subtly shaped innumerable motorists' experiences of history by the road in the BC Interior. People who would never delve into an academic treatise or even a popular work about the past might pause at a Stop of Interest and remember what they read, for the surrounding landscape served as a powerful mnemonic device, linking an easily digestible idea about the past to a particular scene. Any driver who had more than a passing interest in BC history was likely to connect the markers and their limited repertoire of themes with roadside relics, museums, other monuments, and the handful of large-scale historical tourist attractions that began to appear in the Interior during the late 1950s. The first of these was Barkerville Historic Provincial Park.

Calls to Restore Barkerville

The 1958 centennial inspired the BC government to create a major historical tourist attraction in the old Cariboo goldfields, an endeavour in which the Parks Branch played a central role. Since 1945, it had proven itself to be the government agency with expertise in developing scenic, natural, and recreational attractions, and also in managing landscape aesthetics. It was therefore no surprise that the government chose the Parks Branch to handle the Barkerville project, tasking it with imposing and maintaining an appealing old-timey aesthetic that evoked the atmosphere of the colonial gold rush.

For years, Cariboo boosters, business groups, tourism promoters, and history enthusiasts had been pressuring Victoria to preserve and develop Barkerville. During the mid-1950s, the BC Historical Association, the Cariboo Historical Society, the Wells-Barkerville Historical Society, Quesnel's village commissioners, the Anglican Diocese of the Cariboo, the Chinese Freemasons, and the Wells and District Board of Trade had all lobbied the Province to take action.[26] Many BC newspapers printed articles, editorials, and photo features that reinforced these calls for preservation. *Northwest Digest* was an enthusiastic and consistent supporter of the project. Its January 1958 issue carried a guest editorial titled "Barkerville: Is It Worth Preserving?" in which journalist Stan Rough described a family trip to Barkerville the previous summer. Rough identified St. Saviour's Anglican Church, the private museum in the Kelly Hotel, and the old cemetery as being of "special interest" to visitors. He also described meeting several old-timers who were "veritable encyclopedias" of local history. Nevertheless, he concluded that a "visit to Barkerville today is rather a disappointment":

> Barkerville at the present time is a nondescript collection of old buildings that a fire could wipe out in a few hours ... There are no facilities for tourists to eat or stay overnight. The road to the old [Richfield] courthouse where Judge Begbie held court is almost overgrown [and] the building is now just a windowless frame. Today Barkerville tells little of its former bustling days. Second growth has covered up the surrounding hillsides and underbrush has partly covered the churned-up gravel on the floor of the narrow valley itself.[27]

"Why save Barkerville with its weather beaten church, windowless houses, and false-front stores?" Rough asked rhetorically. "Why not leave

Barkerville in the late 1950s. University of Victoria Archives, Chester P. Lyons fonds.

Barkerville to burn down some day or its buildings to collapse one by one under the weight of winter snows?" In addressing these questions, he invoked what had been a common refrain among scholarly and popular historians since the 1920s: the Cariboo gold rush was British Columbia's foundational event, and thus the old ghost town must be saved because it embodied "the spirit of the pioneers who played so vital a role in opening so majestic a province."[28] Rough's lament echoed F.W. Lindsay's 1951 editorial that had criticized the future-mindedness of the postwar boom. By embracing the new and failing to attend to the old – including places such as Barkerville – residents of the northern Interior were neglecting not only their patrimony but also a potential economic asset. There had to be a practical, constructive use for a ghost town seemingly bypassed by modernity, some way to salvage value from its weathered structures. Simply allowing it to rot, burn, or collapse would be wasteful, for its aura of authenticity clearly had potential to draw tourists from within British Columbia and farther afield.

It seemed that only a few ingredients were needed to transform Barkerville into a significant tourist attraction. The two most important were the preservation of its oldest, most distinctive buildings and the modernization of the road from Quesnel. The road was closely intertwined with both auto tourism and truck logging in the north Cariboo during the mid- and late 1950s. District boosters saw it as imperative to get both kinds of traffic into Wells and Barkerville because production at the Cariboo Gold Quartz mine was rapidly tailing off, and virtually all the other mines in the district had shut down. Logging activity was slowly picking up, and there were rumours that a planer mill might be built at Wells, but the growth of the forest industry was hobbled by the primitive condition of the road. Loggers, mill owners, and merchants from the north Cariboo petitioned Victoria to improve the road so that it could accommodate heavy multi-axle logging trucks; they wanted it treated as an arterial highway, even though it came to a dead end at Barkerville. The Wells Board of Trade supported these efforts and pointed out that luring more auto tourists to Barkerville would strengthen the case for upgrading the road while at the same time securing customers for the handful of businesses that remained in the goldfields.[29]

Cariboo MLA Ralph Chetwynd was an important ally in the campaign to preserve and promote Barkerville. A former publicity man for the PGE, Chetwynd was the Social Credit minister for trade and railways. In a February 1956 speech to the Legislature, he suggested that the Province allocate $10,000 to help preserve the crumbling townsite.[30] The Centennial Committee subsequently recommended that Victoria undertake a special project to preserve and interpret Barkerville, and senior Parks Branch officials threw their support behind this idea.[31] Chetwynd died before the scheme advanced very far, but Barkerville's cause was picked up by his colleague Ray Williston, MLA for Prince George. As minister of lands and forests, Williston was no doubt aware that forestry interests in the north Cariboo wanted the Quesnel-Barkerville road upgraded to accommodate heavy logging trucks. He also sat on the Centennial Committee. On his recommendation, Premier Bennett approved a project that would develop Barkerville into a major historical tourist attraction. The timing was propitious, for the Cariboo Gold Quartz mine in Wells stopped production on its main shaft beneath Cow Mountain in 1958.[32]

Planning Barkerville as a Tourist Attraction

The Historic Sites and Publications Subcommittee was not invited to participate in the Barkerville project. Experts on British Columbia's past were not required for this undertaking – what the government needed were experts in engineering, architectural preservation, and the management of landscape aesthetics. The provincial secretary's office placed a reserve over the townsite as a preliminary step toward its purchase and long-term "restoration." The Parks Branch was then given responsibility for the planning and on-site work; it was widely expected that the branch would one day be assigned to manage the province's most significant and accessible designated historic sites. Ches Lyons was sent to investigate Barkerville's development prospects in June 1958, accompanied by Dennis Podmore, an expert on property acquisition. Over the summer of 1958, Lyons and Podmore drew up an ambitious three-stage plan for turning Barkerville into a regional attraction. The first stage was to make it safe for and appealing to visitors. The second was to acquire and stabilize its remaining gold-rush-era buildings, which would be accomplished in two or three years. The third stage, expected to span a decade or more, was to return the townsite to its appearance during the 1870s, after the fire of 1868 had destroyed most of the original town. This plan was in keeping with the wider Canadian enthusiasm for the immersive "pioneer village" attractions that Alan Gordon documents for the 1950s and 1960s.[33] It was also in keeping with the broader Fordist impulse to steer regional economic development through state investment in infrastructure.

The Parks Branch initiated a major clean-up of Barkerville.[34] "Years of neglect and indifference had resulted in the town becoming littered with unsightly debris," Lyons reported. "This atmosphere of disrepair stimulated vandalism and enhanced the general public belief that anything which could be picked up was available for the taking." Residents had long dumped their garbage at the edge of Williams Creek so that it would be washed away by spring freshets. Campers had set up their own unofficial campsites at the outskirts of town, leaving behind litter and unsanitary latrines. The water system for the fire hydrants had fallen into disrepair, as had the power line from Wells. Lyons complained that the utility poles erected in the 1930s were "most unsightly" and recommended their removal. Barkerville had just one cafe and not a single public toilet. The cemetery was badly overgrown, with many of its old headboards almost illegible.

"Emergency measures" undertaken in 1958 included clearing a large parking lot at the lower end of town, building a rudimentary ten-unit campground, and installing five pit toilets. The Forest Service upgraded the firefighting equipment of the Wells Volunteer Fire Brigade, thereby giving Barkerville's old wooden buildings better protection against their traditional nemesis. Brush and weeds were cleared from overgrown alleyways, revealing artifacts that had been protected from souvenir hunters by a luxuriant growth of stinging nettles. Brush was also removed from

Barkerville residents collecting artifacts for donation to the Parks Branch, 1958. University of Victoria Archives, Chester P. Lyons fonds.

the cemetery, and several badly weathered headboards were temporarily removed for repair. The Parks Branch erected a series of plywood signs to identify buildings and other features that were associated with the 1860s gold rush. Although the signs were seen solely as a short-term fix, they were carefully designed to "enhance the pioneer atmosphere."

Parks Branch staff continued this "systematic" clean-up campaign through the 1958 summer travel season and into the fall. Lyons reported that giving the town a "cared for look" reduced the incidence of vandalism and trespassing. It also made for "very good public relations" with the few remaining residents, impressing on them the high cultural value that the government placed on the town. Parks staff made a point of consulting with local history enthusiasts, property owners, and old-timers, including Bill Hong, Fred Ludditt, and the Kelly, Wendle, and Tregillus families. This helped bring in more artifacts and information that could be used in the restoration. It also helped pave the way for an amicable program of property acquisition.

Ches Lyons's development plan called for Barkerville to be divided into three zones. The historic upper town, where most of the oldest buildings stood, would be preserved and gradually made to look the way it had during the 1870s. The lower section, which contained mostly newer structures, would be cleared and dedicated to visitor facilities such as parking and camping. An administration area, with workshops, office, and eventu-

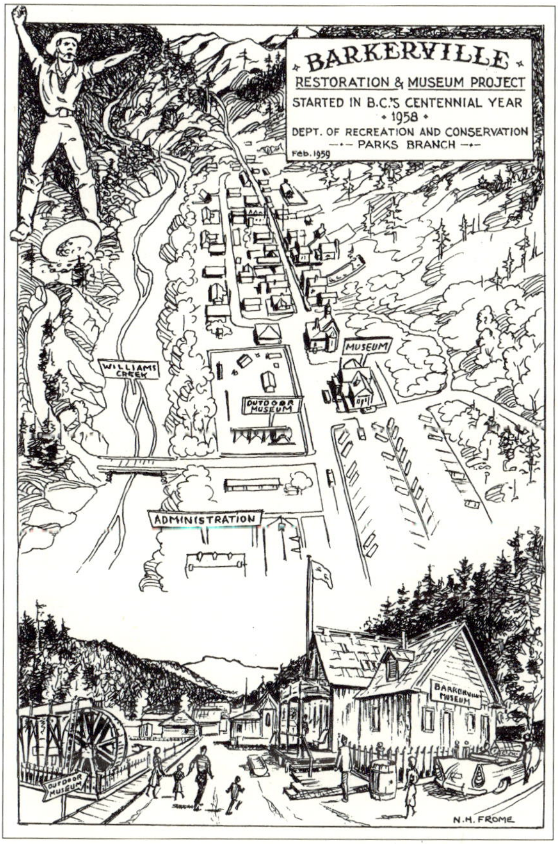

Parks Branch plan for development at Barkerville, 1959.

ally an indoor interpretative centre, would separate these two zones. Isolating the new visitor services from the oldest section of town was seen as vitally important because the sight of cars and camping facilities would detract from the desired atmosphere.[35] In order to properly tell visitors "the Barkerville story," Ches Lyons also recommended that the government preserve historic landscape features located beyond the immediate vicinity of the townsite. He identified Cottonwood House, eighteen miles east of Quesnel, and the remnants of Stanley, seven miles west of Wells, as sites that could feasibly be made into satellites of the main attraction at Barkerville. The Richfield courthouse, one mile up Williams Creek, was particularly worthy of protection. It had captured visitors' imagination for decades, and there had been several proposals to preserve it or turn it into some kind of museum.[36] By getting control of these Barkerville satellites and preserving their atmosphere of bygone days, the Parks Branch could arrange for the motoring public to travel a veritable corridor of historical features from the moment they turned off the main highway at Quesnel. Thus, driving the Quesnel-Barkerville road would evoke journeying along the old Cariboo Wagon Road. For most people, the detritus left over from the 1930s mining boom was indistinguishable from that of the 1860s: ditches and culverts; churned-up creeks; collapsing cabins; the mouldering remnants of old flumes and trestles; heaps of tailings partially grown over with brush. The series of attractions would help make the 110-mile round trip to Barkerville less daunting. Given all the work that Lyons had undertaken with roadside attractions in provincial parks, as well as with the Stop of Interest program, it is no surprise that he recognized the importance of treating the road to Barkerville as an experiential corridor.

Barkerville Historic Park

Publicity about the government's plans for Barkerville was intentionally minimized during the summer of 1958 to make property acquisition easier. Nevertheless, guest registers kept in St. Saviour's Church and the museum in the Kelly Hotel saloon show that about five thousand sightseers visited Barkerville that summer. Most were British Columbians: approximately a third came from the northern Interior and another third from the Coast. The small, rudimentary campground that Parks Branch staff had set up on the lower edge of town was full every night and usually beyond capacity on weekends. As experience in provincial parks such as Manning had repeatedly shown since 1945, such heavy use was a strong indicator that additional facilities would soon be required.

Accorded Class A status, Barkerville Historic Provincial Park was established in January 1959. Ranger Les Cook, who had previously worked in isolated Wells Gray Provincial Park and on the Stop of Interest program, was appointed its first superintendent. Shortly after, Deputy Provincial Secretary Lawrie Wallace formed the Barkerville Restoration Advisory Committee (BRAC) as an arm's-length government agency that would co-ordinate the restoration program between cabinet, the Parks Branch, other government departments, and various Cariboo business and historical organizations.[37] BRAC also deliberated on the park's larger role in the economy of the northern Interior. At one of its first meetings, it passed a motion stating that if Barkerville were to fulfill its potential, "it would be desirable to have the road [from Quesnel] hard-surfaced to make the

Barkerville Historic Provincial Park, 1961. Malcolm Faviell photograph. Courtesy of Mark Faviell.

drive an attractive one." BRAC generally stayed in the background, working to get good publicity and substantial budget allocations for the park, while allowing the Parks Branch considerable leeway in planning and day-to-day management.[38]

The provincial government spent $35,000 acquiring property at Barkerville in 1958 and 1959. Another $13,500 went to the purchase of Cottonwood Ranch on the Quesnel-Barkerville road, which included the 1864 roadhouse.[39] Attendance at Barkerville leapt from five thousand in 1958 to ten thousand in 1959 and then to twenty-five thousand in 1961, with visitation spurred by coverage in magazines such as *Northwest Digest* and *Beautiful British Columbia,* the lavishly illustrated full-colour quarterly that the provincial government started publishing in 1959.[40] Barkerville's appearance changed little in 1959 and 1960. About twenty-five old-timers remained in town, and its narrow main street was still lined with utility wires and parked automobiles. Most of the Parks Branch's work happened out of view, with staff and contractors repairing the water system and the roofs and foundations of many old buildings. A handful of relatively intact structures had displays of artifacts and mannequins set up in their front rooms so that visitors could peer through the windows and see tableaux of the 1870s.

The pace of development picked up in 1961, when the Parks Branch began preparing for a large influx of visitors during the summer of 1962, which would mark the centennial of the discovery of gold on Williams Creek. In the administration zone, work got under way on a new interpretation centre that would replace the museum in the Kelly Hotel saloon. A washroom building with running water and flush toilets was built beside the main parking lot. In the upper town, several buildings were jacked up and shifted to empty lots, where they better fit the restoration plan. The Parks Branch experimented with trucking abandoned buildings in from distant ghost towns such as Quesnel Forks, but this proved impractical due to the long distance and rough roads involved. Trees and brush were cleared from around the Richfield courthouse, and repairs were made to its roof and foundation.[41] There was still nowhere in Barkerville for visitors to purchase food or drinks, and it lacked a venue for performances, so the Parks Branch decided to solve these problems by constructing replicas of several disappeared edifices. An empty lot across from St. Saviour's Church was used to build the Wake-Up-Jake Saloon Café, where a concessionaire would sell refreshments and light meals. A few doors farther up the street, major renovations and additions were made to the 1930s-era community hall so that it could become a "new" Theatre Royal – an eminently suitable scheme, as the hall occupied the site of the original theatre. Parks Branch staff also built a replica of a Cornish pump waterwheel beside Williams Creek to demonstrate gold mining techniques to visitors.[42]

Special government funding for the Barkerville centennial allowed the branch to start making the park's historic zone look as it had during the 1870s. The goal was to have visitors feel as if they were stepping back in time when they entered the townsite, so utility lines were pulled down and the poles removed, and efforts were made to eliminate the presence of automobiles (as discussed below). In the lower town, several squatters' cabins built during the interwar years were loaded onto sledges and skidded away with a caterpillar tractor during the winter of 1961–62, and the remaining buildings were demolished to make way for more parking lots and campsites. By the spring of 1962, most traces of the 1930s-era lower town had been erased. Road access to the park from Wells was reorganized, with the result that motorists who entered Barkerville no longer passed the HSMBC cairn that had been placed beside the original road in 1929. The cairn was cut off from traffic, isolated on the hillside above the new parking lots. Preparations for Barkerville's centennial year extended beyond the boundaries of the park. Parks Branch staff collaborated with the Wells Volunteer Fire Brigade to demolish a number of abandoned, eyesore cabins and shacks that were visible along the Quesnel-Barkerville road.[43] Fifty-five miles west of the park, a large, eye-catching sign was put up at the point where the road split off from the main Cariboo Highway. It showed a prospector discovering gold in his pan amidst a mountain setting, and it listed amenities available at the end of the road, such as campgrounds and the hotels and cafes in Wells. Farther afield, Parks Branch staff erected more than a dozen "Cariboo Wagon Road" signs along the highway between Yale and Quesnel, emblazoned with the familiar old-timey wagon wheel motif. These were positioned near prominent historical landmarks and places where motorists could still discern traces of the famous wagon road.[44]

Boards of trade in Wells and Quesnel petitioned the premier and senior cabinet ministers to improve the Quesnel-Barkerville road in the lead-up to the 1962 centennial. Though it was now surfaced with gravel for its entire length, it still had many rough, winding, and narrow sections, and they pointed to the danger of having pleasure travellers share such a road with loaded logging trucks. Boosters stated that many tourists complained about the road, as well as the lack of a loop trip option, and many were said to have turned back for Quesnel before reaching Barkerville.[45] The petitioners warned that the poor condition of the road would "greatly color the impression of our province gained by visitors." One BC resident who complimented the government for its restoration work at Barkerville added a critical comment about the road: "It is the worst stretch for dust that I encountered anywhere in a wide circuit of the province this summer. I am reliably told that U.S. visitors will not drive over it." He predicted that it would be "the greatest hindrance" to the success of Barkerville Park, a veritable Achilles heel.[46]

Boosters and tourism promoters had good reason to worry about how local roads would influence the Cariboo's reputation. In May 1961, the *Vancouver Sun* printed a very unflattering article by columnist Jack Scott about a trip that he and cartoonist Len Norris had recently taken along the Cariboo Highway. Scott declared himself "deeply disturbed" by the changes that had occurred along the highway corridor since the end of the war. He deplored the road as "an unholy mess ... a route on which stretches of unparalleled beauty are punctuated by clots of ugly, helter skelter slums." The famous Clinton Hotel was gone, as were many other gold-rush-era roadhouses that Scott had become familiar with when travelling through the region during the interwar years. He complained that the surviving relics of the old days were now "fatally embraced in the new, the cheap, the temporary":

> In their place is a jumble of jerry-built motels and drive-in burger joints and auto wreckers who advertise their wares with the piled-up corpses of broken cars and haphazard shacks and trailers and cheerless coffee shops loud with rock and roll, and garages, banks, and supermarkets built without a thought to complementing terrain or landscape, and bleak hotels with loud, grim beer parlors and lumber yards and piles of tires and the junk of rusted machinery apparently calculatingly placed to be on exhibit and a mass of crude signs.[47]

Such criticism grabbed the attention of Cariboo residents who recognized the economic importance of tourism and the experiences of history (and nature) by the road. Newspapers throughout the northern Interior called for Victoria to implement zoning restrictions that would provide some control over roadside development, thereby fending off eyesores and maintaining an uncluttered old-timey or naturalistic aesthetic.[48] The provincial government did add one significant natural attraction to the north Cariboo in the lead-up to Barkerville's 1962 centennial. In the fall of 1961, it established Bowron Lake Provincial Park, the first large park in the Cariboo. Like Barkerville, it was accessible only from the Quesnel-Barkerville road, but it promised to increase tourist and recreational traffic in the district during the summer months.

Barkerville's 1962 centennial drew on the same themes as the 1958 centennial celebrations, including rugged individualism, frontier transportation, and the struggle to wrest resource wealth from an isolated, seemingly hostile environment. A few significant changes were made to the appearance of the townsite, but the most dramatic was not structural. Instead, it was the Parks Branch decision to make Barkerville into a "living museum" by adding actors who wore period costume and roamed the streets and buildings, performing as residents of the 1870s. The Parks Branch was swept up in what Alan Gordon identifies as a national trend during the 1950s and 1960s, whereby living museums were established as major cultural-historical attractions that were differentiated from each other as much by their use of regional iconography as by the history they claimed to portray. Actors added bustle to static buildings and fixed displays. Like the Stop of Interest markers, history as presented at Barkerville was colourful and fun rather than instructional and detail-oriented.[49] Entry to the old town remained free, but visitors could pay a small fee to watch a period costume song-and-dance performance at the replica Theatre Royal, complete with a troupe of high-kicking hurdy-gurdy girls. Most observers concluded that the actors – whose performances did not strive for authenticity but were not permitted to spoof or caricature Barkervillians of the 1870s – helped bring history to life and did not detract from the site.[50] Premier Bennett attended Barkerville in August 1962 to open its new indoor interpretive centre. From the government's perspective, the timing for this celebration of resource-based boom-town history could not have been better, for earlier that summer it had announced that Canadian Forest Products and the British Reed Paper Group were proceeding with plans to build the Interior's first pulp mill at Prince George.[51]

Barkerville was an enormously popular tourist destination in 1962. It outdrew the Provincial Museum in downtown Victoria, with attendance more than quadrupling to 107,000. Its campgrounds, parking lots, and other visitor facilities were overflowing throughout the summer, as were private campgrounds, autocourts, motels, and diners in Wells and Quesnel. Coast media outlets were full of praise for the park. The *Vancouver Province* attributed its "tremendous feeling of atmosphere" to the recently implemented prohibition on automobiles in the old town and to the Parks Branch's myriad other efforts to "keep all signs of modernity out of sight." *Vancouver Sun* columnist Jack Scott, who in 1961 had bemoaned the loss of historical features along the Cariboo Highway, reported that Barkerville "exudes the authentic atmosphere of the dramatic events that transpired here ... You step from your car directly into the past. It is as ageless as the silent mountains that rim the valley."[52] The few criticisms of Barkerville inevitably revolved around the Quesnel-Barkerville road rather than the park itself. Visitors disliked returning to Quesnel by the same route they had come in on. The *Sun* complained about "the choking dust cloud that greets the motorist, thoroughly spoiled by the asphalt ribbon of the Cariboo Highway, when he hits the first leg of the [road] eastward from Quesnel." Clearly, tourists who made the journey to Barkerville were inspired to learn about the Cariboo Wagon Road, but they had no wish to experience nineteenth-century travel conditions for themselves.[53]

Clearing Barkerville's Main Street

During the early and mid-1960s, one of the biggest challenges to making Barkerville Park look, sound, and feel authentic was the presence of automobiles in the historic townsite. This was particularly true along its narrow main street, which was lined by its oldest and most famous buildings. Visitors found it difficult to imagine themselves stepping back in time to the 1870s when cars and trucks were parked up and down the street, and

Barkerville, 1961, showing power lines and automobiles. Malcolm Faviell photograph. Courtesy of Mark Faviell.

in front of the picturesque St. Saviour's Church and the Masonic Hall. The main street remained a public right-of-way, leading up Williams Creek to the site of Richfield and dozens of mineral claims. Most of these claims had been dormant for years, and the road above town was practically overgrown in spots. However, the establishment of the park had not extinguished these mineral claims – in fact, several dozen were grandfathered inside it. Nor had it extinguished miners and prospectors' right of access to the area above town. The road that traversed the townsite and led up to Richfield remained a public right-of-way after 1959.

Before Barkerville became a provincial park, the Department of Mines had expressed concern about how its change in status would affect prospecting and mining operations in the surrounding hills, particularly if the price of gold were to rise in future. It worried that Parks Branch staff might try to prevent the use of Barkerville's main street by vehicles that needed access to claims in the hills above town. "Hauling on the roads [of Barkerville] must not be denied," a senior Mines official insisted in a November 1958 memo. He also optimistically suggested that mining in the vicinity of the new park could heighten, rather than disrupt, the atmosphere that the Parks Branch hoped to cultivate: "Current mining activities as items of tourist interest should be welcomed, and in no way hampered through the presence of the park, for they are of as great interest value as the relics of the past."[54]

From 1958 to 1961, the Parks Branch carefully avoided disputes with prospectors and the Department of Mines over the use of public rights-of-way inside Barkerville Park. There were still a few dozen old-timers living in the townsite, some of whom owned cars and pickups, so this go-easy policy was practical for more than one reason. Although tourists and sightseers were permitted to drive up and down the main street, they were strongly encouraged to leave their cars in the parking lot and proceed on foot. Many who did so complained about the incongruous presence of automobiles and other modern features such as power lines. One who otherwise showered compliments on Barkerville recommended that parking be banned on its main street. "This is for the benefit of the shutterbug," he explained. "It so spoils our pictures of these old buildings to see a row of new cars along the street."[55] These kinds of comments lent support to the Parks Branch's belief that automobiles should be kept out of the townsite.

It was during the lead-up to Barkerville's 1962 centennial that conflict broke out between the Parks Branch and local miners, who were supported by the Department of Mines. The initial flashpoint was the mile-long road that led from Barkerville to Richfield. In 1960, the minister of recreation and conservation had requested that the boundaries of Barkerville Park be extended to encompass the Richfield courthouse. However, it was unclear whether the road that linked the townsite and the courthouse could legally be made part of the park. It was a remnant of the old Cariboo Wagon Road and thus something of a historical artifact in and of itself, but it was also a public right-of-way and officially classified as a mining road by the Department of Highways. As a result, the courthouse was made a separate provincial park – one of the smallest in British Columbia – until the problem of connecting it with Barkerville Park could be resolved. The Parks Branch had several reasons for wanting to obtain control over the road. One was safety. Many visitors walked up to Richfield, and though vehicle traffic was light the potential for accidents remained a concern. Pedestrian and vehicular traffic were thought to mix poorly on the road due to its narrowness, lack of verges, and short sightlines.[56] A second reason involved the aesthetics of commerce. Controlling the road would let the branch restrict the activities of two miners whose claims bordered on the right-of-way and who had started private gold panning businesses, inviting visitors to try their hand at panning in a trough full of Williams Creek gravel in exchange for a small fee.[57] The third reason was to facilitate a stagecoach service between Barkerville and Richfield. Stagecoach mania remained strong in British Columbia after the 1958 centennial, and in the summer of 1961 the Parks Branch began running a replica four-horse, twelve-passenger BX stagecoach in the park. Passengers were driven up and down the main street and over to the old cemetery, but the distances were fairly short. The branch wanted to offer longer rides during the 1962 centennial year. It particularly wanted the option of taking visitors up Williams Creek to see the Richfield courthouse, a key attraction that was inaccessible to people who were unable (or unwilling) to make the two-mile return walk.

For safety reasons, and also for aesthetics, the Parks Branch needed to control the road before it could begin stage service to Richfield. The experience of riding in a replica nineteenth-century stagecoach would not be safe or feel very authentic if it entailed meeting pickup trucks loaded with drilling gear, ore samples, and modern-day prospectors. In a memo to Parks Branch headquarters, Superintendent Les Cook argued that the road itself should be treated as a historical artifact. Several sections would need repairs before it could safely accommodate a loaded stagecoach, and Cook recommended that this work be done by a crew wielding hand tools because using a caterpillar tractor threatened to "lose the authenticity of the old road."[58]

Lobbying from the Parks Branch and Barkerville Restoration Advisory Committee convinced the Department of Highways to legally close the streets of Barkerville to vehicular traffic in June 1962, just in time for the summer influx of visitors. A gate was placed across the road at the administration building, and only staff and mineral claim holders with valid parks use permits were allowed to drive through. Even then, they were obliged to take the back street to avoid disrupting main street's atmosphere. This closure was originally meant to be seasonal and temporary, with the townsite off-limits to traffic until the last day of September 1962. However, the Parks Branch's decision to permanently keep Barkerville an open-air "living" museum made it necessary to extend the traffic ban: reconciling a streetscape populated by actors dressed in 1870s costume with the passage of jeeps and heavy-duty pickups was simply not possible. The prohibition on unapproved automobile traffic in the historic zone was made permanent during the fall of 1963, and the following summer the Parks Branch began running its replica BX stagecoach between St. Saviour's Church and the Richfield courthouse.[59]

From the start, enforcing the ban proved difficult. Some local old-timers were slow to accept the Parks Branch regulations. In August 1963, Superintendent Les Cook reported that Wells resident Bill Hong continued to drive his pickup truck into and around the townsite to conduct his duties as district fire marshal. "We have to do a fair amount of explaining to visitors as to why his vehicle can be parked in town ... while everyone else has to walk," Cook complained. The ban on automobile traffic also led to strained relations among park staff, prospectors, mineral claim holders, the Department of Mines, and anyone else who had business in the hills above Barkerville. Shouting matches erupted between park employees and miners who failed to check in at the administration building or keep off the main street. There were accusations of physical intimidation and threats of lawsuits.[60] Similar conflicts arose when the campgrounds filled beyond capacity, which became increasingly common during the summers: 175,000 people visited the park in 1966. Many motorists who reached Barkerville late in the day, only to discover that its small campground was full, often proved reluctant to return to Quesnel and therefore set up their tents in places where camping was not permitted, including the picnic site, the museum parking lot, or just outside the park gates. The strain of dealing with unruly miners and tourists who refused to drive or park or camp where they were supposed to contributed to Superintendent Cook's decision to transfer to Parks headquarters in Victoria, where he oversaw the Stop of Interest program in the lead-up to Canada's 1967 centennial. These difficulties continued all through the 1960s, with every uptick in gold prices fuelling worries about a new incursion of miners. Particularly worrisome was the prospect that diamond drilling and cat stripping might be conducted within view (or earshot) of the Richfield courthouse. The Parks Branch had been given the authority to restrict certain activities in the park – even to restrict miners' usually privileged right to come and go – but there were limits to this power. Though the provincial government had found a way to extract tourist gold from the isolated ghost town of Barkerville, that did not extend to preventing miners from searching for real gold in the surrounding hills.

Once Barkerville became a provincial park, it quickly proved a valuable asset to the Fordist state, a piece of tourist infrastructure that could draw thousands of motorists over the Cariboo Highway and up the dead-end road from Quesnel. It helped increase certain kinds of economic activity in the northern Interior, bringing extra profits for many merchants and owners of roadside businesses. It also helped to justify other economic developments in the region, including improvement of the Quesnel-Barkerville road, which benefitted the forest industry, and the establishment of nearby Bowron Lake Provincial Park, which helped lure outdoor recreationalists. As attested to by its popularity, Barkerville also seemed to offer an appealing, resonant, or at least entertaining and easily palatable lesson about British Columbia's past, though imposing and maintaining its aesthetic was not without difficulties. Nor was it a quick or inexpensive process: "restoration" continued through the 1970s, with extensive work done not only in the townsite but also at Richfield and Cottonwood House, the park's two satellite attractions. Nevertheless, Barkerville Historic Provincial Park proved such an asset to the Fordist state – and the motoring public responded so enthusiastically – that it decided to develop similar facilities in other, more accessible parts of the BC Interior during the 1960s.

8

Mixed Fortunes in the BC Old Rush

In the late 1950s and the 1960s, the landscapes along several arterial highways were "filled in" with historical attractions. The state expanded the Stop of Interest program and developed additional history-themed parks along the lines of Barkerville. It also helped numerous local historical societies establish their own museums and churned out reams of history-themed publicity material. For their part, boosters and roadside businesses also continued to capitalize on the motoring public's taste for frontier history.

The Kootenay River valley, just to the north of Cranbrook, and the Revelstoke and Upper Arrow Lake district, both experienced enormous changes during the 1960s, and many of them were linked to state-supported megaprojects. The 1960s saw the Celgar pulp mill start operation in Castlegar, 150 miles south of Revelstoke at the confluence of the Kootenay and Columbia Rivers. Work also commenced on a pulp mill at Skookumchuck, thirty-five miles north of Cranbrook. The highways that led into these communities were frequently crowded with logging trucks, and when the wind was right they were awash with sulphurous emissions from the mills, colloquially referred to as "the smell of money." Even more dramatically, the Kootenay and Columbia River valleys both saw the construction of enormous new dams and the associated clearance of massive reservoir areas during the 1960s. These corporate and state-sponsored megaprojects tended to overshadow a series of smaller but nevertheless important infrastructure projects, including the building of new highways and modernization of existing ones. In the eastern Interior, the new section of the Trans-Canada

Highway between Revelstoke and Golden via the sublime Rogers Pass was the road that received the most attention, but other districts were also significantly affected by changes to the highway network.

Many Schemes for History by the Road

On the heels of the 1958 centennial celebrations, the provincial government was inundated with requests and proposals for aid with marking, preserving, restoring, and promoting old buildings and other historical landscape features. The centennial's array of events and projects had made frontier, pioneering, gold rush, and transportation-related themes more popular than ever before, and the success of Barkerville provided a useful template. The 1958 festivities had also underlined the importance of tying historical attractions to the highway network. Pitches arrived from every corner of the province. Some came from districts in which selling goods and services to the motoring public was already part of the economy. For example, from the Fraser Canyon and Cariboo Highway corridors came calls for the government to preserve St. John the Divine Anglican Church in Yale and the roadhouse at Ashcroft Manor, both of which dated from the 1860s.[1] Proposals also came from areas in which auto tourism was not important to the economy, but where new and improved highways made it feasible to imagine it becoming so.

Deputy Provincial Secretary Lawrie Wallace received so many requests for assistance that in late 1962 he asked cabinet for instructions on how to address them. Wallace believed that many were worthy of consideration; he also believed that some of the most accessible and intact historic sites could be tied together to form a BC-wide system, akin to what had been done with the provincial parks and Stop of Interest markers. He was supported by Parks Branch director H.G. McWilliams, who argued that such an approach would help achieve "desirable standards of authenticity and continuity."[2] The Social Credit government was not so enthusiastic. It instructed Wallace to leave small projects in the hands of local historical societies and to avoid initiating new ones without first getting cabinet approval. State-supported historical tourist attractions were not to be set up just anywhere, for they were expensive, long-term commitments, and they had to be incorporated into larger regional economic development strategies.

Dozens of local museums were established throughout the Interior during the late 1950s, the 1960s, and the early 1970s, most of which benefitted from provincial and federal funding programs that were associated with the 1958, 1966, 1967, and 1971 centennials. Almost all of them were situated beside major thoroughfares. For example, Princeton's Pioneer Museum, a 1958 centennial project, stood near the centre of town on a lot donated by autocourt owner Elmer Burr, whose father, Edgar, had supported the establishment of a provincial park along the Hope-Princeton Highway during the early 1930s. In Quesnel, the Cariboo Historical Society finally managed to open a museum in the mid-1960s, helped by the fact that Barkerville had become a major regional tourist draw. The Quesnel Museum shared a building with the local tourist information bureau and was located beside the Cariboo Highway in a municipal park named after long-time booster and MLA Louis LeBourdais.[3]

The growing involvement of government agencies, historical societies, and local museums in cultivating historical attractions and landscape features did not mean that commercial operators no longer had a part to play. Indeed, most local museum initiatives were either driven or supported by boosters, businesses, and boards of trade in the expectation that they would help attract pleasure travellers, who would purchase food, gas, lodging, and other goods and services during their visit. Some owners of roadside businesses also kept trying to profit from the public enthusiasm for frontier themes. After 1958, dozens of campgrounds, autocourts, motels, diners, cafes, and other concerns were inspired to use Wild West themes and gold rush iconography to appeal to passing motorists. The roadsides became festooned with eye-catching references to explorers, prospectors, cowboys, pioneers, stagecoaches, wagon wheels, and old trails. Quesnel alone had the Old Cariboo Cabin Camp, the Billy Barker Inn, the Gold Pan Motel, and the Mule Train Auto Court. The Interior also gained a clutch of privately owned roadside museums, curiosity collections, and simulated forts, all trying to cash in on the new tourist gold rush (or "old rush"). Most did not include an actual historical building; replicas and simulations proliferated even as the real thing continued to disappear, like the old roadhouses along the Cariboo Highway.

This proliferation was accompanied by a flood of publications related to British Columbia's past, including travelogues, pamphlets, road guides, brochures, and popular histories – even restaurant placemats. Typically inexpensive and portable, they could be folded into a glove compartment alongside road maps and insurance papers. They eschewed the "boring" conventions of scholarly writing, such as the focus on politics and economics that characterized Margaret Ormsby's *British Columbia: A History* (1958). Instead, they told rollicking stories about the romantic, adventuresome,

History on the Highways, published by the *Vancouver Province* and BC Government Travel Bureau, 1966. Courtesy of Pacific Newspaper Group.

rip-roaring days of the fur trade, the gold rush, and railroad construction. Common themes included crime and conflict, hostile environments, heroic infrastructure, and ruggedly masculine individuals. Lost mines and misplaced caches of gold were popular topics, as if the landscape were littered with treasure that was just waiting to be discovered by some especially perceptive individual. The thrills and travails of travel by animal and steam power – which were foreign to a fast-growing percentage of British Columbians – were also frequently described. These publications were typically illustrated with historical photographs and maps that showed how ghost towns, historic sites, and the transportation routes of yesteryear related to the modern-day highway network. They were, in that sense, guides to history by the road.[4]

Fort Steele Historic Park

After Barkerville, Fort Steele was the biggest, most expensive, and most ambitious historical tourist attraction developed in the BC Interior during the postwar years. Like Barkerville, it was a ghost town "restored" by the provincial government, and it was tied even more closely to the expansion and improvement of the highway network. Whereas Barkerville became popular despite being the isolated terminus of an unpaved, dead-end secondary road, Fort Steele was just a few minutes' drive from the southern transprovincial highway and the growing regional centre of Cranbrook. After 1967, it was also traversed by an important new north-south highway.

Like Barkerville, Fort Steele originated in an 1860s gold rush, at Wild Horse Creek. A tributary of the upper Kootenay, Wild Horse was the site of a placer rush between 1864 and 1867. As was so often the case, the diggings were shallow and the rush short-lived, and only a few miners remained in the district by 1880, as well as the Galbraith family, who operated a cable ferry across the fast-flowing Kootenay. In the mid-1880s, the construction of the Canadian Pacific Railway (CPR) far to the north brought another flurry of activity to the upper Kootenay and Columbia River valleys, with loggers, ranchers, and hydraulic gold miners moving in. A colonization road was built to link Galbraith's Ferry and the CPR mainline at Golden, 140 miles to the north, and sternwheel steamboats plied the upper Columbia and Kootenay Rivers. The growing number of white settlers moving into the upper Kootenay River valley led to tension with the Indigenous residents, so Ottawa dispatched a division of the North West Mounted Police (NWMP) to the vicinity of Galbraith's Ferry to forestall violence. The first NWMP post in British Columbia was built in 1887 under the supervision of Superintendent Sam Steele. The detachment stayed in the area for one year, during which Indian reserves were demarcated, the ferry across the Kootenay was replaced by a bridge, and the name of the community changed from Galbraith's Ferry to Fort Steele.

For the next decade, Fort Steele was the commercial and administrative centre of the southeastern Interior. However, its prosperity was fleeting. At the turn of the century, the CPR's east-west BC Southern branch line was built ten miles to the south, and the new town of Cranbrook quickly eclipsed Fort Steele; by 1902, their respective populations were 2,000 and 150. In 1904, the district courthouse and other government offices were moved from Fort Steele to Cranbrook, and two years later a fire wiped out much of the older town's remaining commercial section. Many surviving buildings were subsequently allowed to fall into disrepair, and others were relocated. By the 1920s, the only NWMP structure left at Wild Horse Creek was a log building that had served as the officers' quarters. It was used as a private residence, then as a storehouse, and eventually as a chicken coop.

The CPR built its north-south Kootenay Central branch line through Fort Steele in 1912, but the bulk of the district's rail and road traffic went up the other side of the Kootenay River valley, between Cranbrook and the burgeoning town of Kimberley, where the CPR was developing the enormous Sullivan lead-silver mine. There were enough farms, ranches, and hydraulic operations left near Fort Steele to keep a school and several businesses open, including a post office, a general store, and the Windsor Hotel, with its associated saloon. However, Fort Steele's glory days lay behind it. As the town gradually faded, many of its buildings were abandoned and left to decay.[5]

Few tourists drove through Fort Steele during the interwar years, due to its location on an obscure, poor-quality side road. The townsite was just far enough off the beaten track to dissuade casual travellers from stopping by. One motorist who went out of his way to visit in the early 1920s was Regina land agent R.V. Bing. The Bing family paused in Fort Steele to purchase camping supplies at the general store, and the storekeeper – "a real old-timer of the place" – regaled them with tales of the town's past, "when large finds of gold were common and the place was crowded with prospectors, lumbermen and trappers." Bing discerned few obvious traces of the gold rush and reported in his diary that there were "no buildings of any interest left standing."[6] In 1929, the Historic Sites and Monuments Board of Canada (HSMBC) erected a cairn and plaque at Fort Steele to identify the site of the 1887 NWMP barracks. Few motorists saw this monument, however. For the next thirty years, Fort Steele was a place that auto tourists either intentionally sought out or stumbled upon after making a wrong turn, a special discovery that provided a romantic contrast to the bustling mining and railroad towns of Cranbrook and Kimberley. Less than fifty people lived in Fort Steele by 1945, the school closed in 1954, and the beer hall in the decrepit Windsor Hotel lasted only a couple of years longer.[7]

The 1958 Centennial Committee erected a gold-on-green Stop of Interest marker at Fort Steele to commemorate the Wild Horse gold rush and Galbraith's Ferry – the site was hard to pass over, what with its connection to the themes of gold mining, law and order, and frontier transportation. This was not enough to satisfy boosters and history buffs in the east Kootenays, however. After Victoria's development plan for Barkerville became public knowledge, they lobbied for a similar project at Fort Steele, which was the most intact and accessible of the region's numerous ghost towns. In many ways, it was an ideal site for a major historical tourist attraction, located just a short drive from the southern transprovincial

The Windsor Hotel at Fort Steele, early 1960s. Author's collection.

highway, the city of Cranbrook, American border crossings, and the national parks in the Rockies. Fort Steele's biggest drawback remained its location on the opposite side of the Kootenay River valley from the arterial road that connected Cranbrook with Kimberley and points north. At that moment, Barkerville had yet to demonstrate that a major historical tourist attraction could be both successful and situated far from an arterial highway.

The first proposal to "restore" Fort Steele came from private operators in 1958. Tom Andruschuk and the Sinclair brothers were building contractors based in Radium Hot Springs, and through a mixture of preservation and reconstruction they hoped to make Fort Steele look like "a thriving Gold Rush Community ... exactly as it was at the turn of the century." They bought the boarded-up Windsor Hotel, which had been built in 1894 and was one of the few large buildings left in Fort Steele. They then applied to purchase all the vacant Crown land in the townsite. Their application was turned down, probably because government officials doubted the ability of small private operators to carry out such an ambitious project.[8] By 1959, the *Cranbrook Courier, Nelson Daily News,* and East Kootenay Historical Society were urging Victoria to develop Fort Steele into a major tourist draw. Several boards of trade threw their support behind this proposal, arguing that the east Kootenays deserved to

Fort Steele streetscape, 1959. University of Victoria Archives, Chester P. Lyons fonds.

have their own state-operated historical park, particularly because the region had suffered a series of economic setbacks, with coal mines recently closed in Fernie and preliminary negotiations for the Columbia River Treaty casting a pall of uncertainty over everything. The fact that Nelson-Creston MLA Wesley Black was the provincial secretary and therefore responsible for historic sites was seen as a key political factor in favour of the scheme.[9]

In response to this regional lobby, the minister of recreation and conservation promised to investigate "what might be done to perpetuate, in some degree, the colourful history of Ft. Steele."[10] The Parks Branch dispatched Ches Lyons to inspect the dusty, rundown townsite in the spring of 1960. Unlike the dozens of elaborate reconnaissance reports that Lyons had produced since the early 1940s, his report on Fort Steele was a straightforward inventory. It identified about fifty structures, including numerous homes (most abandoned, a few still occupied), an array of collapsing sheds, lean-tos, and outhouses, and several larger edifices, such as the Windsor Hotel, Masonic Hall, and Catholic and Presbyterian churches. Lyons stated that fewer than a dozen buildings appeared to date from the nineteenth century, but he made no recommendation about the advisability of trying to duplicate at Fort Steele the kind of effort then under way at Barkerville or how the site might be developed as a provincial park. The cursory nature of his report suggests that the Social Credit government had already decided to proceed with a restoration project that would give the east Kootenays (and the southern transprovincial highway) their own major historical tourist attraction.[11]

A crucial factor in cabinet's decision to proceed with the Fort Steele project was the fact that significant changes were planned for the road network in the district north of Cranbrook. Since the end of the war, the volume of automobile traffic had mushroomed in the upper Kootenay River valley, including heavy trucks that hauled logs to the large Crestbrook Timber sawmill in Cranbrook. In the late 1950s, Crestbrook applied for a tree farm licence covering a huge tract in the upper Kootenay watershed and began seeking financial backing to develop a pulp mill, which, if approved, would lead to even more heavy hauling on district roads. All of this traffic funnelled along the main street of Kimberley, the lively mining town that lay across the valley from moribund Fort Steele. To safely speed the flow of traffic, provincial engineers planned to divert it away from Kimberley by upgrading the secondary road through Fort Steele, where fewer people lived and property prices were lower. The little-used gravel road would become the main corridor northward from Cranbrook, a paved highway with modern standards of curvature, gradient, and sightlines. A key feature of this project would be the construction of a large new bridge at Fort Steele and the realignment of the road through the dilapidated townsite.[12]

This infrastructure plan promised to transform the relationship between the motoring public and the ghost town at Fort Steele. For decades, the trickle of traffic that ventured into it had passed through the centre of town on gravel-surfaced streets before descending a steep cutbank, making a sharp turn, and crossing a set of railroad tracks that lay at the foot of the narrow, timber-truss bridge over the Kootenay River. By the late 1950s, this set-up was antiquated, even for a secondary road. The proximity of steep hill, sharp turn, level crossing, and bridge was very unsafe, and the bridge itself could not handle logging trucks or commercial transports. Even though the streets of Fort Steele were broad and essentially bereft of traffic, they were unsuitable for large vehicles or high speeds. To improve the situation, the Department of Highways planned to carve a broad new right-of-way through the centre of town, which would provide an approach to a wide concrete bridge over both the Kootenay River and the CPR's Kootenay Central branch line. The new highway would effectively bisect the town and required the expropriation of many properties. The fact that the state envisioned such an extensive property acquisition program made it feasible to contemplate the refurbishment of Fort Steele. The townsite was set to go from obscure backwater to an easily accessible centre of attention and thus a potential tourism asset for southeastern British Columbia.

American industrialist Bill Mead was a key backer of the Fort Steele project. The biggest private landowner in the vicinity, he used the Wild Horse Ranch on the north edge of town as a summer home and hobby farm. In May 1960, he contacted the Department of Recreation and Conservation with an offer to donate some of his property in support of turning the decaying townsite into a "living museum" that would reproduce "in strict detail [the] town of Fort Steele in its early days." Citing Williamsburg in Virginia and Westfield Village in Massachusetts as examples of what he had in mind, Mead suggested that Fort Steele be made into a "working, income-producing village in the style of 1860."[13] Aware that the new highway would run through the townsite, he recommended that its northern section (where most of the oldest structures were located) should become a "historic zone" that tourists would pay to enter. Victoria would purchase the private properties in that part of the townsite and allow a non-profit foundation to lease stores and workshops to craftspeople, who would sell their products to visitors. These artisans would live in prefabricated aluminum-skinned homes in a residential zone on the south side of the highway. Mead predicted that Hollywood studios would clamour to rent the historic townsite as a movie set, if it were "rebuilt" with a high enough degree of verisimilitude. "If Fort Steele is recreated as outlined above, it would be an additional fabulous attraction for British Columbia," he declared.[14]

Mead's scheme (and offer to donate land) piqued the interest of the provincial secretary's office and the Barkerville Restoration Advisory Committee. They identified placer gold mining and the "world-famous" Royal Canadian Mounted Police (RCMP) as two key themes that could be commemorated at Fort Steele. The NWMP, the predecessor of the RCMP, had been stationed at Wild Horse Creek for just one year, but incorporating the force into the site would tie it to the popular Wild West theme of "law and order" and to other police-related attractions in western Canada, such as Fort Macleod in Alberta and Fort Battleford in Saskatchewan. The RCMP promised full co-operation on the project. Commemorating the force's historical presence in the southern Interior would enable it to generate good publicity about itself: in 1960, the RCMP was struggling with a protracted campaign of nude protests, arsons, and bombings in the southern Interior, waged by the Sons of Freedom, a radical Doukhobor sect.[15]

The provincial government spent $10,000 to acquire private property at Fort Steele during the winter of 1960–61, and in the spring it established Fort Steele Historic Provincial Park, 140 acres with a Class A designation.[16] Shortly thereafter, the Fort Steele Restoration Foundation was created as an offshoot of the Barkerville Restoration Advisory Committee with many of the same government ministers, bureaucrats, and publicity men involved. As at Barkerville, the Parks Branch was responsible for most of the planning and groundwork.[17] Fort Steele saw relatively little development during the early 1960s because virtually nothing could be done until the Department of Highways finalized its plans for the new highway that would transect the townsite. The Parks Branch had only partial control over the park during these years. Several long-time residents continued to live within it, and a light but steady flow of automobile traffic continued to traverse its gravelled streets. In the summer months of the early 1960s, approximately a hundred cars passed through Fort Steele each day; traffic engineers projected that the number would grow twelvefold once the new highway redirected traffic away from Kimberley.[18]

The Parks Branch drew up tentative plans for developing Fort Steele and set about securing and stabilizing its various old buildings. The foundations of many structures were repaired. The former NWMP officers' quarters were relocated from Bill Mead's Wild Horse Ranch by jacking up the decaying log building, loading it onto an oversize trailer, and then depositing it in the northwest corner of the park near the old HSMBC cairn. In response to reports of vandalism and overzealous "souvenir hunting," one of Fort Steele's remaining residents was hired to act as caretaker. He was instructed to warn away trespassers and to report offenders' licence plate numbers to the RCMP in Cranbrook.[19]

Many tourists went out of their way to visit Fort Steele during the early 1960s, their curiosity aroused by the government's announcement that it intended to restore the ghost town in a manner akin to Barkerville. But publicity outstripped the actual work, and many visitors left disappointed. Little was done to identify or explain the significance of the old buildings, and most were boarded up to prevent trespassing and vandalism. There were no picnic tables or public toilets – the general store was the only polite option available to visitors who needed a washroom, and its limited septic capacity was soon at risk of being overwhelmed. Expecting a rapid increase in visitation – especially after attendance at Barkerville leapt from 25,000 in 1961 to 107,000 in 1962 – area residents and the MLA for

Cranbrook urged the Parks Branch to install interpretive signs and basic visitor facilities like those in other roadside parks of British Columbia.[20]

Shortly after Fort Steele Park was established, Bill Mead's motives for supporting the project were revealed as not entirely altruistic. He asked for the park boundaries to be adjusted so that he could retain a strip of land bordering on the surveyed route of the future highway. Mead hoped to develop a motel, gas station, and diner on the edge of the park, and planned to subdivide part of Wild Horse Ranch into half-acre lots for recreational homes. He even had an idea for a roadside attraction of his own: a frontage road he called the "Fabulous Mile of Architecture," where examples of North American architecture would be displayed, ranging from pioneer log cabins to a "Frank Lloyd Wright type space building made of aluminum." Fearing that these ventures might detract from the park and make a bad impression on the motoring public, Parks Branch staff asked the Department of Highways to exercise strict control over access points and commercial development for two miles in each direction from the park.[21]

In 1963, Highways announced that in future drivers would need to enter and exit Fort Steele Park from a single access point. It would not be allowed to interfere with through-traffic, meaning that there could be no confusing sprawl or unapproved access points. However, Highways could not indicate precisely where the single entrance should be located, and this compelled the Parks Branch to keep most of its development plans on hold.[22] The Department of Highways started to expropriate properties at Fort Steele in the winter of 1963–64, and the Parks Branch requested that it preserve all the old buildings it acquired, including those on the south side of the future highway right-of-way, because they could be jacked onto trailers and moved to help fill in the historic townsite, where there were many empty lots. By the early 1960s, moving very large buildings in this manner had become feasible, and there was far more room to manoeuvre in sprawling Fort Steele than in the cramped confines of Barkerville.

The Parks Branch began to erect a timber palisade around the edge of Fort Steele Park during the 1964 summer tourist season, despite the fact that the 1887 NWMP post had lacked such fortifications. This structure was intended to achieve several things. First, it would draw the eye: timber palisades were shorthand for "Wild West," having been stock features of Hollywood westerns for decades. Second, it would hide the park's new service yard and administrative area from view. Third, it would help screen parts of the historic townsite from the new highway. By obscuring the sights and sounds of high-speed automobile traffic, the palisade would create a sense of separation between past and present. The gateway to the historic section of the park was considered a very important feature: a kind of portal to the past, it gave visitors the sense that they were leaving the twentieth century behind in the parking lot. Planners wanted to build an impressive bastion or blockhouse around the gate, but their preferred locations for the gateway were repeatedly deemed to conflict with Highways plans for access to the park.[23]

Allan Hunter of Cranbrook was hired as Fort Steele's first curator in 1965. Like Bill Mead, he had been a major supporter of making the townsite into a historic attraction. Hunter had been collecting artifacts related to the east Kootenays since the 1950s and at one point had even purchased the Windsor Hotel to save it from being demolished. In his role as curator, he continued to amass artifacts ranging from diaries to buildings. He also co-ordinated the appearance of the townsite with Superintendent Norman Blackburn. Their goal was to make it look somewhat as it had during the boom times of the early and mid-1890s. One of Hunter's priorities was a "general clean up," which entailed removing old cars, gas pumps, metal signs that advertised pop and cigarettes, and other objects that were incommensurate with an 1890s atmosphere. Several buildings that were identified as being "in very bad condition" were torn down and burned after being stripped of salvageable material, but Hunter believed that too much "cleaning" might disrupt the air of picturesque decay. He insisted that a handful of badly dilapidated structures be left to moulder so as to "portray an authentic ghost town atmosphere."[24]

In the summer of 1965, the Parks Branch acquired a relic that would become a signature landmark at Fort Steele Park. A large, weathered waterwheel from a Cornish pump had been found at an abandoned gold mining operation on nearby Perry Creek. After being jacked onto a flatbed trailer and hauled to Fort Steele, it was unloaded in the park's southwestern corner on a bluff that overlooked the Kootenay River – a location that would be very prominent once the new highway bridge was built. The waterwheel was a veritable beacon of old-timey-ness, a familiar icon of gold mining history that resembled the waterwheels at Quesnel and Barkerville. Staff expected it to "catch the public's eye when approaching," thus giving motorists a few extra moments to consider pulling off the road to visit the historic townsite.[25]

The Department of Highways finalized its plans for the new Kootenay River crossing and highway through Fort Steele during the winter of 1965–66. After the spring thaw, contractors started preparing the roadbed and building the concrete bridge abutments. The new road would traverse part

Fort Steele Historic Provincial Park in the late 1960s, showing old bridge and route of new highway at right. United Specialties postcard. Author's collection.

of the townsite in a cut, which required substantial excavation. Park planners arranged for the construction contractors to deposit much of the resulting waste material inside the park. A caterpillar subsequently graded it flat to create a parking lot with room for about three hundred cars, around which barriers were erected to prevent people from driving into restricted areas. Commencement of highway construction pushed the Parks Branch's Fort Steele program into high gear. Staff rushed to complete the palisade and its elaborate blockhouses and gate. Work also started on a new but old-looking museum building that would house artifacts and interpretive displays. The remaining residents had their homes relocated to the south side of the highway, and contractors scrambled to move historic buildings into, out of, and within the park, including the very large Masonic Hall and Presbyterian church. To help fill out the emerging townscape, park staff proposed to truck in old buildings from as far away as the Lake Windermere district, seventy miles to the north.[26]

At Fort Steele, unlike at Barkerville, the Parks Branch could prepare for the day when all motorists would be excluded from the park's historic zone. There would be no miners in incongruous-looking pickup trucks, which meant that rides in horse-drawn wagons and stagecoaches could safely be offered to visitors.[27] The branch briefly planned to add a dash of exoticism and local colour by constructing a "typical Indian village" in partnership with the federal Department of Indian Affairs. This would have strongly differentiated Fort Steele from Barkerville, which had no First Nations content. However, with the rise of First Nations political and justice movements during the late 1960s, and changing attitudes toward Indigenous peoples and issues, this scheme was deemed inappropriate and dropped.[28] Instead, the branch decided to build a two-mile loop of railroad track in the northeast corner of the park. Steam locomotives had become rare sights in western North America since the switch to diesel power during the late 1940s and the 1950s, and the travelling public was increasingly less familiar with railways due to the sharp postwar decline in passenger service. Transportation-related themes had been common at the province's roadside historical attractions since the late 1920s, so a short railroad with functioning antique steam locomotives was considered an appealing and appropriate way to draw visitors into Fort Steele.

The new steel-reinforced concrete bridge over the Kootenay at Fort Steele opened in May 1967, seven years after the Department of Highways had started planning to reorganize the road network north of Cranbrook. The removal of automobile traffic from the streets of Fort Steele allowed the Parks Branch to accelerate its restoration-related program and also dramatically changed visitors' experiences of the site. Engine noise and the dust stirred up by passing vehicles were eliminated, and now that chromed, tail-finned automobiles had been rerouted, it was much easier to imagine the townsite as representative of frontier life in the 1890s. The Parks Branch started plans to turn Fort Steele into an open-air living museum like Barkerville. Once drivers were cut off from the centre of the park, efforts were required to draw them in. Signs were needed along the new highway to flag the proximity of a major government-designated historical attraction and to indicate the location of its entrance. The park superintendent received many complaints from drivers who overshot the turn-off. "The travelling public is on to our large entrance sign too quickly," he reported to headquarters. "They have to turn around and come back, or just pass on by and think about coming for a visit the next time they visit this part of the world." The high-speed traffic and lack of pullouts on the new highway made doubling back difficult or unappealing and correspondingly increased the need for signs to advertise Fort Steele.[29]

The grand opening for Fort Steele Park was held on 24 June 1967. Premier W.A.C. Bennett flew in to officiate the event, which included opening the new museum building that most of the park's 100,000 visitors

Palisade and gatehouses at Fort Steele, late 1960s. Dorse McTaggart photograph, courtesy of Walter Lanz. Author's collection.

would explore that year. The proceedings coincided with the ribbon cutting for the new bridge over the Kootenay River – the crucial piece of infrastructure that in some ways had made the park and restoration project possible – and also with the groundbreaking ceremony for the new $42 million Crestbrook Forest Industries pulp and paper mill at Skookumchuck, twenty miles north of Fort Steele. The mill was a joint venture by Crestbrook Timber, Mitsubishi, and the Honshu Paper Manufacturing Company, which owned paper mills around the world. This weekend extravaganza of nominally discrete but actually quite closely connected opening ceremonies marked a major success for the Fordist state, which had paid for much of the expensive infrastructure that made them feasible. A big historical attraction such as Fort Steele was part of the modernization and diversification of the Interior economy. A key asset that would fuel the growth of the service and tourism industries, it was thus a kind of cultural counterpart to the new pulp mill.

Fort Steele Park quickly proved popular, drawing an average of 125,000 visitors per year during the late 1960s. As a tourist attraction, it had significant advantages over Barkerville. Probably the most important was its ease of access. Indeed, the same first-class highway that carried pleasure travellers past the park during the summer months also permitted heavy logging trucks to haul timber to the Crestbrook mill at Skookumchuck on a year-round basis. In addition to bringing in tourists and other members of the motoring public, then, Fort Steele Park helped create a sense of continuity around the dramatic transformations of both the environment and the economy in the east Kootenays. In commemorating the gold rushes of the 1860s and 1890s, it suggested antecedents to the massive tree farm licences and pulp mills of the 1960s. In commemorating Sam Steele and the North West Mounted Police, it suggested precursors for an active state that helped to facilitate the process of resource extraction. And in commemorating travel by stagecoach and steam locomotive, it suggested the profound importance of transportation infrastructure to the province's past and, by extension, to its present and future as well.

Three Valley Gap and Columbia Village

Barkerville and Fort Steele were outstanding examples of what the Fordist state could accomplish, but it did not support the development of every ghost town in the Interior during the 1960s. Nor did every ghost town attraction that it did support achieve the success of Barkerville and Fort Steele. As noted at the start of this chapter, several private museums and curiosity collections were established along the highways of the Interior during the late 1950s and the 1960s. There were also several proposed historical attractions that failed to come to fruition even though they were supported by the government. This final section examines these kinds of developments in the Revelstoke district: first the privately owned ghost town at Three Valley Gap and then the failed Columbia Village outdoor museum.

The Revelstoke district experienced many significant changes during the 1950s and 1960s. In 1952, the provincial government announced that it would grant Columbia Cellulose an enormous tree farm licence in the Selkirk Mountains, which would be used to supply the Celgar pulp mill it intended to build at Castlegar. This was followed by news that the Big Bend Highway would be replaced by a route through the Selkirks, the little-noticed destruction of Hamber Park, the opening of the new Rogers Pass route, massive timber clearing efforts in the High Arrow and Mica reservoirs, and the construction of enormous dams on the Columbia River upstream and downstream from Revelstoke. Amidst these changes, the district saw a large amount of new commercial development. Autocourts and motels were built on the edge of Revelstoke, two full-service hotels opened in the town centre, and new gas stations, diners, banks, and government buildings were erected. Revelstoke also gained a new mascot, when Wooden Head, the famous Big Bend Highway landmark, was salvaged from Boat Encampment before it was flooded out and relocated to a perch overlooking the new Trans-Canada Highway. Amidst the boom and bustle, the members of the Revelstoke Historical Association, like those of many historical associations in the BC Interior during these years, dreamt of opening their own museum that would promote the community to passing travellers while also preserving papers, images, and objects related to its past.

The first major historical tourist attraction built near Revelstoke was attached to a private commercial operation at Three Valley Lake, twelve miles west of town on the Trans-Canada. It was owned by Gordon and Ethel Bell, who purchased the land in 1956, shortly after the Trans-Canada's modernization was announced. Four years later, they opened a small roadside motel and cafe called Three Valley Gap, and in keeping with the times incorporated various historical themes and symbols into the venture. Their emblem, for example, was a bearded, pistol-packing prospector leading a burro loaded with a pick, shovel, and gold pan. The Bells also built a very small "museum" in a shed across the parking lot from their motel and cafe. Gordon Bell was keen on vintage automobiles, so a Model T Ford was one of the first things it displayed. Business increased sharply after the paved, all-season Rogers Pass route replaced the unpopular, roundabout Big Bend Highway in 1962. The Bells expanded their cafe and motel, added gas pumps and a souvenir shop, and bought another twenty acres. They also expanded their collection of historical artifacts, gradually assembling their own private ghost town. They gathered old farm implements, home fixtures, wagons, and vintage automobiles, as well as historic buildings from the region between Revelstoke and Salmon Arm. These included pioneer log cabins, a Finnish-style duplex barn from Malakwa, the one-room schoolhouse from Craigellachie (which had been scheduled for demolition to make way for highway widening), and the three-storey Hotel Bellevue from Sicamous, thirty miles to the west, which had closed in the early 1950s after being bypassed by a realignment of the Trans-Canada.

The Bells arranged their Frontier Mountain Town so that some of the old buildings faced onto the highway, where they would catch the eye of passing motorists – hinting at what lay within was thought to be the best advertisement. Driving in the confined, heavily wooded mountain terrain around Revelstoke could be tiring and lonely, and many people broke up the long trek between Kamloops and Revelstoke by spending an hour visiting the simulated ghost town, even though they were charged an entry fee to do so. The most elaborate private historical attraction developed in

Frontier Mountain Town at Three Valley Gap, late 1960s. George Hunter photograph, courtesy of Three Valley Gap and Canadian Souvenir Sales. Author's collection.

the Interior during the postwar years, Three Valley Gap became a familiar sight and popular stopping place on the drive across the central Interior.[30] It was also a purely synthetic affair. The Frontier Mountain Town was not meant to be a reconstruction of any specific place or period, and all of its artifacts and old buildings had been brought from elsewhere. Three Valley Gap's commercial success reflected the general enthusiasm for ghost towns following the 1958 centennial. It also emphasized the importance of being located in a spot that was visible and easily accessible from a major road.

Three Valley Gap and several nearby attractions sprang up during a period when the Revelstoke district was becoming more familiar to western Canada's motoring public. Tourism and roadside commercial services became much more important to the Revelstoke economy during the 1960s, and this coincided with local history enthusiasts' desire to rescue landscape features that were going to be destroyed by the reservoirs associated with the Columbia River dams. According to the preliminary terms of the Columbia River Treaty, the High Arrow Dam would be the first major dam built on the BC section of the Columbia. Situated a few miles north of Castlegar, it would create a reservoir that at full pool would extend 150 miles upstream, reaching all the way to the southern outskirts of Revelstoke. The announcement of the High Arrow Dam project spurred historians and history buffs to salvage records, artifacts, buildings, and anything else they deemed significant to or representative of the Arrow Lakes region's past. In 1960, the BC Historical Association urged the provincial government to collect historical information about the many small communities that would be partially or entirely inundated by High Arrow, "including moving historical buildings where judged advisable." Wilson Duff and British Columbia's new Archaeological Sites Advisory Board asked BC Hydro to fund surveys of archaeological sites in the proposed reservoir areas, starting with the one that would form behind the High Arrow Dam.[31]

BC Hydro had plans for clearing the High Arrow reservoir area by the time construction got under way in early 1965. Huge swathes of timber were to be removed, as well as buildings and communities. Two thousand people were expected to have their homes, farms, and businesses flooded out by the High Arrow component of the Columbia River Treaty megaproject. BC Hydro, the provincial Crown corporation responsible for building and operating the dams, had established departments to coordinate property expropriation and resettlement. It planned to rebuild several of the larger Arrow Lakes villages on higher ground, which would entail moving some homes and businesses and replacing others. Other communities would not be rebuilt: very small places such as Arrowhead, Arrow Park, and Renata. Several hundred displaced people were expected to move to new subdivisions that BC Hydro had staked out in Revelstoke, Nakusp, and Castlegar.[32]

In 1965, BC Hydro planners contacted the Parks Branch and the provincial secretary's office about the possibility of developing a tourist information centre and "regional museum" beside the Trans-Canada Highway at Revelstoke. This proposal was promoted by James Wood Wilson, who was in charge of long-term planning for the power authority's resettlement department. Wilson told Deputy Provincial Secretary Lawrie Wallace that BC Hydro was "quite willing to look out for and make available to a Museum any buildings and effects of historical value which we acquire in the [expropriation] process." He suggested that the museum could describe the history of "development" in the Arrow Lakes through the use of "full size original exhibits" – mining machinery, logging equipment, agricultural implements, old buildings, and railway rolling stock would appropriately commemorate the region's history of transportation and natural resource extraction.[33] Wilson urged the Parks Branch to reach a quick decision regarding his proposal. He pointed out that "strategically located land" was becoming scarce in the Revelstoke area due to commercial development and property speculation along the Trans-Canada corridor. Also, the longer that old buildings sat vacant, the greater the chance that they might be damaged or even destroyed by vandals. Most importantly, BC Hydro's property acquisition program in the Arrow Lakes was rapidly accelerating. A huge clearcutting effort would soon be under way in the flood zone, and BC Hydro's demolition contractors were expected to start bulldozing and burning the structures on expropriated properties during the winter of 1965–66. Wilson wanted to ensure that any especially valuable or representative buildings and other structures would be identified and marked for preservation before these clearances began.[34]

Senior politicians and Parks Branch officials were keen on the idea of a third major historic park in the Interior. In the northern Interior, the Cariboo Highway gave access to Barkerville, and the southern transprovincial highway had Fort Steele, but there was no equivalent in the central Interior. Bob Broadland, who was in charge of the historic provincial parks, judged Revelstoke "a natural for a regional museum" due to its location on the Trans-Canada and its proximity to popular national parks. He also recognized that this would be a big project, probably as expensive and complicated as those at Barkerville and Fort Steele, even with BC Hydro's offer to donate the buildings for free. At Barkerville and Fort Steele, the provincial government had acquired, through a mixture of purchase and expropriation, relatively intact ghost towns that contained streets and alleys, buildings, artifacts, and other historical features. By comparison, Columbia Village, as the proposed Revelstoke museum came to be known, would be purely synthetic, akin to the Bell family's Frontier Mountain Town at nearby Three Valley Lake. Suitable land would need to be acquired and cleared. All of the old buildings and other artifacts would need to be transported to the museum site from throughout the Revelstoke and Arrow Lakes region, and then arranged in a convincingly evocative manner. No one in the Parks Branch appears to have entertained any serious qualms about the authenticity of the project. No complaints had been voiced at Fort Steele, where old buildings were being trucked hither and thither, or at Barkerville, where squatters' cabins had been removed from the lower town and replicas of landmarks such as the Theatre Royal had been erected. Nevertheless, this kind of development was bound to be expensive when conducted on a large scale and with buildings and other structures being transported long distances over secondary roads.[35]

In the summer of 1965, cabinet gave the Parks Branch approval to begin planning for the acquisition of land, buildings, and artifacts for the Columbia Village project. Bob Broadland travelled to Revelstoke to meet BC Hydro's property acquisition department and members of the Revelstoke Historical Association. They showed him several sites where a museum could be developed and also many of the old buildings and other structures that were slated for demolition in the flood zone between Revelstoke and the village of Arrowhead, twenty-five miles to the south. Arrowhead, located at the point where the Columbia flowed into Upper Arrow Lake, had had a very large sawmill in the 1900s and still possessed a number of turn-of-the-century buildings in good condition. The Revelstoke Historical Association (RHA) had already identified a handful of buildings that it wanted to save, including cabins, houses, barns, and former businesses. Broadland knew how adept contractors were becoming at moving large structures by truck and trailer, so he added several more to this list, including Arrowhead's general store and Anglican church. In his report to Parks Branch headquarters, he urged that a museum site be found soon so that the selected buildings could be moved to safety.[36]

Unfortunately for its advocates, the Columbia Village project was struck by a series of delays at the very moment that it needed to be expedited. These delays were related to financing and site acquisition. A significant setback was suffered in early 1966, when BC Hydro – which was an arm's-length Crown corporation – declined to match the financial contribution that the provincial government proposed to make toward the project. In a letter to Deputy Provincial Secretary Lawrie Wallace, BC Hydro planner James Wood Wilson pointed out that the power authority had never offered to help *pay* for Columbia Village. It was willing to donate buildings and objects that it had acquired through expropriation, to donate surplus land for a museum site, and even to have its contractors help relocate buildings from the flood zone. But it had never promised cash for the project. Shortly after, Wilson quit his job as resettlement planner, and with his departure the museum scheme lost its biggest supporter inside BC Hydro.[37]

Enthusiasm for the Columbia Village project was growing in Revelstoke, even as it became increasingly less clear who was going to pay for it. The RHA predicted that Columbia Village would quickly outdraw Barkerville, what with the huge volume of traffic passing through town each year on the modernized Trans-Canada. The association envisioned Columbia Village as a "living museum," with actors dressed in period costume, buildings that visitors could enter, and a bustling streetscape. For a centrepiece attraction, the RHA hoped to restore a sternwheel steamboat that could take visitors for short cruises on the future High Arrow reservoir – a ride into the past that would be appropriate to Arrow Lakes history in the same way that stagecoaches were to Barkerville's. The RHA was presumably thinking of the SS *Minto,* a decommissioned CPR lake steamer whose battered hulk had been beached at Galena Bay on

Hulk of the *Minto* ashore at Galena Bay, mid-1960s. Courtesy of BC Hydro.

Upper Arrow Lake since the late 1950s. The Nakusp-based Arrow Lakes Historical Society had already tried and failed to turn the old vessel into an attraction, but the *Minto* had subsequently been purchased by a local history aficionado who still hoped to restore it one day.[38]

The vision that Parks Branch planners put forward for Columbia Village resembled that of the Revelstoke Historical Association. Bob Broadland predicted that a large ghost-town-type outdoor museum at Revelstoke would become "one of the major tourist attractions adjacent to the Trans-Canada Highway." He also agreed that transportation-related themes such as steamboating on the Arrow Lakes and the construction of the CPR through the Selkirks would be especially appropriate for such a museum, given its setting. By the mid-1960s, heroic infrastructure as the key to unlocking the resource wealth of the Interior had been a common theme in scholarly and popular historical writing for thirty years. Furthermore, tourists who reached Revelstoke by way of the Kicking Horse and Rogers Passes (if coming from the Prairies) or the Fraser and Thompson River canyons and Three Valley Lake (if coming from the Coast) would be primed for narratives about how the prospectors and railroad builders of yesteryear had struggled to traverse rugged environments.[39]

Broadland's enthusiasm for Columbia Village was not enough to overcome the problem of finding a site that was both accessible and big enough.

The Parks Branch estimated that it needed seventy-five acres of relatively flat land to assemble Columbia Village, but properties of such size had become prohibitively expensive along the Trans-Canada corridor near Revelstoke since the Rogers Pass had replaced the unpopular Big Bend route. Several locations were flagged as potentially useable, but they proved either to have significant shortcomings or to be tied up with BC Hydro's dam development program. For example, the City of Revelstoke offered to donate a ninety-acre lot several miles north of town on the Big Bend Highway. It had the necessary amount of flat land, and though it was a fair distance north of the Trans-Canada, Broadland predicted that the Mica Dam would one day be a tourist attraction in and of itself, thus helping to bring motorists that way. However, the Columbia River was constricted, rocky, and fast flowing at that point, which put paid to the steamboating venture that Broadland and the RHA agreed should be a major draw. Several promising parcels of Crown land proved to be scheduled for inundation, including one that could also have accommodated a large campground. Another had been claimed by the City of Revelstoke for a new dump. Still others had been reserved for the resettlement of Arrow Lakes residents who would be displaced by flooding. Local boosters and history enthusiasts scrambled to help the Parks Branch find a suitable spot for Columbia Village. Their ranks included Mayor Arvid Lundell, a former Social Credit MLA and publisher of the *Revelstoke Review,* and RHA member Estelle Dickey, widow of arch-Revelstoke booster and postcard photographer Earle Dickey, who had lobbied for the preservation of scenic timber along the Big Bend Highway during the 1930s.[40]

The delays associated with acquiring both funding and a site need not have proven fatal to Columbia Village. Unfortunately, they coincided with the fact that construction of the High Arrow Dam was six months ahead of schedule. As megaprojects go, High Arrow was relatively simple to build. It was just a short distance from Castlegar, had no power-generating facilities, and was only 170 feet tall (versus 800 feet for the dam planned at Mica Creek). In February 1967, Estelle Dickey warned the Parks Branch that "we can expect to have the water up here ... by 1968." Members of the RHA hurried to remove artifacts from the flood zone and pleaded with the Parks Branch to finalize a location for Columbia Village, so that the old buildings BC Hydro had left standing at Arrowhead and other points inside the reservoir could be hauled to high ground before it was too late.[41]

During the spring of 1968, as the floodwaters began rising behind the completed High Arrow Dam, BC Hydro's demolition contractors made one last sweep through the valley. They bulldozed and burned the homes, barns, and other structures that had been left standing at Arrowhead, Sidmouth, 12 Mile, Greenslide, and Mount Cartier, including buildings that the Parks Branch and RHA had earmarked for Columbia Village.[42] With the museum project looking dead in the water, the owner of the SS *Minto* allowed BC Hydro to tow it offshore at Galena Bay and set it ablaze, destroying what could have become the signature attraction of Columbia Village. The *Minto*'s Viking funeral became a popular symbol of the passing of an era, as the Arrow Lakes region was transformed by pulp mills, paved highways, and hydroelectric reservoirs. Few local residents knew of the plans to incorporate the *Minto* into a major government-supported attraction at Revelstoke. Making the loss especially frustrating for history enthusiasts and tourism promoters in that town was the fact that BC Hydro had blocked the RHA and the Bell family at Three Valley Gap from using their meagre resources to salvage even a few old buildings from the flood zone.[43]

Columbia Village would have gone forward if the Parks Branch had managed to acquire a suitable piece of property. Proximity to the heavily travelled Trans-Canada Highway makes it reasonable to assume that visitation levels would have been even higher than at Fort Steele and Barkerville – perhaps high enough to offset the extra start-up costs associated with land acquisition. Yet by 1970, even without a major historically themed attraction on the Trans-Canada, the highways of the BC Interior seemed to be increasingly awash with old-timey ghost town parks, outdoor museums, living museums, and local museums. These were complemented by an array of monuments, markers, and state-designated historical sites. In the early 1960s, a palisaded "frontier town" was built at Cultus Lake in the Fraser Valley. During the late 1960s, the Kamloops Museum Association collaborated with the Kamloops Board of Trade to build an open-air museum with a palisade wall in Riverside Park. It housed wagons, tractors, and other large items that were too big to store in the city's 1955 museum. In Prince George, a group of history enthusiasts and tourism promoters decided to build a replica of the North West Company's 1807 Fort George trading post. When they learned that Fort George had in fact been a modest collection of storehouses, they deemed this too boring and proceeded to erect a large stockade with prominent blockhouses and a palisade. In the late 1960s, a private company proposed to turn the entire village of Clinton into a historical attraction that would span both sides of the Cariboo Highway. Under this scheme, eye-catching palisades would have been installed at the points where the highway entered the village, and all the storefronts lining the highway would have been renovated to make Clinton look as it might have done during the gold rush days.

History through the Rearview Mirror

History by the road was big business in the BC Interior by 1970, remaking the image of dozens of communities as large and small players sought to benefit from the "old rush" generated by the motoring public's sustained enthusiasm for locally distinctive yet culturally familiar landscape features. The 1970s would see the establishment and preservation of many more attractions, as the Parks Branch and then its successor agency the Heritage Conservation Branch (established in 1977) continued to acquire properties, erect Stop of Interest markers, and provide support to local museums. Almost all the major historical venues that the provincial government added were related to the fur trade, the gold rush, and pioneering. All, including the Keremeos Grist Mill, St. John the Divine Church at Yale, and Hat Creek Ranch near Cache Creek, stood beside or just a short distance from an arterial road.

The new living museums helped fill out what by the late 1970s was a sprawling and professionally managed system of state-built attractions, complementing the bigger, more expensive "destination" assets of the 1960s and further adorning the highway network that enabled British Columbians to see them. With their carefully cultivated ambiance and publicity generated by government agencies and private promoters alike, they captured the attention of both residents and visitors. It is impossible to gauge precisely how they shaped public understanding of the Interior's history, but there is no doubt that they were immensely popular places to get out of the car and learn something about the landscapes and communities being driven through. Their automobile-free spaces, old (looking) wooden structures, and muscle- and steam-powered conveyances transported visitors to the past. In the midst of the postwar resource boom, their commemoration of boom towns of yesteryear drove home the essential role of natural resource extraction in the Interior economy. In celebrating solitary figures such as the prospector, stagecoach driver, cowboy on the open range, and boom-town merchant, they also provided reassuring lessons about the place of the enterprising individual at a time when impersonal megaprojects, international corporations, and complex bureaucracies were increasingly at the centre of modern life. At the same time, by marking forlorn mining camps and forgotten fur trade posts, they subtly, implicitly gestured toward progress by contrasting the failures of a past laissez-faire political economy (and cut-and-run treatment of the environment) against the active, stabilizing role played by the enlightened Fordist state. They were tourist attractions but also province-building devices in the cultural sense, generating shared experiences that by their association with specific places and the process of journeying to reach them were more appealing and memorable than most classroom lessons or history books.

The paths to the past traced by Route B show that history by the road in the BC Interior did not begin with the 1958 centennial celebrations and the state's active role in them. More than thirty years earlier, as the Interior was being opened up to large numbers of motorists from the Coast and points farther afield, its roadsides were being seeded with a range of historical landscape features by businesses, boosters, and the Historic Sites and Monuments Board of Canada. That such an array of interested parties was engaged in this practice, to the point that it became unremarkable, demonstrates the wider cultural and business impulse to cultivate the past during these years. This project was tightly connected to automobility, to the travel patterns and viewing habits of a fast-growing proportion of the public. It had its heyday during the late 1950s and the 1960s, with a proliferation of purpose-built attractions, large and small, public and private. "Old" proved a kind of replacement for gold, and though it was not as economically valuable or influential in terms of community formation, it contributed significantly to the service sector in parts of the Interior that might otherwise have withered. Today, Barkerville, Fort Steele, and several other "restored" ghost towns have served as roadside attractions for more than half a century, which is substantially longer than the romantic frontier boom times that they themselves evoke. They have proven durable assets for British Columbia and have significant histories *as* historical attractions. Some are even the objects of nostalgia, as suggested by the fact that new series of Stop of Interest signs were created for the province's 2008 sesquicentennial and then again in 2016. Many of these green-on-gold markers replaced earlier ones that had been vandalized, stolen for their value as scrap, or – in a large number of cases – bypassed or removed to make way for subsequent rounds of highway modernization.

Conclusion

Looking Back on British Columbia by the Road

Nature and history in the BC Interior during the mid-twentieth century were closely bound up with and structured by automobility – the system of objects, spaces, images, habits, and practices that surrounded private automobiles and public roads. Motorists experienced the landscapes of the Interior in a very different way than steamboat and railway passengers did, in that they were nominally free to choose their own route, pace, and schedule, pausing when and where they liked. They came to see and know their province by the road: in the sense of driving along a massive, expensive network built and maintained by the state, and in the sense of viewing landscapes that, in a growing number of cases, had been prepared specifically for them.

As the motoring public became a larger, more diverse, and more politically and economically important group over the course of the century, the manner in which they saw the province became a pressing concern for the incipient and then fully formed Fordist state. Politicians and bureaucrats became increasingly road-minded, seeing good roads and appealing landscapes as assets that could draw tourists and stimulate other types of consumption, while legitimating the state in the eyes of citizens and assuaging concerns about resource use and modernization. In the early 1940s, the provincial government began to develop a park system that would be accessible to drivers, establishing hundreds of parks along arterial highways during the next thirty years. Two of the largest, most automobile-accessible examples, Manning and Hamber, stand out as cases that reveal the intricacy of the interests and agendas that could converge on park development and management. In the late 1950s, the government launched a similar program with historic sites, which – provided they caught the motoring public's interest at the right time and in the right way – also came to serve as important amenities. Part of automobility was, then, a public pedagogy that accounted for new, modern ways of experiencing time and space, and, by extension, nature and history. State-built infrastructure combined with the selective efforts of various groups to manipulate and modify roadside landscapes in a manner that ineluctably shaped how the public perceived particular places and entire regions.

An enormously complex and diffuse system, automobility was one of the major economic engines of twentieth-century North America. This was true in British Columbia, even though the province had only a peripheral role in the production of automobiles (as a supplier of raw materials). In the BC Interior, as in most parts of North America, it was automobile travel – people's actual use of cars, trucks, and roads, and consumption of goods and services associated with doing so – that played the bigger role. A society did not need to *make* automobiles in order to be *remade,* in good measure, by them. People drove in the Interior for all kinds of reasons. Some hauled timber, produce, and freight. Others commuted to work. Some drove to maintain family ties, or for pleasure, for recreation, for an escape from everyday routines and surroundings. Regardless of why they took to the road, they were part of a larger community – the motoring public. As citizens and as consumers, they shared interests and experiences that were specific to the province, regions, and communities in which they lived. At the same time, they also shared many interests and experiences with other motorists, making them part of a much larger public and a continental – even global – culture of automobility. For many or even most BC residents and visitors, driving became an important and very modern way of experiencing and imagining the landscapes and communities of the Interior, even in instances where they were drawn to antimodern themes.

For all the flexibility that was associated with driving, the state determined much of what motorists saw because it selected, prepared, and maintained the expensive paths that automobiles had to follow. The sense of personal freedom commonly associated with driving was, in practice, effectively inseparable from the public road network. Motorists who journeyed between Coast and Interior had little choice but to take the Fraser Canyon route until the long-delayed Hope-Princeton Highway was completed in 1949. Similarly, circumnavigating the Big Bend of the Columbia was impossible until the state built a road there in the 1930s, and then impossible again after the state allowed it to be flooded in the early 1970s. To be clear, this is not to suggest that the state determined the *meanings* that drivers attached to their landscape experiences. Rather, it is simply to contend that the landscapes visible from arterial roads formed a vast public facade that came to be imbued with special cultural, political, and economic significance precisely because so many people saw it in a seemingly free and unstructured manner. It was a widely shared experience, something that a very large number of British Columbians had in common – particularly those who were white and middle class. Thus, the opening ceremonies that were organized for the Big Bend Highway in 1940, the Hope-Princeton in 1949, the Rogers Pass route in 1962, and the new bridge over the Kootenay River at Fort Steele in 1967 were not just photo opportunities for grandstanding politicians: they were also very real instances of the Fordist state opening new possibilities to the motoring public as well as to big and small businesses.

British Columbia's Fordist state did not make its decisions about the expansion and improvement of the highway network in isolation. Politicians and government agencies were lobbied by parties who wanted the development of road infrastructure steered to their advantage. These included business owners, tourism promoters, agricultural producers, land companies, mining companies, and forestry companies. They were joined by myriad other parties who had interests in promoting automobile travel or in making British Columbia look good to the motoring public, such as automobile dealers, oil companies, community boosters, outdoor recreationalists, and history enthusiasts. Victoria also had to co-ordinate with or at least take into account the road-building priorities of provinces and states that bordered against British Columbia, as well as the federal government, which was responsible for roads in national parks and Indian reserves.

Just as roads were pressing political and economic concerns in mid-twentieth-century British Columbia, so were the shared landscape experiences and "lessons" that the public picked up while travelling along them. Perhaps the best evidence of how pervasive this Fordist visual pedagogy was can be found in those cases where people expressed concerns about the "view from the road" before the road in question had even been built, as with the Hope-Princeton and Big Bend Highways during the 1930s, and with the new section of road through Fort Steele. They foresaw that roads would act as a kind of cultural infrastructure, shaping the views of large numbers of people over the decades, and therefore scrambled to preserve landscape features that would represent their values or interests.

Studying automobility as a system – as simultaneously an imposing socio-economic structure manifest in physical infrastructure, a political practice generating rival and enduring interests, *and* a way of experiencing time and space that often translated into disparate aesthetic choices and preferences – helps to illuminate new relationships that emerged during the mid-twentieth century. In isolation, a debate about a certain park or historic site might be interpreted as a purely local contest between rival interests, but once it is placed in its more general context, we can appreciate not only the clash of opinions, but the shared languages of aesthetic naturalism and easily digested public history in which they were expressed. Furthermore, for all the multiplicity of agents and interests at work in automobility in British Columbia, the *absence* of sustained debate about whether or how the state should manage roadside landscapes is particularly instructive: it indicates a widely shared vision whereby it was taken for granted that the landscapes visible along arterial highways should be regulated and developed in accordance with the travel patterns and viewing habits of the motoring public.

Fordism – the political-economic moment in which the state acted to smooth out capitalism's tendency toward crisis by balancing mass production and mass consumption – provides a useful unifying theme for mid-century automobility and for the multiple ways that politicians and senior officials of British Columbia's blacktop state became invested in roads. The road network was of course intended to facilitate commercial activity and natural resource extraction, and also to provide communication between far-flung communities. This was province building in the familiar economic and social sense. But modifying and managing roadside landscapes so that they would appeal to, attract, and reassure the motoring public also came to be seen as another legitimate (even necessary) way to get the best possible return from British Columbia's expensive modern highway infrastructure. Here the construction of roads and management of landscapes can be seen as province building in cultural terms. The accumulation and legitimation functions of the Fordist state were smoothly aligned in successful projects, such as Manning Park, Barkerville, and Fort Steele. But just as revealing of the underlying structures at work are the instances in which the alignment did not slot into place, such as the failure to launch of Columbia Village or the long, strange fiasco of Hamber Park and the Big Bend Highway. In these cases, fragmentation within the Fordist state itself resulted in the failure of what might have become significant assets.

Modernity and Nature by the Road

An important element of Fordist modernity in mid-twentieth-century Canada was the ideal of recreational democracy, the notion that all citizens were entitled to enjoy time off for leisure – particularly if it included an element of healthful self-improvement, as with participation in outdoor sports or strenuous, contemplative encounters with nature. Whether rattled by urban turmoil, worn down by the drudgery of the farm, or – particularly after the Second World War – bored stiff by the suburbs, British Columbians were believed to require therapeutic places where they could recover their depleted energies, all the better to engage anew with the stresses and strains of modern life. Martin Allerdale Grainger's horseback excursions into the southern Cascade Mountains exemplified the beneficial practice of roughing it, as he sought mental revivification in the high country. These kinds of activities had a long history in British Columbia, going back to the trails and alpine huts that the Canadian Pacific Railway built around its mountain resorts in the 1880s. However, mass automobility brought new antidotes to modernity within the reach of masses of people, ranging from the leisurely Sunday drive in the country to the extended car-camping trip. Automobility was often hailed as a triumph of democracy, egalitarianism, and expert planning because private automobiles and public roads enabled the masses to enjoy places and experiences that had previously been accessible only to an elite. That Manning Park's campgrounds should be free of charge early on and designed so that a screen of brush and timber separated campers from both the highway and each other suggested the down-to-earth ways that recreational democracy was realized in practice. It was deemed important, in the apt phrase of planner Roy Lowery, that provincial parks should provide visitors with an "atmosphere of congeniality and freedom."[1]

However, as more and more motorists travelled to and through these special places, particularly after the Second World War, their sheer numbers made any definitive escape from modernity an ever-more-unlikely prospect. At Manning, managers struggled to keep up with visitor demand almost from the moment that the Hope-Princeton Highway threw the park open to the motoring public. Manning's success gradually threatened to undermine the naturalistic, anti-modern aesthetic that had helped make it so popular in the first place. The same thing happened at many other road-accessible parks, including Barkerville, whose attendance rose more than tenfold during its first four years as a provincial park and threatened its cultivated frontier atmosphere. By the mid-1960s, there was a growing likelihood that British Columbians who sought to escape from the everyday routines and spaces of their home communities by taking a road trip through the Interior would find themselves on a busy highway bound for a dusty, crowded campground, passing businesses and attractions with overflowing parking lots all along the way, while making note of familiar historical landmarks that had been bypassed or otherwise obscured due to a highway improvement project. The landscapes of BC parks and historic sites were not static, even though they were presented and often perceived as such. Working behind the scenery as aesthetic managers, Parks Branch staff strove to maintain appearances and meet the expectations of the public.

British Columbia's park planners believed that the motoring public deserved a break from industry and even capitalism itself when they visited a park or an officially designated historic site. It was thought improper to have too many reminders within parks of the resource extraction industries that drove the province's economy and that of the Interior in particular. Even though logging and prospecting were allowed inside the provincial parks under certain strict conditions, it was vitally important that this be hidden by buffer zones, and access roads were to be kept to a minimum and made as inconspicuous as possible. Evidence of road construction and recent habitation was also concealed, and commercial activity was stringently regulated. Even such benign modern phenomena as utility lines, aluminum-skinned trailers, and telephone booths seemed examples of scenic defacement, to be screened from view of the highway. Though rarely stated as such, the working premise was that drivers should experience their surroundings (although not the highway itself) as something timeless and untouched by the very modernity that had allowed them access to such sites.

The Parks Division initially considered developing Manning Park as a therapeutic space where well-heeled city dwellers might restore themselves in the rugged quietude of its alpine heights. One early park supporter even disparaged the motoring public, dismissing them as too lazy and uncultured to get out of their cars and properly encounter nature. However, the rise of recreational democracy as an ideal of the Fordist state during the Second World War entailed a demand that the park be replanned as a more democratic space, oriented toward the more numerous and fast-growing motoring public. This meant a new aesthetic of nature, one that replaced the elite pursuit of the rarefied high country with an emphasis on the scenes and attractions that would be visible from the Hope-Princeton Highway, which ran along the valley floor.

Park managers assigned great significance to the look of the highway corridor and devoted much time and effort to planning and policing it. They worried about "unsightly commercialism" and feared that the owners of auto camps and other businesses would disrupt the naturalistic aesthetic they were attempting to impose. Human interventions that were visible to the public must not clash with the natural surroundings – they must not be a blot on the landscape. Unspoken but understood was the sharp distinction between a blot and an attraction, an eyesore and an asset. Ideally, human interventions would blend in with their surroundings, as the provincial government sought to do when it built the rustic Pinewoods concession complex.

Pinewoods, as the most built-up part of Manning Park, and the place where motorists were most likely to pause, was the site of controversies over signage, hazardous traffic conditions, expanded visitor facilities, and overwhelmed utilities. However, the earlier debate regarding the effort to establish a beer parlour in the concession complex is especially noteworthy because it revealed certain assumptions about class and propriety. Importing elements of "rough" working-class culture into "nature" was deemed tantamount to desecration, for nature was imagined to be congenial, not to beer-drinking workers, but to their more refined and temperate social betters. A beer parlour in Manning was both a morally *and* an aesthetically dubious proposition, one that threatened to corrupt its value as a provincial asset. The fear of not having complete aesthetic control over the concession complex ultimately drove Victoria to assume direct responsibility for its development. Ironically, when the Social Credit government of Bill Bennett privatized Pinewoods in the early 1980s, the new owners' decision to open a pub there proved almost as controversial as the selling off of a state-developed asset.

In their role as aesthetic managers, park staff manipulated many aspects of Manning's landscapes with the intention of shaping the motoring public's views. They removed trees in some places and planted them in others. They built parking lots and access roads that made it easy for drivers to visit Sumallo Grove, Rhododendron Flats, and the Lightning Lakes. They manipulated animal habitat to make some species more visible and others less visible. Planners even supplemented real animals with representations of animals, such as the bear and marmot sign-sculptures that marked the entry points to Manning and the stuffed animals displayed in the nature house interpretation centre. Perhaps the best example of the lengths to which the Parks Division would go was the 1950 addition of the mile-wide, ten-mile-long parkway to the western boundary of Manning, which gave it control over a series of scenic, natural, and historical attractions, while at the same time downplaying or minimizing the desolation of the Big Burn.

When nature by the road failed to conform to pre-existing scripts or appeal to the tastes of the motoring public, state planners' verdicts could verge on the absolute. Hamber Park was downgraded from Class A to Class B status just a few years after it was established, and it was ultimately truncated, in large part because the experience of driving the Big Bend Highway had been widely deemed unpleasant. In a way, the undifferentiated, seemingly endless, almost claustrophobic forests of the Big Bend country were *too* natural – too unimproved – for their own good. Neither the road nor the surrounding landscapes made the province look good to drivers. Judged harshly in a damning reconnaissance report drawn up by planners who spent a scant thirty-six hours exploring the section of it that was visible from the highway (the same planners who had lavished attention on Manning just two years earlier), Hamber was handicapped from the outset by the aesthetic experiences afforded by the lonely, roundabout, gravel-surfaced road that had made it accessible. The Parks Division's half-hearted attempts to effect a redemption through stagecraft proved unavailing, and Hamber slid into obscurity through the 1940s and 1950s, unknown to the public, until the state found a higher purpose for the Big Bend country. As both Manning and Hamber illustrated, a certain "normal" nature in western Canada depended intimately upon a particular visual-vehicular relationship.

In their internal communications and by their actions on the ground, park managers readily admitted that the "nature" experienced by the motoring public consisted largely of what was visible from the highway. In some places, as in many parts of the Big Bend country, this was merely a thin strip, no wider than a few feet. In other places, as along the shores of icy Kinbasket Lake, it stretched as far as the eye could see. The nature of parks was first and foremost what drivers saw, not the land as it actually was beyond sight of the highway – those "backcountry" areas were managed in a much different way. Under conditions of mid-century modernity, the visual – whether on television or through the windshield – triumphed over the other senses, and to a high degree roads and parks followed the rules of the society of the spectacle. Those that failed to follow these rules – Hamber Park providing a key example – might ultimately be extinguished, not because they were not "natural" but because insufficient effort had been vested in making them appealing. Neither Manning nor Hamber had been thought intrinsically scenic after they were first accessible by road. Had the Parks Division lavished attention on Hamber the way it did on Manning, and had the Big Bend Highway been paved, widened, and lined with pullouts, viewpoints, and businesses, it seems reasonable to imagine that destroying the park and flooding the highway might have been more difficult than they were.

The nature of "beautiful British Columbia" was something that many residents and visitors came to respect and even revere during the period 1920–70, as suggested by the complaints that ordinary motorists made to the government about eyesores and developments that they believed transgressed its essential qualities. Yet, as the case of Hamber Park suggests, such reverence went only so far and was contingent. Even the sublimity of a spectacular stand of tall and ancient timber, which the state had promised to preserve "in perpetuity," was no guarantee of protection if the land could be put to a more profitable use. In the span of three decades, the provincial and federal governments went from agreeing that the roadside timber between Kinbasket Lake and Boat Encampment should be preserved as an attraction to a perfunctory acceptance of its destruction by logging, fires, and flooding to advance a "high modern" hydroelectric megaproject.

Modernity and History by the Road

Whereas the development of British Columbia's provincial parks was tightly controlled by the state, historical sites were cultivated by a variety of parties between 1925 and 1955. Most commemorated the adventurers and explorers of the past in hopes of advancing their own business interests. Some sought to entice motorists into a roadhouse or auto camp, whereas others hoped to make them linger in a certain community. Many looked to the state to support their (usually modest) ventures, indirectly during the interwar years, when employing the past as a drawing card for travellers was still highly novel, and more directly after 1945.

History by the road during this period often took the form of isolated phenomena – special events, roadside curiosities, plaques, markers – that singly and together offered a way of enjoying that vague, soothing quality here called old-timey-ness. Rustic wagons stationed beside the road, old canoes and waterwheels displayed near a town centre – these remnants from the days before petroleum-powered transportation might evoke an atmosphere of yesteryear, but they did not demand any in-depth reading or critical reflection about the province's often tumultuous past. In such cases, it was important that history be eye catching, lively, and accessible but not necessarily that it be accurate or profound. Plaques commemorated long-gone places and characters whose stories could be presented as uplifting or romantic: the fur trade posts and gold camps of bygone days, for example, or the road and bridge builders who left their mark on the land. Generally, however, those for whom modernity had imposed heavy costs – such as the First Nations families living on small Indian reserves in the Fraser and Thompson Canyons or the old bachelors of Barkerville – were largely forgotten. That modernity might be volatile, disorienting, and even tragic was not an idea that boosters, entrepreneurs, or agencies of the state were likely to develop in their treatment of either nature or history. When First Nations groups erected monuments in close proximity to the Fraser Canyon Highway at I:yem and Lytton during the interwar years, both of which asserted ongoing land claims while also referring to historical events, they were overlooked in motoring guidebooks and related literature, which speaks to the highly selective nature of history by the road.

Even stagnant areas whose economic backwardness was palpable – such as the Cariboo Plateau during the mid- and late 1920s – could be converted into attractions if they were easily accessible and properly promoted. Decrepitude and backwardness could be transmuted into assets. Old buildings and the detritus of the gold rush and wagon road days could be reframed as romantic and colourful. Where the scenery failed to inspire, as in the Cariboo, the old-timey might replace it as a draw for the travelling public.

State history making was less common than entrepreneurial history making during the interwar years and early 1950s, but what little there was tended, unsurprisingly, to sing the praises of order, material progress, and scientific and administrative enlightenment, all underwritten or directly organized by an active, benevolent state. The Historic Sites and Monuments Board of Canada's (HSMBC) cairns at Yale and Barkerville and the Royal Engineers cairn at the Alexandra Bridge all celebrated the theme of heroic infrastructure, with the state and its agents presented as having opened up the Interior to commodity extraction, communication, and colonization. For drivers on the Cariboo Highway, which for lengthy stretches ran along the route of the Cariboo Wagon Road, these monuments were particularly evocative, especially given the number of stopping places that had direct links to gold rush days. In this rolling narrative, monuments such as the one at Quesnel that commemorated the Collins Overland Telegraph placed the BC hinterlands within the much larger picture of the West's beneficent modernization and unification of the entire world.

It was typical that the 1929 unveiling of the HSMBC monument in Barkerville involved a large motorcade heading over the Quesnel-Barkerville road and was accompanied by the first appearance of a flying machine in the district. Stories that diverged markedly from the official narrative – such as those involving the colonial appropriation of Indigenous land – were excluded. Indeed, history by the road was remarkably silent on First Nations communities during the interwar period and only barely audible during the postwar decades. How First Nations people responded to the motoring public's enthusiasm for distinctive signs of pastness and requirement for food, gas, and lodging merits future attention from historians, as does the larger question of how automobility affected and was incorporated into their communities.

The BC government did not take an active role in cultivating history by the road until 1958. There were occasional gestures, however. For example, when the elderly prospector Charlie Bonnevier and his packhorse were invited to participate in the opening ceremony for the Hope-Princeton Highway in 1949, their carefully orchestrated appearance highlighted the new highway's credentials as a state project that built and improved upon the past while opening uncharted prospects to the public. Also in Manning Park, the Parks Division invoked history when it converted remnants of the Dewdney Trail seventeen miles beyond Hope into a roadside attraction. Characteristically, this part of the trail was selected because it was visible from the highway, whereas more intact portions elsewhere were ignored and allowed to fall into disrepair.

History by the road became less didactic and increasingly recreational during the postwar years. Repeatedly, one comes across depictions of the BC Interior that are reminiscent of a Hollywood western, with romantic frontier folksiness converted into palisaded picturesqueness. Stagecoaches, covered freight wagons, grizzled prospectors – they had long been scripted as parts of the Interior's public past, yet as history became increasingly recreational, BC history was undoubtedly reshaped by Hollywood's massively influential Wild West. It was entirely fitting that early advocates of the Fort Steele project contemplated the site's value as a film set and that its peeled log palisades and blockhouses, though concealing a prosaic service yard and administrative area, were also designed after taking account of Wild West stereotypes.

With the centenary celebrations of 1958, the state began to develop historical tourist attractions. Ironically, the Barkerville project was possible only because of the Fordist state, for which it was just one of several economic development ventures in a hinterland region. This town-sized monument to pioneer individualism and gold mining entrepreneurship existed only because the modern state had the capacity to create and sustain it: over the previous three decades, all local efforts to establish a museum or preserve the townsite had come to nothing. Contrary to appearances, then, Barkerville was of a piece with a slew of state megaprojects, such as the new dams in the Kootenay and Columbia River valleys and only slightly less impressive renovations to the province's transportation networks. By the 1960s, these kinds of major historical attractions were big business in the Interior, pieces of cultural infrastructure that served as strategic components of regional development.

The official reading of the past typically emphasized beneficent and necessary progress, and though Barkerville could justifiably be seen as an indication of modernity's broken promises and the human costs of a boom-and-bust economy, in this framework it stood for the spirit of optimism, the buoyancy of unfettered enterprise, and the essential place of the little guy in British Columbia. This was especially the case after its 1962 transformation into a living museum. The Fordist state used historical sites to valorize frontier archetypes, thereby reassuring small producers and businesspeople who were alarmed by the Interior's headlong rush into high modernity. It was similarly fitting that Fort Steele Historic Park was crafted in large measure to commemorate the gold rushes of the 1860s and 1890s, those antecedents of the province's post-1945 resource boom, and that it also entailed commemorating Sam Steele and the Mounties, who had allowed resource extraction to proceed in an orderly, profitable way.

The presentation of history still had to look appealing and had to function smoothly within the province's tourism and transportation infrastructure. The Stop of Interest markers erected in 1958 and subsequent years would be of little use or interest if they were boring and did not align with attractive, distinctive, or at least characteristic landscape features. When they thought about roadside attractions, the planners in the Parks Branch and Department of Highways understood their role as one of adapting historical themes to certain pre-determined vantage points. With this systematic Stop of Interest program, probably more than with any other instance of history by the road in the BC Interior, popular understandings of the past can be seen quite literally as an extension of the highway network.

Many historians have posited that automobility was a kind of long revolution that affected all of North America, but regional cultures of automobility have so far been sorely understudied. Each region was affected in markedly different ways, according to its position within an emerging continent-wide transportation network as well as its distinctive geography and the legacies of its past. Automobility in the BC Interior had its own shape and raised its own issues. In many respects, it is easier to appreciate the salience of automobility in such places, with their unevenly developed economies and sparse and widely spaced populations, than in densely settled cities. Often "the highway" was a rural community's most tangible (if not only) connection to the wider, modern world. For historians, who too often write the province's twentieth-century history without paying careful attention to the rural and wildland areas of the Interior, the questions raised by automobility deserve to be foregrounded. The swift rise and long endurance of the Social Credit government in the 1950s and 1960s, for example, which was seemingly out of step with the province's persisting class-based divisions, makes more sense if we remember that for many British Columbians, even working-class British Columbians, the modernization of the highway network and cultivation of appealing roadside landscapes and amenities were powerful proofs of a government that understood the practical needs and popular desires of "the people." Good roads and good government were closely tied together in the mid-twentieth century, and resourceful, ribbon-cutting, blacktop-minded politicians could deftly insist that the voting public appreciate the connection. The hypothesis that British Columbia's distinctive culture of automobility played a central role in entrenching Social Credit rule during the 1950s and 1960s seems all the more plausible when considered in the broader context of Fordism. Consider also the example of truck logging, which most historians have so far neglected. Few would deny the great regional significance of the forest industry, yet without a Fordist infrastructure of access roads and paved arterial highways, it could hardly have undergone its postwar modernization. The massive expansion of the Interior forest industry – a mainstay of British Columbia's postwar economy and also one of its biggest environmental changes – is a topic that needs to be considered as much in the context of automobility as in that of the industry per se.

Forestry capitalists were just one group among many that sought to exploit the new configurations implicit in automobility. Some had their own, relatively modest economic objectives, and historians need to learn more about the development of the BC service industry. For the various businesses that sold food, gas, and lodging along arterial routes such as the Fraser Canyon and Cariboo Highways, proximity to "the road" meant proximity to that most cherished of postwar dreams – an independent middle-class lifestyle. Many such dreams were dashed against the cold realities of a market that fluctuated wildly between the mid-1920s and the late 1940s, yet others paid off, particularly with the explosion of pleasure travel after the Second World War. At a time when corporations were becoming dominant in Canada as never before, the roadside offered niches in which families, franchisees, and individual entrepreneurs could enjoy a modest competence. In a political and symbolic sense, they testified to the persisting power of individualism, even at a time when corporations dwarfed all competitors. And such small businesses, often united in local service clubs and boards of trade, could in turn help their fellow citizens appreciate that publicly funded highways meant opportunities for little people as well as for the major corporate interests that were often their biggest beneficiaries. Many small towns developed signs, mascots, and symbols that solidified their links to the road and differentiated them from neighbouring communities. Thus, far from appearing to gratify the interests of a particular group, the expansion and improvement of the provincial highway network could appear to be the economic advantage of everyone.

Automobility was material spaces and objects, and also a culture – a vast system of signs, symbols, and practices. It meant that some sights became sites – beacons of the beautiful or the significant, surrounded by markers, often provided by the state, that authenticated their superior aesthetic status. Beauty might lie in the eye of the beholder, and this study has taken care to document cases in which individuals stubbornly insisted on finding beautiful that which most British Columbians dismissed as dull and uninspiring (and vice versa). Yet, when beauty became a business – when drivers en masse determined the fate of a given destination, whose reputation for dullness or excitement often preceded it – then new hierarchies of place developed around the geography of the highway network, with pre-existing aesthetics of the sublime and the beautiful brought to bear upon particular scenes and sites. Images, imagery, image-making practices: no matter how seemingly ethereal and abstract, these had concrete, real-world effects, as projects mounted by the state succeeded and failed in part according to how they looked and the emotional and aesthetic experiences they provided. There was even, one might say, a politics of beauty at work in postwar British Columbia (soon to become *Beautiful* British Columbia, as was stamped on all provincial licence plates after 1964). It mandated a government concerned about its popular legitimacy to provide naturalistic or old-timey-looking buffer strips along the roadside, so that evidence of its even greater concern to maintain capitalist accumulation, in the shape of clearcut logging and other resource extraction activities, remained out of sight. It fell to agencies of the Fordist state to effect such compromises, ones that scholars have developed at a high level of abstraction, but ones that, as this study has demonstrated, were literally enacted on the ground and by the road, ultimately becoming a commonsense part of everyday life in modern British Columbia.

Notes

Introduction

1 Taylor, *The Automobile Saga,* 58–66, ch. 5.

2 Historical geographer Cole Harris observes that as late as 1930, the provincial road network was but "a weak complement to a system of inland transportation still based primarily on railways and steamboats." Harris, *The Resettlement,* 173.

3 The best overview of Fordism remains David Harvey, *The Condition of Postmodernity* (Oxford: Basil Blackwell, 1989), part 2. For an example of how a Fordist framework can effectively be applied to modern Canadian socio-economic history, see Hak, *Capital and Labour.*

4 Barman, *The West beyond the West,* 1–12. Gordon Hak suggests that the Interior's perceived lack of socio-economic and geographic cohesion helps explain its relative neglect by BC historians. Hak, *Capital and Labour,* 16, 32.

5 Harris, *The Resettlement,* 192. Representations of the province's landscapes were certainly tied to those lines in the late nineteenth century, with painters, photographers, and travel writers piggybacking along major lines of commodity circulation; hence the crucial role that the "Canadian Pacific Railway school" of artists played in shaping the early province's place in the popular-imagination. See, for example, Roger Boulet, *Vistas: Artists on the Canadian Pacific Railway* (Calgary: Glenbow Museum, 2009); Schwartz and Koltun, "A Visual Cliché," 113–28; and Tippett and Cole, *From Desolation to Splendour.*

6 See, for example, Philpott, *Vacationland;* and Wyckoff, *On the Road Again.*

7 For some important scholarly treatments of landscape, see Jackson, *Discovering the Vernacular Landscape;* Matless, *Landscape and Englishness;* Tuan, *Space and Place;* and Wiley, *Landscape.*

8 Barman, *The West beyond the West,* 363.

9 On automobility as a non-linear system that could generate the preconditions for its own expansion, see Urry, "The System of Automobility," 25–40; and Dennis and Urry, *After the Car.*

10 On the automobile as a political vehicle in liberal contexts, see Seiler, "Statist Means to Individualist Ends," 5–36; and Seiler, "'So That We as a Race Might,'" 1091–1117. For far-right contexts, see Dimendberg, "The Will to Motorization," 90–137; Virilio, *Speed and Politics;* and Zeller, *Driving Germany.*

11 A culture of time and space is the set of experiential co-ordinates that are associated with a specific historical social formation. Many historians who have employed this concept have privileged literary and artistic production, with the effect of distancing the experience of modernity from common material and social conditions. See, for example, Kern, *The Culture of Time and Space.* In contrast, historical geographers who take a materialist approach argue that the time-space compression created by accelerated circulation of commodities and capital (via transportation and communication technologies and infrastructure) was the driving force behind modern cultures of time and space. Harvey, *The Condition of Postmodernity,* chs. 14–17; Warf, *Time-Space Compression.*

12 Railways symbolically epitomized and concretely facilitated industrial capitalism, and helped give rise to a new culture of time and space through the sense of time-space compression or "annihilation of space by time" generated by expanded markets and accelerated commodity circulation. As railways became the dominant mode of long-distance overland travel, communities, regions, and entire nations came to be known in the popular imagination as they were experienced by travellers moving over the rails. Schivelbusch, *The Railway Journey.* See also Beaumont and Freeman, *The Railway and Modernity;* Freeman, *Railways and the Victorian Imagination;* and Stilgoe, *Metropolitan Corridor.* According to Karl Marx, "the more production comes to be based on exchange value, and thus on exchange, the more important for production do the physical conditions of exchange become – the means of communication and transport. By its very nature, capital strives to go beyond every spatial limitation. Hence the creation of physical conditions of exchange – of the means of communication and transport – becomes a necessity for it to an incomparably greater degree: space must be annihilated by time." Marx, "Outlines of the Critique," 448.

13 See, for example, Duffy, *The Speed Handbook;* Virilio, *The Art of the Motor;* and Virilio, "Dromoscopy," 10–22.

14 On the popularity of auto touring among North American elites prior to 1920, see Belasco, *Americans on the Road,* chs. 1–2; and McCarthy, *Auto Mania,* ch. 1. On the touring car as a means of getting in touch with nature, see Barnett, "Drive-By Viewing," 30–54.

15 Kathleen Franz, *Tinkering: Consumers Reinvent the Early Automobile* (Philadelphia: University of Pennsylvania Press, 2005); McCarthy, *Auto Mania;* Packer, *Mobility without Mayhem;* Seiler, *Republic of Drivers;* Scharff, *Taking the Wheel.* Also see Shaffer, *See America First.* For a trans-Atlantic perspective, see Mom, *Atlantic Automobilism.*

16 Merriman, *Driving Spaces;* Zeller, *Driving Germany.* Also see Mauch and Zeller, *The World beyond the Windshield;* and Wolfe, *Autos and Progress.*

17 The most comprehensive survey of such changes is Christopher Wells, *Car Country: An Environmental History* (Seattle: University of Washington Press, 2012). John Jakle and Keith Sculle have produced an invaluable series of historical geographies about America's common roadside commercial features, including *America's Main Street Hotels; Fast Food; The Gas Station in America; Lots of Parking; Signs in America's Auto Age;* and also Jakle, Sculle, and Rogers, *The Motel in America.* Also see Belasco, *Americans on the Road;* Gudis, *Buyways;* Liebs, *Main Street to Miracle Mile;* and Schlereth, *Reading the Road.*

18 On roadside advertising, see Gudis, *Buyways;* Jakle and Sculle, *Signs in America's Auto Age;* Liebs, *Main Street to Miracle Mile;* and Martin Treu, *Signs, Streets, and Storefronts: A History*

of Architecture and Graphics along America's Commercial Corridors (Baltimore: Johns Hopkins University Press, 2012). On automobility, place-image, and local and regional identity in America, see Leib, "Identity, Banal Nationalism," 37–52; Marling, *Colossus of Roads;* and Whisnant, *Super-Scenic Motorway.*

19 On motoring experiences of nature, see Barnett, "Drive-By Viewing"; Belasco, *Americans on the Road;* Carr, *Mission 66;* Carr, *Wilderness by Design;* Colten and Dilsaver, "The Hidden Landscape," 27–50; Louter, *Windshield Wilderness;* Sutter, *Driven Wild;* Whisnant, *Super-Scenic Motorway;* and White, *Home on the Road.*

20 Anastakis, *Car Nation;* Francis, *A Road for Canada;* Monaghan, *Canada's New Main Street;* Tremblay, *La culture de l'automobilité au Canada.* For a cultural and business history of that quintessentially Canadian roadside business, the donut shop, see Penfold, *The Donut.* There has been surprisingly little research done on automobility on a regional scale in Canada. For many years, Stephen Davies's study of motoring in southern Ontario was the only major provincial-scale work. Davies, "Ontario and the Automobile." However, recent work on Quebec's motoring culture indicates a growing recognition of distinctive regional trajectories. Maude-Emmanuelle Lambert, "À travers le pare-brise: la création des territoires touristiques à l'ère de l'automobile (Québec et Ontario, 1920-1967)" (PhD diss., Université de Montréal, 2013); Etienne Faugier, "L'économie de la vitesse: l'automobilisme et ses enjeux dans le département du Rhône et la région de Québec (1919-1961)" (PhD diss., Université Lyon 2, 2013). On automobility's key role in the development of regional tourist attractions in Canada, see MacEachern, *Natural Selections;* McKay and Bates, *In the Province of History;* and Stevens, "Cars and Cottages," 26–56.

21 See, for example, Craig, *Trucking;* Harvey, *Carving the Western Path: By River;* Harvey, *Carving the Western Path: Routes;* Harvey, *The Coast Connection;* Scheideman, *Policing the Fringe;* and Frank White, *Milk Spills and One-Log Loads: Memories of a Pioneer Truck Driver* (Vancouver: Harbour, 2013). On BC motoring prior to 1920, see Taylor, *The Automobile Saga.*

22 Belshaw and Purvey, *Private Grief;* Garrish, *Tales from the Back;* Kluckner, *Vanishing British Columbia.* Also see Samantha Morris, "Mapping the Family Road Trip: The Automobile, the Family, and Outdoor Recreation in Postwar British Columbia" (Master's thesis, University of Victoria, 2010).

23 Dawson, *Selling British Columbia;* Duffy, *Evergreen Playground;* O'Brian, "Shaping World Culture," 93–112; White, *It Pays to Play.*

24 Harvey, *The Coast Connection,* 78–81, 90.

25 On the primitive state of BC automobile roads in the interwar years, see Harris, "Moving amidst the Mountains," 20–25. On British Columbia's earliest "good roads" movement, see Taylor, *The Automobile Saga,* ch. 10.

26 Minister of Public Works J.H. King, speech before the Good Roads League of British Columbia, 6 October 1919, quoted in Harvey, *The Coast Connection,* 92.

27 On Revelstoke's tourism boosters and the parkway they proposed for Mount Revelstoke National Park, see Clayton, "'A National Playground,'" 389–408.

28 Regarding the popularity of early commercial operations along the canyon route, see Kluckner, *Vanishing British Columbia,* 114–22.

Route A

1 Louter, *Windshield Wilderness.*

2 On the cultural and economic importance that some Vancouverites attached to improving and then maintaining the landscape in one of the province's most famous and accessible parks, see Kheraj, *Inventing Stanley Park,* chs. 3, 5.

3 An important exception to this is Davis, *National Park Roads.* In the Canadian literature on park history, questions about "the machine in the garden" have tended to be shunted aside in favour of investigating the politics of resource development. When aspects of automobility are touched on, it has usually been in the context of shifting policy and management techniques because of a growing number of (middle- and working-class) visitors who arrived by automobile. The shaping of park landscapes by and for the motoring public has gone largely overlooked. E.J. Hart describes the Canadian Pacific Railway's role in earliest motor touring, in *The Selling of Canada,* and also provides a history of a major guiding and touring company operating out of Banff, in *The Brewster Story.*

4 See, for example, Anderson, *British Columbia's Magnificent Parks;* Wilson, *Talk and Log;* and Youds, "A Park System."

Chapter 1

1 Harvey, *The Coast Connection,* 109.

2 The Okanagan Valley had the highest rate of automobile ownership in the BC Interior in 1918, as described in Taylor, *The Automobile Saga,* 80–81. The poor condition of the region's road network and the need for roundabout detours to reach the Coast are described in Craig, *Trucking,* ch. 4; Currie, *Princeton: 120 Years,* 78; and Harvey, *Carving the Western Path: Routes,* ch. 1.

3 Dendy and Kyle, *A Fruitful Century,* ch. 3, especially 67–71.

4 On the Okanagan Valley's healthful image, see Bennett, "Blossoms and Borders."

5 Minister of Public Works Rolf Bruhn told Premier Tolmie that "a large number of transient unemployed men from the larger centres may be placed on such work as the Lougheed Highway, North Thompson, Big Bend, Hope-Princeton, University area, West Coast Road, etc." As he explained, "it is my opinion that in caring for the unemployed, especially single men and transients, that such men should be employed in various parts of the Province instead of concentrating them in camps in one locality." University of British Columbia Library Special Collections (hereafter UBCSC), Simon Fraser Tolmie fonds, box 8, file 19, Bruhn to Tolmie, 17 June 1931.

6 Two accounts of life in camps along the Hope-Princeton are Jack Rainbow's reminiscences in Smuin, "Relief Camps of the Great Depression," 85–88; and Cawston, "Happy Days in a Relief Camp," 55–62. On the regression of road construction techniques and the cynicism that inefficient "make work" practices engendered among many relief camp workers, see Monaghan, *Canada's New Main Street,* 15; Struthers, *No Fault of Their Own,* 133–35; and Thompson and Seager, *Canada, 1922-1939,* 268–69.

7 UBCSC, Simon Fraser Tolmie fonds, box 8, file 21, Tolmie to C.F. McHardy, 13 January 1932; Bruhn to Tolmie, 4 October 1932.

8 Rothman, "A History of U.S. National Parks," 51–67.

9 Booth, "Life and Times of Martin Grainger"; Drushka, *HR: A Biography,* 72; Robert Griffin and Lorne Hammond, *Stewards of the People's Forests: A Short History of the British Columbia Forest Service* (Victoria: Royal BC Museum, 2014), 64–68; Murray, *Home from the Hill,* part 3.

10 Grainger's "escape from business" is reminiscent of Toronto ad-man Charles Sauriol's routine, which involved a weekly retreat to the quietude of the upper Don River Valley. Bonnell, "An Intimate Understanding of Place," 607–36. Also see Shi, *The Simple Life,* ch. 9. On outdoor recreation and landscape contemplation as a middle-class means of escaping city life in interwar British Columbia, see Routledge, "'Being a Girl without Being a Girl,'" 31–58; and Tippett and Cole, *From Desolation to Splendour,* ch. 8.

11 Grainger's letters describing his travels in the Cascades were posthumously compiled in Grainger, *Riding the Skyline.* His proposed Skyline Club echoed the Trail Riders of the Canadian Rockies, which the CPR organized in the early 1920s as a way of drawing well-heeled riding enthusiasts to Canada's western national parks. See Hart, *The Selling of Canada,* 105–6.

12 Logging at Green Timbers began in the late 1920s, with the last trees removed in early 1930. Sandquist, "The Giant Killers."

13 British Columbia Archives (hereafter BCA), GR-1991 Records with Regard to Parks, reel 1800, Grainger to F.P. Burden, Minister of Lands, 11 June 1930.

14 Regarding Burr and Thomas's involvement, see BCA, GR-1991, reel 1800, "Three Brothers Park on New Highway Defenseless until Province Steps In," undated clipping from *Weekend Province;* Currie, *Princeton: 120 Years,* 77; Obituary for F.E. Burr, *Princeton Similkameen Spotlight,* 2 August 1945; "Grand Old Man Celebrates 90," *Princeton Similkameen Spotlight,* 11 November 1964; and Princeton and District Museum and Archives, clipping files, unpublished obituary for Bert Thomas written by Dave Taylor.

15 See Drushka, *HR: A Biography;* and Hak, *Capital and Labour,* 20–25.

16 Drushka, *HR: A Biography,* 125–26.

17 BCA, GR-1991, reel 1800, H.R. MacMillan to Burden, 14 June 1930.

18 Garnet Willis had been aware of the area's grazing potential for at least a decade, having driven cattle through it in the 1910s and having honeymooned there in 1919. Burn, "With Saddle and Pack-Horse," 41; Estabrooks, *Under the K,* 53–54; Willis, "In Memoriam," 124.

19 BCA, GR-1991, reel 1800, Garnet E. Willis to Premier, 24 June 1930; Willis to William Atkinson, MLA [Penticton], 24 June 1930; BC Sheep Breeders Association to Commissioner of Grazing, 27 November 1930.

20 BCA, GR-1991, reel 1800, T. Hooper, Secretary, Princeton Board of Trade, to Minister of Lands, 26 September 1930. Also see Grainger to Burden, 11 June 1930; and Commissioner of Grazing to M.E. Lauder, Secretary, BC Sheep Breeders Association, 1 December 1930. The exact date that the roadside reserve was put in place is not clear, but its purpose is outlined in British Columbia J.T. Fyles Natural Resources Library (hereafter BCNRL), C.P. Lyons and D.M. Trew, "Reconnaissance and Preliminary Recreation Plan, Ernest C. Manning Park" (Victoria, BC Forest Service, 1943).

21 On the state privileging of agriculture in British Columbia, see Cameron, *Openings: A Meditation;* Murton, *Creating a Modern Countryside;* and Sandwell, "Finding Rural British Columbia," 3–14.

22 BCA, GR-1991, reel 1805, Princeton Board of Trade to N.S. Lougheed, Minister of Public Works, 25 March and 23 April 1931; Grainger to Burden, 22 January 1931; reel 1800, Thomas to Lougheed, 23 March 1931. Also see MacMillan to Pooley, 10 September 1931, cited in Drushka, *HR: A Biography,* 152.

23 BCA, GR-1991, reel 1800, Penticton Board of Trade to A. Wells Gray, Minister of Lands, 1 June 1935; Deputy Minister of Lands H. Cathcart to Chief Forester, June 1935.

24 BCA, GR-1991, reel 1800, B.T. McCauley, Acting Director of the State Game Dept. of Washington, to F.R. Butler, Office of the Game Commission, 17 December 1935; Butler to Attorney General Sloan, 3 January 1936. Also see Prof. T.T. McCabe, University of California, to Butler, 23 December 1935.

25 BCA, GR-1991, reel 1805, Premier to Chief Forester, 2 June 1936; Manning memo to Premier, 5 June 1936.

26 On the work of the Young Men's Forest Training Program and other make-work schemes in BC forests during the Pattullo administration, see Griffin and Hammond, *Stewards of the People's Forests,* 90–94, 99–101; and Rajala, "From 'On-to-Ottawa,'" 118–50.

27 Brown, "The Bennett Government"; Cawston, "Happy Days in a Relief Camp"; Tanner, "Microcosms of Misfortune," 50–51.

28 Report by H.C. Anderson, Assistant District Engineer [Merritt], 30 November 1938, cited in Harvey, *The Coast Connection,* 113. Also see BCA, GR-1222, box 23, file 4, Penticton Board of Trade to Pattullo, 29 October 1937.

29 For example, BCA, GR-1222 Premiers' papers, box 23, file 4, Penticton Board of Trade to Premier Pattullo, 25 March 1937; Penticton Board of Trade to Pattullo, 29 October 1937; and Canadian Legion, Okanagan Zone, to Pattullo, 31 October 1937. Also see "$35,000 to Be All for Princeton Road," *Chilliwack Progress,* 4 August 1937, 6.

30 Currie, *Princeton: 120 Years,* 64; Sheils and Swankey, *Work and Wages,* 39–55.

31 See, for example, BCA, GR-1222, box 33, file 6, Greenwood Board of Trade to Pattullo, 5 June 1940; "Speech by L.H. Eyres, MLA in Provincial Legislature," *Chilliwack Progress,* 27 November 1940, 9. On extended closures of the Fraser Canyon highway in August 1934, January 1935, February and October 1937, January 1938, and December 1939, see Septer, *Flooding and Landslide.* It is noteworthy that during the First World War, the German military identified the Fraser Canyon as a key weak point in Canada's national transportation network. Martin Kitchen, "The German Invasion of Canada in the First World War," *International History Review* 7, no. 2 (May 1985): 245–60.

32 BCA, GR-1991, reel 1800, Assistant Chief Forester G.P. Melrose to Wells Gray, Minister of Lands, 22 April 1941. Regarding Melrose as a key park advocate, also see Lyons, "Tough Going," 37; and Shaw, "Memories," 29. On the province's efforts to lure American tourists during the war, see Dawson, *Selling British Columbia,* ch. 4.

33 BCA, GR-1991, reel 1800, Charles Tupper, MLA [Penticton] to Wells Gray, 6 June 1941. On E.C. Manning's role in park development during the Depression, see Rajala, "From 'On-to-Ottawa.'"

34 BCA, GR-1991, reel 1800, BC Forest Service press release, 18 June 1941.

35 The monument was relocated to the park administration area on the Similkameen Flats in 1947 and later to the Pinewoods concession complex. BCA, GR-1991, reel 1800, C.P. Lyons, undated memo "Re: Public Works Department's Assistance in Constructing Access to Campsites along the Hope-Princeton Highway" [midsummer 1947].

36 Regarding the general conditions in internee road-building camps, see Bella, *Parks for Profit,* 96–102; Shimizu, *The Exiles;* and Waiser, *Park Prisoners,* ch. 5.

37 MacEachern, *Natural Selections,* 161–63. Also see Tillotsen, *The Public at Play.*

38 On the equivalency of "park values" with mountains in western Canada, see MacEachern, *Natural Selections,* 33–37.

39 BCNRL, Lyons and Trew, "Reconnaissance and Preliminary Recreation Plan, Ernest C. Manning Park."

40 The Lightning Lakes were already so popular that in 1945 the area was reported to have suffered "intensive damage from indiscriminate tree cutting, numerous camp fires, and the scattering of tin cans and bottles." BCA, GR-1991, reel 1800, C.P. Lyons memo to Gordon McKenzie and Dave Davidson, 16 August 1945.

41 BCA, GR-1991, reel 1800, F.S. McKinnon memo to E.G. Oldham, 3 August 1945.

42 BCNRL, E.G. Oldham and D.L. McMurchie, "Preliminary Development Plan: Manning Park" (BC Forest Service, September 1945).

43 British Columbia, Department of Lands, Forest Branch, *Report of the Forest Branch* (Victoria: Queen's Printer, 1945), 24; Dawson, *Selling British Columbia,* 126–52.

44 BCA, GR-1991, reel 1800, Vancouver Natural History Society to Lyons, 15 January 1946. Regarding the disdain that some middle-class outdoor recreationalists had for the easy access that roads and automobiles provided to the BC backcountry, see Dummitt, "Risk on the Rocks."

45 BCA, GR-1991, reel 1800, G. Clifford Carl to Lyons, 5 January 1946. Also see Carl, Guiguet, and Hardy, *A Natural History Survey.* In 1947, the province's Dogwood Protection Act was amended to make it illegal to pick or damage wild rhododendrons. Province of British Columbia, "Dogwood Protection Act Amendment Act," *Statutes* (Victoria: Queen's Printer, 1947), 65.

46 BCA, GR-1991, reel 1800, Carl to Lyons, 5 January 1946.

47 Carl's concerns about animal strikes reflected a growing interest in the topic among wildlife biologists during the late 1930s and the 1940s. See, for example, Dickerson, "The Problem of Wildlife Destruction," 104–16; and Simmons, *Feathers and Fur.*

48 BCA, GR-1991, reel 1800, F.W. Gregory, Secretary, Princeton Sub-committee of the Provincial Rehabilitation and Reconstruction Committee, memo to District Forester, Kamloops, 9 July 1945.

49 BCA, GR-1991, reel 1800, District Forester A.E. Parlow to Chief Forester, 31 December 1945.

50 The Parks Division's reluctance to have the roadside reserve lifted prior to completion of the highway is discussed in BCA, GR-1991, reel 1800, Lyons to F. Battye, 21 November 1945.

51 BCA, GR-1991, reel 1800, F.S. McKinnon, memo to Chief Forester, 22 February 1946. Also see Bradley, "The Tower Ranch," 11–18.

52 Cambie Creek is a name that the BC Forest Service and Parks Division used (and that the BC Parks Branch continues to use) to refer to the Similkameen River upstream from the point where the Lightning Lakes empty into it. It is employed here for consistency and to distinguish the narrow, creek-like uppermost part of the river from the wider, more free-flowing sections downstream from that point of confluence.

53 BCA, GR-1991, reel 1800, C.D. Orchard, Chief Forester, to J.F. Walker, Deputy Minister of Mines, 29 October 1946. Also see Orchard to C. Hansen, Summit Mineral Claim, 30 October 1946; E.R. Hughes, Inspector of Mines, to P.J. Mulcahy, Chief Gold Commissioner, 8 November 1946.

54 BCA, GR-1991, reel 1803, E.G. Oldham to Ranger Bob Boyd, 21 May 1949; Oldham to Boyd, 7 November 1949. Title to Hansen's mineral claim was returned to the Crown by Order-in-Council 1408 (31 August 1949).

55 BCA, GR-1991, reel 1800, Lyons to McKinnon, 10 July 1947.

56 Order-in-Council 2055 (17 September 1949). The Parks Division's position on the matter is best laid out in BCA, GR-1991, reel 1800, Lyons, undated memo "Re: Infringements on Park Policies" [October 1947].

57 BCA, GR-1991, reel 1800, McKinnon, memo to Chief Forester, 22 February 1946.
58 BCA, GR-1991, reel 1800, McKinnon to Attorney-General's Department, 1 August 1947.
59 BCA, GR-1991, reel 1803, Lyons, undated memo included in McKinnon to Orchard, 1 March 1948.
60 Campbell, *Demon Rum or Easy Money;* Campbell, *Sit Down and Drink.*
61 BCA, GR-1991, reel 1803, McKinnon, memo to Orchard, 1 March 1948.
62 BCA, GR-1991, reel 1803, Lyons to Armstrong Construction Company, 22 February 1949; Oldham to Armstrong Construction Company, 25 February 1949.
63 "Highway Brings Awakening," *Vancouver Province,* 8 July 1949; "New Road All Weather: Giant Rotary Plows Will 'Eat Up' Snow," *Vancouver Province,* 2 November 1949, 42; Harvey, *Carving the Western Path: Routes,* 98.
64 The Oliver Board of Trade organized a party of between thirty and forty cars from the south Okanagan, which joined an even larger caravan from the central and north Okanagan at Penticton before heading westward to Allison Pass. *Oliver Chronicle and Osoyoos Observer,* 2 February 1949, 1.
65 Gordon Root, "Pioneer Prospector First Man on Road," *Vancouver Province,* 3 November 1949, 30.

Chapter 2

1 *Country Life in British Columbia* 33, no. 11 (November 1949): cover. Vancouver dailies regularly described the Hope-Princeton as a "superhighway" in their coverage leading up to its opening ceremony. For example, see "New Road All Weather," *Vancouver Province,* 42.
2 BCA, MS-2723, Leonard A. Coton papers, diary titled "My Latest and Probably 'Last' Trip," 49.
3 This apparent overstepping of the Parks Division's jurisdiction was not as unusual at it might seem. Interdepartmental rumours in the late 1940s hinted that the division might be asked to manage recreational development and roadside aesthetics along the entire Hope-Princeton Highway. See, for example, BCA, GR-1991, reel 1801, D.M. Trew, undated report "Manning Park Boundaries and Hope-Princeton Highway" [fall 1949].
4 Construction of and early travel on the Dewdney Trail are described in Allison, *A Pioneer Gentlewoman,* ch. 1; and Titley, *The Frontier World,* ch. 1.
5 BCA, GR-1991, reel 1801, Lyons to Stuart Lefeaux, Secretary, Metropolitan Parks Planning Committee (Vancouver), 15 July 1952. Also see reel 1803, Superintendent Bob Boyd to Chief Forester, 24 May 1952.
6 BCA, GR-1991, reel 1800, Clifford Carl, Director, Provincial Museum, to C.P. Lyons, 5 January 1946.
7 The Parks Division's enthusiasm to make the rhododendron grove a roadside attraction was aided by the fact that the ranger in charge of its earliest reconnaissance of the Manning Park area was the botanical enthusiast Ches Lyons, author of the best-selling book *Trees, Shrubs, and Flowers to Know in British Columbia,* which was first published in 1952.
8 BCNRL, Lyons and Trew, "Reconnaissance and Preliminary Recreation Plan, Ernest C. Manning Park," 4.
9 Carl, Guiguet, and Hardy, *A Natural History Survey,* 79.
10 Ibid., 80. Roadside signs that prohibited hunting in Manning Park are described in BCA, GR-1991, reel 1803, F.R. Butler, Commissioner, Office of the Game Commission, to Chief Forester, 22 September 1950.

11 In 1869, Susan and John Allison had travelled through the uppermost Skagit River valley during a forest fire. Allison, *A Pioneer Gentlewoman,* 28–33, 82.

12 BCA, GR-1991, reel 1800, A.E. Parlow to F.S. McKinnon, 24 August 1946; also Lyons, "Tough Going," 42.

13 Lyons, "Tough Going," 42. The sign was later changed from "the guy who dropped it" to "the one who dropped it."

14 Ibid.; BCA, GR-1991, reel 1803, David K. Monk for Eric Druce, Public Relations Division, Forest Service, to E.G. Oldham, 30 October 1950. Also see Boyd to Parks Division re: F.P. [Forest Protection] Road Signs, 17 October 1950.

15 BCA, Trew, "Manning Park Boundaries and Hope-Princeton Highway."

16 On scenic parkways in North American parks, see Carr, *Wilderness by Design;* Mauch and Zeller, *The World beyond the Windshield*; and Whisnant, *Super-Scenic Motorway.*

17 BCA, GR-1991, reel 1801, H.G. McWilliams, undated report "The Possibilities of Reforesting the Burn" [fall 1949].

18 The aesthetic, experiential, and managerial advantages of the parkway scheme are summarized in BCA, GR-1991, reel 1801, C.P. Lyons, undated report "Recommendations for the Proposed Parkway Adjoining Western Boundary of Manning Park" [fall 1950]. Also see BCNRL, "The Planning of Manning Park" (1950).

19 BCA, GR-1991, reel 1803, C.J. Wagner, telegram to Chief Forester, 22 July 1952. The rhododendrons had been protected by statute since 1947, but only after the parkway extension was added to Manning Park could the Parks Division enforce the statute. Province of British Columbia, "Dogwood Protection Act Amendment Act," 65.

20 BCA, GR-1991, reel 1801, D.B. Turner, Director of Conservation, Department of Lands and Forests, to George P. Melrose, Deputy Minister of Lands, 26 October 1950; D.B. Turner, minutes of "Meeting Held in Mr. [George] Melrose's Office – November 10, 1950"; C.P. Lyons, undated report "Parkway Problems" [fall 1950]. On government efforts to remove local people and traces of their presence from parks, see Whisnant, *Super-Scenic Motorway,* ch. 3; Jacoby, *Crimes against Nature;* Ted Binnema and Melanie Niemi, "'Let the Line Be Drawn Now': Wilderness, Conservation, and the Exclusion of Aboriginal People from Banff National Park," *Environmental* History 11, no. 4 (2006): 724–50; and MacEachern, *Natural Selections,* 56–63.

21 On large mammals as North American park attractions, see Biel, *Do (Not) Feed;* and Cronin, *Manufacturing National Park Nature,* ch. 4.

22 BCA, GR-1991, reel 1800, Carl to Lyons, 5 January 1946; reel 1805, Oldham to F.R. Butler, Commissioner, BC Game Commission, 23 April 1951; British Columbia, Department of Lands and Forests, Forest Service, *Report of the Forest Service* (Victoria: Queen's Printer, 1951), 63.

23 BCNRL, R. Lowrey, "Development of Beaver Pond Viewpoint, Manning Park" (Victoria, BC Forest Service, Parks and Recreation Division, 1955).

24 BCNRL, D.J. Spalding, "Wildlife Investigations in Manning Park, Summer 1956" (BC Forest Service, Parks and Recreation Division, October 1956).

25 Ibid. Also Yorke Edwards, undated handwritten initialled comments attached to BCNRL, Spalding, "Wildlife Investigations."

26 On *Bambi*'s significance to wildlife and park policy during the late 1940s and early 1950s, see Cartmill, *A View to a Death,* ch. 9; and Lutts, "The Trouble with Bambi," 160–71.

27 H.G. McWilliams, undated handwritten initialled comments attached to BCNRL, Spalding, "Wildlife Investigations."

28 BCNRL, Spalding, "Wildlife Investigations."
29 BCA, GR-1991, reel 1803, Boyd to Chief Forester, 8 December 1953. Also see Lloyd Brooks, Planning Section, to Ray Lowrey, 20 July 1953.
30 BCA, GR-1991, reel 1803, Lloyd Brooks to Lowrey, 20 July 1953. During the early 1950s, the Parks Division received many complaints about overflowing trashcans in provincial parks in the southern Interior. See, for example, BCNRL, S.E. Park, "Public Reaction Survey, 1954" (Publicity Section, Parks and Recreation Division, BC Forest Service, 1955). Regarding the concealment of park utilities such as garbage dumps, incinerators, power generators, and waterworks, see Colten and Dilsaver, "The Hidden Landscape."
31 BCNRL, Spalding, "Wildlife Investigations."
32 BCA, GR-1991, reel 1803, Boyd to Oldham, 4 April 1956; Oldham to Mr. Bowering, Chief Engineer, Department of Highways, 16 April 1956; Oldham to Bowering, 10 May 1956.
33 BCA, GR-1991, reel 1803, Oldham to Chief Engineer, Department of Public Works, 23 August 1951.
34 Three of the seven sites that the Parks Division had identified in 1947 as suitable for campground development were former or active road construction camps. BCA, GR-1991, reel 1800, C.P. Lyons undated memo "Re: Public Works Department's Assistance in Constructing Access to Campsites along the Hope-Princeton Highway" [midsummer 1947].
35 BCA, GR-1991, reel 1801, C.P. Lyons, undated report "History of the Hillside and Lone Pine Mineral Claims" [summer 1950].
36 BCA, GR-1991, reel 1801, Lyons to G. Allan MacPherson, Canam Mining Corporation, 31 July 1950.
37 BCA, GR-1991, reel 1801, MacPherson to Lyons, 8 August 1950.
38 BCA, GR-1991, reel 1801, E.G. Oldham to Superintendent of Lands, 23 August 1950.
39 The rise of truck logging has received limited scholarly attention. Useful insights can be found in Drushka, *Tie Hackers;* Hak, *Capital and Labour;* and Rajala, *Clearcutting.*
40 Hayes, *Hugh Leir,* 163.
41 BCA, GR-1991, reel 1803, Boyd to H. Leir, Manager, Penticton Sawmills Ltd., 30 June 1952; Leir to Oldham, 2 August 1952. A chronology of the Leir licences is found in GR-1991, reel 1801, McKinnon to John Hewitt, Jr., 28 July 1955.
42 On the scramble to acquire tree farm licences in the early 1950s, see Drushka, *Tie Hackers,* chs. 8–9; and Hak, *Capital and Labour,* ch. 2.
43 BCA, GR-1991, reel 1803, McKinnon to Hewitt, 28 July 1955.
44 BCNRL, Park, "Public Reaction Survey, 1954"; G.D. Taylor, "Public Reaction Survey, 1956" (Publicity Section, Parks and Recreation Division, BC Forest Service); G.D. Taylor, "Some Notes on Recreational Travel through Manning Park on Highway 3, Summer 1956" (Parks and Recreation Division, BC Forest Service, 1956); G.D. Taylor, "E.C. Manning Provincial Park Visitor Study, 1956" (Victoria, BC Forest Service, Parks and Recreations Division, 1957). Also see BCA, GR-1991, reel 1803, Taylor memo re: Manning Park to H.G. McWilliams, 24 January 1957.
45 BCNRL, Taylor, "Public Reaction Survey, 1956," 8–9.
46 BCA, GR-1991, reel 1803, L. Keith, "Report on Campsite Maintenance, Manning Park 1956" (31 August 1956). Also see reel 1801, Moore to Director, attn: C.J. Velay, 13 July 1966; R.H.A. [Ahrens], undated handwritten notes on ibid.; Ahrens to Velay, 11 May 1967.
47 BCNRL, Taylor, "Some Notes on Recreational Travel through Manning Park." Also see BCA, GR-1991, reel 1803, G.D. Taylor, memo re: Manning Park to H.G. McWilliams, Forester, Parks and Recreation Division, 24 January 1957.

48 BCA, GR-1991, reel 1801, Director, Parks Branch, to C.C. Hammond, 12 September 1961; H.G. McWilliams, Director, Parks Branch, to C.J. Velay, Engineering Division, 19 August 1964; McWilliams to R.J. Vitch, District Superintendent, Department of Highways, 20 November 1964.

49 BCA, GR-1991, reel 1801, McWilliams to P.E. Bishop, District Engineer, Department of Highways, 22 February 1965; reel 1805, Kerry Joy, Park Officer, Interpretation, memo re: Manning Park Beaver Pond Roadside Attraction, 21 November 1969. Regarding the questionable legality of many of the access roads to Manning's campgrounds and picnic sites, see P. Bishop, District Engineer, Department of Highways, to Director, Provincial Parks Branch, 20 October 1961; and Bishop to Department of Recreation and Conservation, 18 December 1961.

50 BCA, GR-1991, reel 1803, R.H. Boyd to E.G. Oldham, 4 April 1956.

51 BCA, GR-1991, reel 1803, Oldham to Mr. Bowering, Chief Engineer, Department of Highways, 16 April 1956; Oldham to Bowering, 10 May 1956.

52 BCA, GR-1991, reel 1801, McWilliams, Director, to Mr. Godfrey, Chief Engineer, Department of Highways, 25 August 1966; Godfrey to McWilliams, 1 September 1966.

53 See Lyons, "Tough Going"; Ross, "High Times," 42, 50; British Columbia, Ministry of Lands, Forest Service, *Annual Report of the Forest Service* (Victoria: Queen's Printer, 1957), 26; and BCA, GR-1991, reel 1801, Moore to Director, Parks Branch, attn: C.J. Velay, 30 December 1963.

54 BCA, GR-1991, reel 1801, D.B. Turner to K.B. Blakey, Chief Gold Commissioner, Department of Mines, 9 August 1961; McWilliams to Chief Gold Commissioner, Department of Mines and Petroleum Resources, attn: R.H. McCrimmon, 10 November 1964.

55 BCA, GR-1991, reel 1801, Huston Shake and Shingle Ltd. to District Forester, Management Dept. [Vancouver Forest District], 4 September 1958.

56 Ibid.; BCA, GR-1991, reel 1801, Director, Provincial Parks Branch, to Huston Shake and Single, 22 September 1958.

57 BCA, GR-1991, reel 1801, Moore to Director, Parks Branch, attn: C.J. Velay, 30 December 1963; D.B. Turner, Deputy Minister, to McWilliams, Director, Parks Branch, 3 January 1964.

58 BCA, GR-1991, reel 1801, Moore to Director, Parks Branch, 27 January 1964; Moore to Director, Parks Branch, 27 February 1964.

59 BCA, GR-1991, reel 1801, R.H. Ahrens, Chief, Planning Division, to McWilliams, Director, Parks Branch, 11 March 1964.

60 BCA, GR-1991, reel 1803, Director, Parks Branch, to Boyd, 24 October 1958; reel 1801, Ahrens for Director, Parks Branch, to W.G. Manley, District Commercial Manager, BC Telephone Company, 10 December 1959.

61 BCA, GR-1991, reel 180, McWilliams to Moore, Parks Supervisor, Manning Park, 24 [month indecipherable] 1963. On the modern styling of mobile homes and their association with rural resource industries in the postwar years, see Wallis, *Wheel Estate,* and Hart, Rhodes, and Morgan, *The Unknown World,* ch. 1.

62 BCA, GR-1991, reel 1803, Pelletier to McWilliams, 10 January 1957; McWilliams to Pelletier, 18 January 1957

63 Edwards, "Some Early Finds," 47; British Columbia, Department of Recreation and Conservation, *Report of the Department of Recreation and Conservation* (Victoria: Queen's Printer, 1957), 26. Also see Merilees, "The Beginnings of Interpretation," 16–22.

64 BCA, GR-1991, reel 1803, Lloyd Brooks to McWilliams, 19 March 1957.

65 On the long tradition of rustic architectural styling in Canadian parks, see Mills, *Rustic Building.*
66 BCNRL, M. Pope, "Manning Park, Pinewoods 1957 Motel Landscaping Development Plan" (Victoria, Planning Section, Parks Branch, Department of Recreation and Conservation, May 1958).
67 BCA, GR-1991, reel 1805, J.E. Underhill to Yorke Edwards, 29 June 1966; D.B. Turner, Deputy Minister, to McWilliams, 29 August 1966.
68 BCNRL, Mel Turner, "A Conceptual Plan for the Pinewood Region of Manning Park" (Victoria, Parks Branch, 1973).
69 Blake, *God's Own Junkyard;* Zimring, "'Neon, Junk, and Ruined,'" 94–107.
70 Keeling and Wynn, "'The Park Is a Mess,'" 119–50; Van Huizen, "'Panic Park,'" 67–92.

Chapter 3

1 One Canadian study that takes this approach is Brower, *Lost Tracks.*
2 MacEachern, *Natural Selections.*
3 Harvey, *Carving the Western Path: By River,* 86.
4 Charles Stewart, Minister of the Interior, telegram to Nelson Lougheed, Minister of Public Works, 4 October 1929, cited in Harvey, *Carving the Western Path: By River,* 87–89.
5 On conditions along the Big Bend of the Columbia during the early 1920s, see Freeman, *Down the Columbia.*
6 See Tanner, "Microcosms of Misfortune"; and Brown, "The Bennett Government."
7 BCA, GR-1222, box 97, file 2, J.M. Wardle, Chief Engineer, to H. Cathcart, Deputy Minister of Lands, 31 August 1932, cited in Cathcart to Wardle, 10 April 1933. Also see box 15, file 7, Cathcart to Pattullo, 4 June 1935.
8 On the Banff-Windermere Highway and the origins of Kootenay National Park, see Lothian, *A History,* 1:58–60.
9 BCA, GR-1222, box 97, file 2, [H. Cathcart] Deputy Minister [of Lands], to Wardle, 10 April 1933. The Province responded to Wardle's request only after the BC Forest Service reported that the feasibility of profitable logging in the desired area was uncertain. BCNRL, W.A. Johnston, "Big Bend, Columbia River Reconnaissance" (Victoria, BC Forest Service, 1932).
10 BCA, GR-1222, box 97, file 2, Thomas G. Murphy to Pattullo, 26 January 1934 and 9 June 1934.
11 BCA, GR-1222, box 97, file 2, Pattullo to Murphy, 15 February 1934, forwarding A. Wells Gray, Minister of Lands, memo for Pattullo, 13 February 1934.
12 BCA, GR-1222, box 97, file 2, Murphy to Pattullo, 8 September 1934.
13 BCA, GR-1222, box 15, file 7, [Frank M.] MacPherson [Minister of Public Works] to Murphy, 10 November 1934, attached to Department of Public Works to Pattullo, 30 May 1935.
14 BCA, GR-1222, box 15, file 7, E.A. Boyle, Secretary, Big Bend Highway Committee, to Pattullo, 27 April 1935; W. A. Gordon, City Clerk, City of Revelstoke, to MacPherson, 11 May 1935.
15 BCA, GR-1222, box 15, file 7, Murphy, telegram to Pattullo, 28 May 1935; Pattullo to Murphy, 30 May 1935; Murphy, telegram to Pattullo, 1 June 1935.
16 BCA, GR-1222, box 15, file 7, Pattullo, telegram to Murphy, 4 June 1935. Also see Murphy to Pattullo, 19 June 1935; Pattullo to Murphy, 10 July 1935.

17 BCA, GR-1222, box 15, file 7, Murphy to Pattullo, 19 June 1935; Pattullo to Murphy, 10 July 1935; Alberta Motor Association to Pattullo, 16 July 1936.

18 "Blackened Stumps," *Canadian National Parks Association Newsletter* 43 (Fall 1937); Library and Archives Canada (hereafter LAC), RG-84-A-2-a Parks Canada, reel T-10445, W. Selby Walker, Executive Secretary, Canadian National Parks Association, to J.B. Harkin, 15 April 1935.

19 On Earle Dickey's promotional work and postcard photography in the Revelstoke area, see English, *Reflections.*

20 BCA, MS-0560 William Earle Dickey papers, box 1, file 1, Earle Dickey to William Short, provincial editor, *Vancouver Sun,* 22 June 1937; "Revelstoke Fights to Save Timbers," unidentified newspaper clipping from a Thursday after 22 July 1937. Also see "Save Scenic Grandeur of Big Bend Highway," *Revelstoke Review,* 24 June 1937.

21 Leece, "Making BC History," 30–33; Pass, "'The Wondrous Story,'" 3–38.

22 On Revelstoke merchants' early interest in auto tourism, see Clayton, "'A National Playground.'"

23 Vancouver Public Library Special Collections (hereafter VPLSC), British Columbia Government Travel Bureau, *Official Program: Fourth Annual "See BC First" Motor Caravan* (Victoria: BC Government Travel Bureau, 1940); Monaghan, *Canada's New Main Street,* 23.

24 L.G. Temple, "Mountain Hamlet Is a Memorial to Fur Trade," *Vancouver Sun,* 17 January 1953, 11; Parkin, "Disappearing Highway," 32.

25 UBCSC, British Columbia Government Travel Bureau, *Advertising Campaign for Promotion of Tourist Travel, 1940* (Victoria: BC Government Travel Bureau, 1940).

26 VPLSC, British Columbia Government Travel Bureau, *British Columbia Presents the Big Bend – Trans-Canada Highway* (Victoria, n.d. [1940 or 1941]). Also see *Revelstoke Review* Big Bend souvenir edition, 25 June 1940; and "Colorful History Lies behind Big Bend Highway to Vancouver," *Calgary Herald,* 24 July 1941, 11.

27 Driving conditions on the Big Bend Highway are recalled in Bob Metcalfe, "Goodbye to the Big Bend," *Imperial Oil Review* 46, 4 (August 1962): 16–19; Donovan Clemson, "Goodbye to the Big Bend," *BC Motorist,* January-February 1970, 4; and Parkin, "Disappearing Highway," 31.

28 In May 1940, the Department of Lands identified Kinbasket Lake, Downie Creek, and Boat Encampment as locations along the Big Bend Highway that were suitable for gas stations and other services. However, several years elapsed before any such operation opened. BCA, GR-1222, box 34, file 5, Minister of Lands, memo to Pattullo, 30 May 1940.

29 "Thrilling Holiday for Vacationists by All-Canadian Route," *Revelstoke Review* Big Bend souvenir edition, 25 June 1940, section 1, 1.

30 BCA, GR-1222, box 34, file 5, W.B. Hill to Pattullo, 31 August 1941. Stories about unsafe and unscenic conditions along the Big Bend road can also be found in the pages of the *Revelstoke Review* throughout the summer and fall of 1941.

31 Austin Cross, "The Big Bend Highway," *Ottawa Citizen,* 20 December 1942.

32 BCA, GR-1222, box 34, file 5, Revelstoke Board of Trade to Pattullo, 21 July 1940. On Prairie residents' supposedly hazardous driving habits on the Big Bend Highway and BC mountain roads in general, see "The Prairie Motorist," *Winnipeg Evening Tribune,* 14 September 1940; and Golden Memories Book Committee, *Golden Memories,* 233.

33 "Tourist Thinks Big Bend Highway Needs Much Improvement," *Revelstoke Review,* 17 July 1941.

34 *Revelstoke Review,* 24 July 1941.

35 *Revelstoke Review,* 7 August 1941; "Two Winnipeg Women Drown," *Winnipeg Evening Tribune,* 29 July 1941; "3 Die in BC Crash," *Winnipeg Evening Tribune,* 2 October 1940, 2.

36 See BCA, GR-1222, boxes 24, 33, and 34, for complaints about dangerous conditions on Interior roads during the late 1930s and early 1940s. On the Fraser Canyon's reputation for dangerous traffic and geological instability, see Craig, *Trucking;* A.J. Dalrymple, "Completion of Hope-Princeton Link Is a Boon to BC Farmers," *Farm and Ranch Review,* 1 December 1949, 24; and Septer, *Flooding and Landslide.*

37 In an August 1941 election campaign speech to a crowd in Revelstoke, Pattullo promised to press Ottawa to finish the Big Bend Highway "in a permanent manner." Specifically, he wanted the federal government to pay the estimated $1 million cost of paving the road. *Revelstoke Review,* 7 August 1941.

38 Fisher, *Duff Pattullo,* 132.

39 Hamber Park was created by Order-in-Council 1305 because the Legislature had been dissolved in preparation for an October election. The only trace of consultation with his ministers or staff is a report by the deputy minister of lands that described the proposed park's boundaries and reported an absence of "valuable natural resources capable of profitable development." BCA, GR-1991, reel 1754, H. Cathcart, memo for A. Wells Gray [Minister of Lands], 10 September 1941.

40 A road through the Yellowhead Pass is one development that the Province may have expected in exchange for Hamber and Mount Robson Parks. It had also been suggested that a road from Boat Encampment to the Yellowhead Pass via the Canoe River valley might form a leaping-off point for a future road to Alaska, which was one of Pattullo's pet projects. "Big Bend Road Looms Large in Alaska Highway Plan," *Revelstoke Review,* 27 April 1939; Fisher, "T.D. Pattullo," 9–24.

41 In 1938, federal minister of mines and resources T.A. Crerar had informed the BC minister of lands that because the federal government was concentrating on founding parks in the east, funds would probably not be available for more national parks in the Rockies. BCA, GR-1991, reel 1754, Crerar to A. Wells Gray, 25 August 1938, cited in H. Cathcart, Deputy Minister of Lands, memo to Premier John Hart, 1 December 1944. Also see Taylor, *Negotiating the Past,* 109–11; and MacEachern, *Natural Selections,* 45, 52–53.

42 Dawson, *Selling British Columbia,* 120–26. When Pattullo visited Revelstoke in August 1941, he had already received complaints about the need to make the Big Bend Highway more attractive to auto tourists. *Revelstoke Review,* 7 August 1941.

43 BCA, GR-1991, reel 1754, K.C. McCannel, Assistant District Forester, Nelson, to Chief Forester, 8 October 1941; C.P. Lyons to McCannel, 14 October 1941.

44 BCA, GR-1991, reel 1754, H.J. Hodgins, Assistant Forester [assistant to F.S. McKinnon, head of Forest Economics Division], memo re: Hamber Park, 6 November 1941.

45 A handwritten note on ibid. indicates that the issue was discussed with "G.P.M." and that no further action was taken.

46 On the emergence of the "multi-use" approach to BC forests and parks in the Forest Service during the 1950s, see Rajala, "'Nonsensical and a Contradiction,'" 89–126; and Wilson, *Talk and Log,* ch. 5.

47 Hak, *Capital and Labour,* ch. 6; Rajala, *Clearcutting,* chs. 1–2.

48 Drushka, *Tie Hackers,* chs. 4–5; Golden Memories Book Committee, *Golden Memories,* 59–61.

49 BCA, GR-1991, reel 1754, King to E.T. Kenney, Minister of Lands and Forests, 6 April 1945. A dry goods merchant, King appears to have had a side interest in the logging industry:

an account submitted to a local history of Golden indicates that he owned a logging camp in the Blaeberry River valley north of town during the late 1930s. Golden Memories Book Committee, *Golden Memories,* 299. Regarding the prevalence of "over mature" timber in the Big Bend country, see BCNRL, D.E. Clark, "Reconnaissance Survey: CNR Lands and Canoe River Valley" (Victoria, 1913); and Johnston, "Big Bend, Columbia River Reconnaissance."

50 BCA, GR-1991, reel 1754, Percy [?] to Hart, 19 March 1945.

51 Lyons later referred to the inspection as "cursory in nature." BCA, GR-1991, reel 1754, Lyons, undated memo re: commercial concessions in Hamber Park and Big Bend Highway [1946].

52 BCNRL, C.P. Lyons and D.M. Trew, "Reconnaissance of Hamber Park and the Big Bend Highway" (Victoria, Parks Section, Forest Economics Division, BC Forest Service, 1945), 13.

53 Ibid., 21.

54 "Beauty Spot at Revelstoke Fire Victim," *Calgary Herald,* 12 August 1936, 5. These structures can be seen in the photos contained in LAC, RG-84 (graphic material), 1979–195 NPC, box SC184, Big Bend Highway album.

55 Scholefield and Howay, *British Columbia,* 2:240, citing the *British Columbian* of 2 and 6 June 1866.

56 BCNRL, Lyons and Trew, "Reconnaissance of Hamber Park," 11, 12, 14. The cutbank at Downie Creek offered a fine prospect of Frenchman's Cap and the Columbia River, one of the few places where the river could be seen with an impressive mountain backdrop; by 1945, it had proven the most popular view along the road. Photographs taken from similar perspectives by Earle Dickey, Byron Harmon, and others had been distributed as postcards and published in magazines, newspapers, and government publicity brochures. Such photos were used in the BC Government Travel Bureau's 1940 advertising campaign and for the cover of its first Big Bend Highway pamphlet. Byron Harmon's shots of this view were printed in many Prairie newspapers, including the two-page spread "Mountaineering by Motor" in the *Winnipeg Evening Tribune,* 6 July 1940. Earle Dickey's photos of the view appeared in magazine and newspaper articles such as "The New Northwest Passage," *Drumheller Mail,* 25 June 1936; Torchy Anderson, "Bonanza Highway: Big Bend Road Stirs Ghosts," *Vancouver Province* [late summer 1940]; E.A. Grubb, "The Big Bend Highway: Canada's Great New Mountain Road," *Meccano Magazine,* March 1940; and Corday Mackay, "Along the Big Bend Highway," *The Beaver* 277 (December 1946). Dickey's photos also illustrated several promotional pamphlets published by the Revelstoke Board of Trade, including *In the Switzerland of America: Revelstoke British Columbia, Western Gateway to Canada's Famous National Parks* (Revelstoke: Revelstoke Board of Trade, 1947).

57 Regarding the loss of a road survey party on the lake in 1930, see LAC, RG-84-A-2-a (Golden-Revelstoke Highway), reel T-10445, Constable MacDougall, "Patrol Report: Donald, BC to Kinbasket Lake," forwarded with Christen Junget, Superintendent, RCMP Southern Alberta District, to J.B. Harkin, 1931. Also Sherwood, *Return to Northern,* 113–14.

58 BCNRL, Lyons and Trew, "Reconnaissance of Hamber Park," 18.

59 This information is drawn from ibid., 28–31. The McKinnons, it should be noted, were long-time supporters of the provincial Liberal Party, a connection that may have helped them acquire their property at Boat Encampment. Greene, "Token History," 32–33.

60 BCNRL, Lyons and Trew, "Reconnaissance of Hamber Park," 14, 15, 17.

61 Ibid., 21.
62 Ibid., 22–26.
63 Ibid., 2-3.
64 Ibid., 3.
65 On mountain scenery as an aesthetic norm for Canadian national parks during this period, see MacEachern, *Natural Selections,* 4–6, 38–40. On motorists' expectations of scenery and road quality in North American parks more generally, see Barnett, "Drive-By Viewing"; Carr, *Wilderness by Design;* and Colten and Dilsaver, "The Hidden Landscape."

Chapter 4

1 For example, see Locke, "Civil Society"; MacLaren, "Splendor Sine Occasu," 170; Sandford, *Ecology and Wonder,* 201–2; and Wilson, *Talk and Log,* 95.
2 Ross, *Preparing for Ulysses,* 208–9.
3 Barman, *The West beyond the West,* 273, 365; Dawson, *Selling British Columbia,* 117.
4 BCA, GR-1991, reel 1754, Lyons, undated memo re: commercial concessions in Hamber Park [spring 1946]; Assistant Chief Forester C.C. Ternan for C.D. Orchard to J.H. Munro, 30 May 1946; McKinnon and Lyons, memo re: applications for commercial concessions in Hamber Park, 16 July 1946.
5 BCA, GR-1991, reel 1754, H. Coles, Ranger, Golden, to Chief Forester, 18 November 1947; Lyons to Coles, 21 November 1947. Also see Lyons to W.T. Macdonald-Miller, BC Government Travel Bureau, 7 May 1947.
6 For a critique of the lack of scenic improvement and recreational development along the highway, see BCA, GR-1991, reel 1754, Lyons, memo to F.S. McKinnon, 15 July 1946.
7 On the meanings implicit in mountain views and elevated vistas in North American culture, see Boime, *The Magisterial Gaze;* and Nicholson, *Mountain Gloom.*
8 Golden Memories Book Committee, *Golden Memories,* 72–76, 217; Kay, Patton, and White, "Historical Wildlife Observations," 561–83. Regarding motorists' expectations of seeing animals beside the road in the mountain parks of western North America, see Biel, *Do (Not) Feed;* and Cronin, *Manufacturing National Park Nature,* ch. 4.
9 See, for example, "Killed on Big Bend Highway," *Chilliwack Progress,* 17 July 1940, 1; "Soldier Killed on Army Convoy," *Winnipeg Evening Tribune,* 25 May 1944; "2 Ontario Men Plunge 400 Feet in BC Crash," *Toronto Globe and Mail,* 14 August 1953; "16 Bus Crash Victims Still in Hospital," *Saskatoon Star-Phoenix,* 6 August 1958, 1; and "Jury Finds Bus Death Accidental," *Vancouver Sun,* 14 August 1958, 40.
10 As environmental historian William Cronon notes, prior to the nineteenth century the connotations of the word "wilderness" were anything but positive. It typically referred to landscapes that were fearsome, distasteful, or even terrifying. Cronon, "The Trouble with Wilderness," 70. On the changing cultural meaning of mountain scenery, also see Nicholson, *Mountain Gloom.*
11 Monaghan, *Canada's New Main Street,* 23–24.
12 Golden Memories Book Committee, *Golden Memories,* 215.
13 Greyhound even used private snowplows to keep the treacherous Cascade Highway section of the southern transprovincial route between Rossland and Grand Forks passable in winter. Harvey, *Carving the Western Path: Routes,* 98–100; Lymbery, "Greyhound and Gray Creek," 21–23.

14 BCA, GR-1222, box 63, file 9, Nelson Board of Trade to Premier John Hart, 23 January 1946; file 8, E.T. Love, Secretary-Treasurer, Trans Canada Highway System Association (Yellowhead Route) to Premier Byron Johnson, 29 September 1947. Also see "The Trans-Canada Route: No Single Route Can Adequately Serve the Western Provinces," *Cariboo Digest* 5, 3 (August 1949): 12–15.

15 Francis, *A Road for Canada,* 68–70; Monaghan, *Canada's New Main Street,* 25–30.

16 Monaghan, *Canada's New Main Street,* 35–40, 54–56. On engineers' efforts to improve safety on North American highways during the postwar years, see ibid., 56; Jakle and Sculle, *Motoring,* ch. 8; and Packer, *Mobility without Mayhem,* ch. 1.

17 "New Premier Plans to Cut BC Spending by Millions," *Ottawa Journal,* 3 October 1952, 12; Harvey, *Carving the Western Path: By River,* 99–105. In 1953, the MP for Kootenay West told Parliament that tourist traffic had fallen off on the Big Bend Highway due to its poor state of repair. "Big Bend Repair Declared Urgent," *Edmonton Journal,* 14 May 1953, 44. Also see Roy Brown, "No Fair-Weather Road: National Highway Must Be Open All Year," *Vancouver Sun,* 8 May 1954.

18 British Columbia, Forest Service, *Report of the Forest Service* (Victoria: BC Forest Service, 1950), 45. On the proliferation of these small operations in the first postwar decade, see Baikie and Phillips, *From Gypo to B.T.O.;* Bernsohn, *Cutting Up the North,* ch. 10; Drushka, *Tie Hackers,* ch. 8; and Golden Memories Book Committee, *Golden Memories,* 60.

19 Hak, *Capital and Labour,* 39–40, 51.

20 On the geographic reach of the Interior pulp mill companies, see Bernsohn, *Cutting Up the North;* Hak, *Capital and Labour;* and especially Parent, *Caulkboot Riverdance.* The regional effects of pulp mill development in the Interior have so far received little attention from BC historians, but the Celgar mill is discussed in Farrar, *Castlegar,* 67–76, 91–92.

21 On the Roosdahl truck logging operation, see Golden Memories Book Committee, *Golden Memories,* 60, 214–17; and BCA, GR-1991, reel 1754, Oldham to Ernest Evans, Assistant Commissioner, BC Government Travel Bureau, 25 March 1949.

22 BCA, GR-1991, reel 1754, G.W. Minns, Assistant Forester, Nelson, to Chief Forester, 25 August 1949. The logging company appealed the decision, but park planner Robert Ahrens upheld it to disallow logging in such a prominently visible area. Ahrens, undated report "Examination of Timber Sale Application X47686" [late 1949]; also see Minns to Chief Forester, 5 August 1949, regarding the complexities of managing logging operations in hilly sections of the eastern Columbia River valley, where several elevated portions of the highway gave motorists brief glimpses of expansive tracts of timber.

23 BCA, GR-1991, reel 1754, Trew to Oldham, 25 May 1949; Trew to Oldham, 30 August 1949; Trew to Oldham, 21 July 1950. Also see Trew to Oldham, 10 May 1950. Trew was not the only Forest Service critic of Hamber Park: in 1954, planner George Wood concluded that it should be deleted. BCA, GR-1991, reel 1754, G.A. Wood, "An Analysis of Some Parks of the B.C. Park System" (Victoria, BC Forest Service, 1954).

24 BCA, GR-1991, reel 1754, Oldham to Ontario Government Department of Travel and Publicity, 17 May 1950; Parks and Recreation Division to Dorothy Swindelle, 20 August 1956; Director, Provincial Parks Branch, to Walter H. May, 17 March 1959; Director to D. Brewer, 30 November 1960.

25 On the CPR and its studies of the hydroelectric potential of the Surprise Rapids area of the Columbia River in the late 1920s, see Freeman, *Down the Columbia,* 88–90.

26 Sweetenham, *McNaughton,* 3:237. Also see Swainson, *Conflict over the Columbia,* 54–56, 62.

27 Swainson, *Conflict over the Columbia,* 54–56.
28 The political, legal, and diplomatic aspects of this wrangling are described in Mitchell, *W.A.C. Bennett,* chs. 8–9; Sherman, *Bennett,* chs. 9–10; Swainson, *Conflict over the Columbia;* and Swettenham, *McNaughton,* 3:ch. 6.
29 Regarding the disruptive effects of dam building elsewhere along the BC section of the Columbia River, see Loo, "People in the Way," 161–96; Parr, *Sensing Changes,* ch. 5; and Porteous and Smith, *Domicide,* ch. 5.
30 At an early 1955 hearing of the External Affairs Committee, BC attorney-general Robert Bonner assured the federal government of the Province's intention to press ahead with damming the Columbia. This may have been intended to indicate that Victoria would be asking for the Trans-Canada Highway to be rerouted away from the Big Bend country. Swainson, *Conflict over the Columbia,* 62.
31 BCA, GR-1991, reel 1754, Ahrens to Oldham, 22 June 1954.
32 In 1955, 1.15 million acres were deleted from Tweedsmuir Provincial Park to facilitate hydroelectric power production for the Alcan aluminum smelter at Kitimat. The following year, dam builders were permitted to raise scenic Buttle Lake in Strathcona Provincial Park by thirty feet. Christensen, *Too Good to Be True,* 79–101; Baikie, *Strathcona,* 96–100; Keeling and Wynn, "'The Park Is a Mess.'"
33 The possible alternatives to the Big Bend route and the engineering challenges and cost analyses associated with them are described in Harvey, *Carving the Western Path: By River,* 99–105.
34 It is worth noting that the Department of Highways report was completed at the very moment that Ottawa was prodding the provinces to finish modernizing the Trans-Canada. Since the passage of the Trans-Canada Highway Act in 1949, progress on the project had been embarrassingly slow because most provincial governments (Victoria included) had focused on improving their internal road networks. In 1956, hoping to spur them along, Ottawa offered to pay 90 percent of the cost of building the most difficult 10 percent of the road in each province, on top of the fifty-fifty split in costs promised in the 1949 act. Francis, *A Road for Canada,* 94–101; Monaghan, *Canada's New Main Street,* 67–77.
35 Monaghan, *Canada's New Main Street,* 70–71. Robert Harvey, who was an engineer in the BC Department of Highways during the mid-1950s, recalled "a feeling [in the department that] it was the Columbia River hydro-electric potential, not anything the road men could do, that swung the pendulum" in favour of the Rogers Pass route for the Trans-Canada. Harvey, *Carving the Western Path: By River,* 103.
36 BCA, GR-1991, reel 1754, R.H. Ahrens, Reconnaissance Section [Parks Branch], to Forester-in-Charge, Parks and Recreation Division, 14 November 1956.
37 The undated oral agreement that permitted this is described in BCA, GR-1991, reel 1754, H.G. McWilliams, Director, Provincial Parks Branch, to D.B. Turner, Deputy Minister, Department of Recreation and Conservation, 25 April 1961. Also see Forester, Parks Branch, to District Forester, Nelson, 11 September 1957.
38 BCA, GR-1991, reel 1754, H.G. McWilliams, Director, Provincial Parks Branch, to C.T.W. Hyslop, Superintendent of Lands, Lands Branch, 6 January 1959; E.W. Bassett, Deputy Minister of Lands, "Notice of Cancellation and Establishment of Reserve, Pursuant to Order in Council #213," 6 February 1959. Regarding timber clearance in the southernmost section of Hamber that was to be traversed by the new Trans-Canada right-of-way, see D.F. Martin, Regional Engineer, Department of Highways, to Chief Forester, 16 February 1959; and McWilliams to Right-of-Way Agent, Department of Highways, 11 March 1959.

Also see Ahrens to R. Broadland, 6 January 1959; and G. McNab, Parks Branch Headquarters, to Forest Management Headquarters, 9 March 1960.

39 Problems with logging in Hamber during the late 1950s are described in BCA, GR-1991, reel 1822, W. Roosdahl, Roosdahl Contracting Ltd., to Department of Recreation and Conservation, 17 September 1958; John Robertson, R.H. Pollock Construction Ltd. [Golden], to D.L. McMurchie, Director, Provincial Parks Branch, 21 November 1958; McMurchie to Robertson, 16 December 1958; McMurchie to W. Hepper, District Conservation Officer [Nelson], 19 December 1958; Hepper to McMurchie, 21 April 1959; Marc W. Gormley [Professional Forest Engineer] to McMurchie, 29 April 1959; and Hepper to McMurchie, 8 May 1959. The quote is from McMurchie to Hepper, 19 December 1958.

40 "Reporter Finds Vancouver-Banff Highway Good and Getting Better," *Vancouver Sun,* 22 July 1959; Jack Scott, "Beyond the Hills," *Vancouver Sun,* 18 May 1961, 4; Eric Ramsden, "Fantastic Strip of Blacktop," *Vancouver Province,* 26 September 1960. Also see Paddy Sherman, "Rogers Pass, Where Slide Killed 66: Soon It'll Be Tourist Mecca," *Vancouver Province,* 16 July 1956, 3; "Glacier Had Luxury Hotels When Vancouver Had Shacks," *Vancouver Province,* 17 July 1956, 3; and Ivers Kelly, "'Death Pass' Safe for Tourists," *Vancouver Sun* Progress edition, 30 May 1960, 2.

41 "Highway Failure," *Brandon Sun,* 19 September 1955, 6.

42 Ed McNally, "Canada All the Way," *Weekend Magazine,* July 1960, 17.

43 Metcalfe, "Goodbye to the Big Bend," 16, 19.

44 BCA, GR-1991, reel 1754, Director, Provincial Parks Branch, to W.H. Hepper, 30 September 1960; Director, Parks Branch, to D. Brewer [Montreal], 30 November 1960.

45 BCA, GR-1991, reel 1754, Minister of Lands and Forests to Earle C. Westwood, Minister of Recreation and Conservation, 3 February 1961. Williston's enthusiasm for and hands-on involvement in regional development through expansion of the Interior forest industry is discussed in Wilson, *Talk and Log,* 87–89; and Williston and Keller, *Forests, Power and Policy.*

46 Williston so outranked Westwood in the ministerial hierarchy of W.A.C. Bennett's cabinet that Westwood was likely to interpret a recommendation or request from him as an instruction, as Richard Rajala shows in his study of a conflict between the Forest Service and the BC Fish and Wildlife Branch in the late 1960s. Rajala, "'This Wasteful Use,'" 31–74.

47 BCA, GR-1991, reel 1754, H.G. McWilliams, Director, Provincial Parks Branch, to D.B. Turner, Deputy Minister, Department of Recreation and Conservation, 25 April 1961.

48 On criticism of the provincial government for allowing dam construction to affect Buttle Lake in Strathcona Park, see Keeling and Wynn, "'The Park Is a Mess.'"

49 See, for example, "A Holiday in the Bowron Lakes," *Forest Service Newsletter* 105 (April 1952).

50 Postwar plans for the development of a pulp wood economy in the Cariboo region and northern British Columbia are discussed in Bernsohn, *Cutting Up the North,* chs. 18–20; and Hak, *Capital and Labour,* 38–41.

51 BCA, GR-1991, reel 1754, McWilliams to Turner, 25 April 1961.

52 Order-in-Council 1499, 6 June 1961.

53 British Columbia, Department of Recreation and Conservation, *Annual Report* (Victoria: BC Department of Recreation and Conservation, 1961), 34.

54 On the rise of the wilderness movement in the Pacific Northwest during the 1960s, see Keeling and Wynn, "The Park Is a Mess"; Louter, *Windshield Wilderness,* chs. 3–4; and Van Huizen, "'Panic Park.'"

55 The duelling opening ceremonies are described in Francis, *A Road for Canada*, 1–6.

56 McCourt, *The Road across Canada*, 175.

57 See, for example, *BC Motorist*, September-October 1963, 22; Canada, Department of Northern Affairs and Natural Resources, National Parks Branch, "The Rogers Pass Section, Trans-Canada Highway" (Ottawa, 1963); and Frank Coutant, *Rogers Pass: The Impossible Road through the Impassable Canadian Rockies: The Most Spectacular Mountain Highway in the World* (Vancouver, 1963). The closest thing to an environmental history of the Rogers Pass remains Woods, *Snow War*. A general outline of development in Glacier Park after 1957 can be found in Lothian, *A History*, 1:44–45.

58 The art historian Peter White describes the highway through the Rogers Pass as symbolically representing "the end of the province's historic isolation and its emergence as a fully modern society." Unfortunately, he does not consider how representations of the new road might have been related to western Canadian motorists' experiences of driving the old Big Bend Highway between Golden and Revelstoke. White, *It Pays to Play*, 19–21.

59 Golden Memories Book Committee, *Golden Memories*, 61, 73.

60 Clemson, "Goodbye to the Big Bend." Clemson's photography and penchant for automobile travel are discussed in McDonald, "Two Views of the World," 8–19.

61 Clemson, "Goodbye to the Big Bend." Just a few years later, Clemson described the highway in less charitable terms, recalling it as "singularly lacking in interesting landmarks." Clemson, *Old Wooden Buildings*, 16.

62 BCNRL, G.R. Peterson and I.L. Withler, "Effects on Fish and Game Species of Development of Mica Dam for Hydroelectric Purposes" (Victoria, British Columbia Fish and Wildlife Branch, 1965), 24. Also see British Columbia, Fish and Game Branch, "Report to the BC Game Commission on a Preliminary Survey of the Effects of the Mica Creek Development upon Wildlife" (Victoria, 1954); L. Harding, "Our Mountain Caribou: An Endangered Species?" *BC Outdoors* 31, 2 (1975): 24–31; A. Prince, "Local Knowledge of Columbia River Fisheries in British Columbia, Canada" (Cranbrook, Columbia-Kootenay Fisheries Renewal Partnership, 2001), 6–19.

63 "Mica Clearing a Mammoth Task," *Progress*, Spring 1973, 10. *Progress* was a quarterly magazine put out by BC Hydro's Information Services Department during the years of dam building on the Columbia.

Route B

1 For an instance where another federal government agency helped to construct a historical attraction in the hinterlands of British Columbia during the interwar period, see Darling and Cole, "Totem Pole Restoration," 29–48.

2 One recent monograph that looks closely at the question is John A. Jakle and Keith A. Sculle, *Remembering Roadside America: Preserving the Recent Past* (Knoxville: University of Tennessee Press, 2011), chs. 2–3, 5.

3 Opp and Walsh, "Local Acts of Placing," 10–11.

4 McKay and Bates, *In the Province of History*, especially chs. 1–2.

5 None of the essays in Nicole Neatby and Peter Hodgins's recent anthology about public history and commemoration in Canada examine British Columbia or even western Canada. Nicole Neatby and Peter Hodgins, eds., *Settling and Unsettling Memories: Essays in Canadian Public History* (Toronto: University of Toronto Press, 2012). Several BC historians have studied history writing and history collecting, but they focus on literary and archival

work rather than historical sites and popular experiences of history "on the ground." Budd, "'The Story of the Country'"; Pass, "Pacific Dominion"; Reimer, *Writing British Columbia.*

6 Francis, *The Imaginary Indian,* 181–83.

7 Lutz, *Makúk,* ch. 7, especially 251–55; Miller, *Skyscrapers Hide the Heavens,* 211–22.

8 Hawthorn, Belshaw, and Jamieson, *The Indians of British Columbia,* chs. 14–15.

9 Dippie, *The Vanishing American.*

10 At the turn of the century, Northwest Coast totem poles had been sought after by galleries and museums around the world. During the interwar years, they became tourist icons for British Columbia and western Canada generally. Outdoor collections were assembled in municipal parks in Vancouver, Victoria, Nanaimo, and Prince Rupert. Small coastal communities such as Alert Bay became popular stopping places for cruise ships, famous for their poles and other monumental features. The Canadian National and Canadian Pacific Railways both brought totem poles to their tourist resorts in the Rocky Mountains, and the former co-operated with the federal government to preserve poles along its tracks in the Skeena River valley. That railway companies transported totem poles all the way across the province to adorn their resorts in the Canadian Rockies indicates that they and other tourist interests deemed the cultures of Interior First Nations unsuitable for commodification and profitable use in their promotional campaigns. Cole, *Captured Heritage;* Darling and Cole, "Totem Pole Restoration"; Dawson, *Selling British Columbia,* 163–76; Aldona Jonaitis and Aaron Glass, *The Totem Pole: An Intercultural History* (Seattle: University of Washington Press, 2010).

11 Kelm, *A Wilder West,* chs. 1–2; Robertson, *Imagining Difference.*

12 "Constitution," *Report and Proceedings of the British Columbia Historical Association* 1 (1923): 9.

13 Leece, "Making BC History"; Pass, "'The Wondrous Story.'"

14 Taylor, *Negotiating the Past,* chs. 2–3.

15 Gordon, *Time Travel.*

Chapter 5

1 Dawson, *Selling British Columbia,* chs. 2–3.

2 Skelton, *They Call It,* ch. 16.

3 UBCSC, BC Trans-Provincial Highway Association, *Fraser River Highway: The Only Route for Provincial Highway* (Kamloops: BC Trans-Provincial Highway Association, 1923). On transportation systems and shared landscape experience in the Fraser and Thompson Canyons during the colonial and early provincial periods, see Harris, "The Fraser Canyon," 5–28; and Schwartz and Koltun, "A Visual Cliché," 113–28.

4 In the months before the official announcement, there was widespread speculation that the pendulum had swung away from the Hope-Princeton route, which had been the government's preferred option prior to the war. For example, "Fraser Canyon Favoured for Highway Link," *Prince George Citizen,* 18 March 1924, 1. Technical aspects of building the Canyon Highway are outlined in Harvey, *The Coast Connection,* 90–99.

5 Harvey, *The Coast Connection,* 90–91. Also see Harvey, *Carving the Western Path: By River,* 58–66.

6 Galloway, *The Call of the West,* 49–50. For images of the abandoned wagon road between Hope and Lytton, see BCA, image D-03365; City of Vancouver Archives (hereafter CVA), Williams Bros. Photographers collection, image CVA 586–3772; Major Matthews

collection, image Out P1174. For an example of railway passengers' interest in trackside relics of the old wagon road, see "Fraser Canyon Route Selected," *Chilliwack Progress*, 21 May 1924, 1.

7 Scholefield and Howay, *British Columbia*. Howay referred to the Cariboo Wagon Road as "the Appian Way of British Columbia" in many speeches, articles, and books but seems to have first used the phrase in ibid., 2:96.

8 McKelvie, *Early History*.

9 This column was attributed to Felix Penne, which was the pen name of Vancouver litterateur John Francis Bursill. Hooper, "John Francis Bursill," 17–26.

10 On the impulse to link national identity and territory with pleasure travel in North America during the first quarter of the twentieth century, see Shaffer, *See America First*.

11 Charlotte Gordon, "The Strange Tale of the Cariboo Trail Now Surrendered to Motordom," *Pacific Coast Motorist*, December 1925, 25, 40.

12 "Reopening of Highway an Important Event," *Prince George Citizen*, 11 March 1926, 2; "BC Road Problems Subject of Conference," *Chilliwack Progress*, 16 December 1926, 16.

13 Hutchison, *The Unknown Country*, 355; Fitzroy, *A Canadian Panorama*, 189.

14 Passenger cars were charged one dollar to cross the bridge in the late 1920s, which was equivalent to two hours' wages for a skilled tradesman. The province's earliest long-haul truckers complained that the toll on freight was punitively high and alleged that it was meant to insulate the railroads (including the government-owned Pacific Great Eastern) from competition. Craig, *Trucking*; Kluckner, *Vanishing British Columbia*, 115.

15 Dozens of significant road closures resulting from rockfall, landslides, washouts, debris torrents, avalanches, and floods in the Fraser and Thompson Canyons during the period 1926–45 are cited in Septer, *Flooding and Landslide*.

16 Wragge, "Motoring from Nelson," 32; White, *Milk Spills*, 71; Ernest A. Harris, "Memories of Motoring in the 1930s," *British Columbia Historical News* 22, 4 (Fall 1989): 14. Also see Presto, "An Annual Challenge," 76–83; "Tourists Will Not Drive Over Canyon Highway," *Chilliwack Progress*, 28 April 1932, 5.

17 British Columbia, Provincial Bureau of Information, *Highways, Motor Camps, and Stopping-Places of British Columbia* (Victoria, 1926), 26; F.C.R., "The New Way over the Old Cariboo Road," *Vancouver Province*, 10 June 1926.

18 British Columbia Department of Mines, *Annual Report of the Minister of Mines* (Victoria, 1939), 6–7. The quote is from British Columbia Department of Mines, *Annual Report of the Minister of Mines* (Victoria, 1935), 31. A similar training camp operated on the Fraser River north of Quesnel for several years. See Cooper, "Dominion-Provincial Placer Mining."

19 Barman, "Separate and Unequal," 337–57.

20 VPLSC, Vancouver Sun Resort, Hotel, and Travel Information Bureau, *Road Map of the Famous Cariboo Highway and Okanagan Valley Route* (Vancouver: Vancouver Sun, 1941). On historical buildings at All Hallows, see also *Chilliwack Progress*, 20 April 1938, 1.

21 Taylor, *Negotiating the Past*, 89n97.

22 "The Building of the Cariboo Road: Speech by the Hon. Denis Murphy at Unveiling of Monument at Yale, June 27, 1925," *Report and Proceedings of the British Columbia Historical Association* 3 (1925): 21. The same volume contains a description of the unveiling ceremony: John Forsythe, "Secretary's Report, 1924-25," 13–15. A few months later, Howay also visited the canyon with the motoring public's future views in mind, when he helped lead a group of auto club representatives from British Columbia and the Pacific coast states on a rail

tour through the canyon in advance of the road's completion. "Visit Paid to Fraser Canyon Highway," *Chilliwack Progress,* 7 October 1925, 1.

23 Although there is a literature on the disruptive effects of railroad building on Indigenous people in British Columbia, nothing similar has been done for automobile roads in the twentieth century. See, for example, McDonald, "Bleeding Night and Day"; and Schuurman, "Constructing and Deconstructing."

24 "Stallo Tribe Erects Cross to Ancestors," *Chilliwack Progress,* 17 August 1938, 6. This contemporary account of the monument's unveiling slightly misreported the inscription. The accurate inscription is provided here.

25 Ethnohistorian Amanda Fehr draws out other complex social and religious meanings of the monument, in Fehr, "The Relationships of Place"; and Fehr, "A Subversive Sincerity," 61–82.

26 One of the smaller stone crosses near the 1938 memorial bears the inscription "In memory of Our Ancient Grave. Hundreds of Remains. Cross Made 1937."

27 This ad is in the folding pamphlet VPLSC, Vancouver Sun Resort, *Road Map of the Famous Cariboo.*

28 Knight, *Indians at Work,* ch. 7; Laforet, "The Market in Coiled Basketry." I am indebted to Andrea Laforet, Irene Bjerky, and John Haugen for sharing their unpublished research about the sale of Indigenous basketry in the Fraser Canyon. On interwar scholarly study of this material culture, see Boas et al., "Coiled Basketry," 119–484.

29 "Unveil Cairn at Spuzzum," *Chilliwack Progress,* 5 July 1928, 4. For photographs showing the cairn, its text, and its location in relation to the highway and bridge, see CVA, Major Matthews collection, image BR P32; VPLSC, *Vancouver Province* collection, image 44552; LAC, Department of Mines and Technical Surveys collection, 1960–125 NPC, image TS 11281; and University of Washington Libraries Special Collections, Asahel Curtis Photo Company collection, image CUR1556.

30 Kluckner, *Vanishing British Columbia,* 118–20.

31 On roadside commercial operations in Boston Bar during the interwar years, see Craig, *Trucking;* and Koropecki, *Life in the Tee-Pee,* ch. 6.

32 Hutchison, *The Unknown Country,* 345–55.

33 Laforet, "The Market in Coiled Basketry." For a photo of Rose Skuki (sometimes spelled Skukai) and the store in the early 1940s, see Lytton Museum and Archives, Gwen Miller collection, image A1997.04.097. I thank Andrea Laforet and Richard Forrest and Dorothy Dodge of the Lytton Museum and Archives for sharing information about Rose Skuki and the handicrafts store at the Lytton Indian Reserve.

34 The store proved a very long-lasting venture: in fact, it still operates today, being located just across the street (which was formerly part of the highway) from the band office.

35 Coombs, *By Truck and Bus,* 33.

36 Craig, *Trucking,* 85.

37 The TU Auto Camp display dated from at least the summer of 1930, as indicated by its description in Douglas C. Mitchell, "Through the Land of the Golden Twilight," *Touring Topics* 22, 9 (September 1930): 19. *Touring Topics* was the house journal of the Automobile Club of Southern California. C.P. Lyons confirms that the stagecoach was the property of the TU Auto Camp, in *Milestones on the Mighty Fraser,* 132.

38 Fitzroy, *A Canadian Panorama,* 181.

39 The Dufferin Coach was a distinctive four-horse stagecoach that the BX Company had built especially for the 1876 visit of Lord Dufferin, the governor-general of Canada, to

Yale, Ashcroft, and Kamloops. St. John, *The Sea of Mountains;* West, *Stagecoach and Sternwheel,* 19.

40 "The Dufferin Coach," *Cariboo Observer,* 5 January 1935, 2 (reprinted from unidentified edition of the *Ashcroft Journal*). Also see "Lord Dufferin's Coach Carries Quesnel's Mail," *Prince George Citizen,* 8 November 1923, 4; "Famous Old 'Dufferin Coach' Pride of Cariboo, Lies Rotting in Roadside Field," *Vancouver Province,* 15 March 1925; "Rescue the Dufferin Coach," *Toronto Star Weekly,* 5 February 1927; and "Dufferin Coach Should Be Saved as Historical Relic," *Prince George Citizen,* 31 March 1927, 7.

41 Kathy Paulos, "Family Grateful for Tangible Evidence of Their History," *Ashcroft-Cache Creek Journal,* 6 September 2011, 3; Belton, *Bittersweet Oasis,* 25–26. Cumming had also used the *Journal* to publish a collection of his own Wild West tales: Cumming, *Skookum Chuck Fables.*

42 On the history of Clinton's old timber-framed buildings, see Charles, *At the 47 Mile.*

43 BCA, Photo collection, C-01211; VPLSC, Phillip Timms collection, no. 19225; E. Stuart Davidson, "To the Land of the Golden Twilight in British Columbia," *Chilliwack Progress,* 17 July 1930, 10.

44 Patenaude, *Trails to Gold;* Stangoe, *Cariboo-Chilcotin.*

45 Clemson, *Old Wooden Buildings,* 70. Regarding "long tangents replac[ing] the twists and turns that were such characteristic features of the old road," see D.M. LeBourdais and Louis LeBourdais, "The Road That Gold Built," *Maclean's,* 1 June 1928, 12.

46 The rise of the western dude ranch during the 1920s is outlined in Borne, *The Dude Ranch;* and Rodnitzky, "Recapturing the West," 111–26.

47 The farmer-photographer Donovan Clemson worked in the Cariboo as a young man and recalled that during the late 1920s, "the relics of the [wagon] road, apart from the roadhouses, were not uncommon. A number of stagecoaches were to be seen, some of them repainted and displayed at stopping places." Clemson, *Old Wooden Buildings,* 62.

48 Foster, *One Heart, One Way,* chs. 6–10.

49 "Old Landmark Destroyed by Fire," *Cariboo Observer,* 27 April 1937, 1.

50 Mitchell, "Through the Land," 20.

51 *Vancouver Province,* 7 December 1935, 7.

52 Wragge, "Motoring from Nelson," 32; Patenaude, *Trails to Gold,* 105.

53 BCA, MS-0676, Louis LeBourdais papers, box 6, file 29, Howay to LeBourdais, 11 January and 18 January 1932.

54 *Prince George Citizen,* 2 July 1936, 6; 9 July 1936, 3; Stangoe, *Looking Back,* 13–14.

55 The limited administrative functions centred in isolated, shrinking Quesnel Forks had similarly been relocated to 150 Mile House on the Cariboo Wagon Road in 1908. Elliott, *Gold and Grand Dreams,* 166.

56 Quesnel Old Age Pensioners' Organization, *A Tribute to the Past.*

57 "Mining Prospects at Barkerville," *Cariboo Observer,* 7 May 1927, 1.

58 Futcher, *The Great North Road,* 62–63.

59 Mitchell, "Land of the Golden Twilight," 21.

60 The copper plaque explained that the pump had been donated by a mining company that had last used it in about 1900 and that its move had been paid for by the mining institute, with assistance from the provincial government and the CPR. *Cariboo Observer,* 31 May 1930, 1; "Cornish Pump Dedicated," *Cariboo Observer,* 5 July 1930, 1. Also see BCA, MS-0676, box 1, file 5, LeBourdais to Henry Thomson, 11 January 1939. On the use of waterwheels as a power source in the BC Interior, see Liddicott, *Waterwheels in the Service.*

61 "Cairn Unveiling Drew Crowd to Quesnel Friday," *Prince George Citizen*, 25 August 1932, 1–2, 7; "Unveiling Ceremonies of the Collins Telegraph Cairn," *Cariboo Observer*, 27 August 1932, 1.

62 Regarding the long history of forest fires in the Cariboo goldfields, see BCNRL, W.W. Stevens, "Reconnaissance between Quesnel and Barkerville" (Victoria, British Columbia Forest Service, 1923).

63 Mitchell, "Through the Land," 21.

64 The best descriptions of hydraulic monitoring in the Barkerville district during the 1920s and the roadside detritus of old mining operations are found in Hong, *And So That's How*, especially 39–42. Hydraulic placer mining's long-term effects on the landscape are described in Kennedy, "Fraser River Placer," 35–66.

65 Wragge, "Motoring from Nelson," 33; Mitchell, "Through the Land," 21. On the stagnant economy of the Cariboo goldfields during the 1920s, see Elliott, *Gold and Grand Dreams*, ch. 10; and Skelton, *They Call It*, chs. 13–15. Regarding Lowhee Gulch and other small- and medium-scale placer mining operations during the 1920s, see Hong, *And So That's How*, especially chs. 1 and 17.

66 John Hosie, "Barkerville, August 10, 1929," *Museum and Art Notes* 4, no. 3 (September 1929): 94.

67 Hong, *And So That's How*, chs. 4–5, 19; Skelton, *They Call It*, 216.

68 Wragge, "Motoring from Nelson," 31, 32.

69 T.A.B., "Fire Protection in Old Barkerville," *Cariboo Observer*, 2 April 1927, 1.

70 "Richfield Courthouse Receives Attention," *Cariboo Observer*, 5 November 1927, 4, reprinted from unidentified edition of the *Vancouver Province*. On the Richfield courthouse, also see "Keeping Old Lamps Alight," *Chilliwack Progress*, 5 December 1929, 4, reprinted from unidentified edition of *Journal of Commerce*.

71 BCA, MS-0676, box 3, file 13, undated manuscript on collectors of historical materials in the Barkerville district in early 1930s.

72 "Today's Big Do," *Cariboo Observer*, 10 August 1929, 1; BCA, G C19 B63, J.P. Hampton Bole, "A Trip to Barkerville BC, August 1929."

73 Marshall, *Cariboo Gold*, 31–32; "Harry Jones Will Unveil the Cairn at Barkerville," *Prince George Citizen*, 11 July 1929, 4; "Today's Big Do," *Cariboo Observer*, 10 August 1929, 1; Louis LeBourdais, "Barkerville's Celebration Proved a Huge Success," *Prince George Citizen*, 15 August 1929, 1; T.A.B., "The Unveiling of the Cairn," *Cariboo Observer*, 17 August 1929, 1.

74 Mitchell, "Through the Land," 21.

75 Hutchison, *The Unknown Country*, 363–64. Also Bruce Hutchison, "Adventuring on B.C.'s Great Highway," *Vancouver Province*, 9 February 1930, 7. Margaret Robinson was another visitor who was inspired to detect departed spirits at Barkerville. She drove there for a holiday in 1931 and reported finding it hard to sleep in the "eerie" town, "all alone there with memories of six foot men all sharp shooters who were buried in the nearby cemetery." BCA, H/A/R56, Margaret E. Robinson diaries.

76 On conditions in the goldfields in 1933, see H.G. Lockwood, "An Accurate and Dependable Prospector's and Traveller's Guide to Barkerville of Today: Absolutely Authentic Information" (1933), cited in Skelton, *They Call It*, 209–12. Three accounts of working in BC goldfields during the Depression years are Harris, *Ten Golden Years;* Knight and Knight, *A Very Ordinary Life*, ch. 7; and Fred W. Ludditt, *Campfire Sketches of the Cariboo* (Union Bay: Fred Ludditt, 1974). Also see Wallace, "The Spirit of the Pioneers," 355–74.

77 Statistics drawn from Barman, *The West beyond the West*, 256, 376.

78 Hong, *And So That's How,* ch. 16; Skelton, *They Call It,* 217.

79 Harris, *Ten Golden Years,* 64; Ernie Roberts, "Into the Cariboo by Truck: New Transport on Old Trail," *Vancouver Province,* 14 October 1933, magazine section, 7. On the expansion of trucking in the central and northern Interior during the 1930s generally, see Craig, *Trucking,* ch. 6.

80 Regarding Victoria's efforts to improve the Quesnel-Barkerville road and keep it open throughout the year, see Ludditt, *Campfire Sketches,* 21–23; and Skelton, *They Call It,* ch. 16.

81 British Columbia, Department of Mines, *Annual Report of the Minister of Mines, 1936* (Victoria: Department of Mines, 1937), 4; Futcher, *The Great North Road,* 80–81. Also see Wragge, "Motoring from Nelson," 32.

82 Harris, *Ten Golden Years,* 101–3; Hong, *And So That's How,* 217; Marshall, *Cariboo Gold,* 35; Skelton, *They Call It,* 213–14; "Historic Building at Barkerville Is Torn Down," *Vancouver Province,* 16 February 1936, 16; "Historic Landmark to Be Demolished," *Prince George Citizen,* 23 September 1937, 8; "Barkerville Telegraph Office Goes to Wells," *Cariboo Observer,* 13 August 1938, 1.

83 Futcher, *The Great North Road, 70;* Skelton, *They Call It,* ch. 16, especially 215–17. Also J.B. Eberts, "Barkerville Gold Mecca Again," *Vancouver Sun,* 31 June 1933, 1–2. Pictures of flumes and trestles crossing above the Quesnel-Barkerville road can be found in Hong, *And So That's How,* 78, 99, 102, 108, 123. A photo showing the proximity of the Shamrock Mine to the road and the HSMBC cairn is BCA, A-05444.

84 Hutchison, *The Unknown Country,* 365, 367. Also see Ludditt, *Campfire Sketches,* 31.

85 Barman, *The West beyond the West,* 375.

86 "To Preserve Cemetery," *Prince George Citizen,* 6 August 1942, 7; "Trade Board Meeting Here Well Attended," *Cariboo Observer,* 13 June 1942, 1; "Courthouse at Richfield Diggings to Be Preserved," *Cariboo Observer,* 10 February 1945, 1.

87 Skelton, *The Call It,* ch. 17.

Chapter 6

1 On province building and active government in postwar British Columbia, see Barman, *The West beyond the West,* ch. 12; Mitchell, *W.A.C. Bennett,* ch. 8; and Tomblin, "In Defense of Territory."

2 Giesbrecht, *Heritage Lost;* Shelford, *From Snowshoes to Politics,* ch. 13; Windsor and McVey, "Annihilation of Both," 146–65.

3 Bernsohn, *Cutting Up the North,* 58.

4 Ibid., ch. 10; Drushka, *Tie Hackers,* chs. 7–8; Hak, *Capital and Labour,* 51–64. Gordon Hak has concluded that fathers, sons, and brothers were at the core of most Interior truck logging and gypo sawmill ventures. "Companies were owned by one man or perhaps a few partners who were close to their operations and their workers and involved in the day-to-day physical activities of producing logs." Hak, *Capital and Labour,* 37, 53.

5 Bernsohn, *Cutting Up the North,* chs. 10–11; Drushka, *Tie Hackers,* chs. 7–8; Hak, *Capital and Labour,* 32–40.

6 Bernsohn, *Cutting Up the North,* chs. 12–17; Drushka, *Tie Hackers,* chs. 8–9; Hak, "Populism and the 1952," 277–96.

7 The slogan "Know British Columbia Better" is from a BC Government Travel Bureau advertisement in the guidebook *The Traveller's Digest* (Banff, 1948). On Victoria's postwar

publicity efforts, see Dawson, *Selling British Columbia,* chs. 4–6; Duffy, *Evergreen Playground;* and Mattison, "The British Columbia Government," 79–104.

8 Dawson, *Selling British Columbia.*

9 Barman, *The West beyond the West,* 273.

10 See, for example, BCA, GR-1222, box 84, file 2 passim; "To Repair Canyon Road," *Chilliwack Progress,* 13 September 1950, 1; and "Hope Bureau Find Traffic Evenly Split," *Chilliwack Progress,* 29 August 1951, 15.

11 For the economic consequences of postwar highway modernization on rural areas and small towns, see Bennett, "Highways to Heaven?" 451–67; and Hill, "A Serpent in the Garden," 495–514.

12 See, for example, the editorials in the issues of *Northwest Digest* for January-February and September-October of 1958.

13 "Toll Is Locked Gate Dividing the Province," *Chilliwack Progress,* 17 October 1945, 12; "That Steel Gate at Yale," *Chilliwack Progress,* 6 March 1946, 2.

14 For a sampling of wartime and postwar correspondence on the toll charged at the Alexandra Bridge, see BCA, GR-1222, box 34, file 2, Motor Carrier and Fleet Owners of Western Canada to Premier Pattullo, 18 June 1941; box 55, file 5 passim. The text of the speech announcing the cancellation can be found in BCA, GR-1222, box 63, file 6, undated 1946 speech by the Public Works minister to the Legislature.

15 "Road Victory Won, Hope Seeks Power," *Vancouver Province,* 2 November 1949.

16 BCA, MS-2723, "My Latest and Probably 'Last' Trip," 3. For similar complaints, see also Dorothy G. Taylor, "Why Oh Why?" *Chilliwack Progress,* 23 July 1952, 2; and L.E.B., "Not in My Small Corner," *Chilliwack Progress,* 24 June 1953, 8.

17 Reid, *Mountains, Men, and Rivers,* 167.

18 BCA, MS-2723, "My Latest and Probably 'Last' Trip," 6, 9–10. Also see "Don't Destroy Lytton Jail," *Ashcroft Journal,* 18 June 1953, 2.

19 Laforet, "The Market in Coiled Basketry," 30.

20 Some tourism promoters conducted a campaign to make totem poles the premier symbol of British Columbia during the postwar years. From 1952 through 1954, a stylized thunderbird totem pole was even stamped on the province's passenger licence plates. See Dawson, *Selling British Columbia,* 165–75; and Garrish, *Tales from the Back,* ch. 3.

21 Koropecki, *Life in the Tee-Pee.*

22 Patenaude, *Trails to Gold,* 2:16, 2:30; "Fire Destroys Kersley House," *Cariboo Observer,* 17 February 1955, 1.

23 An overview of the situation at Alexandria is provided in BCA, GR-1661 Records of the Deputy Provincial Secretary, box 4, file 5, J. Hatter, Director, Fish and Game Branch, Department of Recreation and Conservation, to Deputy Minister D.B. Turner, 21 July 1964; and H.G. McWilliams to Lawrie Wallace, 29 July 1964. Thank you to Leslie Middleton and the volunteers at the Quesnel and District Museum and Archives for kindly tracking down information on this business.

24 "Water Wheel under Repair," *Cariboo Observer,* 15 July 1954, 1.

25 "Lets Get Started," *Cariboo Observer,* 16 March 1946, 1; "Louis LeBourdais Cariboo Relics Go to BC Archives at Victoria," *Cariboo Observer,* 18 October 1947, 1.

26 "Commission to Give Lot for Rest Room," *Cariboo Observer,* 16 March 1950, 1.

27 Skelton, *They Call It,* 219.

28 "Historic Stanley Hotel Razed in Early Morning Fire," *Cariboo Observer,* 1 May 1948, 1; "Barkerville's Historic Kelly House Is Damaged by Fire," *Cariboo Observer,* 29 January

1949, 1. Also see B.A. McKelvie, "Barkerville Loses Face," *Vancouver Province,* 16 February 1952, 4.

29 Originally published as *Cariboo Digest,* the magazine changed its name several times. It was rebranded *Northwest Digest* in the early 1950s, then *British Columbia Digest* in the 1960s, and finally *BC Outdoors* in the early 1970s.

30 F.W. Lindsay, "We Never Think," *Northwest Digest,* March 1951, 8.

31 "Keep Our History Alive," *Prince George Citizen,* 31 August 1953, 2.

32 Regarding these markers, see "Rbt. Barlow Passes Suddenly," *Cariboo Observer,* 15 July 1954, 1, 4.

33 "Historic Group Now at B'ville," *Cariboo Observer,* 17 July 1952, 5.

34 "Display Recalls Gold Rush Days," *Prince George Citizen,* 26 July 1951, 4.

35 *Ashcroft Journal,* 2 July 1953, 1; 30 July 1953, 1; "Clinton Museum Opened Friday," *Ashcroft Journal,* 10 September 1953, 1; "Notes and Comments," *British Columbia Historical Quarterly* 17, nos. 3-4 (July-October 1953): 249, 254.

36 On Fred Ludditt's efforts, see Ludditt, *Gold in the Cariboo;* Skelton, *They Call It,* 219; and BCA, GR-1661, box 17, file 1, James McKelvie to Charles V. Axine, 22 August 1964.

37 "To Seek Repairs for Courthouse," *Cariboo Observer,* 5 August 1954, 9.

38 "Landmark Gone, 3 Perish as Famous Hotel Burns," *Prince George Citizen,* 20 May 1958, 12; *Cariboo Observer,* 22 May 1958, 1; Coombs, *By Truck and Bus,* 31; BCA, MS-2723, "My Latest and Probably 'Last' Trip," 9.

39 Ramsey and Turner, *Inn-Side British Columbia,* 13; BCA, GR-1661, box 23, file 3, Lawrie Wallace to W.P. Anderson, Assistant to the President, Standard Oil Company of British Columbia, 19 September 1961.

Chapter 7

1 Reimers, "'BC at Its Most Sparkling,'" 141–42. The period from the mid-1940s to the late 1950s is usually identified as the second golden age of the western movie genre, as epitomized by the films of John Ford and John Wayne. See Loy, *Westerns and American Culture;* and Simmon, *The Invention of the Western Film.*

2 Reimers, "BC at Its Most Sparkling."

3 The provincial secretary, who was a cabinet minister, was nominally responsible for enforcing the provincial Historic Objects Preservation Act (1948), which was followed by the Archaeological and Historic Sites Protection Act (1960). The act of 1960 gave the provincial secretary the power "to designate any site, parcel of land, building, or structure of any kind" as an official archaeological or historic site. No one without a permit from the minister was allowed to "destroy, deface, move, excavate, or alter in any way" these sites, on the threat of a fine. BCA, GR-1661, box 1, file 1.

4 Dawson, "'It's a Landmark,'" 397–416; Kincade, *Saskatchewan Monuments;* Lewis, "On the Trail," 206–9.

5 "Starting Gun Fired for Local Centennial Effort," *Vancouver Sun,* 17 May 1956, 4. Also see "To Stint on Centennial Unforgivable Blunder," *Vancouver Sun,* 11 April 1955, 4.

6 Mitchell, *W.A.C. Bennett,* 260–62; Tomblin, "W.A.C. Bennett," 45–61.

7 British Columbia Centennial Committee, *The Report of the British Columbia Centennial,* 160–61, 166–68, 178–79, 185–98, ch. 7; Reimers, "BC at Its Most Sparkling," 156–61; Stangoe, *Looking Back,* 122–26.

8 Advertising and publicity are outlined in British Columbia Centennial Committee, *The Report of the British Columbia Centennial,* 143–48. On the promotion of the centennial with bumper stickers, windshield decals, and licence plates, see BCA, GR-1448 BC Centennial '58 Committee, box 13, G.B. Rae, President, Screencraft Advertising Ltd., to L.H. McCance, Executive Secretary, BC Centennial Committee, 2 October 1956; box 21, George G. Fleming to L.H. McCance, Executive Secretary, BC Centennial Committee, 11 September 1956; Doug Horan, Publicity Director, BC Centennial Committee, to Local Centennial Committee Chairmen, 17 December 1956. Also see Garrish, *Tales from the Back,* ch. 3.

9 The subcommittee's activities are summarized in British Columbia Centennial Committee, *The Report of the British Columbia Centennial,* 118–32. This synopsis includes the locations and inscriptions of the thirty-eight markers that were erected in 1958.

10 McKelvie and Sage took radically different approaches to writing BC history. McKelvie, who constantly emphasized romance, adventure, conflict, and myth, epitomized the popular approach to the province's past, whereas Sage embodied the professional, academic approach. Reimer, *Writing British Columbia,* ch. 5; Twigg, *The Essentials,* 80–81.

11 Borden, "Wilson Duff," 3–12.

12 In addition to a very popular book on BC flora and fauna, Lyons had authored two guidebooks about the central and southern Interior: *Milestones on the Mighty Fraser* (1949) and *Milestones in Ogopogo Land* (1957).

13 Except where indicated otherwise, the following is drawn from BCA, GR-1448, box 1, "Minutes of First Meeting of Historic Sites and Publications Subcommittee," 25 September 1956.

14 BCA, GR-1448, box 1, Alvin Johnston, Cariboo Historical Society, to Ireland, 15 September 1956. Also see Leo Mader, Boundary Historical Society, to Willard Ireland, 15 August 1956.

15 BCNRL, S.E. Park, "A Recreational Inventory of British Columbia: Historic Sites and Monuments" (Victoria, BC Forest Service, Parks and Recreation Division, 1956). The Historic Sites and Monuments Board of Canada had erected thirty-seven monuments in British Columbia, twelve of which were in the Interior. Five lay along the Cariboo Highway, at Hope, Yale, Alexandria, Quesnel, and Barkerville. Four were spread across the Kootenays, at Fort Steele, near Invermere at the original site of Kootenae House, on the Banff-Windermere Highway at the summit of Sinclair Pass, and on the southern transprovincial highway at the Castlegar ferry. There were also markers at Riverside Park in Kamloops, at Boat Encampment on the Big Bend Highway, and at Westbank on a bluff overlooking Okanagan Lake and Kelowna. Except for the Collins Overland Telegraph monument at Quesnel, all of these markers commemorated people, places, and events associated with western exploration, the fur trade, and the gold rushes of the 1850s and 1860s. The provincial government had erected twenty-nine markers, but only five were in the Interior: at Kamloops, Revelstoke, and Grand Forks, at the site of Fort Sheppard near Trail, and at Lillooet, to mark the original start of the Cariboo Wagon Road.

16 For examples in western Canadian, see Taylor, *Negotiating the Past,* 144–46, regarding the spiralling cost of restoration projects at Manitoba's Lower Fort Garry and Saskatchewan's Fort Battleford in the early 1950s. Closer to home, the planned restoration of Fort Langley in the Fraser Valley had proven beyond the limited technical and financial means of the Native Sons of British Columbia, which by the 1950s was lobbying Ottawa to take over the project.

17 See, for example, L. Lazeo, *Collectors Guide to BC Indian Artifact Sites: Over 160 Locations* (N.p.: L. Lazeo, 1970).

18 The following is drawn from BCA, GR-1448, box 1, "Minutes of Second Meeting of the Historic Sites and Publications Subcommittee," 21 November 1956.

19 The Kootenay Lake Historical Society's efforts to preserve the *Moyie* are described in Turner, *The SS Moyie,* 54–55. On the decline of BC lake and river steamers after the Second World War, see Turner, *Sternwheelers and Steam Tugs.*

20 BCA, GR-1448, box 1, C.P. Lyons, undated draft of statement titled "Historic Sites Marking Programme."

21 Except where noted otherwise, the following is drawn from BCA, GR-1448, box 1, "Minutes of the Third Historic Sites Subcommittee," 5 February 1958.

22 On another Canadian academic historian's frustration with the imperatives of a historical marker program that was oriented toward a popular audience, see McKay, "Liberty, Equality and Tourism," 263–87.

23 BCA, GR-1448, box 1, "Minutes of the Fourth Meeting of the Historic Sites Subcommittee," 14 February 1958; "Minutes of the Fifth Meeting of the Historic Sites Subcommittee," 21 March 1958; "Minutes of the Seventh Meeting of the Historic Sites Subcommittee," 14 May 1958.

24 BCA, GR-1448, box 1, undated list of thirty-four proposed viewpoints.

25 Marker inventories include BC Parks Branch, *Stop, Look, and Learn: "Stop of Interest" Markers in British Columbia* (Victoria: Parks Branch, Department of Recreation and Conservation, 1966); McGill, *101 Stops of Interest;* and McGill, *126 Stops of Interest.*

26 A few history enthusiasts from Quesnel even organized what they hoped would be a headline-grabbing publicity stunt that would prompt the provincial government to save Barkerville. They surreptitiously removed the rot-riddled headboard that marked the grave of Chartres Brew, the first BC police chief, from Barkerville's overgrown cemetery in the hope that someone would mistake its removal for an act of theft or desecration. The resulting press coverage was expected to stir up public interest in the deteriorating townsite. However, the stunt fizzled when no one noticed that the headboard had disappeared. "Headboard Moved for Safe Keeping," *Cariboo Observer,* 25 September 1958, 19; Gordon R. Elliott, Review of *Barkerville Days,* 55–59.

27 Stan Rough, "Barkerville: Is It Worth Preserving?" *Northwest Digest,* January-February 1958, 7.

28 Ibid., 7.

29 "Trade Board Checks Rumors," *Cariboo Observer,* 16 February 1956, 9.

30 "Seeks Grant for Barkerville," *Cariboo Observer,* 16 February 1956, 9. Something of a Cariboo old-timer himself, Ralph Chetwynd was familiar with the changes the region had undergone since the turn of the century. He had come to British Columbia from Britain in 1908 and after first settling in Ashcroft had gone on to manage a large orchard at Walhachin until the outbreak of war. During the interwar years, he got into ranching and cattle transportation in the central Cariboo, which meant doing considerable business with the PGE. From 1942 to 1952, he was the PGE's director of public relations and was made minister of trade and railways after being elected on the Social Credit ticket in 1952.

31 An outline of the Centennial Committee's initial plans for Barkerville can be found in British Columbia Centennial Committee, *Report of the British Columbia Centennial,* 133–36. For examples of Parks Branch officials advocating a restoration program within the structure

of the Department of Recreation and Conservation, see BCA, GR-1991, reel 1725, D.L. MacMurchie, Forester, Provincial Parks Branch, to C.P. Lyons, 6 August 1957; and D.B. Turner, Acting Deputy Minister, Department of Recreation and Conservation, to Lyons, 6 August 1957. Regarding Cariboo residents' continued involvement with Barkerville after the townsite's "takeover" by the provincial government, see Elliott, Review of *Barkerville Days;* and BCA, GR-1661, box 17, file 1, James McKelvie to Charles V. Axine, 22 August 1964.

32 BCA, GR-1991, reel 1725, W.A.C. [Bennett], undated handwritten notes on Willard Ireland, Honorary Secretary, British Columbia Centennial Committee, to Premier Bennett, 6 November 1957. Other documents that refer to the involvement of the premier and senior cabinet members are McWilliams to Land Commissioner, Quesnel, 7 May 1958; Ireland to C.W.T. Hyslop, Superintendent of Lands, 18 November 1957; and Ray Williston to Bennett, 22 November 1957. On Williston's role on the Centennial Committee, see Williston and Keller, *Forests, Power and Policy,* 92–93.

33 Gordon, *Time Travel.*

34 The following is drawn from BCA, GR-1991, reel 1760, undated Ches Lyons report to Centennial Committee [summer 1958]. Also see British Columbia Centennial Committee, *The Report of the British Columbia Centennial,* 133–35.

35 For an architect's interpretation of Ches Lyons's recommendations, see BCA, GR-1661, box 1, file 6, Raymond O. Harrison to Barkerville Restoration Advisory Committee, 10 October 1959.

36 BCA, GR-1991, reel 1725, Ireland to W.A.C. Bennett, 6 November 1957.

37 The park was established on 12 January 1959 by Order-in-Council 26.

38 Regarding the Barkerville Restoration Advisory Committee, see BCA, GR-1661, box 3, file 3, E.F. Fox, Public Relations Department, BC Electric, to Wallace, 19 October 1959, forwarding George Towhill, Public Relations, Canadian National Railways, to Fox, 16 October 1959; and J.A.L. Godfrey, Secretary, Quesnel and District Board of Trade, to Wallace, 19 November 1959.

39 On the protracted negotiations to acquire Cottonwood House, see BCA, GR-1661, box 1, file 3, "Report of the Barkerville Restoration Advisory Committee to the Legislature" (19 February 1962). Regarding attendance in the park's earliest years, see box 1, file 9, Wallace to Donald Mitchell, Manager, Mitchell Press, 7 March 1961.

40 See, for example, Art Downs, "Look What's Happening to Barkerville," *Northwest Digest,* November-December 1959, 11–18; and "Restoration at Barkerville," *Northwest Digest,* January-February 1961, 32–35. *Beautiful British Columbia* was a veritable catalogue of roadside attractions. Its first issue had an article titled "Barkerville Lives On!," and stories involving the Cariboo Highway corridor were common fare during the 1960s.

41 BCA, GR-1661, box 1, file 5, C.P. Lyons, "Barkerville Programme Report" (1960).

42 British Columbia, Department of Recreation and Conservation, *Annual Report* (Victoria: Department of Recreation and Conservation, 1962), 40.

43 BCA, GR-1661, box 1, file 4, E.W. Bassett, Deputy Minister of Lands, to Wallace, 12 May 1961; Wallace to Bassett, 10 August 1961.

44 BCA, GR-1661, box 23, file 3, Lyons to R.H. Nichols, 31 July 1961.

45 The government received several proposals to make a loop trip possible by the construction of new roads to the south of Barkerville, linking it with Williams Lake. See, for example, BCA, GR-1991, reel 1725, K.F. Phillips, Secretary, Williams Lake and District Board of

Trade, to Department of Recreation and Conservation, 14 December 1962; J.A. Dennison, Senior Maintenance Engineer, Department of Highways, to Phillips, 18 December 1962; Broadland to R.L. Colby, BC Government Travel Bureau, 4 September 1964; and GR-1661, box 17, file 1, W.M. Hong to P. Gaglardi, Minister of Highways, 26 April 1966.

46 BCA, GR-1661, box 18, file 6, Quesnel and District Board of Trade and Wells District Board of Trade to Wallace, 19 January 1961; Pete Lowden to Barkerville Historic Restoration Committee, August 1961.

47 Jack Scott and Len Norris, "Beyond the Hills," *Vancouver Sun,* 20 May 1961. On middle-brow critiques of commercial strips elsewhere in Canada at this time, see Penfold, "Are We to Go Literally?" 8–23.

48 See, for example, Lew Griffith, "In One Ear," *Cariboo Observer,* 25 May 1961, 5; and "Stop Penny Chiselling" and "Prevention of More Value," *Cariboo Observer,* 13 July 1961, 6.

49 Gordon, *Time Travel.*

50 Ibid., 206.

51 British Columbia, Department of Recreation and Conservation, *Annual Report* (Victoria: Department of Recreation and Conservation, 1962), 41; Bernsohn, *Cutting Up the North,* ch. 18; Drushka, *Tie Hackers,* 177–78; Hak, *Capital and Labour,* 39.

52 BCA, GR-1661, box 17, file 9, transcript of broadcasts on CKWX by Dorwin Baird, 20 and 21 August 1963; box 18, file 5, clipping of Jack Scott article from *Vancouver Sun,* 13 July 1962; clipping of Mike Tytherleigh article from *Vancouver Province,* 14 July 1962, 5.

53 BCA, Jack Scott article from *Vancouver Sun,* 13 July 1962. Also see Fern E. Crockett, letter to the editor, *Northwest Digest,* March–April 1962, 54.

54 BCA, GR-1991, reel 1725, S.S. Holland, Geologist, Department of Mines, to Dr. H. Sargent, Chief, Mineralogical Branch, Department of Mines, 18 November 1958; K.B. Blakey, Chief Gold Commissioner, Department of Mines, to McWilliams, 9 December 1958; McWilliams to Blakey, 18 December 1958; McWilliams, memo to the Minister re: establishment of Barkerville Historic Park, 19 December 1958.

55 BCA, GR-1991, reel 1725, Roger Pease [New Westminster] to Director, Parks Branch, 11 July 1961; McWilliams to Pease, 1 August 1961.

56 BCA, GR-1661, box 1, file 5, Westwood to Black, 29 January 1960; Black to Westwood, 5 February 1960; GR-1991, reel 1725, D.B. Turner, Deputy Minister, to P.J. Mulcahy, Deputy Minister of Mines, 5 July 1960; Cook to C.P. Lyons, 26 October 1960. The new courthouse park was established on 24 February 1960 by Order-in-Council 457.

57 These "mining" operations were drummed out in 1962, when the Parks Branch began operating its own free, hands-on gold panning display beside Williams Creek. This in turn led to complaints from the Wells Chamber of Commerce that the government was impinging on private enterprise in the vicinity of Barkerville Park. BCA, GR-1661, box 1, file 3, Alfred W. Ludditt, Wells and District Chamber of Commerce, to Wallace, 15 July 1963; file 4, Wallace to McWilliams, 6 January 1961; Lyons to Wallace, 31 January 1961; Wallace to Kiernan, Minister of Mines, 10 March 1961.

58 BCA, GR-1991, reel 1725, Cook to McWilliams, attn: C.P. Lyons, 14 May 1962.

59 The traffic restrictions put in place in 1962 are described most thoroughly in BCA, GR-1991, reel 1725, Wallace to Department of Highways, 31 May 1963. Traffic was permanently banned inside the park (except with Parks Branch permission) by Order-in-Council 1997 of 5 August 1963.

60 BCA, GR-1661, box 17, file 7, Cook to Wallace, 5 August 1963.

Chapter 8

1 BCA, GR-1661, box 1, file 2, Oscar Lohm [Yale] to Westwood, 31 August 1961; file 3, Mary O'Keefe to Les Cook, Barkerville Historic Park, 2 December 1963; box 4, file 5, Bill Hartley, MLA [Merritt] to Wallace, 5 May 1964.

2 BCA, GR-1661, box 1, file 3, Wallace to Black, memo "Re: Acquisition of Historic Sites Policy," 12 December 1962; H.G. McWilliams to Wallace, 16 December 1963.

3 On the history of Princeton's Pioneer Museum, see Gloria Stout, "Museums Have History Too," *Princeton BC News,* Summer 2010, 3.

4 Many of these publications were written by individuals who had helped cultivate roadside history in other ways. The two guidebooks authored by Ches Lyons – *Milestones on the Mighty Fraser* (1949) and *Milestones in Ogopogo Land* (1957) – have already been mentioned; both were reprinted several times. Barkerville booster Fred Ludditt published *Gold in the Cariboo* (1958) and *Barkerville Days* (1969). Bruce Ramsey, who had been allowed to ride shotgun on the '58 Centennial Stagecoach Run, wrote a handful of popular histories, including *Barkerville: A Guide* (1961), *Ghost Towns of British Columbia* (1963), and *History on the Highways* (1966). Art Downs of *Northwest Digest* wrote two very popular books about transportation in the Interior: *Wagon Road North* (1960) and *Paddlewheels on the Frontier* (1967). Former Barkerville resident F.W. Lindsay, whose 1951 *Northwest Digest* article decried the future-mindedness of the BC postwar boom, published a series of booklets about the gold rush days, including *Cariboo Story* (1958), *Cariboo Yarns* (1962), *Outlaws* (1963), and *Cariboo Dream* (1972). *Beautiful British Columbia,* the glossy full-colour quarterly that the Department of Recreation and Conservation started to produce in 1959, also ran dozens of stories on roadside attractions, including ghost towns, as well as the growing number of museums, markers, and designated historical sites.

5 On life in Fort Steele during the period 1910–60, see Miller, *Fort Steele,* 217–27.

6 Fort Steele Heritage Town Archives, R.V. Bing collection, 1921 travel diary, ch. 18; 1923 travel diary, ch. 3.

7 Miller, *Fort Steele,* 6–8.

8 BCA, GR-1661, box 20, file 5, D.C. Sinclair to McWilliams, 10 August 1960; Windermere Valley Museum, David Thompson Memorial Fort collection, Richard T. Andruschuk to Windermere Valley Museum, 11 December 2007.

9 BCA, GR-1991, reel 1750, J.D. McMynn, Secretary-Treasurer, Associated Boards of Trade and Chambers of Commerce of South-Eastern British Columbia, to Earle C. Westwood, Minister of Recreation and Conservation, 10 December 1959. Wesley Black, it is also worth noting, had been a teacher in Creston for fourteen years before getting elected on the Social Credit ticket in 1952 and may well have been predisposed toward the preservation of historical sites for educational purposes.

10 BCA, GR-1991, reel 1750, Westwood to McMynn, 17 December 1959.

11 BCA, GR-1661, box 20, file 3, C.P. Lyons, "List of Buildings in Fort Steele" (29 April 1960). Regarding "gossip" within the government that future legislation would put Fort Steele "and other locations in the province" under the control of the Parks Branch, see box 3, file 3, minutes of the first meeting of the Barkerville Restoration Advisory Committee, 13 October 1959.

12 On Crestbrook Timber's plans to become a major forestry firm in the southern Interior, see Drushka, *Tie Hackers,* 181–82; and Crestbrook Forest Industries, *Our First 100 Years.*

13 BCA, GR-1991, reel 1750, Bill Mead to Earle C. Westwood, Minister of Recreation and Conservation, 7 May 1960.
14 Ibid.
15 BCA, GR-1661, box 20, file 5, Mead to Wallace, 26 September 1960; Wallace to Mead, Mead to Wallace, 11 October 1960; Wallace to Mead, 4 November 1960; Mead to Wallace, 30 December 1960. Regarding the RCMP's public relations efforts during the postwar years, see Dawson, *The Mountie.*
16 Public meetings to discuss the project during this period are described in "Public Notice: Fort Steele Property Owners to Meet" and "Property Owners to Meet: Fort Steele Historic Site to Be Discussed," *Cranbrook Courier,* 5 January 1961, 1, 8; and "Scene of Gold Rush in 1880s: Favor Fort Steele as Historic Site," *Cranbrook Courier,* 12 January 1961, 1.
17 BCA, GR-1991, reel 1750, Director, Provincial Parks Branch, to W.H. Hepper, Nelson District Park Officer, 16 March 1961.
18 BCA, GR-1661, box 20, file 3, Wallace to Mead, 15 November 1963.
19 BCA, GR-1991, reel 1750, Director, Provincial Parks Branch, to Arthur Howard, 19 September 1961.
20 BCA, GR-1991, reel 1750, H.C. McKay [MLA, Cranbrook] to Director of Parks, 11 September 1962; GR-1661, box 20, file 3, Dinty Moore to Wallace, 18 October 1963; box 1, file 3, Ed Leonard to Wesley Black, Minister of Municipal Affairs, January 1964.
21 BCA, GR-1661, box 20, file 5, Mead to Wallace, 17 February 1961; box 20, file 3, Wallace to Mead, 9 January 1963; Willard Ireland to Wallace, 25 January 1963; GR-1991, reel 1750, H.G. McWilliams to Minister of Recreation and Conservation, 10 February 1965; McWilliams to J. Dennison, Department of Highways, 20 May 1966; Dennison to McWilliams, 15 June 1965.
22 BCA, GR-1661, box 19, file 8, Wallace to E.W. Bassett, Deputy Minister of Lands, 29 April 1963; Wallace to Deputy Minister of Highways, 7 November 1963; GR-1991, reel 1750, Broadland to Blackburn, 17 December 1964.
23 BCA, GR-1991, reel 1750, N.O. Blackburn to T.R. Broadland, Planner, Historic Sites, Department of Recreation and Conservation, 26 November 1964; McWilliams to Wallace, 25 March 1965; McWilliams to G.V. Sandiford, Secretary-Manager, Kamloops Tourist Bureau, 22 July 1965.
24 BCA, GR-1661, box 21, file 4, Allan Hunter to Lawrie Wallace, 16 April 1966; GR-1991, reel 1750, Blackburn to Broadland, 25 August 1965.
25 BCA, GR-1991, reel 1750, McWilliams to Wallace, 1 September 1965; McWilliams to Wallace, 23 March 1966.
26 BCA, GR-1991, reel 1750, H.G. McWilliams, Director, Parks Branch, to L.J. Wallace, Deputy Provincial Secretary, 25 March 1965; N.O. Blackburn, "Progress Report: Fort Steele Historic Park" (15 December 1965); reel 1751, Broadland to Blackburn, 2 February 1968.
27 BCA, GR-1991, reel 1751, Blackburn to Broadland, 24 January 1967.
28 See especially BCA, GR-1991, reel 1751, G.H. Perret, Superintendent, Kootenay-Okanagan Agency, Indian Affairs Branch, to Mr. Bailey, BC Forest Service, Cranbrook, 7 April 1966. On the dearth of material related to First Nations at Fort Steele Park during the 1960s and 1970s, see Gordon, *Time Travel,* 292–93.
29 BCA, GR-1991, reel 1750, Blackburn to Broadland, 15 May 1967; Blackburn to Broadland, 17 July 1967.

30 Bell, *Three Valley Gap*. Regarding the highway realignment that cut off access to the Hotel Bellevue in Sicamous, see BCA, GR-1222, box 92, file 9, L.H. Congreve to Premier Byron Johnson, 9 May 1952.

31 BCA, GR-1661, box 1, file 4, John E. Gibbard, Secretary, BC Historical Association, to Wesley Black, 23 December 1960; file 5, Wilson Duff to Wallace, 4 November 1960.

32 Loo, "People in the Way"; Parr, *Sensing Changes,* ch. 5; Porteous and Smith, *Domicide,* ch. 5; Stanley, *Voices from Two Rivers,* chs. 6–10; Wilson, *People in the Way.*

33 BCA, GR-1661, box 7, file 3, J.W. Wilson, Regional Development Coordinator, BC Hydro and Power Authority, to Wallace, 17 March 1965; Wallace to Wesley Black, Provincial Secretary and Minister of Municipal Affairs, 18 March 1965.

34 BCA, GR-1661, box 7, file 3, Wilson to Wallace, 18 May 1965.

35 BCA, GR-1661, box 7, file 3, J.W. Wilson to Wallace, 7 April 1965; Broadland to R.H. Ahrens, Chief, Planning, Parks Branch, 9 April 1965. For offers to donate structures that would otherwise be demolished as part of BC Hydro's reservoir clearing program, see Wilson to Wallace, 7 April 1965; and H.L. Keenleyside, Chairman, BC Hydro and Power Authority, to Wesley Black, 14 April 1965.

36 BCA, GR-1661, box 7, file 3, McWilliams to Wilson, 24 September 1965; Broadland to McWilliams, 12 October 1965. On the history of Arrowhead and other communities along the north end of Upper Arrow Lake, see Parent, *Silent Shores.*

37 BCA, GR-1661, box 7, file 3, Wilson to Wallace, 17 December 1965; file 2, G.W. Fitzpatrick, Senior Community Planner, Land Division, BC Hydro, to Wallace, 21 August 1966.

38 BCA, GR-1661, box 7, file 2, J.P. Corrigan, City Clerk [Revelstoke], to Black, 15 April 1965; Frank Sampson, President, Revelstoke Historical Association, to Black, January 1966. Regarding the remains of the SS *Minto,* see BCA, GR-1661, box 3, file 1, Broadland to Ireland, 23 October 1967.

39 BCA, GR-1661, box 7, file 2, Broadland to McWilliams, 15 September 1966.

40 BCA, GR-1661, box 7, file 2, McWilliams to Wallace, 3 August 1966; G.W. Fitzpatrick, Senior Community Planner, Land Division, BC Hydro, to Wallace, 21 August 1966; Estelle Dickey to Ireland, 19 September 1966; Arvid Lundell to Black, 1 October 1966; Dickey to Ireland, 8 October 1966; R.W. Gross, Manager, Land Division, BC Hydro, to Wallace, 12 October 1966; Dickey to Wallace, 10 April 1968; Wallace to Keenleyside, 29 May 1968.

41 BCA, GR-1661, box 7, file 2, Dickey to Broadland, 22 February 1967. Regarding the construction of the High Arrow Dam, see Stanley, *Voices from Two Rivers,* 169–78.

42 Ada Domke, *12 Mile Remembered: Our Lives before They Burned Our Homesteads: Flooded and Burned Dreams of a Small Community in British Columbia* (Revelstoke: Trafford, 2008), ch. 14.

43 The Parks Branch was surprisingly reluctant to abandon the Columbia Village scheme, even after it had lost the materials with which to assemble the museum. Robert Ahrens, Parks Branch director in 1968, channelled the American government's anxiety about losing face by withdrawing from South Vietnam when he argued, "we don't feel that we can simply pull out and leave the [Revelstoke Historical] Association entirely to its own devices." The Parks Branch encouraged the RHA to seek funding from the recently established Columbia-Shuswap Regional District and promised assistance "in the planning of your Museum." The idea of a large outdoor museum at Revelstoke staggered along for a few more years, but in the spring of 1969 the Parks Branch informed the RHA that no more help would be forthcoming. BCA, GR-1661, box 7, file 2, Ahrens to Dickey, 18 October

1968; file 1, Ahrens to Wallace, 20 February 1969; Ahrens to Wallace, 28 February 1969; Wallace to Dickey, 3 March 1969.

Conclusion

1 BCNRL, Ray Lowery, "Some BC Provincial Park Development Standards" (Victoria, [mid-1950s]).

Bibliography

Archival Sources

British Columbia Archives (BCA)
GR-1222, Premiers' papers
GR-1388, BC Provincial Police, Yale Division
GR-1448, BC Centennial '58 Committee
GR-1661, Records of the Deputy Provincial Secretary
GR-1991, Records with Regards to Parks
MS-0560, William Earle Dickey papers
MS-0676, Louis LeBourdais papers
MS-2723, Leonard A. Coton papers
MS-2793, BC Provincial Police Veterans Association papers

British Columbia J.T. Fyles Natural Resources Library (BCNRL)
Plans, reports, surveys, and other original materials relating to provincial parks and forestry

City of Vancouver Archives (CVA)
Major Matthews collection
Pamphlet collection

Fort Steele Heritage Town Archives
R.V. Bing collection

Kamloops Museum and Archives
Historical articles collection (vertical files)

Library and Archives Canada (LAC)
Department of Mines and Technical Surveys collection
MG-26K, R.B. Bennett papers

RG-24, Department of National Defence, Unemployment Relief
RG-84, Parks Canada

Lytton Museum and Archives
Gwen Miller collection

Princeton and District Museum and Archives
Clipping files

Revelstoke Museum and Archives (RMA)
Earle and Estelle Dickey collection

Touchstones Nelson Museum and Archives
West Kootenay Forest History Project

University of British Columbia Library Special Collections (UBCSC)
Pamphlet collection
Simon Fraser Tolmie fonds

University of Victoria Archives
Chester P. Lyons fonds

University of Washington Libraries Special Collections
Asahel Curtis Photo Company collection

Vancouver Public Library Special Collections (VPLSC)
Donovan Clemson collection
Pamphlet collection

Newspapers

Chilliwack Progress
Golden Star
Prince George Citizen
Princeton Similkameen Spotlight
Quesnel Cariboo Observer
Revelstoke Review
Vancouver Province
Vancouver Sun
Victoria Colonist
Winnipeg Free Press

Other Sources

Allison, Susan. *A Pioneer Gentlewoman in British Columbia: The Recollections of Susan Allison,* ed. Margaret Ormsby. Vancouver: UBC Press, 1976.

Anastakis, Dimitry. *Car Nation: An Illustrated History of Canada's Transformation behind the Wheel.* Toronto: Lorimer, 2008.

Anderson, James D. *British Columbia's Magnificent Parks: The First 100 Years.* Vancouver: Harbour, 2011.

Baikie, Wallace. *Strathcona: A History of British Columbia's First Provincial Park.* Campbell River: Ptarmigan, 1986.

Baikie, Wallace, and Rosemary Phillips. *From Gypo to B.T.O.: The First Twenty-Five Years of the Truck Loggers Association of British Columbia.* Campbell River: Ptarmigan, 1986.

Barman, Jean. "Separate and Unequal: Indian and White Girls at All Hallows School, 1884-1920." In *Children, Teachers, and Schools in the History of British Columbia,* ed. Jean Barman, Neil Sutherland, and J. Donald Wilson, 337–57. Calgary: Detselig, 1995.

–. *The West beyond the West: A History of British Columbia.* Toronto: University of Toronto Press, 1991.

Barnett, Gabrielle. "Drive-By Viewing: Visual Consciousness and Forest Preservation in the Automobile Age." *Technology and Culture* 45, no. 1 (January 2004): 30–54. http://dx.doi.org/10.1353/tech.2004.0004.

Beaumont, Matthew, and Michael Freeman, eds. *The Railway and Modernity: Time, Space, and the Machine Ensemble.* Bern: Peter Lang, 2007.

Belasco, Warren. *Americans on the Road: From Autocamp to Motel, 1910–1945.* Baltimore: Johns Hopkins University Press, 1979.

Bell, Gordon. *Three Valley Gap: British Columbia, Canada.* Revelstoke: Three Valley Lake Chateau, 2003.

Bella, Leslie. *Parks for Profit.* Montreal: Harvest House, 1987.

Belshaw, John, and Diane Purvey. *Private Grief, Public Mourning: The Rise of the Roadside Shrine in British Columbia.* Vancouver: Anvil Press, 2009.

Belton, Brian. *Bittersweet Oasis: A History of Ashcroft, the First 100 Years.* Ashcroft: Village of Ashcroft, 1986.

Bennett, Evan. "Highways to Heaven or Roads to Ruin? The Interstate Highway System and the Fate of Starke, Florida." *Florida Historical Quarterly* 78, no. 4 (Spring 2000): 451–67.

Bennett, Jason. "Blossoms and Borders: Cultivating Apples and a Modern Countryside in the Pacific Northwest, 1890-2001." PhD diss., University of Victoria, 2008.

Bernsohn, Ken. *Cutting Up the North: The History of the Forest Industry in the Northern Interior.* North Vancouver: Hancock House, 1981.

Biel, Alice Wondrak. *Do (Not) Feed the Bears: The Fitful History of Wildlife and Tourists in Yellowstone.* Lawrence: University Press of Kansas, 2006.

Blake, Peter. *God's Own Junkyard: The Planned Deterioration of the American Landscape.* New York: Holt, 1964.

Boas, Franz, H.K. Haberlin, James Teit, and Helen Roberts. "Coiled Basketry in British Columbia and Surrounding Region." In *Forty-First Annual Report of the Bureau of American Ethnology, 1919–1924,* 119–484. Washington, DC: Bureau of American Ethnology, 1928.

Boime, Albert. *The Magisterial Gaze: Manifest Destiny and American Landscape Painting, 1830–1865.* Washington, DC: Smithsonian Institution Press, 1991.

Bonnell, Jennifer. "An Intimate Understanding of Place: Charles Sauriol and Toronto's Don River Valley, 1927-1989." *Canadian Historical Review* 92, no. 4 (December 2011): 607–36. Medline:22229164.

Booth, Janet Katharine. "Life and Times of Martin Grainger." Bachelor's thesis, University of British Columbia, 1985.

Borden, Charles E. "Wilson Duff: His Contributions to the Growth of Archeology in British Columbia." *BC Studies* 33 (Spring 1977): 3–12.

Borne, Lawrence R. *The Dude Ranch: A Complete History.* Albuquerque: University of New Mexico Press, 1983.

Bradley, Ben. "The Tower Ranch on the Hope-Princeton Highway." *Okanagan History: The Report of the Okanagan Historical Society* 74 (2010): 11–18.

British Columbia Centennial Committee. *The Report of the British Columbia Centennial Committee.* Victoria: The Committee, 1959.

Brower, Jennifer. *Lost Tracks: Buffalo National Park, 1909–1939.* Edmonton: AU Press, 2008.

Brown, Lorne Alvin. "The Bennett Government, Political Stability, and the Politics of the Unemployment Relief Camps, 1930-1935." PhD diss., Queen's University, 1983.

Budd, Robert. "'The Story of the Country': Imbert Orchard's Quest for Frontier Folk in BC, 1870–1914." Master's thesis, University of Victoria, 2005.

Burn, Michael. "With Saddle and Pack-Horse on the Sky Line Trail, circa 1919." *Report of the Okanagan Historical Society* 58 (1994): 41–45.

Cameron, Laura. *Openings: A Meditation on History, Method, and Sumas Lake.* Montreal and Kingston: McGill-Queen's University Press, 1997.

Campbell, Robert A. *Demon Rum or Easy Money: Government Control of Liquor in British Columbia from Prohibition to Privatization.* Ottawa: Carleton University Press, 1991.

–. *Sit Down and Drink Your Beer: Regulating Vancouver's Beer Parlours, 1925–1954.* Toronto: University of Toronto Press, 2001.

Carl, G. Clifford, C.J. Guiguet, and George A. Hardy. *A Natural History Survey of the Manning Park Area, British Columbia.* Occasional Papers of the British Columbia Provincial Museum, No. 9. Victoria: British Columbia Provincial Museum, 1952.

Carr, Ethan. *Mission 66: Modernism and the National Park Dilemma.* Amherst: University of Massachusetts Press, 2007.

–. *Wilderness by Design: Landscape Architecture and the National Park Service.* Lincoln: University of Nebraska Press, 1998.

Cartmill, Matt. *A View to a Death in the Morning: Hunting and Nature through History.* Cambridge, MA: Harvard University Press, 1993.

Cawston, Verna B. "Happy Days in a Relief Camp." In *Making History: An Anthology of British Columbia,* ed. Millicent A. Lindo, 55–62. Vancouver: Lindo, 1974.

Charles, Peter. *At the 47 Mile: A History of the Village of Clinton.* Victoria: Orca, 1990.

Christensen, Bev. *Too Good to Be True: Alcan's Kemano Completion Project.* Vancouver: Talon Books, 1995.

Clayton, Jenny. "'A National Playground Both in Summer and Winter': Civic Groups, Ethnic Organizations, and Tourism Promotion in Revelstoke, BC, 1890–1920." *Histoire sociale* 49, no. 99 (June 2016): 389–408. http://dx.doi.org/10.1353/his.2016.0010.

Clemson, Donovan. *Old Wooden Buildings.* Saanichton: Hancock House, 1978.

Cole, Douglas. *Captured Heritage: The Scramble for Northwest Coast Artifacts.* Vancouver: UBC Press, 1985.

Coleman, Jon T. "The Prim Reaper: Muriel Sibell Wolle and the Making of Western Ghost Towns." *Mining History Journal* 8 (2001): 10–17.

Colten, Craig E., and Lary M. Dilsaver. "The Hidden Landscape of Yosemite National Park." *Journal of Cultural Geography* 22, no. 2 (Spring-Summer 2005): 27–50. http://dx.doi.org/10.1080/08873630509478238.

Coombs, W. Gordon. *By Truck and Bus and Romance of Age.* Nanaimo: Evergreen, 1961.

Cooper, Lesley. "Dominion-Provincial Placer Mining Training School, Quesnel Forks, 1938-1939." *Likely Cemetery Society Newsletter,* 1993–94.

Craig, Andy. *Trucking: British Columbia's Trucking History*. Saanichton: Hancock House, 1977.

Crestbrook Forest Industries. *Our First 100 Years, 1898–1998: From Cranbrook Sash and Door Co. to Crestbrook Forest Industries Ltd.* Cranbrook: Crestbrook Forest Industries, 1998.

–. *Manufacturing National Park Nature: Photography, Ecology, and the Wilderness Industry of Jasper*. Vancouver: UBC Press, 2011.

Cronon, William. "The Trouble with Wilderness, or, Getting Back to the Wrong Nature." In *Uncommon Ground: Re-thinking the Human Place in Nature,* ed. William Cronon, 69–90. New York: W.W. Norton, 1995.

Cumming, R.D. *Skookum Chuck Fables: Bits of History, through the Microscope*. Ashcroft: Ashcroft Journal, 1915.

Currie, Laurie. *Princeton: 120 Years*. Princeton, BC: Similkameen Spotlight, 1990.

Darling, David, and Douglas Cole. "Totem Pole Restoration on the Skeena, 1925-30: An Early Exercise in Heritage Conservation." *BC Studies* 47 (Autumn 1980): 29–48.

Davies, Stephen. "Ontario and the Automobile, 1900-1930: Aspects of Technological Integration." PhD diss., McMaster University, 1987.

Davis, Timothy. *National Park Roads: A Legacy in the American Landscape*. Charlottesville: University of Virginia Press, 2016.

Dawson, Bruce. "'It's a Landmark in the Community': The Conservation of Historic Places in Saskatchewan." In *The West and Beyond: New Perspectives on an Imagined Region,* ed. Alvin Finkel, Sarah Carter, and Peter Fortna, 397–416. Edmonton: AU Press, 2010.

Dawson, Michael. *The Mountie from Dime Novel to Disney*. Toronto: Between the Lines, 1998.

–. *Selling British Columbia: Tourism and Consumer Culture, 1890–1970*. Vancouver: UBC Press, 2004.

Dendy, David, and Kathleen M. Kyle. *A Fruitful Century: The British Columbia Fruit Growers' Association, 1889–1989*. Kelowna: BC Fruit Growers' Association, 1990.

Dennis, Kingsley, and John Urry. *After the Car*. London: Polity, 2009.

Dickerson, L. "The Problem of Wildlife Destruction by Automobile Traffic." *Journal of Wildlife Management* 3, no. 2 (1939): 104–16. http://dx.doi.org/10.2307/3796352.

Dimendberg, Edward. "The Will to Motorization: Cinema, Highways, and Modernity." *October* 73 (1995): 90–137. http://dx.doi.org/10.2307/779010.

Dippie, Brian W. *The Vanishing American: White Attitudes and US Indian Policy*. Middletown: Wesleyan University Press, 1982.

Downs, Art. *Paddlewheels on the Frontier: The Story of British Columbia Sternwheel Steamers*. Cloverdale: BC Outdoors Magazine, 1967.

–. *Wagon Road North: The Story of the Cariboo Gold Rush in Historical Photos*. Quesnel: Northwest Digest, 1960.

Drushka, Ken. *HR: A Biography of H.R. MacMillan*. Madeira Park, BC: Harbour, 1995.

–. *Tie Hackers to Timber Harvesters: The History of Logging in British Columbia's Interior*. Madeira Park: Harbour, 1998.

Duffy, Dennis J., ed. *Evergreen Playground: A Road Trip through British Columbia*. Victoria: Royal BC Museum, 2008.

Duffy, Enda. *The Speed Handbook: Velocity, Pleasure, Modernism*. Durham: Duke University Press, 2008.

Dummitt, Christopher. "Risk on the Rocks: Modernity, Manhood, and Mountaineering in Postwar British Columbia." *BC Studies* 141 (Spring 2004): 3–29.

Duncan, Colin A.M. *The Centrality of Agriculture: Between Humankind and the Rest of Nature.* Montreal and Kingston: McGill-Queen's University Press, 1996.

Edwards, Yorke. "Some Early Finds and Follies." In British Columbia, Ministry of Lands and Parks, *Manning Park Memories: Reflections of the Past,* 45–48. Victoria: Ministry of Lands and Parks, 1991.

Elliott, Gordon R. *Quesnel: Commercial Centre of the Cariboo Gold Rush.* Quesnel: Cariboo Historical Society, 1958.

-. Review of *Barkerville Days,* by Fred Ludditt. *BC Studies* 9 (Spring 1971): 55–59.

Elliott, Marie. *Gold and Grand Dreams: Cariboo East in the Early Years.* Victoria: Horsdal and Schubart, 2000.

English, Cathy. *Reflections: Four Decades of Photography by Earle and Estelle Dickey.* Revelstoke: Revelstoke Museum and Archives, 2010.

Estabrooks, Lillian. *Under the K: Memories of Growing Up in Keremeos.* Kelowna: Skookum, 1981.

Evans, Rhys. "Looking at the World through a Windshield: A Historical Geography of the Trucking Industry in British Columbia." Master's thesis, University of British Columbia, 1996.

Farrar, Karen, ed. *Castlegar: A Confluence.* Castlegar: Castlegar and District Heritage Society, 2000.

Fehr, Amanda. "The Relationships of Place: A Study of Change and Continuity in Sto:lo Understandings of I:yem." Master's thesis, University of Saskatchewan, 2008.

–. "A Subversive Sincerity: The I:yem Memorial, Catholicism, and Political Opportunity in S'olh Téméxw." In *Mixed Blessings: Indigenous Encounters with Christianity in Canada,* ed. Tolly Bradford and Chelsea Horton, 61–82. Vancouver: UBC Press, 2016.

Fisher, Robin. *Duff Pattullo of British Columbia.* Toronto: University of Toronto Press, 1991.

–. "T.D. Pattullo and the British Columbia to Alaska Highway." In *The Alaska Highway: Papers of the 40th Anniversary Symposium,* ed. Ken Coates, 9-24. Vancouver: UBC Press, 1985.

Fitzroy, Yvonne. *A Canadian Panorama.* London: Methuen, 1929.

Foster, Chris. *One Heart, One Way: The Life and Legacy of Martin Exeter.* Denver: Foundation House, 1989.

Francis, Dan. *The Imaginary Indian: The Image of the Indian in Canadian Culture.* Vancouver: Arsenal, 1992.

–. *A Road for Canada: The Illustrated Story of the Trans-Canada Highway.* Vancouver: Stanton, Atkins, and Dosil, 2006.

Freeman, Lewis R. *Down the Columbia.* New York: Dodd, Mead, 1921.

Freeman, Michael. *Railways and the Victorian Imagination.* New Haven: Yale University Press, 1999. <Author: 2001 in a note that I shortened.>

Futcher, Winnifred. *The Great North Road to the Cariboo.* Vancouver: Wrigley, 1938.

Galloway, C.F.J. *The Call of the West: Letters from British Columbia.* London: T. Fisher Unwin, 1916.

Garrish, Christopher. *Tales from the Back Bumper: A Century of British Columbia's History as Seen through the Province's License Plates.* Victoria: Heritage House, 2013.

Giesbrecht, Jean Clark. *Heritage Lost: A People's History of the Ootsa Lake Region, 1905–1975.* Likely: Quesnel Lake, 1994.

Golden Memories Book Committee. *Golden Memories.* Golden, BC: Golden and District Historical Society, 2000.

Gordon, Alan. *Time Travel: Tourism and the Rise of the Living History Museum in Mid-Twentieth-Century Canada.* Vancouver: UBC Press, 2016.

Grainger, Martin Allerdale. *Riding the Skyline.* Victoria: Horsdal and Schubart, 1994.

Greene, Ronald. "Token History: McKinnon Bros. of Revelstoke." *BC Historical News* 37, no. 2 (Spring 2004): 32–33.

Gudis, Catherine. *Buyways: Billboards, Automobiles, and the American Landscape.* New York: Routledge, 2004.

Hak, Gordon. *Capital and Labour in the British Columbia Forest Industry, 1934–74.* Vancouver: UBC Press, 2007.

–. "Populism and the 1952 Social Credit Breakthrough in British Columbia." *Canadian Historical Review* 85, no. 2 (June 2004): 277–96. http://dx.doi.org/10.3138/CHR.85.2.277.

Harris, Cole. "The Fraser Canyon Encountered." *BC Studies* 94 (Summer 1992): 5–28.

–. "Moving amidst the Mountains, 1870-1933." *BC Studies* 58 (Summer 1983): 3–39.

–. *The Resettlement of British Columbia: Essays on Colonialism and Geographical Change.* Vancouver: UBC Press, 1997.

Harris, W. Howard. *Ten Golden Years: Barkerville-Wells, 1932–1942.* Quesnel: Little Shepherd, 1984.

Hart, E.J. *The Brewster Story: From Pack Train to Tour Bus.* Banff: Brewster Transport, 1981.

–. *The Selling of Canada: The CPR and the Beginnings of Canadian Tourism.* Banff: Altitude, 1983.

Hart, John Fraser, Michelle J. Rhodes, and John T. Morgan. *The Unknown World of the Mobile Home.* Baltimore: Johns Hopkins University Press, 2002.

Harvey, R.G. *Carving the Western Path: By River, Rail, and Road through BC's Southern Mountains.* Surrey: Heritage House, 1998.

–. *Carving the Western Path: Routes to Remember.* Surrey: Heritage House, 2006.

–. *The Coast Connection.* Lantzville: Oolichan, 1994.

Hawthorn, H.B., C.S. Belshaw, and S.M. Jamieson. *The Indians of British Columbia: A Study of Contemporary Social Adjustment.* Toronto: University of Toronto Press, 1958.

Hayes, Charles. *Hugh Leir: The Remarkable Enigma.* Okanagan Falls: Rima, 1999.

Hill, A. Suzanne. "A Serpent in the Garden: Implications of Highway Development in Canada's Niagara Fruit Belt." *Journal of Historical Sociology* 15, no. 4 (December 2002): 495–514. http://dx.doi.org/10.1111/1467-6443.00189.

Hong, W.M. *And So That's How It Happened: Recollections of Stanley and Barkerville, 1900–1975,* ed. Gary Seale and Eileen Seale. Quesnel: W.M. Hong, 1978.

Hooper, Jacqueline. "John Francis Bursill: Founder of the Vagabonds Club." *British Columbia Literary Quarterly* 32, no. 1 (July 1968): 17–26.

Howay, Frederic W. *The Early History of the Fraser River Mines.* Archives of British Columbia Memoir No. 6. Victoria: King's Printer, 1926.

Hutchison, Bruce. *The Unknown Country: Canada and Her People.* New York: Coward-McCann, 1942.

Jackson, John Brinckerhoff. *Discovering the Vernacular Landscape.* New Haven: Yale University Press, 1984.

Jacoby, Karl. *Crimes against Nature: Squatters, Poachers, Thieves and the Hidden History of American Conservation.* Berkeley: University of California Press, 2001.

Jakle, John A., and Keith A. Sculle. *America's Main Street Hotels: Transiency and Community in the Early Auto Age.* Charlottesville: University of Virginia Press, 2009.

–. *Fast Food: Roadside Restaurants in the Automobile Age*. Baltimore: Johns Hopkins University Press, 1999.

–. *The Gas Station in America*. Baltimore: Johns Hopkins University Press, 1994.

–. *Lots of Parking: Land Use in a Car Culture*. Charlottesville: University of Virginia Press, 2004.

–. *Motoring: The Highway Experience in America*. Athens: University of Georgia Press, 2008.

–. *Signs in America's Auto Age: Signatures of Landscape and Place*. Iowa City: University of Iowa Press, 2004.

Jakle, John A., Keith A. Sculle, and Jefferson S. Rogers. *The Motel in America*. Baltimore: Johns Hopkins University Press, 1996.

Kay, Charles E., Brian Patton, and Cliff A. White. "Historical Wildlife Observations in the Canadian Rockies: Implications for Ecological Integrity." *Canadian Field Naturalist* 114 (2000): 561–83.

Keeling, Arn, and Graeme Wynn. "'The Park Is a Mess': Development and Degradation in British Columbia's First Provincial Park." *BC Studies* 170 (2011): 119–50.

Kelm, Mary-Ellen. *A Wilder West: Rodeo in Western Canada*. Vancouver: UBC Press, 2011.

Kennedy, Michael. "Fraser River Placer Mining Landscapes." *BC Studies* 160 (Winter 2008–09): 35–66.

Kern, Stephen. *The Culture of Time and Space, 1880–1918*. New Haven: Harvard University Press, 1983.

Kheraj, Sean. *Inventing Stanley Park: An Environmental History*. Vancouver: UBC Press, 2013.

Kincade, Winifred. *Saskatchewan Monuments*. Regina: School Aids and Text Book Publishing, 1963.

Kluckner, Michael. *Vanishing British Columbia*. Vancouver: UBC Press, 2005.

Knight, Rolf. *Indians at Work: An Informal History of Native Labour in British Columbia*. Vancouver: New Star Books, 1996.

Knight, Rolf, and Phyllis Knight. *A Very Ordinary Life*. Vancouver: New Star Books, 1974.

Koropecki, June. *Life in the Tee-Pee*. Lytton: Freedom Graphics, 2010.

Laforet, Andrea. "The Market in Coiled Basketry." Unpublished paper, 2011.

Leece, Robert. "Making BC History: The Native Sons of British Columbia." *BC Historical News* 29, no. 1 (Winter 1995–96): 30–33.

Leib, Jonathan. "Identity, Banal Nationalism, Contestation, and North American License Plates." *Geographical Review* 101, no. 1 (January 2011): 37–52. http://dx.doi.org/10.1111/j.1931-0846.2011.00071.x.

Lewis, Wallace. "On the Trail: Commemorating the Lewis and Clark Expedition in the Twentieth Century." In *Lewis and Clark: Legacies, Memories, and New Perspectives*, ed. Kris Fresonke and Mark Spence, 198–213. Berkeley: University of California Press, 2004. http://dx.doi.org/10.1525/california/9780520228399.003.0010.

Liddicott, Wallace L. *Waterwheels in the Service of British Columbia's Pioneers*. Keremeos: Wallace L. Liddicott, 1996.

Liebs, Chester. *Main Street to Miracle Mile: American Roadside Architectures*. Boston: Little, Brown, 1985.

Lindsay, F.W. *Cariboo Story*. Quesnel: Quesnel Advertiser, 1958.

Locke, Harvey. "Civil Society and Protected Areas." Paper presented at the Parks for Tomorrow Conference, University of Calgary, July 2008.

Loo, Tina. "People in the Way: Modernity, Environment, and Society on the Arrow Lakes." *BC Studies* 142–43 (Summer–Autumn 2004): 161–96.

Lothian, W.F. *A History of Canada's National Parks.* 4 vols. Ottawa: Indian and Northern Affairs, Parks Canada, 1976–81.

Louter, David. *Windshield Wilderness: Cars, Roads, and Nature in Washington's National Parks.* Seattle: University of Washington Press, 2006.

Loy, R. Philip. *Westerns and American Culture, 1930–1955.* Jefferson, NC: McFarland, 2001.

Ludditt, A.W. *Campfire Sketches of the Cariboo.* Union Bay: Fred Ludditt, 1974.

–. *Gold in the Cariboo.* Vancouver: Evergreen, 1958.

Lutts, Ralph. "The Trouble with Bambi: Walt Disney's Bambi and the American Vision of Nature." *Forest and Conservation History* 36, no. 4 (October 1992): 160–71. http://dx.doi.org/10.2307/3983677.

Lutz, John Sutton. *Makúk: A New History of Aboriginal-White Relations.* Vancouver: UBC Press, 2008.

Lymbery, Tom. "Greyhound and Gray Creek." *BC Historical News* 43, no. 1 (Spring 2010): 21–23.

Lyons, Ches P. *Milestones in Ogopogo Land.* Vancouver: Evergreen, 1957.

–. *Milestones on the Mighty Fraser.* Toronto: Dent, 1949.

–. "Tough Going." In British Columbia, Ministry of Lands and Parks, *Manning Park Memories: Reflections of the Past,* 37–44. Victoria: Ministry of Lands and Parks, 1991.

–. *Trees, Shrubs, and Flowers to Know in British Columbia.* Toronto: Dent, 1952.

MacEachern, Alan. *Natural Selections: National Parks in Atlantic Canada, 1935–1970.* Montreal and Kingston: McGill-Queen's University Press, 2001.

MacLaren, I.S. "Splendor Sine Occasu: Salvaging Boat Encampment." *Canadian Literature* 170–71 (Autumn-Winter 2001): 162–87.

Marling, Karal Ann. *The Colossus of Roads: Myth and Symbol along the American Highway.* Minneapolis: University of Minnesota Press, 1984.

Marshall, J.T. *Cariboo Gold: An Episode in the History of Freemasonry: The Story of Cariboo Lodge No. 469 Holding under the Grand Lodge of Scotland, and Cariboo Lodge, No. 4, under the Grand Lodge of British Columbia.* Victoria: Canadian Masonic Research Association, 1967.

Marx, Karl. "Outlines of the Critique of Political Economy (The Grundrisse)." In *Karl Marx and Fredrick Engels, Collected Works,* vol. 28: 49-540. New York: International, 1986.

Matless, David. *Landscape and Englishness.* London: Reaktion, 1998.

Mattison, David. "The British Columbia Government Travel Bureau and Motion Picture Production, 1937-1947." In *Flashback: People and Institutions in Canadian Film History,* ed. Gene Walz, 79–104. Montreal: Mediatexte, 1986.

Mauch, Christof, and Thomas Zeller, eds. *The World beyond the Windshield: Roads and Landscapes in the United States and Europe.* Athens/Stuttgart: Ohio University Press/Franz Steiner Verlag, 2008.

McCarthy, Tom. *Auto Mania: Cars, Consumers, and the Environment.* New Haven: Yale University Press, 2007.

McCourt, Edward. *The Road across Canada.* Toronto: Macmillan, 1965.

McDonald, James A. "Bleeding Night and Day: The Construction of the Grand Trunk Pacific Railway across Tsimshian Reserve Lands." *Canadian Journal of Native Studies* 10, no. 1 (1990): 33-69.

McDonald, Yvonne. "Two Views of the World: Photographer-Author Donovan Clemson." *Report of the Okanagan Historical Society* 62 (1998): 8–19.
McGill, David. *101 Stops of Interest in Beautiful British Columbia*. N.p.: Agency Press, 1970.
–. *126 Stops of Interest in Beautiful British Columbia*. Aldergrove: Frontier, 1979.
McKay, Ian. "Liberty, Equality and Tourism: D.C. Harvey, Prince Edward Island, and the Power of Tourism/History." *Histoire sociale* 49, no. 99 (June 2016): 263–87. http://dx.doi.org/10.1353/his.2016.0000.
McKay, Ian, and Robin Bates. *In the Province of History: The Making of the Public Past in Twentieth Century Nova Scotia*. Montreal and Kingston: McGill-Queen's University Press, 2010.
McKelvie, Bruce. *The Black Canyon: A Story of '58*. Toronto: Dent, 1927.
–. *Early History of the Province of British Columbia*. Toronto: Dent, 1926.
Merilees, Bill. "The Beginnings of Interpretation in BC's Parks." *British Columbia History* 47, no. 2 (Summer 2014): 16–22.
Merriman, Peter. *Driving Spaces: A Cultural-Historical Geography of England's M1 Motorway*. Oxford: Blackwell, 2007. http://dx.doi.org/10.1002/9780470762448.
Miller, J.R. *Skyscrapers Hide the Heavens: A History of Indian-White Relations in Canada*. Toronto: University of Toronto Press, 1991.
Miller, Naomi. *Fort Steele: Gold Rush to Boom Town*. Surrey: Heritage House, 2002.
Mills, Edward. *Rustic Building in Canada's National Parks, 1887–1950*. Ottawa: Parks Canada, National Historic Sites Directorate, 1994.
Mitchell, David J. *W.A.C. Bennett and the Rise of British Columbia*. Vancouver: Douglas and McIntyre, 1995.
Mom, Gijs. *Atlantic Automobilism: Emergence and Persistence of the Car, 1895–1940*. New York: Berghahn, 2014.
Monaghan, David W. *Canada's New Main Street: The Trans-Canada Highway as Idea and Reality, 1912–1956*. Ottawa: Canada Science and Technology Museum, 2002.
Morrissey, Katherine G. *Mental Territories: Mapping the Inland Empire*. Ithaca: Cornell University Press, 1997.
Murray, Peter. *Home from the Hill: Three Gentlemen Adventurers*. Victoria: Horsdal and Schubart, 1994.
Murton, James. *Creating a Modern Countryside: Liberalism and Land Settlement in British Columbia*. Vancouver: UBC Press, 2007.
Nicholson, Marjorie Hope. *Mountain Gloom and Mountain Glory: The Development of the Aesthetics of the Infinite*. Ithaca: Cornell University Press, 1959.
O'Brian, John. "Shaping World Culture: Postwar Postcards in British Columbia." *BC Studies* 131 (Autumn 2001): 93–112.
Opp, James, and John C. Walsh. "Local Acts of Placing and Remembering." In *Placing Memory and Remembering Place in Canada*, ed. James Opp and John C. Walsh, 2–21. Vancouver: UBC Press, 2010.
Ormsby, Margaret A. *British Columbia: A History*. Toronto: Macmillan, 1958.
–. "T. Dufferin Pattullo and the Little New Deal." *Canadian Historical Review* 40, no. 4 (December 1962): 277–97.
Packer, Jeremy. *Mobility without Mayhem: Safety, Cars, and Citizenship*. Durham: Duke University Press, 2008. http://dx.doi.org/10.1215/9780822388906.
Parent, Milton. *Caulkboot Riverdance: Working the Columbia, Canada's Wildest Log Drive*. Nakusp: Arrow Lakes Historical Society, 2006.

–. *Silent Shores and Sunken Ships*. Nakusp: Arrow Lakes Historical Society, 1997.

Parkin, Tom. "Disappearing Highway." *BC Historical News* 28, no. 4 (Fall 1995): 31–32.

Parr, Joy. *Sensing Changes: Technologies, Environments, and the Everyday, 1953–2003*. Vancouver: UBC Press, 2010.

Pass, Forrest. "Pacific Dominion: British Columbia and the Making of Canadian Nationalism, 1858-1958." PhD diss., University of Western Ontario, 2009.

–. "'The Wondrous Story and Traditions of the Country': The Native Sons of British Columbia and the Role of Myth in the Formation of an Urban Middle Class." *BC Studies* 151 (Fall 2006): 3–38.

Patenaude, Branwen. *Trails to Gold: Roadhouses of the Cariboo*. Vol. 2. Surrey: Heritage House, 1996.

Penfold, Steve. "Are We to Go Literally to the Hot Dogs? Parking Lots, Drive-Ins, and the Critique of Progress in Toronto's Suburbs, 1965-1975." *Urban History Review* 33, no. 1 (Fall 2004): 8–23. http://dx.doi.org/10.7202/1015671ar.

–. *The Donut: A Canadian History*. Toronto: University of Toronto Press, 2008.

Philpott, William. *Vacationland: Tourism and the Environment in the Colorado High Country*. Seattle: University of Washington Press, 2013.

Porteous, J. Douglas, and Sandra E. Smith. *Domicide: The Global Destruction of Home*. Montreal and Kingston: McGill-Queen's University Press, 2001.

Presto, Sylvia. "An Annual Challenge: Travelling the Fraser Canyon." *Okanagan History: Report of the Okanagan Historical Society* 77 (2013): 76–83.

Quesnel Old Age Pensioners' Organization. *A Tribute to the Past*. Quesnel: Old Age Pensioners' Organization, Branch 77, 1985.

Rajala, Richard A. *Clearcutting the Pacific Rain Forest: Production, Science, and Regulation*. Vancouver: UBC Press, 1998.

–. "From 'On to Ottawa' to 'Bloody Sunday': Unemployment Relief and British Columbia Forests, 1935–1939." In *Framing Canadian Federalism: Historical Essays in Honour of John T. Saywell*, ed. Dimitry Anastakis and Penny Bryden, 118–50. Toronto: University of Toronto Press, 2009.

–. "'Nonsensical and a Contradiction in Terms': Multiple Use Forestry, Clearcutting, and the Politics of Salmon Habitat in British Columbia, 1945–1970." *BC Studies* 183 (Autumn 2014): 89–126.

–. "'This Wasteful Use of a River': Log Driving, Conservation, and British Columbia's Stellako River Controversy, 1965–72." *BC Studies* 165 (Spring 2010): 31–74.

Ramsey, Bruce. *Barkerville: A Guide in Word and Picture to the Fabulous Gold Camp of the Cariboo*. Vancouver: Mitchell, 1961.

–. *Ghost Towns of British Columbia*. Vancouver: Mitchell, 1963.

–. *History on the Highways*. Vancouver: Vancouver Province and BC Government Travel Bureau, 1966.

Ramsey, Bruce, and Ormond Turner. *Inn-Side British Columbia by Automobile*. Vancouver: Standard Oil Company of British Columbia and British Columbia Hotels Association, 1962.

Reid, J.H. Stewart. *Mountains, Men, and Rivers: British Columbia in Legend and Story*. Toronto: Ryerson, 1954.

Reimer, Chad. *Writing British Columbia History, 1784–1958*. Vancouver: UBC Press, 2009.

Reimers, Mia. "'BC at Its Most Sparkling, Colourful Best': Post-war Province Building through Centennial Celebrations." PhD diss., University of Victoria, 2007.

Robertson, Leslie. *Imagining Difference: Legend, Curse, and Spectacle in a Canadian Mining Town.* Vancouver: UBC Press, 2005.

Rodnitzky, Jerome L. "Recapturing the West: The Dude Ranch in American Life." *Arizona and the West* 10, no. 2 (Summer 1968): 111–26.

Ross, Davis R.B. *Preparing for Ulysses: Politics and Veterans during World War Two.* New York: Columbia University Press, 1969.

Ross, Gail. "High Times." In British Columbia, Ministry of Lands and Parks, *Manning Park Memories: Reflections of the Past,* 49–52. Victoria: Ministry of Lands and Parks, 1991.

Rothman, Hal. "A History of U.S. National Parks and Economic Development." In *National Parks and Rural Development,* ed. Gary Machlis and Donald Field, 51-66. Washington, DC: Island Press, 2000.

Routledge, Karen. "'Being a Girl without Being a Girl': Gender and Mountaineering on Mount Waddington, 1926–36." *BC Studies* 141 (Spring 2004): 31–58.

Sandford, Robert William. *Ecology and Wonder in the Canadian Rocky Mountain Parks World Heritage Site.* Calgary: AU Press, 2010.

Sandquist, David J. "The Giant Killers: Forestry, Conservation and Recreation in the Green Timbers Forest, Surrey, British Columbia to 1930." Master's thesis, Simon Fraser University, 2000.

Sandwell, R.W. "Finding Rural British Columbia." In *Beyond the City Limits: Rural History in British Columbia,* ed. R.W. Sandwell, 3–14. Vancouver: UBC Press, 1999.

Scharff, Virginia. *Taking the Wheel: Women and the Coming of the Motor Age.* Albuquerque: University of New Mexico Press, 1992.

Scheideman, Charles. *Policing the Fringe: The Curious Life of a Small-Town Mountie.* Madeira Park: Harbour, 2009.

Schivelbusch, Wolfgang. *The Railway Journey: The Industrialization of Time and Space in the 19th Century.* Berkeley: University of California Press, 1986. German original published 1977.

Schlereth, Thomas. *Reading the Road: US 40 and the American Landscape.* Knoxville: University of Tennessee Press, 1997.

Scholefield, E.O.S., and F. Howay. *British Columbia from the Earliest Times to the Present.* 2 vols. Vancouver: S.J. Clarke, 1914.

Schuurman, Nadine. "Constructing and Deconstructing the Railway through Reserves in British Columbia." *Native Studies Review* 13, no. 1 (2000): 19–40.

Schwartz, Joan M., and Lily Koltun. "A Visual Cliché: Five Views of Yale." *BC Studies* 52 (Winter 1981–82): 113–28.

Seiler, Cotten. *Republic of Drivers: A Cultural History of Automobility in America.* Chicago: University of Chicago Press, 2008. http://dx.doi.org/10.7208/chicago/9780226745657.001.0001.

–. "'So That We as a Race Might Have Something Authentic to Travel By': African American Automobility and Cold-War Liberalism." *American Quarterly* 58, no. 4 (2006): 1091–117.

–. "Statist Means to Individualist Ends: Subjectivity, Automobility, and the Cold War State." *American Studies* (Lawrence, KS) 44, no. 3 (2003): 5–36.

Septer, Dirk. *Flooding and Landslide Events in Southern British Columbia, 1808–2006.* Victoria: British Columbia Ministry of Environment, 2007.

Shaffer, Marguerite S. *See America First: Tourism and National Identity, 1880–1940.* Washington, DC: Smithsonian Institution Press, 2001.

Shaw, Louise. "Memories." In British Columbia, Ministry of Lands and Parks, *Manning Park Memories: Reflections of the Past,* 29–36. Victoria: Ministry of Lands and Parks, 1991.

Sheils, Jean Evans, and Ben Swankey. *Work and Wages: A Semi-documentary Account of the Life and Times of Arthur H. (Slim) Evans.* Vancouver: Trade Union Research Bureau, 1977.

Shelford, Cyril. *From Snowshoes to Politics.* Victoria: Orca, 1987.

Sherman, Paddy. *Bennett.* Toronto: McClelland and Stewart, 1966.

Sherwood, Jay. *Return to Northern British Columbia: A Photojournal of Frank Swannell, 1929–39.* Victoria: Royal BC Museum, 2010.

Shi, David. *The Simple Life: Plain Living and High Thinking in American Culture.* New York: Oxford University Press, 1985.

Shimizu, Yon. *The Exiles: An Archival History of the World War II Japanese Road Camps in British Columbia and Ontario.* Wallaceburg, ON: Shimizu Consulting, 1993.

Simmon, Scott. *The Invention of the Western Film: A Cultural History of the Genre's First Half-Century.* Cambridge: Cambridge University Press, 2003.

Simmons, J. *Feathers and Fur on the Turnpike.* Boston: Christopher Publishing House, 1938.

Skelton, Robin. *They Call It the Cariboo.* Victoria: Sono Nis, 1980.

Smuin, Dorothy. "Relief Camps of the Great Depression." *Report of the Okanagan Historical Society* 63 (1999): 85–88.

St. John, Molyneux. *The Sea of Mountains: An Account of Lord Dufferin's Tour through British Columbia in 1876.* London: Hurst and Blackett, 1877.

Stangoe, Irene. *Cariboo-Chilcotin: Pioneer People and Places.* Surrey: Heritage House, 1994.

–. *Looking Back at the Cariboo-Chilcotin.* Surrey: Heritage House, 1997.

Stanley, Meg. *Voices from Two Rivers: Harnessing the Power of the Peace and Columbia.* Vancouver: Douglas and McIntyre and BC Hydro Power Pioneers Association, 2010.

Stevens, Peter A. "Cars and Cottages: The Automotive Transformation of Ontario's Summer Home Tradition." *Ontario History* 100, no. 1 (Spring 2008): 26–56.

Stilgoe, John R. *Metropolitan Corridor: Railroads and the American Scene.* New Haven: Yale University Press, 1983.

Struthers, James. *No Fault of Their Own: Unemployment and the Canadian Welfare State, 1914–1941.* Toronto: University of Toronto Press, 1983.

Sutter, Paul S. *Driven Wild: How the Fight against Automobiles Launched the Modern Wilderness Movement.* Seattle: University of Washington Press, 2002.

Swainson, Neil. *Conflict over the Columbia: The Canadian Background to an Historic Treaty.* Ottawa/Montreal and Kingston: Institute of Public Administration of Canada/ McGill-Queen's University Press, 1979.

Sweetenham, John. *McNaughton.* 3 vols. Toronto: Ryerson Press, 1969.

Tanner, Thomas William. "Microcosms of Misfortune: Canada's Unemployment Relief Camps Administered by the Department of National Defence, 1932-1936." Master's thesis, University of Western Ontario, 1965.

Taylor, C.J. *Negotiating the Past: The Making of Canada's National Historic Parks and Sites.* Montreal and Kingston: McGill-Queen's University Press, 1990.

Taylor, G.W. *The Automobile Saga of British Columbia, 1864–1914.* Victoria: Morriss, 1984.

Thompson, John Herd, and Allen Seager. *Canada, 1922–1939: Decades of Discord.* Toronto: McClelland and Stewart, 1985.

Tillotsen, Shirley. *The Public at Play: Gender and the Politics of Recreation in Post-war Ontario.* Toronto: University of Toronto Press, 2000.

Tippett, Maria, and Douglas Cole. *From Desolation to Splendour: Changing Perceptions of the British Columbia Landscape.* Toronto: Clarke, Irwin, 1977.

Titley, Brian. *The Frontier World of Edgar Dewdney.* Vancouver: UBC Press, 1999.

Tomblin, S.G. "In Defense of Territory: Province-Building under W.A.C. Bennett." PhD diss., University of British Columbia, 1985.

–. "W.A.C. Bennett and Province-Building in British Columbia." *BC Studies* 85 (Spring 1990): 45–61.

Tremblay, Robert. *La culture de l'automobilité au Canada: Modes de vie, aménagement des paysages et univers symboliques le long des routes, 1945-2000.* Ottawa: Canadian Science and Technology Museum, 2006.

Tuan, Yi-Fu. *Space and Place: The Perspective of Experience.* London: Edward Arnold, 1977.

Turner, Robert D. *The SS Moyie: Memories of the Oldest Sternwheeler.* Victoria: Sono Nis, 1991.

–. *Sternwheelers and Steam Tugs: An Illustrated History of the Canadian Pacific Railway's British Columbia Lake and River Service.* Victoria: Sono Nis, 1984.

Twigg, Alan. *The Essentials: 150 Great BC Books and Authors.* Vancouver: Ronsdale, 2010.

Urry, John. *Sociology beyond Societies: Mobilities for the Twenty-First Century.* London: Routledge, 2000.

–. "The System of Automobility." *Theory, Culture and Society* 21, no. 4–5 (2004): 25–40.

Van Huizen, Philip. "'Panic Park': Environmental Protest and the Politics of Parks in British Columbia's Skagit Valley." *BC Studies* 170 (Summer 2011): 67–92.

Virilio, Paul. *The Art of the Motor,* trans. Julie Rose. Minneapolis: University of Minnesota Press, 1995.

–. "Dromoscopy, or the Ecstasy of Enormities." Trans. Edward R. O'Neill. *Wide Angle* 20, no. 3 (1998): 10–22.

–. *Speed and Politics.* New York: Semiotext(e), 1986.

Waiser, Bill. *Park Prisoners: The Untold Story of Western Canada's National Parks, 1915–1946.* Calgary: Fifth House, 1995.

Wallace, Charles Miller. "The Spirit of the Pioneers Still Rules: Arizona's Automobile Gold Rush of the 1930s." *Journal of Arizona History* 38, no. 4 (Winter 1997): 355–74.

Wallis, Allan D. *Wheel Estate: The Rise and Decline of Mobile Homes.* New York: Oxford University Press, 1991.

Warf, Barney. *Time-Space Compression: Historical Geographies.* London: Routledge, 2008.

West, Willis J. *Stagecoach and Sternwheel Days in the Cariboo and Central BC.* Surrey: Heritage House, 1985.

Whisnant, Anne Mitchell. *Super-Scenic Motorway: A Blue Ridge Parkway History.* Chapel Hill: University of North Carolina Press, 2006.

White, Peter. *It Pays to Play: British Columbia in Postcards, 1950s-1980s.* Vancouver: Arsenal Pulp and Presentation House Gallery, 1996.

White, Roger B. *Home on the Road: The Motor Home in America.* Washington, DC: Smithsonian Institution Press, 2000.

Wiley, John. *Landscape.* London: Routledge, 2007.

Willis, Grant. "In Memoriam: Garnet Edward Willis." *Report of the Okanagan Historical Society* 50 (1986): 124.

Williston, Eileen, and Betty Keller. *Forests, Power and Policy: The Legacy of Ray Williston.* Prince George: Caitlin, 1997.

Wilson, J.W. *People in the Way: The Human Aspects of the Columbia River Project.* Toronto: University of Toronto Press, 1973.

Wilson, Jeremy. *Talk and Log: Wilderness Politics in British Columbia, 1965–95.* Vancouver: UBC Press, 1998.

Windsor, J.E., and J.A. McVey. "Annihilation of Both Place and Sense of Place: The Experience of the Cheslatta T'En Canadian First Nation within the Context of Large-Scale Environmental Projects." *Geographical Journal* 171, no. 2 (June 2005): 146–65. http://dx.doi.org/10.1111/j.1475-4959.2005.00156.x.

Wolfe, Joel. *Autos and Progress: The Brazilian Search for Modernity.* New York: Oxford University Press, 2010.

Woods, John G. *Snow War: An Illustrated History of Rogers Pass, Glacier National Park, BC.* Toronto: National and Provincial Parks Association of Canada, 1985.

Wragge, Edmund C. "Motoring from Nelson to the Cariboo, 1926." *BC Historical News* 28, no. 3 (Summer 1995): 30–32.

Wyckoff, William K. *On the Road Again: Montana's Changing Landscape.* Seattle: University of Washington Press, 2006.

Youds, James. "A Park System as an Evolving Cultural Institution: A Case Study of the British Columbia Provincial Park System, 1890-1941." Master's thesis, University of Waterloo, 1978.

Zeller, Thomas. *Driving Germany: The Landscape of the German Autobahn.* Oxford: Berghahn, 2007.

Zimring, Carl A. "'Neon, Junk, and Ruined Landscape': Competing Visions of America's Roadsides and the Highway Beautification Act of 1965." In *The World beyond the Windshield: Roads and Landscapes in the United States and Europe,* ed. Christof Mauch and Thomas Zeller, 94–107. Athens/Stuttgart: Ohio University Press/Franz Steiner Verlag, 2008.

Index